essentials of
marketing

PAUL BAINES | CHRIS FILL | KELLY PAGE

OXFORD
UNIVERSITY PRESS

OXFORD
UNIVERSITY PRESS

Great Clarendon Street, Oxford, OX2 6DP,
United Kingdom

Oxford University Press is a department of the University of Oxford.
It furthers the University's objective of excellence in research, scholarship,
and education by publishing worldwide. Oxford is a registered trade mark of
Oxford University Press in the UK and in certain other countries

British Library Cataloguing in Publication Data

Data available

Library of Congress Cataloging in Publication Data

Data available

ISBN 978-0-19-964650-0

Printed in Great Britain by Bell & Bain Ltd, Glasgow

To Mark, my brother, an early mentor and constant guide

Paul Baines

To my fabulous Karen

Chris Fill

To Michael, for being my why

Kelly Page

Brief Contents

Detailed Contents

Part 4 Principles of Relational Marketing

List of Case Insights

Chapter 1: Systembolaget
Hear from Fredrik Thor to find out how a state alcohol monopoly with a prohibition remit can market itself.

Chapter 2: Michelin Tyres
Helen Tattersall explains how Michelin conducts environmental scanning to keep abreast of the marketing environment.

Chapter 3: BRAND sense agency
CEO Simon Harrop considers how adopting a multi-sensory approach can help to build brands that have deeper emotional connections with their consumers.

Chapter 4: i to i research
Hear from Claire Spencer about the challenges i to i encountered when devising the research programme into public support during London's bid process for the 2012 Olympic Games.

Chapter 5: Innocent Drinks
We speak to Dan Germain, Head of Creative, to find out what strategies Innocent will use to market its water/juice drinks.

Chapter 6: Stagecoach
As one of the largest bus operators in the UK, Stagecoach needs to know who its customers are. Hear from Elaine Rosscraig to find out more about its segmentation, targeting, and positioning strategy.

Chapter 7: 3M
3M is renowned for its innovative products, including the Post-it, Scotch Cellophane, and the world's first water-proof sandpaper. With global sales of US$30 billion, Andrew Hicks explains how it goes about developing innovative products such as the 3M Visual Attention Service (VAS).

Chapter 8: P&O Ferries
The rise in low-cost airlines and ferry operators has created challenging market conditions for P&O Ferries. Simon Johnson explains how it makes its crucial pricing decisions.

Chapter 9: the London Eye
Visited by an average of 10,000 people a day, the London Eye is the UK's most popular paid-for visitor attraction. Helen Bull explains how marketing communications have played a key role in its success.

Chapter 10: ZSL London Zoo
Why did London Zoo become ZSL London Zoo? James Bailey explains all.

Chapter 11: HMV
How is HMV adapting to changing customer and market expectations? We speak to Gennaro Castaldo to learn more about HMV's product and channel offering.

Chapter 12: RAKBANK
The National Bank of Ras Al-Khaimah (RAKBANK), in the United Arab Emirates (UAE), operates in the fiercely competitive credit card market. Banali Malhotra explains what strategy it should adopt to attract and retain customers.

Acknowledgements

All books are a collective endeavour, and this book and its associated digital learning resources are no exception. It takes a lot of people to design, write, produce, sell, and market a marketing textbook. On the editorial side, we would like to thank Peter Hooper for his early work on developing the original blueprint and proposal for the book, Sarah Lodge, Helen Cook, and Francesca Griffin for their sterling work on the editorial development of the book, Sian Jenkins for production, Claire Dickinson and Gemma Wakefield for design, Mathew Emery and Stuart Keltie and their fantastic teams on sales, and Marianne Lightowler and Tristan Jones on marketing. We would also like to thank the postgraduate marketing students at Cranfield School of Management and at Cardiff University for helping to choose the final front cover design for the book. We would like to thank Ning Baines for helping with the writing of the test bank, multiple-choice questions, and updating the web links, and Paolo Antonetti for his help with sourcing YouTube clips and material for the marketing resource bank.

The authors and publishers would also like to thank:

- Dr Frauke Mattison Thompson, Lecturer in Marketing, King's College London;
- Malcolm McDonald, Emeritus Professor, Cranfield University;
- Robert P. Ormrod, Associate Professor, Aarhus University; and
- Dr Ian Richardson, Stockholm University, School of Business.

Whilst every effort has been made to source permissions for the material contained herein, any errors contained within the text remain the responsibility of the authors alone.

QR-Code images are used throughout this book. QR-Code is a registered trademark of DENSO WAVE INCORPORATED. If your mobile device does not have a QR-Code reader, visit http://www.mobile-barcodes.com/qr-code-software for advice.

Preface

Welcome to *Essentials of Marketing*. You may be wondering why you should buy this marketing textbook. The answer is that our research with expert marketing lecturers and marketing students has indicated to us that you need:

- a concise, but rigorous, textbook that offers real value for money—which is particularly important in European countries in which many marketing courses are shorter than those in the UK and run for only one semester;
- an inspirational text with which you can really engage, taking your experience of marketing as a starting point and building on this;
- to be able to gain insights into what marketing practitioners actually do and the decisions that they have to make—accordingly, each chapter of the text begins with a real-life marketing challenge appropriate to the chapter;
- a book that recognizes the need to go further than the traditional '4Ps' approach and reflects on newer, contemporary perspectives, whilst still covering classical perspectives, theories, and frameworks of marketing;
- help with identifying, locating, and reading seminal research papers on important topic areas; and
- to be taught marketing in a creative and visual way.

Essentials of Marketing has been developed to meet these needs. It is a truly integrated print and digital learning package for introductory marketing modules. It comprises a textbook packed with learning features, combining authority with a lively and engaging writing style. There is a diverse range of electronic resources matched to the contents of the textbook, available on the book's **Online Resource Centre**. The purpose of this learning package is to bring contemporary marketing perspectives to life.

Essentials of Marketing covers the basic concepts from classical marketing perspectives, but contrasts these with newer perspectives from the relational and service-dominant schools of marketing, helping you to develop your knowledge and understanding of marketing. Each chapter contains a mix of digital, international, business-to-business, and consumer marketing market insights. Digital marketing insights, in particular, are distributed throughout the text and the online resources, rather than presented as a separate chapter; this approach reflects its integral nature in the practice and study of marketing.

Who Should Use this Book?

The key audiences for this book are:

- undergraduate students in universities and colleges of higher and further education, who are taught in English—although the case material and the examples are deliberately European and international in scope, so that international students can benefit;

- postgraduate students on Masters degree (MBA and MSc/MA) programmes with a strong marketing component, who will find this text invaluable, particularly because of the case insights adopted in each chapter in the book and the associated video 'solutions' filmed for each case, available through your lecturers; and
- non-specialist students studying a one-semester course in marketing as part of an engineering, business, finance, or other management degree.

How to Use this Textbook

We aim to enhance your learning by providing a holistic marketing learning system, incorporating the key components that you need to understand core marketing principles. We hope not only that this text and its associated **Online Resource Centre** will facilitate and enhance your learning, making it enjoyable along the way, but also that you will find it useful to use this text and to refer back to it throughout your student experiences of marketing.

Key features of this book and the **Online Resource Centre** therefore include:

- a real marketing dilemma with which each chapter opens, encouraging you to consider how you might tackle the marketing challenges facing practitioners at organizations including Innocent, RAKBANK, 3M, and Systembolaget;
- up-to-date market insight examples featuring organizations including WOMAD, Groupon, Foursquare, IKEA, and HTC;
- essential, core content tailored specifically for shorter modules and courses, whilst also providing access to a wealth of digital resources to enhance student understanding;
- coverage of the latest developments in digital marketing and social media, integrated throughout the chapters, reflecting the integral role that digital marketing now plays in contemporary marketing practice; and
- links to seminal papers to help you to take your learning further, and to introduce you to classic and contemporary influential contributions.

The text is also accompanied by access to a wealth of online resources, including podcasts, and tips and advice on employability from top recruitment agencies, as well as a variety of Internet activities and multiple-choice questions for students, and a test bank of multiple-choice and assessment questions for lecturers.

We genuinely hope that you enjoy using this text. If you want to give us tips on how we can improve your learning experience, please feel free to email us at bfpinsights@oup.com. We would love to hear from you.

Good luck in your studies!

Paul Baines
Chris Fill
Kelly Page

 ## Practitioner Insights (free for all registered adopting lecturers)

Bespoke video case material features top marketers at organizations, including HMV, Innocent, and Systembolaget (Sweden's only retailer of alcohol), who explain how they actually deal with the marketing dilemmas outlined in the chapter's Case Insight. Once you have read the Case Insight and formulated your own strategy for tackling the marketing challenge, your lecturer can show the short video interview in class to give you a true insight into marketing in action.

Case Insight 1.1

Fredrik Thor for Systembolaget AB

Systembolaget AB was the world's first alcohol monopoly. It has a government mandate to limit the harm that might come to Swedish society from alcohol consumption. We speak to Fredrik Thor, to find out how a state alcohol monopoly with a prohibition remit can possibly market itself.

It all started in 1850 with the formation in Dalarna, Sweden, of a company that was granted exclusive rights to operate outlets for the sale and serving of alcoholic drinks. This was the world's first ever alcohol monopoly and it worked so well that the model spread nationwide. In 1955, the various local monopolies were merged to form a single one: Systemaktiebolaget.

Systembolaget's mandate is to help to limit the medical and social harm caused by alcohol and thereby to improve public health. It aims to do this by limiting alcohol availability through: the number of retail outlets (opening hours and selling rules); not endeavouring to maximize profits; not promoting additional sales; being brand-neutral; providing good customer service; and being financially efficient. But if the company is essentially designed to limit societal harm from alcohol—in effect, implementing and ensuring compliance with the government's alcohol policy—how can it market alcoholic products responsibly?

The company's marketing communication is steered by legislation, such as the Swedish Marketing Practices Act and the Swedish Alcohol Act, by Systembolaget's agreement with the state, and by the company's own internal guidelines for marketing communication in relation to alcohol products.

So, the monopoly exists to ensure that alcohol-related problems are, as far as possible, minimized. If it were abolished, it is generally believed that people would drink more and social problems would increase. But the monopoly isn't a given: it will continue to exist only as long as it has public support. Therefore the company

A refreshing lack of promotional material at Systembolaget

does everything it can to ensure that when you visit us, you like what you get.

The goal of all of our communication measures has been to persuade more Swedes to support the monopoly—or at least to ensure that more people understand why it exists. The problem was in 2002, only 48 per cent of Swedes actually supported the monopoly; a risky proportion of the public, in other words, didn't. As Systembolaget's President said: 'If everyone knows why it exists, and people still don't want it, we shouldn't have an alcohol monopoly. But it would be awful if it were to be abolished because no one understood why it existed.'

The company therefore defined a concrete goal in its strategic plan to boost support for the monopoly to 54 per cent over the course of two years.

1 The question is: how does an alcohol monopoly increase public support for its existence without promoting alcohol consumption?

 ## Marketing videos collection

Students and lecturers can access a wealth of carefully selected marketing videos sourced from the likes of TED and YouTube.

YouTube Resource Title: Systembolaget promotional "feast"
Brand and/or Topic: Systembolaget
Resource Description: TV Ad about responsible drinking from Systembolaget
Channel: Systembolaget
Link (URL): http://www.youtube.com/watch?v=5kFSOUeK3hw

YouTube Resource Title: What is marketing?
Brand and/or Topic: Marketing
Resource Description: Professor of the Department of Marketing Management of ESADE's Chair of Design Management.
Channel: esade
Link (URL): http://www.youtube.com/watch?v=h7FIWC2NdEM

Marketing Resource Bank (free for all registered adopting lecturers)

A suite of marketing tools and video clips accompanied by detailed teaching notes, including examples of viral marketing, online games, and TV advertisements, provides a diverse collection of practical examples to illustrate key theories in each chapter.

Chapter 01: Marketing Principles and Society
MRB 1.1: Systembolaget AB
MRB 1.2: RM Customer Success
MRB 1.3: CIM & UK Marketing Standards

Chapter 02: The Marketing Environment
MRB 2.1: Michelin Man: World Of Mobility
MRB 2.3 IBM & the Smarter Planet

Web links

Each chapter is accompanied by a suite of web links to marketing-related and commercial sites to expand your general understanding of marketing.

Marketing Related Organizations

Chartered Institute of Marketing (CIM)
http://www.cim.co.uk/
CIM is the world's largest professional body of marketing, with 50,0
worldwide. We share a passion for marketing, we lead the develop
standards and practice, and we champion the big issues and new
world. The Chartered Institute of Marketing's Mission Statement: T
body on marketing practice, standards and associated knowledge
basis and for this to be acknowledged by governments, marketers
and others.

American Marketing Association (AMA)
http://www.marketingpower.com/
The American Marketing Association, one of the largest profession
marketers, has 38,000 members worldwide in every area of marke
decades the AMA has been the leading source for information, kno
development in the marketing profession. The AMA's website, Mari
supplies marketing professionals and AMA members with the infor
services required to succeed in their jobs and careers.

Market Insights

Bang up to date, topical examples including WOMAD, iTunes, Foursquare, and Twitter, help you to apply marketing theory to real brands and products.

Market Insight 6.3   (continued)

reviews and reading other reviews, inviting friends, exploring other venues in the area, creating lists, and even following other people's lists (such as a list of 'Top ten restaurants in the area'). Furthermore, consumers are offered the option of recommending certain venues and observing trends.

On the merchant side, once registered with Foursquare, a business is able to use the mobile loyalty programme as a platform from which to engage consumers in a variety of different ways. For example, the venue may add a 'loyalty special' for those who check in with their mobile phone more than five times, or a 'newbie special' for first-time check-ins if the objective is to create new

business. Another innovative way in which to get the most from Foursquare is to offer 'last minute specials' on a day that business is slow. Check-in services seem to be present a robust way for retailers to segment out their customer base based on geography and behaviour.

As check-ins become more mainstream, the potential for targeted segmentation is growing with the following implications.

- *Loyalty*—Businesses are able to create robust customer loyalty programmes based on frequency of patronage, and to micro-segment and offer individualized rewards at a much cheaper cost than traditional loyalty programmes.
- *Brand awareness*—The sharing of check-ins on social media sites such as Twitter or Facebook is invaluable: it represents the ability to reach a more targeted audience via a medium (word of mouth) that is arguably more powerful than traditional advertising.
- *Promotion driving traffic*—Businesses are able to promote as needed to drive traffic on an individual level—with no need to dilute the brand by promoting to the entire customer base.

The Foursquare mobile loyalty platform is so much more than simply another customer loyalty reward programme or social network. For many customers, this type of marketing brings a new and innovative way in which to shop and be entertained wherever you are.

1 Why do you think retailers would use Foursquare to target customers?

2 How do you think customers could be segmented based on the data and information that Foursquare provides merchants?

3 Think of your own mobile phone use behaviour. What characteristics do you think a business on Foursquare might use to segment people like you?

Foursquare: the location-based social networking service
Source: © foursquare 2012

How to Use this Package to Test Understanding

Throughout each chapter there are suggestions to go online to access the wealth of marketing resources. In addition, in each chapter you'll find a QR code which links directly to the accompanying online student resources where you can test and expand your knowledge.

Discussion questions

Have a go at answering the online discussion questions to help you develop skills in analysis and debate.

> **1.** Having read the Case Insight at the beginning of this chapter, drinks to develop their brand?
>
> **2.** Find three examples of mission statements and associated or these examples, discuss the value of formulating a mission st: likely to arise from setting organisational level goals.

Multiple-choice questions

This bank of questions provides instant feedback to help you identify which areas require further study.

> **Question 1**
>
> Which of the following statements is correct?
>
> ✔ **Your Answer:**
>
> **d)** Marketing is the activity, set of institutions, and processes communicating, delivering, and exchanging offerings that hav clients, partners, and society at large

Worksheets

Each chapter invites you to complete an online worksheet, to enhance your understanding of marketing theories by undertaking various marketing tasks.

> **Worksheet Summary**
>
> Visit the **Online Resource Centre** and complete Worksheet 6.1. This will aid in learning about the STP process used to develop to whom to market, in what way, and while differentiating from the competition.

Podcasts

Revise on the go with our author audio podcasts summarizing each chapter.

> - Chapter 01: Marketing Principles and Society
>   [MP3: 5.17MB, 5.38 mins]
>
> - Chapter 02: The Marketing Environment
>   [MP3: 5.99MB, 6.32 mins]
>
> - Chapter 03: Consumer Buying Behaviour
>   [MP3: 6.06MB, 6.37 mins]

Review questions

After you've finished reading each chapter, try to answer the review questions to test your understanding of the chapter's central themes.

> **Review Questions**
>
> 1 Define 'price', 'cost', 'quality', and 'value' in your own words.
> 2 Explain the concept of 'price elasticity of demand', giving examples of products that are price elastic and products that are price inelastic.
> 3 What pricing policies are most appropriate for which situations?
> 4 What are the main business-to-business pricing policies?
> 5 What are the main two approaches to pricing for new products and services?

Test bank (free for all adopting lecturers)

This ready-made electronic testing resource is fully customizable and will help you save time creating assessments for your students.

1 of 5

Chapter 01 - Question 01
The key focus of the American Marketing Associatio...
- ○ organizational activities
- ○ product components
- ○ Shareholder returns
- ○ Stakeholder value

Essay questions (free for all registered adopting lecturers)

Set your students stimulating essay questions.

Question 1
What is marketing? Compare and contrast the American the Chartered Institute of Marketing definitions of marke

Answer guidance
The CIM defines marketing as: "The management process o satisfying customer requirements profitably" (CIM, 2001). In concentrates on "customer value" by defining marketing as: institutions, and processes for creating, communicating, deli offerings that have value for customers, clients, partners, an 2007).

The CIM and AMA definitions recognize marketing as a "ma "organizational process" although, in reality, many firms orga department rather than across all departments (Sheth and S AMA definitions are similar in that they stress the importanc of determining their requirements, or needs. The CIM defini "requirements" and the AMA to "delivering value". Neither th refers explicitly to products, as it is now widely recognized ir requirements are delivered through offerings whether these ideas or some combination of the three.

 Tutorial activities (free for all registered adopting lecturers)

Drawing on the Marketing Resource Bank and video collection, the tutorial activities have been designed for seminars and tutorials, and offer lots of ideas for integrating the textbook and its resources into your teaching.

Chapter Reference
Chapter 1: Marketing Principles & Society

Overview
This activity introduces students to marketing and encoura...
as a target market be it consumers, customers, purchasers
have been marketed.

Learning Outcomes
Students should demonstrate:
- an understanding of the marketing concept;
- awareness of the differing definitions of marketing;
- knowledge of the process of marketing and the differing activities.

Answer guidance (free for all registered adopting lecturers)

Teaching notes accompany all essay and discussion questions, and offer suggested answers.

1. Having read the Case Insight at the beginning of this chapt Systembolaget to use marketing in the future to: a) maintai alcohol monopoly? b) ensure that customers drink respons

Pointers

- To provide insight to this discussion question, review the m concept of market orientation from Chapter 1. In addition, r marketing has on society towards the end of the chapter.

How to Use this Package to Take Learning Further

@ Marketing and your career

Hear from graduate employment and recruitment specialists about the skills and attributes you'll need to succeed in your job applications and future career.

Research Insights

Each chapter signposts seminal journal articles and books to help broaden your understanding of the chapter topics. These can all be accessed online via the web links.

Research Insight 1.2

To take your learning further, you might wish to read the following influential paper:

Vargo, S. L. and Lusch, R. F. (2004) 'Evolving to a new dominant logic for marketing', *Journal of Marketing*, 39(Oct): 32–9.

This ground-breaking article redefined how marketers should perceive offerings, arguing that marketing needed to move beyond outmoded concepts derived from economics of tangible resources ('goods'), embedded value, and transactions, towards intangible resources, the co-creation of values, and relationships.

Visit the **Online Resource Centre** to read the abstract and to access the full paper.

@ Internet activities

These activities encourage you to undertake web based research to enhance your understanding.

Chapter Reference
Chapter 1: Marketing Principles and Society

Overview
This activity will introduce you to an example of the positive impact society when undertaken ethically and responsibly.

Activity Description
Visit the Fairtrade Labelling Organisations (FLO) International webs use of marketing to raise awareness of their activities for fairtrade

Website
http://www.fairtrade.net
Fairtrade Labelling Organizations (FLO) International is an NGO inv traders in a labelling initiative which awards companies with fairtrad pay a fair price to producers in lesser developed countries for the p The organization's mission is to ensure the economic independenc of small farmer organizations and their members, through Fairtrade

In addition to the lecturer support materials already mentioned, we also provide (free for all registered adopting lecturers):

@ PowerPoint slides

Fully customizable slides accompany each chapter.

The Marketing Mix

The Original developed by Borden in his teaching but not written up until 1964:

- Product planning
- Pricing
- Branding
- Channels of distribution
- Personal selling
- Advertising
- Promotions
- Packaging
- Display
- Servicing
- Physical handling
- Fact finding and analysis (Borden, 1964).

The Shortened simplified version by Eugene McCarthy and now more commonly used:

- Product
- Place (distribution)
- Price and
- Promotion (McCarthy, 1960).

@ Video guide

Transcripts are provided of all the practitioner clips in addition to a breakdown, showing time blocks, of the Academic Insight videos.

CHAPTER 1 – Marketing Principles and Society Systembolaget – Fredrik Thor, Brand Manager

8min 34secs in total

0min17secs
Interviewer: Can you tell me about the history of Systembol

Fredrik Thor: First, my name is Fredrik Thor and I Systembolaget, I have been here for eight years but it all running a bit longer than I have been here. At that time Sw pure alcohol per person per year and this was a huge pu bolaget, that means company in Swedish, was formed by

@ Figures

Figures from the textbook are provided online.

Part 1

Marketing
Fundamentals

Marketing Principles and Society

1

Learning outcomes

After reading this chapter, you will be able to:

- define the marketing concept;

- explain how marketing has developed over the last century;

- describe the four major contexts of marketing application—that is, consumer goods, business to business, services, and not-for-profit marketing;

- assess critically the impact that marketing has on society.

Fredrik Thor for Systembolaget AB

Systembolaget AB was the world's first alcohol monopoly. It has a government mandate to limit the harm that might come to Swedish society from alcohol consumption. We speak to Fredrik Thor, to find out how a state alcohol monopoly with a prohibition remit can possibly market itself.

It all started in 1850 with the formation in Dalarna, Sweden, of a company that was granted exclusive rights to operate outlets for the sale and serving of alcoholic drinks. This was the world's first ever alcohol monopoly and it worked so well that the model spread nationwide. In 1955, the various local monopolies were merged to form a single one: Systemaktiebolaget.

Systembolaget's mandate is to help to limit the medical and social harm caused by alcohol and thereby to improve public health. It aims to do this by limiting alcohol availability through: the number of retail outlets (opening hours and selling rules); not endeavouring to maximize profits; not promoting additional sales; being brand-neutral; providing good customer service; and being financially efficient. But if the company is essentially designed to limit societal harm from alcohol—in effect, implementing and ensuring compliance with the government's alcohol policy—how can it market alcoholic products responsibly?

The company's marketing communication is steered by legislation, such as the Swedish Marketing Practices Act and the Swedish Alcohol Act, by Systembolaget's agreement with the state, and by the company's own internal guidelines for marketing communication in relation to alcohol products.

So, the monopoly exists to ensure that alcohol-related problems are, as far as possible, minimized. If it were abolished, it is generally believed that people would drink more and social problems would increase. But the monopoly isn't a given: it will continue to exist only as long as it has public support. Therefore the company

A refreshing lack of promotional material at Systembolaget

does everything it can to ensure that when you visit us, you like what you get.

The goal of all of our communication measures has been to persuade more Swedes to support the monopoly—or at least to ensure that more people understand why it exists. The problem was in 2002, only 48 per cent of Swedes actually supported the monopoly; a risky proportion of the public, in other words, didn't. As Systembolaget's President said: 'If everyone knows why it exists, and people still don't want it, we shouldn't have an alcohol monopoly. But it would be awful if it were to be abolished because no one understood why it existed.'

The company therefore defined a concrete goal in its strategic plan to boost support for the monopoly to 54 per cent over the course of two years.

1 **The question is: how does an alcohol monopoly increase public support for its existence without promoting alcohol consumption?**

■ Introduction

How have companies marketed their products and services to you in the past? Consider the smartphones you buy, the sports teams you follow, the music you listen to, and the holidays you take. Why did you decide to buy these offerings? Each one has been marketed to you to cater for a particular need that you have at a particular time. Consider how the offering was distributed to you. What component parts is it made of? What contribution does each of these offerings make to society? How useful are they really? These are just some of the questions that marketers might ask themselves when designing, developing, and delivering products to the **customer**, and determining whether or not the customer's wants and needs have been met.

In this chapter, we develop our understanding of marketing principles and marketing's impact upon society by defining 'marketing', and by comparing and contrasting definitions from the American, British, and French perspectives. We explore how marketing is different in the business-to-**consumer** (B2C), business-to-business (B2B), and services marketing sectors, and how marketing thinking has changed to redefine all offerings as essentially service-based. The core principles of marketing, incorporating the **marketing mix**, the principle of marketing exchange, **market orientation**, and **relationship marketing**, are all considered. How marketing impacts upon society is also detailed, and, finally, we explore the need to reflect on marketing activities critically and ethically, as both marketers and consumers, by considering their impact on society from positive and negative perspectives.

■ What is Marketing?

Consider your own experience of being marketed to throughout your own life. So far, you have probably been subjected to millions of marketing communications messages, bought many hundreds of thousands of products and services, been involved in thousands of customer service telephone calls, and visited tens of thousands of shops, retail outlets, and websites. You're already a pretty experienced customer, so you've experienced one side of the marketing exchange—consumption—already. The key question is to explain how professionals perform the other side of marketing—in other words, how to market products to customers. Remember: most customers are just like you and will be just as discriminating as you are when buying an offering. If they don't like it, they won't buy it.

In order to explain how we go about marketing offerings to customers, we must first describe exactly what 'marketing' is. There are many definitions of marketing, but we present three for easy reference in Table 1.1.

The Chartered Institute of Marketing (CIM) and American Marketing Association (AMA) definitions recognize marketing as a 'management process' and an 'activity', although many firms organize marketing as a discrete department rather than across all departments (Sheth and Sisodia, 2005). The CIM and AMA definitions are similar, because they stress the importance of considering the customer, and of determining their requirements or needs. The CIM definition refers to customer 'requirements' and the AMA to 'delivering value'. The French definition, by contrast, refers to developing an offer of superior value. Neither the AMA nor the CIM definition refers explicitly to products, while the French definition explicitly discusses

Table 1.1	Definitions of marketing
Defining institution/author	**Definition**
The Chartered Institute of Marketing (CIM)	'The management process of anticipating, identifying and satisfying customer requirements profitably' (CIM, 2001)
The American Marketing Association (AMA)	'Marketing is the activity, set of institutions, and processes for creating communicating, delivering, and exchanging offerings that have value for customers, clients, partners, and society at large' (AMA, 2007)
A French perspective	*'Le marketing est l'effort d'adaptation des organisations à des marchés concurrentiels, pour influencer en leur faveur le comportement de leurs publics, par une offre dont la valeur perçue est durablement supérieure à celle des concurrents'* [broadly, 'Marketing is the endeavour of adapting organizations to their competitive markets in order to influence, in their favour, the behaviour of their publics, with an offer the perceived value of which is durably superior to that of the competition'] (Lendrevie et al., 2006)

an 'offer'. This is important because recent research has suggested that we should consider all offerings as essentially service-based, because they serve customers' psychological needs, which are intangible.

go online

Visit the **Online Resource Centre**, and follow the web links to the CIM and AMA websites to read more about their views on 'What is marketing?'

Both the CIM and AMA definitions discuss meeting customers' needs or adding value to customers. Both definitions recognize the need for marketers to undertake **environmental scanning** activity (see Chapter 2) and marketing research (see Chapter 4) to satisfy customers, and in the long term to anticipate customers' needs.

The French definition talks of influencing the behaviour of the publics, rather than customers, recognizing the wider remit of marketing in modern society. The challenge, according to the French definition, is to develop an offering that is 'durably superior' to that of the competition. This definition therefore explicitly recognizes the importance of market segmentation and **positioning** concepts (see Chapter 6).

The CIM definition (which is probably now somewhat obsolete as a result) suggests that marketing is a process with only a profit motive, and we would usually understand this to be a financial profit rather than a gain in society, for example as in the case of a charity's or government department's use of marketing.

The AMA definition is clearer, arguing that marketing is a process undertaken to benefit 'clients, partners, and society at large'.

All of this clearly illustrates how the concept of marketing finally formally changed in the 2000s to one that recognized that commercial organizations must assess the social impacts of their businesses or risk damage to their reputation, and also that marketing can be used by organizations with purely social motives, as well as those with profit motives or some combination of the two. Marketing is increasingly used by not-for-profit organizations and **social entrepreneurs**. The relationship between customers in a not-for-profit and a for-profit organization is different, because the offerings are different and because the missions of the organizations concerned are different. Nevertheless, the broad principles of how marketing is used in both are the same.

Visit the **Online Resource Centre** and complete Internet Activity 1.1 to learn more about the two leading professional marketing associations.

go online

■ What's the Difference between Customers and Consumers?

We've talked a lot about customers, but what actually is a 'customer'? And is there a difference between a 'customer' and a 'consumer'?

We define a 'customer' as a buyer, a purchaser, a patron, a client, or a shopper. A customer is someone who buys from a shop, a website, a business, and, increasingly, another customer, for example via eBay or Amazon exchange. The difference between a customer and a consumer is that while a customer purchases or obtains a product, service, or idea, a consumer uses it (or eats it, in the case of food).

To illustrate the example, consider Lego® Marvel™ Superheroes. In this case, the customer is the chief shopper, the mother/father, or guardian, and the consumer is the child. The customer and consumer can be the same person: for example, a girl buying the cinema tickets for herself and her boyfriend online to see the next big blockbuster movie is both the customer

In this instance, you would expect the chief shopper to be the mother/father/guardian and the consumer to be a child.

Source: ™ & © 2012 Marvel & Subs. LEGO and the LEGO logo are trademarks of the LEGO Group © 2012 The LEGO Group.

and consumer. Another example is when a person uses an airline: if he or she buys the ticket himself or herself, he or she is the customer; if someone else buys the ticket for the person, he or she is the consumer. The airline companies are themselves the customers of big aeroplane manufacturers such as Boeing or Airbus, who are themselves customers of suppliers such as Pratt and Whitney or Rolls-Royce (for the jet engines, for example).

■ Market Orientation

Just how close to the customer should a company aim to be? This is the principle of 'market orientation' and it lies at the heart of what marketing is about. Developing a market orientation is argued to make organizations more profitable, especially when there is limited competition, unchanging customer wants and needs, fast-paced technological change, and strong economies in operation (Kohli and Jaworski, 1990).

But developing a *market* orientation is not the same as developing a *marketing* orientation. So what's the difference? A company with a marketing orientation would be a company that increases the importance of marketing within the organization, perhaps by appointing a marketing person to its board of directors (or trustees, in the case of a charity).

Developing a market orientation refers to 'the organisationwide generation of market intelligence pertaining to current and future customer needs, dissemination of the intelligence across the departments, and organisationwide responsiveness to it' (Kohli and Jaworski, 1990). So a market orientation doesn't only involve marketing, but also involves all aspects of a company, gathering and responding to market intelligence (that is, customers' verbalized needs and preferences, data from customer surveys, sales data, website click-through rates and traffic, and information gleaned informally from discussions with customers and trade partners).

Developing a market orientation means developing:

- *customer orientation*—which is concerned with creating superior value by continuously developing and redeveloping product and service offerings to meet customer needs, meaning that we must measure customer satisfaction on a continuous basis, and train and develop front-line service staff accordingly;

- *competitor orientation*—which requires an organization to develop an understanding of its competitors' short-term strengths and weaknesses, and its long-term capabilities and strategies (Slater and Narver, 1994); and

- *interfunctional coordination*—which requires all of the functions within an organization to work together to achieve these goals for long-term profit (as shown in Figure 1.1).

Achieving a market orientation so that an organization is internally responsive to changes in the marketplace can take an organization four years or more and requires the support of top senior management, the development of teams to gather the necessary market intelligence data and design appropriate market-based reward systems, and management to implement the recommendations made as a result (Kohli and Jaworski, 1990).

Developing market orientation is a capability—something that not all companies are able to do. Those organizations that manage to do so are those that are better at **market sensing**—that is, at understanding the strategic implications of the market for a particular organization

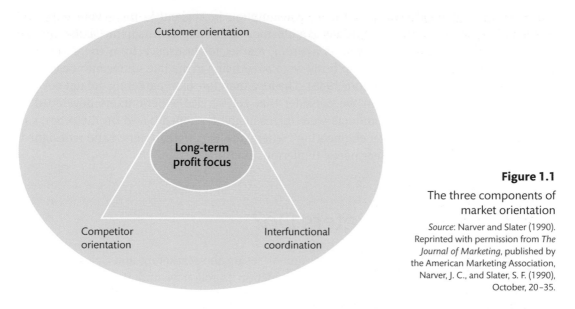

Figure 1.1

The three components of market orientation

Source: Narver and Slater (1990). Reprinted with permission from *The Journal of Marketing*, published by the American Marketing Association, Narver, J. C., and Slater, S. F. (1990), October, 20–35.

—and acting upon the information collected through environmental scanning. (This topic is covered fully in Chapter 2.) Apple, the organization behind numerous consumer electronic innovations including the iPod, iPad, and iTunes, has developed a very strong market orientation by aligning its company to the task of developing and designing products that disrupt product categories by completely redefining how customers' needs are met. For example, iTunes revolutionized music sales, allowing consumers to buy music by downloading it using their computers rather than having to visit a retailer to purchase the physical CD.

■ A History of Marketing

Most marketing historians regard marketing as an invention of the twentieth century (Keith, 1960) and most marketing texts present the development of marketing as a four-stage sequence as follows.

1 *Production period (1890s–1920s)* This period was characterized by a focus on physical production and supply, during which time demand exceeded supply, there was little competition, and the range of products was limited. This phase took place after the Industrial Revolution.

2 *Sales period (1920s–50s)* This period was characterized by a focus on personal selling, supported by market research and advertising. This phase took place after the First World War.

3 *Marketing period (1950s–80s)* This period was characterized by a more advanced focus on the customer's needs. It took place after the Second World War.

4 *Societal marketing period (1980s to present)* This period was characterized by a stronger focus on social and ethical concerns in marketing. This phase is taking place during the 'information revolution' of the late twentieth century (Enright, 2002).

However, there is good evidence of mass consumption in England in the seventeenth and eighteenth centuries, and the operations of guildsmen and entrepreneurs in the sixteenth- and eighteenth-century markets, as well as a strong market for insurance from the early eighteenth century (Enright, 2002). Soap firms were advertising in the late nineteenth century in the UK, US, and Germany (Fullerton, 1988). The idea therefore that marketing did not develop until the 1950s is wrong, when we consider that self-service supermarkets developed in America from the 1930s and products were increasingly developed based on the process of what was then called 'consumer engineering', where products were designed and redesigned, using research, to meet customer needs (Fullerton, 1988).

■ What Do Marketers Do?

To answer this question, the British government set up the Marketing and Sales Standards Setting Body (MSSSB) to map the marketing function (a role now undertaken by the Skills CfA). Its consultation indicated that marketing covers eight areas (see Figure 1.2), each of which is interlinked with **stakeholder** requirements. Generally, the senior marketer or marketing director will guide and direct these eight functions, while the marketing manager will manage them, the marketing executive will undertake the actions necessary to fulfil these functions, and the marketing assistant will support the marketing executive. The marketing department of the future, however, increasingly needs to embrace the rapid evolution of digital channels (such as Facebook and Twitter) and the increasing availability of customer data that derives from marketing research, customer relationship management (CRM) systems, sales force data, and web statistics (Clawson, 2011). This means that marketers will increasingly need to have skills and capabilities in social media marketing.

Figure 1.2

A functional map for marketing

Source: The Marketing and Sales Standards Setting Body (2010). Reproduced with the kind permission of Dr Chahid Fourali, Head of MSSSB.

Principles of Marketing

Marketing managers use a number of general concepts that help them to frame their actions as they develop marketing plans and undertake marketing tactics. We cover these concepts next in the chronological order in which they were developed including the marketing mix for products (4Ps) in the 1950s–60s, the concept of exchange in marketing in the 1970s, the marketing mix for services (7Ps) in the 1980s, market orientation and relationship marketing developed mainly in the 1990s, and **co-creation** developed mainly in the 2000s.

Research Insight 1.1

To take your learning further, you might wish to read the following influential paper:

Borden, N. H. (1964) 'The concept of the marketing mix', *Journal of Advertising Research*, 4: 2–7.

The marketing mix is the most famous concept in marketing. This easy-to-read article explains how marketing managers act as 'mixers of ingredients' in developing their brand policies and programmes. The concept of the marketing mix, popularized as the '4P's, remains popular amongst managers today, although the advent of relationship marketing and co-creation has challenged the impersonal notion of marketers as manipulators of marketing policies and consumers as passive recipients.

Visit the **Online Resource Centre** to read the abstract and to access the full paper.

The Marketing Mix and the 4Ps

What are the responsibilities of the marketing manager? To outline these, Neil Borden developed the marketing mix in his teaching at Harvard University in the 1950s. The idea came from the idea that marketing managers were 'mixers of ingredients'—chefs who concocted a unique marketing recipe to fit the requirements of their customers' needs.

The emphasis was on the creative fashioning of a mix of marketing procedures and policies to develop a profitable enterprise. Borden (1964) composed a twelve-item list of elements that the manufacturer should consider when developing its marketing mix policies and procedures, as follows.

1 Product planning
2 Pricing
3 Branding
4 Channels of distribution
5 Personal selling

6 Advertising

7 Promotions

8 Packaging

9 Display

10 Servicing

11 Physical handling

12 Fact finding and analysis

This useful list was simplified and amended by Eugene McCarthy (1960) to the more memorable, but rigid, 4Ps, as follows (see Figure 1.3).

- *Product*—that is, the offering and how it meets the customer's need, its packaging and labelling (see Chapter 7)
- *Place* (distribution)—that is, the way in which the product meets customers' needs (see Chapter 11)
- *Price*—that is, the cost to the customer and the cost plus profit to the seller (see Chapter 8)
- *Promotion*—that is, how the product's benefits and features are conveyed to the potential buyer (see Chapter 9 and Chapter 10)

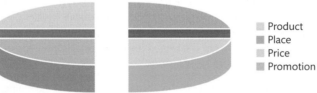

Figure 1.3

The 4Ps of the marketing mix

- Product
- Place
- Price
- Promotion

The intention was to create a simpler framework around which managers could develop their planning. Although there was some recognition that all of these elements might be interlinked (for example, promotion based on the price paid by the consumer), McCarthy's framework did not take such interplay between these mix components into account. Market Insight 1.1 gives an example of why the Nokia smartphone product needs redeveloping.

Although some commentators have argued that the 4Ps framework is of very limited use, we include it here because managers still use the framework extensively when devising their product plans.

Market Insight 1.1

Nokia's Burning Platform

In 2011, Finnish company Nokia posted an operating loss of €1.07 billion, compared with a profit of €745 million the previous year. Nokia's smartphone sales were particularly badly hit as consumers turned away from Nokia's legacy Symbian platform phones to competitors, such as Apple's iPhone and Google Android-enabled phones such as those made by HTC. Research in Motion's Blackberry smartphone has also suffered a similar fate, losing considerable market share, and its own long-term future as an independent company looks increasingly uncertain: its co-chief executives both stepped down from office in 2012. During 2011, Nokia is believed to have lost as much as 7 per cent of market share, giving it about 24 per cent of the global smartphone market by early 2012. To arrest the problem, Nokia announced a joint venture with Microsoft to offer Windows-only platform smartphones (the Lumia 800 was its first product), but sales have been slow.

The problem is that Nokia's customers have shifted to new platforms such as Apple's iPhone and Google Android-enabled phones over the time that it has taken Nokia to develop the joint venture with Microsoft. Nevertheless, a leaked Microsoft briefing suggests that the new version of Windows mobile version 8, apparently codenamed 'Apollo', will allow major innovations such as contactless payment systems, improved data synchronization (for example, between phones and gaming consoles and music collections), and new screen resolutions. However, with Apple's iPhone 5 and new versions of Android already works in progress, how the smartphone product will pan out is difficult to forecast. What is clear is that the competition is fierce. The question is: what new products will Nokia have to develop to keep its punters ringing its tune?

For a discussion of competitive strategy in the smartphone market, see Market Insight 5.3.

Sources: Richmond (2012); Rushton (2012); Taylor (2012); Thomas (2012)

1 Why do you think Nokia clung onto its Symbian smartphone platform for so long despite its decreasing market share?

2 How can Nokia use the 4Ps to build market share for its Windows-enabled smartphones?

3 Which of the 4Ps do you think is most important in rebuilding Nokia's share of the global smartphone market?

■ Marketing as Exchange

Marketing is a two-way process. It's not only about the marketing organization doing all of the work; the customer also has a strong input. In fact, not only must customers specify how we might satisfy their needs as marketers, because marketers are not mind readers, but they must also pay for the product or service.

Around the middle of the 1970s, there was increasing belief that the underlying phenomenon in marketing related to the exchange process between buyers and sellers and associated supply chain intermediaries. Exchange relationships might not only be economic, such as a consumer buying groceries, but social as well, such as the service undertaken by the social worker on behalf of society paid for by government (Bagozzi, 1975). This recognition of the importance of the underlying relationship within marketing has led to the broadening of the concept of marketing and the emergence of the relationship marketing school of marketing (which we consider further in Chapter 12).

There are three main types of buyer–seller exchange in marketing. Figure 1.4 outlines these two-way (**dyadic**) exchanges as follows.

1 In the first exchange type, the exchange takes place between the police, who protect the general public from fire and provide emergency planning activity and services, and the

Figure 1.4

Simple marketing exchange processes

public, who support them in return, sometimes politically through signing petitions to keep them in service in a particular locale, and especially through their national and local taxes (see also Market Insight 1.4).

2 In the second exchange type, the one with which we're probably more familiar as consumers, we enter a shop—say, H&M—and purchase the necessary goods by paying for these with money or by credit/debit card.

3 In the third type of exchange, we have a manufacturer and a retailer. Here, the retailer (perhaps London's Hamleys toyshop) purchases goods from the manufacturer (for example, Mattel) through a credit facility (such as 'payment in 30 days'); it expects any damaged goods to be returnable and wants the goods delivered on certain types of pallet at a certain height, within a particular time limit. In return, the retailer undertakes to pay a wholesale (that is, a trade discounted) price.

However, few exchanges in marketing are as simple as those presented in Figure 1.4. They might well involve other individual transactions and multiple combinations. For example, (2) and (3) can be combined to indicate a simple supply chain for, say, a toy manufacturer selling through to shops that sell on to the general public, their customers. Understanding how exchanges take place between the various members of the supply chain allows us to understand where we can add or reduce value in the customer experience.

We can imagine that what is exchanged in a service context (such as purchasing a holiday) is different from a product context (for example, buying a DVD). By the end of the 1970s, it was recognized that the traditional 4Ps approach to marketing planning based on physical products (such as salt, CDs, alcoholic drinks) was not particularly useful for either the physical product offering with a strong service component (for example, laptop computers with extended warranty, or services with little or no physical component, such as spa and massage, hairdressing, sports spectatorship). (We consider the differences between services and physical goods marketing in Chapter 12.)

To illustrate how marketing needed to market services differently, Booms and Bitner (1981) incorporated a further 3Ps into the marketing mix, as follows (see Figure 1.5).

- *Physical evidence*—This aspect emphasizes that the tangible components of services are strategically important: for example, potential university students often assess whether or not they want to attend a university and a particular course by requesting a copy of brochures and course outlines, looking at graduate employability statistics, or by visiting the campus.

Not even a storm would keep DHL from delivering on time!

Source: DHL International GmbH

- *Process*—This aspect emphasizes the importance of the service delivery. When processes are standardized, it is easier to manage customer expectations: for example, DHL International GmbH, the German international express, overland transport, and air freight company, is a master at producing a standardized menu of service options, such as track and trace delivery services, which are remarkably consistent around the world.

- *People*—This aspect emphasizes the importance of customer service personnel. How they interact with customers, and how satisfied customers are as a result, is of strategic importance. (See Chapter 12 for a more detailed discussion of the extended mix.)

Consider how the extended marketing mix is used in the airline industry. For example, the process component of the services marketing mix within the airline sector has been revolutionized through Internet ticket booking and online check-in services. The traditional middleman, the travel agency, has had to alter its customer proposition radically now that the major national carriers (such as SAS, Emirates, British Airways) offer their services directly via Internet to compete with lower-cost airlines also offering their services directly to the public via the Internet at substantially lower prices. The travel agencies have put their own services online, customizing their holiday offerings in a bid to differentiate their services from the airlines and add value for the customer, offering better deals on insurance, identifying best flight connections, providing advice on best airlines, and offering affiliate hotel deals (Saren, 2006).

Market Insight 1.2

Thomas Cook: Piecemeal or Package?

Thomas Cook, the tour operator, was founded in the 1840s when founder Thomas Cook began organizing, first, temperance meetings for those who had given up drinking alcohol, and then meetings of workers to visit the Great Exhibition in London in 1851. The company's first trips overseas were to France in 1855 and to Egypt to see the Pyramids in 1869. The company pioneered the idea of the package holiday—a holiday product that took the hassle out of organizing a holiday by taking care of every aspect of a tourist's travel programme, including organizing the airline, the hotel, the transfers to and from the hotel, and even day-trips in-country. Over the twentieth century, the company was built into a substantial business and was owned variously by the Belgian owner of the glamorous Orient Express in the 1920s, by British railway companies in the 1940s (which were subsequently nationalized), by a German company in the early 2000s, and finally merging with, first, the MyTravel Group in 2007, and then with the UK's The Co-operative Group's high-street travel business in 2011, giving the joint entity a high-street presence of some 1,200 outlets.

Problems arose during the Arab Spring in 2011, when political unrest in Egypt and Tunisia damaged the company's holiday bookings. The Icelandic ash cloud in April 2011, airline strikes, fears of flu pandemics, and the flooding in Thailand all disrupted business that year. In November 2011, the company's share price plummeted by 75 per cent in a single day after the company revealed that it needed extra financing to plug a gap in revenues created by the lack of demand for its holiday packages. However, Thomas Cook has a longer-term problem: customers are cutting out the middlemen in the supply chain. Customers are increasingly shifting towards booking their own holidays directly online (through companies such as Expedia and Hostelworld), including booking individual components such as transfers, hotels and flights. To some extent, this trend towards online booking is also driven by the meteoric rise of another former middleman: the airlines, including low-cost airlines such as easyJet and Ryanair, the largest of which now fly to an increasing range of destinations at relatively cheap prices.

The key consideration for Thomas Cook is: how does it maintain demand for its package holidays when many customers are increasingly turning to planning their holidays themselves piecemeal?

Maintaining demand for package holidays is a key challenge for Thomas Cook

Sources: Guthrie and Blitz (2011); BBC News (2011)

1 **Do you think that Thomas Cook can still provide value for customers in organizing package holidays for them? Why (not)?**

2 **Do you think that there is a still a segment of customers who are happy for their holidays to be completely organized for them? What do you think the characteristics of such customers are likely to be?**

3 **How do you organize your own holidays and why: piecemeal, using the Internet, or package, using a tour operator?**

The people, process, and physical evidence components of the service marketing mix are fundamental in the development of the overall airline service offering. Of course, we should recognize that airlines do not offer everyone the same level of service. Most airlines offer an economy service, an economy-plus service (with slightly more seating space), and a business-class service (with even more seating space, a better meal, and personalized cabin crew service), while first class with Emirates, for example, offers the use of in-flight 'shower spas' and onboard lounges for both business and first-class passengers.

Table 1.2 provides a summary of the marketing mix for the airline industry.

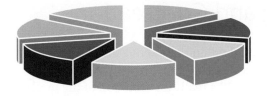

- Product
- Place
- Price
- Promotion
- Physical evidence
- People
- Process

Figure 1.5

The extended marketing mix for services: the 7Ps

Table 1.2 The marketing mix: the airline industry

Marketing aspect	Airline industry
Basic customer need	Safe long- and short-haul transportation, domestic and international
Target market	Mass consumer market (economy class); businesspeople (business class); high-net-worth individuals (first class)
Product offering	Typically, differentiated based on class of passenger, with seat size, check-in, and boarding times reducing, quality of food increasing, and levels of ancillary services (e.g. limousine service, in-flight shower spa) increasing as we move from economy through business to first class
	Some carriers focus on 'no-frills' basic services (e.g. easyJet, Ryanair, Norwegian Air Shuttle, Germanwings)
Price	Substantial differences in price exist depending on class of service, type of carrier, and purchasing approach (e.g. via Internet is cheaper)
Principal promotional tools	(1) Internet advertising; (2) proprietary websites; (3) newspapers and magazines; (4) billboards
Distribution	Increasingly purchased via the Internet, including third-party brokerages such as Expedia, as well as through travel agents, the once-dominant but now increasingly redundant medium
Process	Self-service via Internet or aided by travel agent in retail location
	Travel options increasingly customized to the customer's needs, including size of baggage allowance, class of travel, increasing availability of alternative locations
Physical evidence	Airline loyalty cards and souvenirs, in-flight magazines, in-flight entertainment services, food and snack meals, grooming and toiletry products provided, and airlines' lounges
People	Combination of check-in staff, customer service personnel, and cabin crew/pilot teams, all of whom interface with the customer at different points in the experience

Relationship Marketing and Co-creation

If marketing is about exchange, as we outlined earlier, shouldn't marketing also be concerned with relationships between those parties that are exchanging value? This was the principal idea behind the development of relationship marketing. It is really an evolution of the marketing concept from the need to engage in transactions towards the need to develop long-term customer relationships. Relationship marketing concerns not only the development of longer-lasting relationships with customers, but also the development of stronger relationships with other external markets, including:

- suppliers;
- potential employees;
- recruiters;
- referral markets—where they exist, for example retail banks partly relying on professional services organizations, including estate agents for mortgage referrals;
- influence markets—such as government bodies for companies and organizations in the public sector, regulatory authorities, and so on; and
- internal markets—such as existing employees (see Chapter 12).

Relationship marketing concerns the integration of customer service, quality assurance, and marketing activity (Payne, 1993). Consequently, companies employing a relationship marketing approach stress customer retention rather than customer acquisition. Customer retention is a particularly important strategic activity in marketing mass consumer services. Research has demonstrated that when a company retains loyal customers, it is more likely to be profitable compared with competitors who do not, because loyal customers:

- will increase their purchases over time;
- are cheaper to promote to;
- are happy to refer it to others; and
- are prepared to pay a (small) price premium (Reichheld and Sasser, 1990).

(We consider relationship marketing further in Chapter 12.)

This can be demonstrated by the fact that mobile telecommunication providers in Europe, such as Vodafone and Orange, focus on persuading customers to spend more, for example by buying data packages in addition to voice packages and SMS (short messaging services), rather than persuading potential customers who haven't got a mobile phone to buy one (not least because many people in Western markets have at least one or more mobiles anyway). Retention programmes focus marketing activity on customer experience, rewarding loyalty, customer relationship management (CRM), and sales promotion activities in areas such as utilities and telecommunications, but also in the travel industry and retail banking, among others.

Companies have been urged to develop long-term interactive relationships before (Gummesson, 1987). However, the idea that we need to rethink the way in which marketing activity is organized is a good one and suggests moving away from simply adopting the 4Ps towards adopting an interactive marketing approach, paying more attention to the customer base rather than simply market share (Grönroos, 1994). (We consider relationship and services marketing in more detail in Chapter 12.)

More recently, there has been a realization that organizations can go way beyond simply developing strong relationships between buyers and sellers towards the co-creation of value between those buyers and sellers. This requires the customer and the seller organization to learn about each others' needs and to manage their encounters, to enhance the value of the end-product, often in an iterative process (Payne et al., 2008). A good example is the way in which Boeing developed the Dreamliner aeroplane by working in conjunction both with its suppliers (Rolls Royce supplied some of its engines, for example) to envisage the final aeroplane product and also with its potential passengers, by designing a website through which potential passengers could specify how they felt the plane should be laid out. Central to the idea of co-creation is the notion that all offerings, whether they are physical goods or services, are actually services, since they meet our psychological needs in some way. For example, even though a bottle of, say, San Pellegrino water is a good or a physical product, it provides a service in that it quenches our thirst. It is only since the early 2000s that we have begun to see this idea of offerings from this service-dominant, as opposed to product-dominant, perspective (see Research Insight 1.2).

San Pellegrino: the mineral water from Italy

Research Insight 1.2

To take your learning further, you might wish to read the following influential paper:

Vargo, S. L. and Lusch, R. F. (2004) 'Evolving to a new dominant logic for marketing', *Journal of Marketing*, 39(Oct): 32–9.

This ground-breaking article redefined how marketers should perceive offerings, arguing that marketing needed to move beyond outmoded concepts derived from economics of tangible resources ('goods'), embedded value, and transactions, towards intangible resources, the co-creation of values, and relationships.

@ Visit the **Online Resource Centre** to read the abstract and to access the full paper.

Marketing in Context

Does the practice of marketing change depending on whether we are marketing goods or services, and to consumers or businesses? Most textbooks on marketing focus on the marketing offering being essentially a product, rather than a service, experience, or an idea. Yet we've known since the 1960s that services were making important contributions to the US economy (Regan, 1963), and no doubt to other major economies. While the product has been the focus of marketing practice and theory, it should no longer be so. Figure 1.6 shows clearly how important services are to a wide variety of economies around the world, including those in the developed world (such as Sweden), the developing world (such as Thailand), and in the least developed countries (such as Namibia). Even in China and the United Arab Emirates (UAE), services make up more than 35 per cent of the economy—a substantial contribution.

Marketing techniques need to be adapted to the specific sector in which they are used (Blois, 1974). The context, whether it is industrial (that is, B2B), consumer (that is, retail), or services-based (either B2B services such as accountancy or B2B products such as manufacturing components), or used in the not-for-profit context, has an impact upon the marketing tools and techniques that we need to use. Whether offerings are B2B or B2C, they may principally be either product or service, but all offerings combine some elements of the two. (We discuss the intangible nature of services further in Chapter 12.)

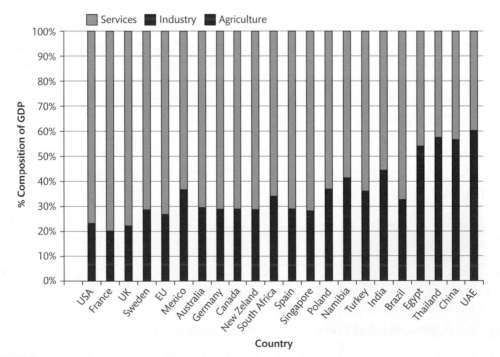

Figure 1.6

Estimated gross domestic product (GDP) % composition by sector for selected countries (year)

Note: All data for 2011, except Singapore and EU, for 2010.

Source: Data taken from CIA World Factbook, http://www.cia.gov. Reproduced with the kind permission of CIA World Factbook.

Having identified four unique contexts of marketing, consumer goods, industrial (B2B), services and not-for-profit, we briefly discuss how each of these contexts affects how we undertake marketing activity.

The Consumer Goods Perspective

Bucklin (1963) defined 'consumer goods' as either:

- convenience goods (purchased frequently with minimum effort);
- shopping goods (purchased selectively based on suitability, quality, price, and style); or
- speciality goods (purchased highly selectively because only that product was capable of meeting a specific need).

Examples of consumer goods industries might include the retail car market, the luxury goods market, and multiple retail grocery. Examples of companies operating in this sector might include car manufacturer Ford, French fashion house Louis Vuitton Moët Hennessey (LVMH), and Wal-Mart, the American supermarket chain.

The consumer goods perspective of marketing has been dominant in the history and study of marketing. The concept is concerned with ideas of the 'marketing mix' and the 4Ps. The consumer goods perspective, borrowing heavily from neoclassical economics, assumes there are comparatively few suppliers within a particular industry, all rivals for the **aggregated demand** (that is, the demand totalled at the population level rather than at the individual level). In fast-moving consumer goods (FMCG) markets, the price at which a good is sold is clearly defined. The product exchanged is tangible (that is, it has physical form), and exchanged between buyer and seller through retail distribution outlets. Consumption takes place at a later and different point in time, with demand stimulated through the 'promotional mix'—that is, advertising, personal selling, direct marketing, and public relations (PR) (see Chapter 9).

The focus of marketing in this context is on how to facilitate the rapid exchange of goods, the effectiveness of the marketing in determining the match between supplier offering and customer demand, and efficiency in managing the distribution of the product through the supply chain. Of particular importance in the consumer goods marketing context are the principles and practice of channel management and retailing (see Chapter 11), since this is the principal means by which customers acquire their consumer goods.

Because of the need to stimulate demand from consumers, focus is placed on the importance of advertising (see Chapter 10), to stimulate demand, and market research (see Chapter 4), to determine how to develop appropriate consumer products and how they are received by the consumers once they're launched into the marketplace. More recently, the Internet and other digital mechanisms have greatly increased the way in which customers receive information about their goods, and the ways in which retailers reorder goods and services from their suppliers.

The Services Perspective

The services perspective in marketing is organized around the idea that markets are increasingly characterized not by physical goods, but by intangible services. Around the late 1970s and early 1980s, there was recognition that the standard goods marketing approach was ill-suited to the marketing of services. Services marketing thinkers suggested that the intangible, performance-dependent, nature of services substantially affected the way in which they should be marketed (Shostack, 1977). There was a focus on the quality of service offered as a result (Grönroos, 1984), as well as a focus on the difference between customer perceptions of actual service quality and their expectations of service quality (Parasuraman et al., 1985).

Some commentators have questioned the use of the product analogy altogether in services marketing (Grönroos, 1998; Vargo and Lusch, 2004). Quite simply, they argue that there are significant differences and similarities between goods and services, in that services:

- cannot be protected by patent;
- do not make use of packaging;
- lack a physical display; and
- cannot be demonstrated in the same way.

Others have argued that there are major similarities, including the need to:

- work at full capacity;
- develop trade and service marks;
- use promotional media;
- use personal selling techniques; and
- approach pricing based on cost and value (Judd, 1968).

The Business-to-Business Perspective

Many marketing textbooks overemphasize consumer goods marketing, paying inadequate attention to industrial/organizational marketing. Business-to-business marketing is essentially different from consumer marketing because the customer is a business rather than an individual household or chief shopper, for example. Business-to-business marketing requires marketers to deal with more sophisticated customers who may buy in volume, as part of a decision-making unit (with other buyers and technicians), who are trained to buy/procure professionally, and who are rewarded for buying the right products and services at the right price (see Chapter 3).

Much B2B marketing activity revolves around the need to develop strong prospects for your company's products and services, and to ensure effective supply chain management operations to develop the market for a B2B product and to ensure that it is delivered appropriately. Because buyers typically purchase in large volumes of product or complex 'bundles' of services (for example, customized IT software solutions sold by the German company SAP), tight specifications are usually produced with which suppliers must comply. Buyers try to ensure that they obtain the best supplier possible by offering suppliers a contract to supply for a set period of time through a bidding process.

In public sector markets, the **procurement** (that is, purchasing) process is bound by strict legal guidelines for product and service contracts valued over a set amount. This process creates substantial rivalry, with firms often submitting bids that they cannot then fulfil either because they've underpriced themselves or because they've over-promised what they can deliver—a phenomenon known as the 'winner's curse', since the winning company ends up servicing an unprofitable contract (Fleisher and Bensoussan, 2004).

The emphasis in B2B markets is strongly focused on the development and building of mutually satisfying relationships based on commitment and trust (Morgan and Hunt, 1994), to win the contract in the first place and then to deliver it to the customer's specifications. Whether or not a firm meets these specifications is in part linked to the **logistics** function (that is, its warehousing, inventory management, delivery) of the firm, be it product- or service-focused. Consequently, B2B marketers can create a competitive advantage if they develop a strong linkage between the marketing and logistics functions, developing a strong customer service proposition through:

- cycle time order reduction;
- accurate invoicing procedures;
- reliable delivery;
- effective claims procedures;
- inventory availability;
- good condition of goods/effective service delivery;
- few order size constraints or limited customization of services;
- effective/planned salesperson visits;
- convenient ordering systems/provision of order status information;
- flexible delivery times; and
- strong after-sales support (Christopher, 1986).

The Not-for-Profit Perspective

There are some key differences in how marketing is used in the not-for-profit and for-profit environments, particularly in relation to marketing communications. Not-for-profit environments can include the charitable sector, government, social enterprise, and social marketing. In the last case, marketing is used to advance social causes: for example, a government might advertise that it is important to eat five or six portions of vegetables per day in order to improve citizens' health.

Rothschild (1979) indicates that key differences between not-for-profit and for-profit marketing include the following.

- *Product*—With not-for profit 'products', there is typically a weaker unique selling proposition (USP)—that is, weaker direct benefits—making it more difficult to direct customer or target audience behaviour in the way desired. For example, giving to charity provides us with a sense of 'doing good', but this feeling may not be sufficient to induce many people to give.
- *Price*—This important component of the marketing mix has different connotations in not-for-profit situations. For example, in a political marketing context, what is the price in relation to marketing a political party? Is it the effort needed to go out and vote, or the opportunity costs for that voter's household of voting for one party's economic promises versus those of another? In relation to charities, the amount donated is often left to the discretion of the donor and is, in fact, largely determined by the donor, rather than specified by the seller, as in a commercial transaction.
- *Involvement*—Whilst we speak of 'high' and 'low' involvement in commercial situations in relation to the extent to which consumers become involved with a product or service in

order to learn more about it during the purchasing process, the involvement in non-business situations displays more extreme tendencies. People either really engage with a charity or political party or cause, for example, or show strong reactions against them.

- *Segmentation*—In the not-for-profit environment, it may be necessary to develop a campaign to drive behaviour in all targets rather than a specific audience, as in commercial markets. For example, a road safety campaign might seek to encourage all adults to drive at the speed limit rather than a specific audience. Nevertheless, there may well be a subgroup that needs a specific targeted message, for example young male drivers who may persistently break the speed limit. But the point is that the general message is applicable to all. The London Metropolitan Police Service's 'Operation Trident' uses advertising techniques to reduce black-on-black crime in London (see Market Insight 1.3).

Although for-profit or private-sector organizations need to interact with a range of stakeholders in order to achieve their business goals, their focus is primarily on target market customers and shareholders. What is different about not-for-profit organizations is that they are concerned with a wider group of interested parties, which we term 'stakeholders'. Stakeholders are those groups with whom the organization has a relationship and which impact upon the operations of the organization, and they include shareholders (or trustees), regulatory bodies, other charity or not-for-profit partners, supply chain partners, employees, and customers. In private companies, revenue is distributed from customers to shareholders, initially converted into profits by the organization, and shareholders are rewarded with a dividend, as a share of the profits earned. Private companies have stakeholders also, but those stakeholders are less likely to have influence on how an organization's profits are distributed. In commercial firms, this remains the remit of the shareholder group.

Not-for-profit organizations also provide products and services, but their customers or users do not always pay the full costs incurred by the organization to provide it. Many not-for-profit organizations rely on a range of stakeholders to provide the finance to support the organization. Instead of revenue from customers being used to reward shareholders, there are often no profits to be redistributed, because those who help to fund the organization do not require a return on their resource provision. For example, central government, local council taxpayers, lottery funding for special projects, and business rate taxes, to name but four sources of income, fund city councils in the UK. Charities are supported by individual and corporate donations. Museums, for example, may rely on a mixture of grants, lottery allocations, entrance fees, and individual donations and bequests.

Market Insight 1.3

Marketing the Law

Operation Trident was set up by London's Metropolitan Police Service in 1998 after a spate of shootings in the black communities of the London Boroughs of Brent and Lambeth. The unit has a focus on gun crime and a special focus on drug-related gun crime. After a successful launch, its operation was later extended to the whole of London. Around 75 per cent of London's gun crime involves black victims and black suspects. What is different about Trident's approach is that part of its remit has been to disrupt gun crime by dissuading people from getting involved in the first place and to inform on suspects through the placement of adverts on billboards in targeted areas, on the radio (Choice FM, using celebrity endorsers), viral rap videos, adverts in the cinema and on MTV, and at community events, such as the Urban Music Festival at Earl's Court. One Trident campaign centred around the tagline 'You don't need a gun to get it', with celebrity role models outlining how respect can be earned as an alternative to street violence.

Trident has spent around £250,000 per year on media and advertising, arguably to very good effect. After the 2005 campaign, with the tagline 'Don't get blood on your hands—if you know about a gun, call Crimestoppers anonymously', gun crime calls increased by 86 per cent. In 2007, the Trident advertising campaign 'Stop the guns' won the Institute of Practitioners in Advertising (IPA) Grand Prix Award and a Gold Award at the IPA 2007 Effectiveness Awards. (The campaign has now rebranded as 'Drop the weapons', to include knife crime.)

Trident has historically struggled to maintain its trust within the black community, partly because only around 8 per cent of its officers were from the black community (in 2008). Despite substantial cuts to other areas of the Metropolitan Police budget (arising from the UK government's 2010–15 austerity Budget) and threats to disband Trident, the unit continues to exist, although it no longer spends funds on high-profile advertising and PR campaigns. This may be a serious mistake, as 'Stop snitching' leaflets outlining how the police will ruin witnesses' lives have appeared on one South London estate after police appealed for witnesses following the murder of teenager Sylvester Akalapara in December 2010.

Lee Jasper, former director of police and equalities and former chair of the Trident Independent Advisory Group, says:

> Cuts to Trident budgets have resulted in them ending their massively effective advertising and community engagements campaigns. That was a critical error. The Trident posters provided massive reassurance, boosted community confidence and community events led by the Independent Trident Advisers (IAG) gave Trident the edge in the war of misinformation that is the battle ground between criminals and the police in trying to maintain community confidence.

Sources: BBC News (2006); Benady (2007); Fisk (2008); Davenport (2010); Jasper (2011); http://www.droptheweapons.org; http://www.ipaeffectivenessawards.co.uk/Gold-Award-Winners/Stop-the-guns

1 If you were the senior police officer in charge of Operation Trident, how would you use marketing and PR in future campaigns to reduce gun crime in London?

2 Do you think that the use of the police budget for advertising is a better use of the money than the employment of further police officers or not? Justify your answer.

3 How important do you think it is that the police counter the 'Stop snitching' campaign with their own communication campaign?

What Impact Does Marketing Have on Society?

The marketing industry makes considerable contributions to society. Wilkie and Moore (1999) describe how the complexities of the 'aggregate marketing system' work using the example of how marketing brings together all of the ingredients of a typical breakfast to American households.

Consider the individual ingredients of that American breakfast: for example, coffee or tea, together with pancakes and syrup (and the necessary ingredients required here), the cups and plates to contain the food, the hotplate or grill to heat the food, and so on. The aggregate marketing system is truly amazing when reflected on in this way. We should remember that there are over 313 million people in the US, with over 100 million households (Wilkie and Moore, 1999), each of which is brought its own unique mixture of products and services that come together to form an individual breakfast for any one particular person. The system in most countries around the world works very well because we're not generally starving and we don't have to ration our food to preserve the amount that we eat to be fair to others. Certain countries in Africa, North Korea, and parts of China, for example, do have people dying of hunger, but these countries often experience imperfections in supply and demand because of political circumstances (such as war, dictatorship, famine) and environmental conditions (for example, drought).

Marketing plays a key role in developing and transforming society. Consider how different your life would be without television, invented in 1929–32 by Scotland's Baird Television Development Company and Germany's Telefunken. Consider how different your life would be without the credit card, invented by America's Diner's Club in 1950. Of course, these are large, disruptive innovations, but how much is your own life improved by the invention of artificial sweeteners, invented by Finland's Cultor in 1969? Most people would now be completely lost without their mobile phones, first developed by Japan's NTT in 1979. In more modern times, the invention of social networking by Facebook in 2004 has had a huge impact on marketing and society.

Research Insight 1.3

To take your learning further, you might wish to read the following influential paper:

Wilkie, W. L. and Moore, E. S. (1999) 'Marketing's contributions to society', *Journal of Marketing*, 63(Special Issue): 198–218.

This excellent article describes how marketing operates as an aggregated system within society. The article explains how marketing impacts upon, and contributes to, society by considering how offerings flow through it, contributing both positively and negatively to individual well-being and the economy. The article concludes that the marketing system adapts and changes to the needs of modern society, but contributes greatly to it.

@ Visit the **Online Resource Centre** to read the abstract and to access the full paper.

Is the Future Bright for the Electric Car?

The race is on to produce the Wünderkind of the car industry, an all-singing, all-dancing, good-looking electric car. Silent and pollution-free, with engineering underpinned by green technologies, the car must not compromise on performance, looks, or handling. The change has come about because of greater public concern and the need for European legislation concerning vehicle fuel emissions to combat global warming. Since car drivers are collectively a major user of oil to power their cars, a shift to electric seems obvious. Problems with oil supply in the Middle East, since the OPEC crises of the 1970s to the modern day, have worsened the situation.

Toyota Motor introduced the first successful green car technology with the hybrid Prius in 1997, combining a petrol engine with an electric battery; other manufacturers (such as Honda, Ford, and Chevrolet) in the industry swiftly followed. The car performed at similar speeds to a traditional car, but with greater fuel economy.

Sleek, powerful, and green: the Tesla sports car

It used the petrol engine when it needed high performance and the battery when it didn't. A number of car manufacturers already sell electric vehicles, including the Citroën C-Zero, Mitsubishi IMEV, Nissan Leaf, Peugeot IOn, Smart ED, Tata Vista, and the Tesla sports car. Hyundai, Chevrolet, Renault, Vauxhall, Audi, Ford, Morgan, Smart, and Toyota all planned to release pure electric vehicles in 2012, with BMW, Porsche and Vauxhall following in 2013.

What is interesting is that the business model will change: instead of buying petrol at a station, the purchaser of an electric vehicle will either be able to lease the battery with a subscription to an energy supplier, or own the whole car outright and charge up the battery separately as necessary. The critical questions will be:

- will there be a large enough network of recharging stations?
- will the time/price taken to recharge offset the time/price to fill up with unleaded fuel?
- will the car perform as well as any hybrid/non-electric vehicle?

What is likely is that manufacturers will need to undertake very large campaigns to persuade motorists if they genuinely want them to switch to the new technology. Humans are, after all. creatures of habit.

Sources: Toyota (2006); Renault (2009); SMMT (2011)

1 **Why do you think it has taken so long to develop the fully electric car?**

2 **Do you think motorists will switch quickly or slowly to the new technology? Why?**

3 **What other well-known products or services have taken advantage of society's movement towards stronger environmental values? What are these values?**

What would we do without these products in today's world? In each case, we enjoy these products because innovative individuals and companies brought these products to us, as consumers. Take the tin can for storing food, for example: we couldn't conceive of not having this device now and yet it is only around 200 years old. Prior to that, food was stored in earthenware pots and spoiled at a much faster rate. Could you imagine ketchup not existing? It was brought to us by Heinz, but based on an ancient Chinese fish sauce recipe called *ketsiap*! Of course, in each of these cases, the invention has been an extraordinary success. But the aggregate marketing system not only serves to bring consumers those products and services that truly meet their needs, but it also serves to stop the failures from getting through as well (see Chapter 7). The aggregate marketing system serves to impede products because they don't meet consumer needs. So it serves a number of benefits to society, including the following:

- the promotion and delivery of desired products and services;
- the provision of a forum for market learning (we can see what does and what doesn't get through the system);
- the stimulation of market demand;
- the offering of a wide scope for choice of products and services by offering a close/customized fit with consumer needs;
- the facilitation of purchases (or acquisitions generally, for example if no payment is made directly, as in the case of public services);
- time savings and the promotion of efficiency in customer requirement matching;
- the bringing of new products and services, and improvements, to market to meet latent and unserved needs; and
- the search for customer satisfaction for repeat purchases (Wilkie and Moore, 1999).

Nevertheless, the marketing function within society does not always serve the common good. Marketing is frequently criticized for doing precisely the opposite: it has been charged with being unethical in nature and manipulative, and with creating wants and needs when none previously existed (Packard, 1960).

The Critical Marketing Perspective

Because marketing's contributions to society are not necessarily all good, it is important that we develop a critical approach to understanding marketing. This allows us constantly to evaluate and re-evaluate marketing, to improve it, so that marketing continues to operate in a desirable manner within society. While the aggregate marketing system distributes life-saving medicines, food, and important utilities, such as heat and light, it also distributes alcohol, tobacco, and gambling products, for example—products that we might regard as dangerous to our health and well-being. Of course, in many cultures around the world, people enjoy drinking, smoking, and gambling. However, we are fooling ourselves, especially if we use these to excess, if we think that our use of these is really satisfying our own needs and not causing ourselves harm.

Unless told otherwise by government, the aggregate marketing system would distribute anything. Were prostitution and soft drugs, such as cannabis, to be made legal in Britain, the aggregate marketing system would distribute them. It already does this in the Netherlands, for example, where these practices are no longer illegal. In that sense, the aggregate marketing system in itself is inherently *amoral*—that is, without morals. It is not *immoral*—that is, designed to harm—but simply amoral, designed without any sensitivity to whether it harms or not. The system is made moral only by the decisions of government and other institutional actors who may act upon and regulate the aggregate marketing system.

Some might consider the very ideology of marketing to be rooted in big business, mass consumer sovereignty, excess supply over demand, and ever-increasing consumption (Brownlie and Saren, 1992). In other words, they may say that we consume far too much and that marketing companies are to blame for it! This argument, mooted at the very start of the 1990s, was far-sighted for its time and has developed some considerable backing in the 2000s, with governments around the world working to regulate the fast food industry, for example, to ensure that it delivers a healthier product to the marketplace (or at least that it informs the consumer of the inherent risks). Interestingly, politicians and leaders in some cities have becomes so sick of advertising billboards and posters that they have either limited them, as in the historic city of Rome (Kingston, 2011), or banned them completely, as in the city of São Paolo in Brazil, where all advertising has been banned since the mayor introduced a 'Clean City Law' in 2006 (Jefferson, 2011).

So what else might we be over-consuming because of marketers? There are many other controversies in marketing, some of which include the following.

- What is a fair price for companies and organizations in wealthier countries to pay suppliers in poorer countries?
- Where is the line between persuading customers and manipulating customers to purchase products, services, and ideas? Is some marketing promotion really simply corporate propaganda?
- To what extent should the goods, services, and ideas of one country be marketed over the goods, services, and ideas of another country? What are the cultural implications?
- How much should we consume of any one particular good, service, or idea? When should governments step in to limit consumption?
- Are some groups more susceptible than others to certain types of marketing promotion? If they are, at what point and how should they be protected?
- Are some producers or buyer groups more powerful than others and what impact, if any, does this have upon society?
- Does the aggregate marketing system itself advantage some groups over others and what are the implications for society?

A critical approach to marketing can help us to understand the nature of marketing knowledge. 'Marketing can then be learned from the many varieties of market that exist rather than concentrating on branded, mass consumption products in developed economies' (Easton, 2002), as marketing is so often portrayed. Adopting a critical approach to understanding marketing serves us well and is in keeping with how managers actually learn the discipline in practice (Easton, 2002).

Critiquing marketing helps to consider:

- how marketing knowledge is developed and the extent to which this is based on our contemporary social world (for example, much of current marketing knowledge is based on American practice and research, and what implications does this have for the rest of the world?);
- how the historical and cultural conditions in which we operate, as consumers and as students of marketing, impact on how we see marketing as a discipline;
- the need for continuous re-examination of the categories and frameworks that we use to understand marketing; and
- how marketing can benefit from other intellectual perspectives, such as social anthropology, social psychology (see Burton, 2001).

In this chapter, we have aimed to explore marketing from the perspective of how it interacts with and has developed in society. We see marketing as a force within society in itself—as a form of virus because of the way in which it replicates itself (Gladwell, 2002). We consider marketing as a management process, operating as a holistic process, within and outside the firm or organization that is using it. Of course, it is currently fashionable, and perhaps always was, to criticize marketing in general and **capitalism** in particular (Packard, 1960; Klein, 1999). But the move from a production-led to a consumer-led society has undoubtedly arisen because of marketing, as the following quote illustrates:

> The power of market forces and that of marketing to virtually shape every aspect of a society's mores [customs], attitudes and culture should not be underestimated. Used wisely and with restraint, marketing can harness and channel the vast energies of the free market system for the good of consumers, corporations and for society as a whole. Used recklessly, it can cause significant harm to all those entities. Thus, marketing is like a potent drug with potentially serious side effects.
>
> (Sheth and Sisodia, 2006: 326)

⟨◈⟩ Chapter Summary

To consolidate your learning, the key points from this chapter can be summarized as follows.

■ **Define the marketing concept**

Marketing is the process by which organizations anticipate and satisfy their customers' needs to both parties' benefit. It involves mutual exchange of benefits. Over the last twenty years, the marketing concept has been altered to recognize the importance of the long-term customer relationship to organizations.

■ **Explain how marketing has developed over the last century**

While some writers have suggested a simple production era–sales era–marketing era development for marketing over the twentieth century, others recognize that marketing has existed in different forms in different countries. Nevertheless, there is an increasing recognition that marketing is now a more systematic organizational activity as a result of market research and sophisticated promotional activity than it has been before. There is also a move towards recognizing the need for companies and organizations to behave responsibly in relation to society.

■ **Describe the four major contexts of marketing application—that is, consumer goods, business to business, services, and not-for-profit marketing**

Marketing divides into four types, recognizing that marketing activities are designed based on the context in which an organization operates. The consumer goods marketing approach has traditionally been dominant, stressing the 4Ps and the marketing mix. Business-to-business (B2B) marketing focuses on principles of relationship marketing and buyer–seller relationships. Services marketing stresses the intangible nature of the product, the need to manage customer expectations, and levels of service quality. Not-for-profit marketing stresses the need to understand the needs of multiple stakeholders.

■ **Assess critically the impact that marketing has on society**

The aggregate marketing system also has its faults, allowing the promotion and distribution of products and services that could be bad for us, and the over-consumption of products that, in moderation, are good for us. We propose adopting a critical marketing perspective as a natural approach to learning marketing. As society is changing, new critical approaches to marketing are increasingly developing (such as the Fairtrade movement).

Review Questions

1 How do we define the marketing concept?
2 How do the American Marketing Association (AMA) and the Chartered Institute of Marketing (CIM) definitions of marketing differ?
3 What is the 'marketing mix'?
4 What are the four major contexts of marketing application?
5 What is the idea of service-dominant logic in marketing?
6 How does marketing contribute positively and negatively to society?

Scan this image to go online and access the chapter's multiple-choice questions, web links, Internet activities, and more!

Worksheet Summary

Visit the **Online Resource Centre** and complete Worksheet 1.1. This will help you to learn about how managers can use McCarthy's 4Ps framework to market goods, and Bitner and Boom's 7Ps framework to market services.

References

American Marketing Association (AMA) (2007) 'Definition of marketing', available online at http://www.marketingpower.com/Community/ARC/Pages/Additional/Definition/default.aspx?sq=definition+of+marketing [accessed 5 February 2012].

Bagozzi, R. P. (1975) 'Marketing as exchange', *Journal of Marketing*, 39(4): 32–9.

BBC News (2006) 'Q&A: Operation Trident', 14 September, available online at http://news.bbc.co.uk/1/hi/uk/5342246.stm [accessed 6 February 2012].

BBC News (2011) 'Profile: Thomas Cook', 22 November, available online at http://www.bbc.co.uk/news/business-15835839 [accessed 11 February 2012].

Benady, D. (2007) 'Gun crime: selling an anti-gun culture', 29 November, *Marketing Week*, p. 24.

Blois, K. J. (1974) 'The marketing of services: an approach', *European Journal of Marketing*, 8(2): 137–45.

Booms, B. H. and Bitner, M. J. (1981) 'Marketing strategies and organisation structures for service firms', in J. H. Donnelly and W. R. George (eds) *Marketing of Services*, Chicago, IL: AMA, pp. 47–51.

Borden, N. H. (1964) 'The concept of the marketing mix', *Journal of Advertising Research*, 4: 2–7.

Brownlie, D. and Saren, M. (1992) 'The four Ps of the marketing concept: prescriptive, polemical, permanent, and problematic', *European Journal of Marketing*, 26(4): 34–47.

Bucklin, L. P. (1963) 'Retail strategy and the classification of consumer goods', *Journal of Marketing*, Jan: 51–6.

Burton, D. (2001) 'Critical marketing theory: the blueprint?', *European Journal of Marketing*, 35(5/6): 722–43.

Chartered Institute of Marketing (CIM) (2001) 'Resource Glossary: Marketing', available online at http://www.cim.co.uk/resources/glossary/home.aspx [accessed 5 February 2012].

Christopher, M. (1986) 'Reaching the customer: strategies for marketing and customer service', *Journal of Marketing Management*, 2(1): 63–71.

Clawson, T. (2011) 'Shaping the marketing department of the future', *Marketing*, 12 October, pp. 39–40.

Davenport, J. (2010) 'Operation Trident to be spared in Met budget cuts', *Evening Standard*, 23 November, available online at http://www.thisislondon.co.uk/standard/article-23900153-operation-trident-to-be-spared-in-met-budget-cuts.do [accessed 6 February 2012].

Easton, G. (2002) 'Marketing: a critical realist approach', *Journal of Business Research*, 55: 103–9.

Enright, M. (2002) 'Marketing and conflicting dates for its emergence: Hotchkiss, Bartels and the fifties school of alternative accounts', *Journal of Marketing Management*, 18: 445–61.

Fisk, P. (2008) 'Ten years of Operation Trident', *Time Out London*, 19 February, available online at http://www.timeout.com/london/big-smoke/features/4285/Ten_years_of_Operation_Trident.html#articleAfterMpu [accessed 6 February 2012].

Fleisher, C. S. and Bensoussan, B. E. (2002) *Strategic and Competitive Analysis*, Englewood Cliffs, NJ: Prentice-Hall.

Fullerton, R. A. (1988) 'How modern is modern marketing? Marketing's evolution and the myth of the "Production Era"', *Journal of Marketing*, 52(Jan): 108–25.

Gladwell, M. (2002) *The Tipping Point: How Little Things Can Make a Big Difference*, London: Abacus Books.

Grönroos, C. (1984) 'A service quality model and its marketing implications', *European Journal of Marketing*, 18(4): 36–44.

Grönroos, C. (1994) 'From marketing mix to relationship marketing: towards a paradigm shift in marketing', *Management Decision*, 32(2): 4–20.

Grönroos, C. (1998) 'Marketing services: a case of a missing product', *Journal of Business and Industrial Marketing*, 13(4/5): 322–38.

Gummesson, E. (1987) 'The new marketing: developing long-term interactive relationships', *Long Range Planning*, 20(4): 10–20.

Guthrie, J. and Blitz, R. (2011) 'Egyptian heat brings chill for Thomas Cook', *Financial Times*, 26–27 November, p. 17.

Jasper, L. (2011) 'Trident failures feed "stop snitching" campaign', *Lee Jasper Official Blog*, 20 February, available online at http://leejasper.blogspot.com/2011/01/trident-failures-feed-stop-snitching.html [accessed 6 February 2012].

Jefferson, C. (2011) 'A happy, flourishing city with no advertising', *Good Cities*, 22 December, available online at http://www.good.is/post/a-happy-flourishing-city-with-no-advertising/ [accessed 10 February 2012].

Judd, R. C. (1968) 'Similarities and differences in product and service retailing', *Journal of Retailing*, 43(4): 1–9.

Keith, R. J. (1960) 'The marketing revolution', *Journal of Marketing*, 24(Jan): 35–8.

Kingston, T. (2011) 'Romans revolt over billboard jungle', *The Guardian*, 27 December, p. 27.

Klein, N. (1999) *No Logo*, London: Flamingo.

Kohli, A. K. and Jaworski, B. J. (1990) 'Market orientation: the construct, research propositions and managerial implications', *Journal of Marketing*, 54(Apr): 1–18.

Lendrevie, J., Lévy, J., and Lindon, D. (2006) *Mercator: Théorie et Pratique du Marketing*, 8th edn, Paris: Dunod.

Marketing and Sales Standards Setting Body (MSSSB) (2010) *Developing World-Class Standards for the Marketing Profession*, Cookham: Chartered Institute of Marketing.

McCarthy, E. J. (1960) *Basic Marketing*, Homewood, IL: Irwin.

Morgan. R. M. and Hunt, S. D. (1994) 'The commitment–trust theory of relationship marketing', *Journal of Marketing*, 58(3): 20–38.

Narver, J. C. and Slater, S. F. (1990) 'The effect of a market orientation on business profitability', *Journal of Marketing*, Oct: 20–35.

Packard, V. O. (1960) *The Hidden Persuaders*, Harmondsworth: Penguin Books.

Parasuraman, A., Berry, L. L., and Zeithaml, V. A. (1985) 'A conceptual model of service quality and its implications for further research', *Journal of Marketing*, 49(3): 41–50.

Payne, A. F. (1993) *The Essence of Services Marketing*, Hemel Hempstead: Prentice-Hall.

Payne, A. F., Storbacka, K., and Frow, P. (2008) 'Managing the co-creation of value', *Journal of the Academy of Marketing Science*, 36: 83–96.

Regan, W. J. (1963) 'The service revolution', *Journal of Marketing*, 27: 57–62.

Reichheld, F. F. and Sasser Jr, W. E. (1990) 'Zero defections: quality comes to services', *Harvard Business Review*, Sept–Oct: 105–11.

Renault (2009) 'Drive the Change', available online at http://www.renault-ze.com/uk/ [accessed 17 April 2010].

Richmond, S. (2012) 'Microsoft Windows Phone 8 details leak', *The Telegraph*, 3 February, available online at http://www.telegraph.co.uk/technology/microsoft/9058937/Microsoft-Windows-Phone-8-details-leak.html [accessed 5 February 2012].

Rothschild, M. L. (1979) 'Marketing communications in non-business situations or why it's so hard to sell brotherhood like soap', *Journal of Marketing*, 43(2): 11–20.

Rushton, K. (2012) 'Nokia slides to €1bn loss as sales tumble', *The Telegraph*, 26 January, available online at http://www.telegraph.co.uk/finance/newsbysector/mediatechnologyandtelecoms/telecoms/9041388/Nokia-slides-to-1bn-loss-as-sales-tumble.html [accessed 5 February 2012].

Saren, M. (2006) *Marketing Graffiti: The View from the Street*, Oxford: Butterworth-Heinemann.

Sheth, J. N. and Sisodia, R. J. (2005) 'A dangerous divergence: marketing and society', *Journal of Public Policy and Marketing*, 24(1): 160–2.

Sheth, J. N. and Sisodia, R. J. (2006) 'Introduction. How to reform marketing', in J. N. Sheth and R. J. Sisodia (eds) *Does Marketing Need Reform? Fresh Perspectives on the Future*, Armonk, NY: M. E. Sharpe, pp. 3–12.

Shostack, G. L. (1977) 'Breaking free from product marketing', *Journal of Marketing*, 41(Apr): 73–8.

Slater, S. F. and Narver, J. C. (1994) 'Market orientation, customer value and superior performance', *Business Horizons*, Mar–Apr: 22–7.

Society of Motor Manufacturers and Traders (SMMT) (2011) 'Electric Car Guide 2011: Questions and Answers', available online at https://www.smmt.co.uk/shop/electric-car-guide-2011/ [accessed 6 February 2012].

Taylor, P. (2012) 'Glory days an old memory in RIM's new world', *Financial Times*, 24 January, p. 19.

Thomas, D. (2012) 'Windows platform fails to curb Nokia's slide', *Financial Times*, 26 January, available online at http://www.ft.com/cms/s/2/f03520d8-481a-11e1-a4e5-00144feabdc0.html#axzz1IXzCpfO4 [accessed 5 February 2012].

Toyota (2006) 'Hybrid Synergy Drive', available online at http://www.toyota.co.uk/cgi-bin/toyota/bv/frame_start.jsp?id=HSD_mainnav [accessed 17 April 2010].

Vargo, S. L. and Lusch, R. F. (2004) 'Evolving to a new service dominant logic for marketing', *Journal of Marketing*, 68(Jan): 1–17.

Wilkie, W. L. and Moore, E. S. (1999) 'Marketing's contributions to society', *Journal of Marketing*, 63(Special Issue): 198–218.

2

The Global Marketing Environment

Learning outcomes

After reading this chapter, you will be able to:

- define the global marketing environment;

- explain PESTLE analysis and show how it is used to understand the external environment;

- explain the environmental scanning process;

- analyse the performance environment using an appropriate model; and

- understand the importance of analysing an organization's internal environment, and identify the key resources and capabilities.

Case Insight 2.1

Helen Tattersall for Michelin Tyres

Michelin Tyres has been established for over a century and is now active in more than 170 countries. How does it keep abreast of the marketing environment? We speak to Helen Tattersall to find out more.

The Michelin Tyre Company Ltd, first incorporated in 1905, was set up in 1889 by two brothers, André and Edouard Michelin. Now active in more than 170 countries, Michelin operates across all continents of the world, manufacturing and selling tyres for all kinds of vehicles, publishing maps and guides, and operating specialist digital services. Most people recognize our world famous mascot, Bibendum, 'The Michelin man', looking good considering his age! My own division is concerned with tyres made for heavy goods vehicles over 3.5 tonnes, including trucks, coaches, and buses. In the UK and the Republic of Ireland, we have an extensive sales force supporting thousands of tyre distributors, from tyres used in cars and trucks, to those used in specialist industrial and earth-moving equipment.

To conduct environmental scanning, we adopt several approaches. We use joint panels with key national and regional trade journals, conducting telephone questionnaires with customers on challenges, issues, and developments in the haulage industry. Our sales force in the UK and Ireland is responsible for collecting market intelligence, especially on competitors' actions and products.

We work with the Road Haulage Association and the Freight Transport Association, which offers us a chance to mix with customers in a non-selling environment, and we belong to the EuroPool organization, an independent body that acts on behalf of all European tyre manufacturers. Here, we declare our sales on a monthly basis and it sends back to us details of our market share. In addition, we conduct our own annual surveys with

distribution partners (including ATS Euromaster—a Michelin group company—and independent tyre dealers). We use the results of these surveys to track industry market shares with sales revenues. Finally, we analyse and test competitors' tyre products at our research and development centre.

Our scanning activity has picked up lots of challenges, for example rising fuel costs, changes in haulage patterns resulting from an increase in Internet shopping, new legislation around driving and emission standards, and changing patterns of labour with the increase in Eastern European drivers (often bringing with them their cheaper fuel). However, the biggest challenge that we have experienced in the last four or five years is the strong competition from cheap imported tyre manufacturers from emerging economies in the east, including India, China, and Korea. These new tyre brands sell very cheaply because of the low manufacturing and labour costs in these countries. Although we knew these brands were coming, we were very surprised by how rapidly customers adopted them.

The Bibendum brand, looking good for 100 years old!

1 If you were faced with unexpected competition of this type, what would you do?

■ Introduction

Have you ever wondered why some organizations collapse and others don't? How do companies keep up with the many changes that occur in politics, markets, and economies? What processes do they use to try to anticipate changes in technologies? How do they know which factors will impact on their businesses and which won't? We consider such questions in this chapter.

The operating environment for all organizations, whether they are commercial, charitable, or in the public sector, is never static and predictable. In this chapter, we examine the nature of the marketing environment, determine environment-related issues, and provide a context for developing marketing strategies (see Chapter 5).

Consider the degree to which an organization can influence the various environmental forces acting on it. The external environment consists of political, social, and technological influences, and organizations usually have very limited influence on each of these. The performance environment consists of competitors, suppliers, and indirect service providers who shape the way in which an organization achieves its objectives. Here, organizations have a much stronger level of influence. The internal environment concerns the resources, processes, and policies with which an organization manages to achieve its goals. These elements can be influenced directly by an organization. Each of these three marketing environments is discussed in this chapter (see Figure 2.1).

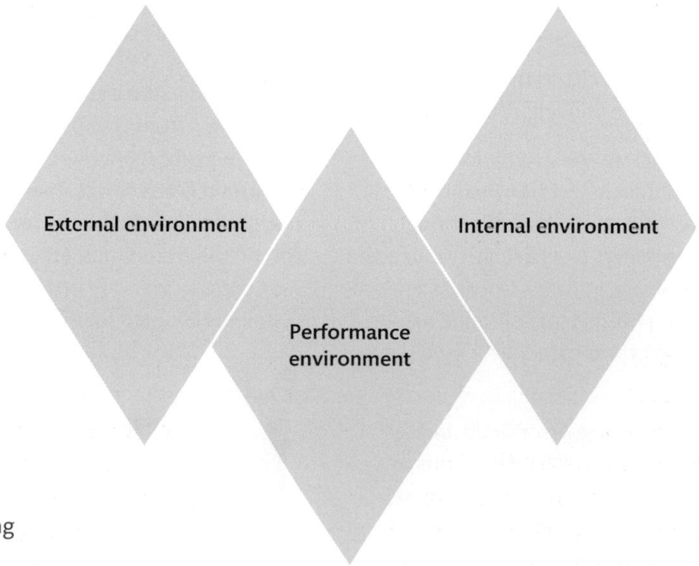

Figure 2.1

The three marketing environments

External environment

Performance environment

Internal environment

Figure 2.2
The external marketing environment

Understanding the External Environment

The external environment is characterized in two main ways: in the first, the elements do not have an immediate impact on the performance of an organization, although they might do in the longer term; in the second, although the elements can influence an organization, it is not possible to control them. This suggests that the level of risk attached to the external environment is potentially high. To make sense of the external environment, we use the well-known acronym, **PESTLE**. This is by far the easiest and one of the most popular frameworks with which to examine the external environment.

PESTLE refers to the 'political', 'economic', 'social', 'technological', 'legal', and 'ecological' environments, as shown as Figure 2.2.

The Political Environment

When we conduct environmental scanning programmes, we consider the firm or organization's **political environment**. Although the legal environment relates to the laws and regulations associated with consumers and business practices, the political environment relates to the period of interaction between business, society, and government before those laws are enacted, when they are still being formed or are in dispute. Political environmental analysis is a critical phase in environmental scanning, because companies can detect potential legal and regulatory changes in their industries, and have a chance to impede, influence, and alter that legislation. Most marketing strategy textbooks teach that the political environment is largely uncontrollable. However, this is not always the case. There are circumstances in which an organization, or an industry coalition, can affect legislation in its own favour—or at least respond more flexibly to changes in legislation than do its competitors. There is increasingly an understanding that business–government relations, properly undertaken, can be a source of **sustainable competitive advantage** (Baines and Viney, 2010). In other words, organizations can outperform other organizations over time if they can manage their relationships with government and regulatory bodies better than do their competitors (Hillman et al., 2004).

Market Insight 2.1 offers an example of a business–government relations campaign.

WikiLeaks Reveals Shell's Lobbying Strategy

When Bradley Manning, an intelligence analyst in the US army, allegedly released secret US embassy diplomatic cables to WikiLeaks, an online whistleblower publishing private and classified media in February 2010, he could not have imagined the international furore that would result, and how it would lead to his eventual arrest and trial for 'aiding the enemy'—a crime punishable with the death penalty. In total, Manning is alleged to have released more than 250,000 documents to WikiLeaks, which in turn released its content in redacted form to major newspaper groups around the world, including *The New York Times* (US), *The Guardian* (UK), *El Pais* (Spain), *Le Monde* (France), and *Der Spiegel* (Germany), thereby ensuring a global audience.

Inside one cable dated October 2009 is a conversation between Royal Dutch Shell's then executive vice-president for Sub-Saharan Africa, Ann Pickard, and the then US ambassador to Nigeria, Robin Sanders. They discussed the passage of the imminent Petroleum Industry Bill, which was set to introduce regulations banning gas flaring (which had potential cost and security implications to the tune of US$4 billion for Shell-operated companies in Nigeria), regulating the governance of international joint ventures (between Nigerian National Petroleum Corporation and international oil companies such as Shell, Exxon Mobil, and Chevron), and redefining how companies will hold onto their exploration and production blocks (Shell was worried it could lose 80 per cent of its 'acreage'). Clearly, there was a lot at stake for Shell (and US oil majors such as Chevron and Exxon Mobil). Pickard and the US ambassador discussed how the US Joint House Committee on Petroleum Upstream and Downstream and the Justice Department were working on the Bill. Because Pickard could not get the ear of Yar-Adua, then President of Nigeria, she asked the US ambassador if he could 'deliver low-level messages of concern'.

In the cables, the conversation turned to how Pickard believed that the Nigerian government had contacted China and Russia to discuss potentially selling rights for exploration and production for some of Nigeria's oil blocks, and had provided Shell data on which they could base their bids. The Chinese came back with an offer, which the Nigerian government declined, because it was too low. What was particularly revealing, according to the cables, was the fact that Pickard said that Shell had picked up this competitive intelligence because the 'Government of Nigeria had forgotten that Shell had seconded people to all the relevant ministries and that Shell had access to everything that was being done in those ministries'. For some, Shell's influence in Nigeria is no surprise given that 'Shell's presence in Nigeria is older than the Nigerian state itself': Shell was granted its first oil exploration and production licence in 1913.

Shell, on the other hand, would argue that Shell-operated companies in Nigeria make a major contribution to the Nigerian economy and labour force. For example, Shell's Nigerian joint venture (in which it is the minority shareholder) contributed close to US$31 billion to the Government of Nigeria between 2006 and 2010, and its offshore business close to US$4 billion over the same period, supplied about 21 per cent of Nigeria's total oil and gas production in 2010, employed 6,000 people in Nigeria (90 per cent of whom are Nigerian), and has contributed over US$250 million to the Niger Delta Development Commission over the nine years from 2002 to 2010 to aid the region's development. Given its financial exposure to Nigerian oil and gas production, and the income derived from that industry, why wouldn't it want to seek to influence the Nigerian government?

Sources: Anon. (2010); Nwajiaku-Dahou (2010); Shell (2011); BBC News (2012)

1 Over two years later, the Petroleum Industry Bill had still not been passed. To what extent do you think this was due to the lobbying activity?

2 Do you think it is ethical for Shell to influence Nigerian government oil and gas policy in this way? Why?

3 How does the pervasive nature of modern digital media impact on how transparent companies should be in their lobbying activities?

Companies or organizations sometimes make the decision to influence governments in collaboration with other organizations. For example, Japanese automotive manufacturers Nissan and Honda lobbied the European Commission to recognize cars assembled in the UK largely from Japanese parts as European in the early 1990s to offset import quotas on certain Japanese goods (Kewley, 2002). There have been many successful examples of other lobbying campaigns, such as that of the Shopping Hours Reform Council (SHRC), consisting mainly of large supermarket chains, which managed to lobby the then UK Conservative government to make Sunday trading legal in July 1994 (Harris et al., 1999).

There are several ways in which marketers might conduct business–government relations, including the following.

- Lobbyist firms, with key industry knowledge, can be engaged permanently or as needed.
- Public relations (PR) consultancies, such as Weber Shandwick, can be commissioned for their political services.
- A politician may be paid a fee to give political advice on matters of importance to an organization, where this is legal within that particular jurisdiction and that politician is not serving directly within the government in question on the same portfolio as that on which he or she is advising.
- An in-house PR manager might handle government relations directly.
- An industry association might be contacted to lobby on behalf of members: in the European financial services industry, for example, groups include the European Banking Federation (EBF), the European Savings Bank Group (ESBG), and the European Association of Co-operative Banks (EACB).
- Where it is legal, a politician may be invited directly to join the board of directors, board of trustees, or board of advisers of an organization.

Working with parliaments, civil servants, and governments in different countries gives rise to serious difficulties, particularly where a company or organization has limited knowledge of the market. It is therefore important not only to try to change or influence the political environment, but also to understand how changes in it might affect your own organization. A case study by Melewar et al. (2008) showed the impact of the then newly enlarged European Union on Fjord Seafood, a Norwegian company, and one of the world's largest salmon producers. When ten new countries joined the EU, structural changes were likely to have profound effects on Fjord Seafood's export sales, the nature of its international marketing strategy, and all aspects of its marketing mix. A key consideration was therefore whether it could sell a standardized product across the EU or whether it would need to tailor the product to individual countries. In China, private sector organizations, including those investing from overseas, are required to house a Communist Party branch within them, which may serve to hinder or expedite their relationships with local and national government stakeholders (Anon., 2012).

The Economic Environment

Companies and organizations should develop an understanding of the economic environment because a country's economic circumstances have an impact on what economists term 'factor prices' within a particular industry for a particular firm or organization. These factors could include raw material, labour, building, and other capital costs, or any other input to a business.

The external environment of a firm is affected by the following items.

- *Wage inflation*—Annual wages increases in a particular sector will depend on the availability and supply of labour in that sector.
- *Price inflation*—How much consumers pay for goods and services depends on the rate of supply of those goods and services. If supply is scarce, there is usually an increase in the price of that consumer good or service (such as petrol).
- **Gross domestic product (GDP)** *per capita*—The combined output of goods and services in a particular nation is useful for determining relative wealth per member of the population, compared between nations as GDP per capita at **purchasing power parity (PPP)**.
- *Income, sales, and corporation taxes*—These taxes substantially affect how we market goods and services.
- *Exchange rates*—The relative value of a currency vis-à-vis another currency is an important calculation for businesses operating in foreign markets or those investing in foreign currencies.
- *Export quota controls and duties*—There are often restrictions placed on the amounts (quotas) of goods/services any particular firm/industry can import into a country, depending on which trading bloc is being exported to and the taxes that apply.

We might also need to understand how prices or labour costs change if we are importing our goods and services, or components of them, from another country—that is, our factor prices. This is known as the 'rate of price (or wage) inflation'. The difficulty comes in comparing prices from one country to another. Should we simply compare costs (what you pay for a good or service) and prices of goods (the price at which you sell a good, or what you pay as a consumer) through the exchange rate at any one particular time? Apparently not, since this is itself subject to political and other pressures. What economists tend to do is calculate prices for a particular basket of goods—a fixed list of common items—and compare the two. This is known as the 'purchasing power parity (PPP) exchange rate'. This rate then allows us to compare directly the relative costs between two countries for a given item.

Firms usually have little impact on the macroeconomic environment, since they have little control over macroeconomic variables. The challenge is to foresee economic changes that might affect the firm's activities. If a Swedish computer company imports silicon chips from Japan and pays for them in Swedish kronor, but the exchange rate for yen is rising against the Swedish krona, then it might source silicon chips from another country to ensure that its own prices are relatively unaffected.

Similarly, if inflation drives consumer prices higher in a particularly country, it may mean that the price of goods becomes more expensive, forcing a drop in sales. Typically, during a recession (as occurred in many European countries around 2008 and again in 2012, for the UK and Spain, for example), consumers tend to purchase fewer goods and increase their savings, and prices tend to fall further as producers attempt to stimulate demand. But prices can also increase during a recession. Surveys of consumer expectations of inflation, forecasts of foreign exchange rates, wage forecasts, and lots of other financial information are frequently available from government central banks.

Visit the **Online Resource Centre** and complete Internet Activity 2.1 to learn more about how the contribution of service industries to the UK's national economy has changed over the last ten years.

go online

The Socio-Cultural Environment

Companies that fail to recognize changes in the socio-cultural environment and fail to change their goods/service mix accordingly can fail. Levi's, the jeans company, has lost its way since its heyday in the 1990s when the brand alone was reputedly worth nearly US$7 billion; it was worth only around US$920 million in 2010 (Millward Brown, 2010). Companies must monitor the changing nature of households, demographics, lifestyles, and family structures, and changing **values** in society.

Demographics and Lifestyles

Changes in population proportions impact on a company's marketing activity. In the UK, immigration from Poland after EU enlargement increased the Polish population from fewer than 100,000 in 2001 to more than 500,000 people by the end of 2010 (ONS, 2011). Some supermarkets specifically target the Polish population in the UK using adverts in Polish and by stocking Polish products such as borsch, meatballs, pickled vegetables, and sauerkraut soup (BBC News, 2006). Off-licences in the UK have also seen increased sales of vodka, particularly Polish vodkas such as Wyborawa (Neate, 2008). According to the UN Population Division (2011), India's population is set to reach around 1.72 billion, China is set to reach 1.21 billion, America is due to reach 421 million, and the UK only 74 million by 2060. Notably, some countries' populations are set to fall (such as Japan and Russia). What implications will these changes have for different consumer and industrial sectors?

But it isn't only the absolute number of people within a population that matters to the marketer; we are also concerned with the ages of those different people. Figure 2.3 illustrates the relative differences in age structure in a variety of selected countries.

The figure shows clearly the relatively large proportion of people in the 65+ age bracket (the 'silver', or 'grey', market). Those countries with comparatively younger citizens include African and Middle Eastern countries, such as Namibia, South Africa, and Egypt. The changes and relative differences in age structure in different countries correspond with different size markets for brand propositions relevant to these particular communities of citizens. Clearly, the market for private pensions in Europe is likely to increase substantially as national governments and the EU move towards developing appropriate schemes, which should bode well for insurance and pension groups. But this is just one example; there are a whole host of goods and services that might be targeted at these different groups.

People's lifestyles are also changing. In Europe, the trend is towards marrying later and there is a greater tendency to divorce than in previous generations. In some countries, citizens are increasingly living alone, for example in single-person households. There is a rise in industrialized nations of same-sex civil marriages or partnerships, as well in the adoption of bisexual and transgender lifestyles. Some countries and states within countries have legitimized these more than others (for example, UK, India, and California in the US). Nevertheless, marketing activity is sometimes purely targeted at this group by companies, but is also becoming increasingly mainstreamed: Lloyds TSB, Ikea, Pepsi, and Heinz all launched campaigns in 2010 depicting or targeting gay people (Costa, 2010).

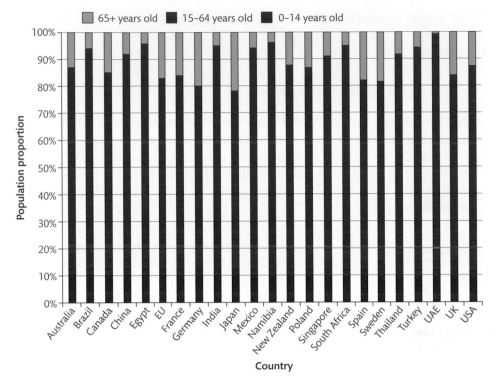

Figure 2.3

Population proportion estimates by age in selected countries

Note: 2011 estimates excluding EU 2009 estimate; row totals may not add up to 100% as a result of rounding.

Source: CIA World Factbook

The Technological Environment

The emergence of new technologies can substantially affect not only high-technology businesses, but also non-technology businesses. Examples include those aspects of technology that impact upon productivity and business efficiency (such as changes in energy, transportation, and information and communication technologies, or ICT). New social media technologies are increasingly changing the way in which companies go to market through moves towards more email, mobile, and web-based marketing, and greater efficiency in direct and database marketing techniques (Sclater, 2005). We are likely to see changes in mobile telecommunications (so-called **near-field communications**) allowing companies to communicate with users' mobile phones to share point-of-sale (POS) information such as price, product, and promotional information. Changes in technology particularly affect high-technology industries, in which firms must decide whether they wish to dominate that market by pushing their own particular technology standards and especially in which new technology renders existing standards obsolete (for example, cloud computing and digital music files, the MP3 player and the tape and vinyl record manufacturing industries).

As marketers scanning the technological environment, we are particularly interested in research and development (R&D) trends, particularly those of our competitors. Strategies to ascertain these can involve regular searches of patent registration, trademarks, and copyright assignations, as well as maintaining a general interest in technological and scientific advances

Spotify—the digital music service that plays music directly from the cloud
Source: Courtesy of Spotify

to determine their potential impact on product and service redesign. Firms' actions vis-à-vis one another are shaped by technological opportunity within the technological environment (Wilson, 1977). For example, in the pharmaceutical and chemical industries, companies have long developed new compounds based on modifications of compounds registered for patents by their competitors in a process known as **reverse engineering**.

But the reverse engineering principle does not solely operate within these industries. Companies in other industries frequently develop new product and service formulations based on their competitors' products and services, through 'me too', or imitation, marketing strategy. In fact, this kind of imitation lies at the heart of the inability of firms to turn their technological advances into sustainable competitive advantages (Rao, 2005). The problem is that as soon as they introduce a new product or service variant, it is quickly copied. The trick is *continually* to introduce new products and services, and to stay as close to the consumer as possible.

The difficulty for most firms is how to determine whether or not to invest in radical new technologies. Fear of obsolescence is usually a greater incentive to invest in new technologies than the lure of enhancement of existing offerings (Chandy et al., 2003). Companies are particularly concerned about the impact of technological changes on the life cycles of their offerings. However, innovation becomes a necessary condition in the strategic marketing decision making of high-technology firms. For less technology-intensive firms, innovation of some form, whether it is process- or product/service-focused, or at least rapid adoption of new product/service variants based on competitors' offerings, is still usually necessary to stay ahead of the competition.

Howe (2006) refers to this phenomenon as **crowdsourcing**. Whitla (2009) suggests that the role and process of crowdsourcing is to identify a task or group of tasks that are currently conducted in-house. These activities are then released to a 'crowd' of outsiders who are invited to perform the task on behalf of the company (for a fee or prize). This invitation might either be truly open to everyone or restricted in some way to ensure that those who respond are only those qualified to undertake the task. This new approach can help marketers to gain insights into both new product/service development and marketing communications, as Market Insight 2.2 demonstrates.

Market Insight 2.2

The Wisdom of Crowds

Crowdsourcing is increasingly being engaged for a variety of different marketing uses, including for the development of new products, creative ideas for a print and TV advert campaign, and for solving R&D problems.

The development of a successful beer for women in Britain has been a difficult marketing challenge. Only 13 per cent of beer is drunk by women in Britain compared to 36 per cent of beer in Ireland. Previous attempts to produce a women-friendly beer incorporating tastes of fruit and green tea failed, so Molson Coors has now developed a clear, low-calorie beer after undertaking a survey of 30,000 female drinkers. But what do you call a clear, light beer for women? That's where Molson Coors thought women could help again, by giving them the chance to name it—and so they did, calling it Animée.

Unilever offered US$10,000 in a competition to develop ideas for its next Peperami print and TV advert campaign, based on its quirky character 'Animal', a living representation of the pork salami snack. Using a crowdsourcing website, http://www.ideabounty.com and its production house SmartWorks, Unilever asked for an 'unapologetic, unexpected, and incredibly memorable piece of communication'. The Unilever team

For the ladies by ladies: Animée—light, fruity, and less gassy

Source: Courtesy of Red

was so impressed with the submissions that it received that instead of picking one winning idea, it actually selected two!

InnoCentive, a company spun out of pharmaceutical giant Eli Lilly, is an open source innovation and crowdsourcing pioneer, launched in 2001. It works by posting R&D and scientific challenges on its website for its crowd of users to solve. Winning contributors are paid a large financial incentive and InnoCentive takes a fee for hosting the challenge. According to analysis for InnoCentive by Forrester Consulting, the benefits from posting R&D challenges to InnoCentive's network rather than using internal staff, paying outside consultants, or awarding university grants for a large consumer products organization were substantial, including the achievement of: costs savings, a faster go-to-market process, a more innovative culture, and a smoother intellectual property transfer process.

If the benefits of sourcing expertise from outside your organization are so great, what does this mean for the workforces of the future?

Sources: Forrester Consulting (2009); Molson Coors (2011); Taylor (2010); http://www.ideabounty.com/blog/post/2485/peperami-picks-two-winning-ideas

1 **Why has crowdsourcing become so popular amongst marketers?**

2 **What are the disadvantages of crowdsourcing advertising content?**

3 **Why do you think crowdsourcing can reduce new product development process times to get new offerings to market?**

The Legal Environment

The legal environment covers every aspect of an organization's business. Laws and regulation are enacted in most countries, covering issues ranging from the transparency of pricing, the prevention of restrictive trade practices, product safety, good practice in packaging and labelling, and the abuse of a dominant market position, to codes of practice in advertising, to take just a small selection.

Product Safety, Packaging, and Labelling

In the European Union, product safety is covered by the General Product Safety Directive to protect consumer health and safety both for member states within the EU, and importers from third-party countries to the EU or their EU agent representatives. Where products pose serious risks to consumer health, the European Commission can take action, imposing fines and criminal sentences for those contravening the Directive. The General Product Safety Directive does not cover food safety; this is subject to another EU Directive, which has established a European Food Safety Authority (EFSA), and a set of regulations covering food safety. As a company operating in these sectors, it is important to keep up with changes in legislation. Failure to do so could jeopardize the business.

In the pharmaceutical industry, regulations govern testing, approval, manufacturing, labelling, and the marketing of drugs. Most countries also place restrictions on the prices that pharmaceutical companies can charge for drugs and so, in Japan, price regulations are stipulated for individual products, while in the UK strict controls are placed on the overall profitability of products supplied by a specific company to the National Health Service (NHS), under the Pharmaceutical Price Regulation Scheme, until 2014. Companies that develop cosmetics and fragrances are required to comply with legislative measures designed to protect the cosmetic user, and so need to ensure that products remain cosmetics and are not reclassified under different regulations, such as those related to medicines.

Codes of Practice in Advertising

Advertising standards differ around the world. In some countries, for example the UK, advertising is self-regulated—that is, by the advertising industry itself. In other countries, advertising is restricted by government legislation. In the UK, advertising is regulated by the Advertising Standards Authority (ASA), which has a mission to apply codes of practice in advertising and to uphold advertising standards for consumers, business, and the general public (see Market Insight 2.3). Such self-regulatory agencies operate in other countries, such as the Bureau de Vérification de la Publicité in France. In the EU, the European Advertising Standards Alliance (EASA) oversees both statutory and self-regulatory provision in most European countries, and even non-European countries, covering Russia, Canada, the US, New Zealand, and Turkey.

In most countries, broadcast communications codes of practice exist covering both radio and television, typically with specific regulations for alcohol advertising, usually specifying that claims cannot be made in relation to sexual prowess, fitness or health, courage or strength. Restrictions on advertising exist for the advertising of alcohol products around the world: for example, alcohol products cannot be advertised before 10 pm in Thailand. France restricts advertising for alcoholic beverages by obliging manufacturers to show a government health warning on all advertisements using the wording 'The abuse of alcohol is dangerous for your health. Consume with moderation' [here in translation] and by banning TV advertising (although it does not ban online advertising for alcohol products). Many breweries and distillers around the world have begun voluntarily to place the message 'drink responsibly' or a derivative thereof in the copy of their adverts accordingly.

Government health warnings also apply to tobacco products; tobacco advertising is now virtually banned in all marketing communication forms in most of the world's countries. Consumers are dissuaded from smoking not only through high taxes placed on tobacco to reduce consumption and through public restrictions on where people can smoke (for example, in Ireland, the UK, and Sweden), but also through legislation banning and restricting advertising and requiring the placing of government health warnings on packages. In some countries, these government health warnings provide stark warning and graphic pictures (such as in Canada and Australia).

Market Insight 2.3

ASA Bans Touched-Up L'Oréal Ad

Codes of advertising are divided into broadcast and non-broadcast practice. In the UK, the British Code of Non-broadcast Advertising, Sales Promotion, and Direct Marketing (the CAP Code) regulates the content of marketing communications, the administration of sales promotions, and the suitability of promotional items, the delivery of products ordered through an advertisement, and the use of personal information in direct marketing; it does not, however, consider editorial content. The Committee of Advertising Practice creates, revises, and enforces the CAP Code (hence its name), and comprises organizations that represent the advertising, sales promotion, direct marketing, and online/offline media industries. The CAP Code aims to ensure that advertising is legal, decent, honest, and truthful, to ensure consumer confidence in the advertising industry. In the UK, the ASA receives complaints from members of the public and adjudicates these.

In 2011, in one such adjudication, L'Oréal (UK) used an advert for 'Teint Miracle' foundation by Lancôme featuring Hollywood star, Julia Roberts, making the claim that the foundation could reproduce the natural light that emanates from beautiful skin. However, the ASA received a complaint from Liberal Democrat, Jo Swinson MP. Swinson complained that the images of the actress for the advert were digitally enhanced. L'Oréal stated that it had used a photographer, Mario Testino, well known for taking flattering photographs. It admitted to having digitally enhanced the images using post-production techniques, but stated that this had had no material impact on the final images used. It would not provide before and after pictures, stating that this would contravene its contract with the actress. In adjudication, the ASA upheld the complaint on the basis that it believed that the advert had made a misleading and exaggerated claim.

Source: ASA (2011); Sweney (2011)

1 Do you think that the advertising industry should be allowed to regulate itself or be regulated by government? Why?

2 In this example, do you agree with the judgement of the ASA? Does it matter if fashion companies digitally enhance images of models?

3 Can you remember an advert you've seen recently that seriously offended you? What was it?

Rachel's Organic yoghurts: even the packaging looks tasty!

Source: Courtesy of Rachel's Organics, http://www.rachelsorganic.co.uk

The Ecological Environment

In the 1990s, companies were concerned with 'green' marketing, and since the early 2000s they have been concerned with the concept of 'sustainability'. Increasingly, consumers are worried about the impact of companies on their ecological environments. They are demanding more 'organic' food, incorporating principles of better welfare for the animals that they consume as food products, and less interference with the natural processes of growing fruit and vegetables (for example, the use of pesticides and chemical fertilizers). But this ecological impact is being felt across many different industries, consumer and business to business (B2B).

For example, consumers are concerned that products are not sourced from countries with coercive labour policies, such as parts of Latin America, the Far East, and Africa. They are also keen to ensure that companies are not damaging the environment themselves or causing harm to consumers. There has been a rise in demand for 'fair trade' products. Around the world, Fairtrade International trademarks goods as a guarantee to indicate that a particular good has been sourced from disadvantaged producers in developing countries at fair prices. Sales of Fairtrade products include coffee, tea, banana, cocoa, flowers, wine, cotton, honey, and many others. Increasingly, despite having to pay more, consumers do trust ethical goods, but that level of trust varies across different countries (see Figure 2.4), and what's more, sales of Fairtrade products in the UK have surpassed £1 billion, despite the recession (Milmo, 2011).

Companies need to decide how to incorporate changing trends in sustainability into their organizational processes. Orsato (2006) suggests that a company can do this by adopting one of the following four strategies.

- *Eco-efficiency*—This involves developing lower costs through organizational processes, such as the promotion of resource productivity (for example, energy efficiency) and better utilization of by-products. Supermarket chains in Norway and other Scandinavian countries have long encouraged recycling, and British supermarkets for the last few years have charged for plastic shopping bags in a bid to reduce their consumption.

- *Beyond compliance leadership*—This involves the adoption of a differentiation strategy through organizational processes, such as certified schemes to demonstrate ecological credentials, environmental excellence (for example, adoption of UN Global Compact principles or the international standard ISO14001). This approach should be adopted by firms supplying industrial markets.

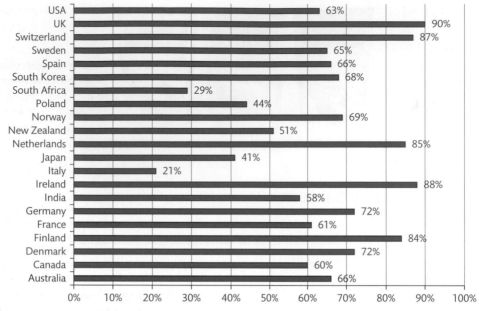

Figure 2.4

% levels of trust in Fairtrade goods by consumers by country

Note: Base, 17,000 consumers answering 3+4 on a scale of 1–4, in which 1= 'Do not trust at all' at 4= 'A lot of trust'.

Source: Fairtrade Foundation (2012)

Tesco's 'Less CO$_2$' initiative: every little helps!

Source: Courtesy of Tesco

- *Eco-branding*—This involves the differentiation of a firm's products or services to promote environmental responsibility. Examples include Marks and Spencer's 'Plan A' initiative, the Thai King Bhumibol's Golden Place brand, or Renault's ZE electric car range.

- *Environmental cost leadership*—This is achieved through offerings that give greater environmental benefits at lower prices. This strategy suits firms operating in ecologically sensitive markets with high **price sensitivity** (such as the packaging and chemical industries).

Whatever your company and industry, ecological trends in marketing look set to stay and further develop as the sustainability debate rages on and companies use it to develop their own competitive strategies. It is important to assess how this movement towards greener and sustainable marketing is affecting your own industry to ensure that your company is either not adversely affected by these changes or can take advantage of the opportunities.

Information about each of these sub-environments needs to be gathered in order to make an assessment about the potential impact on the organization. All organizations should monitor all PESTLE elements, but some individual elements may be of particular importance. For example, pharmaceutical organizations (such as AstraZeneca) regularly need to monitor legal and regulatory developments (such as labelling, patents, and testing), major retailers (such as Zara and H&M) must monitor economic and ecological changes (such as consumer discretionary spending and ecological buying habits), and road haulage companies might watch for changes that impact on transport (for example, congestion charging and diesel duty), whilst music distributors must watch for changes in technology and associated social and cultural developments (such as cloud computing and the increasing obsolescence of the CD).

Environmental Scanning

To understand how the external environment is changing, organizations should put in place processes to inform them of market developments. This process is 'environmental scanning'. Environmental scanning is the process of gathering information about a company's external events and relationships, to assist top management in its decision-making and developing its future course of action (Aguilar, 1967). It is the internal communication of external information about issues potentially influencing an organization's decision-making process, focusing on the identification of emerging issues, situations, and potential threats in the external environment (Albright, 2004). Environmental scanning is a key component of strategic marketing planning (see Chapter 5). The development of an organization's strategic options is dependent on first determining the opportunities and threats in the environment, and auditing an organization's resources.

We can gather information in environmental scanning exercises using company reports, newspapers, industry reports and magazines, government reports, and marketing intelligence reports (such as by Euromonitor and Mintel). Visit the **Online Resource Centre** and follow the web links to learn more about the information and services offered provided by Datamonitor, Euromonitor, and Mintel. In addition, 'soft' personal sources of information

go online

obtained through networking are important, such as contacts at trade fairs, particularly for competitive, and legal and regulatory, information. Verbal sources of information can be critical in fast-changing environments (May et al., 2000) when reports from government, industry, or specific businesses have been written and disseminated.

Conversely, small manufacturing companies, for example, tend to scan three important areas of information in environmental scanning activities, which, according to Beal (2000) include:

- *customer and competitor information*—including competitors' prices, competitors' new product introductions, competitors' advertising/promotional programmes, competitors' entry into new markets and new product technologies, customers' buying habits, customers' product preferences, and customers' demands and desires;
- *company resources and capabilities*—including companies' R&D capabilities and resources, companies' advertising and promotions resources, companies' sales capabilities/resources, companies' financial capabilities/resources, and companies' management capabilities/resources; and
- *suppliers of labour and funds*—including availability of external financing, availability of labour, and new manufacturing technologies.

For larger companies, or small companies operating in global environments, because of the increased complexity, there is an even greater need to undertake effective environmental scanning exercises. Firms operating in international markets should monitor their competitors' export performance, involvement in exporting, and their export intention, in addition to monitoring changes in technology, in products, in economic conditions, and in socio-political conditions (Lim et al., 1996). A study on Thai small-to-medium-sized food-processing companies has indicated that environmental scanning is critical to new product development success in sectors with high technological turbulence (Ngamkroeckjoti and Speece, 2008).

go online

Visit the **Online Resource Centre** and complete Internet Activity 2.2 to learn more about a number of sources that can be useful when conducting a scan of the marketing environment.

Although the scanning process seems relatively straightforward and simply a matter of collecting the 'right' information, barriers to effective environmental scanning occur because it is difficult to determine what the 'right' information actually is. In addition, data gathering can be time-consuming. In such cases, the information gathered ceases to provide a useful input to strategic marketing decision-making. In addition, multinational corporations may see opportunities and desire organizational change, and collect the right data, to take advantage of those opportunities, but fail actually to undertake such opportunities because of **switching costs** and organizational inertia related to production, sourcing, and other business operations. Most commentators on environmental scanning assume that managers take advantage of environmental changes reactively rather than actually bring about environmental change for their own gain. There are competing views on how organizations interact and react with their environment, and their adaptability to it.

Research Insight 2.1

To take your learning further, you might wish to read the following influential paper:

Levitt, T. (1960) 'Marketing myopia', *Harvard Business Review*, July–Aug: 45–56.

This is perhaps the most famous and celebrated article ever written on marketing. It has twice been reprinted in the *Harvard Business Review*. The central thesis of the article, as true today as it was in the 1960s, is that companies must monitor change in the external environment and keep abreast of their customers' needs or they risk decline.

@ Visit the **Online Resource Centre** to read the abstract and to access the full paper.

■ Understanding the Performance Environment

The performance environment, or the micro-environment, consists of those organizations that either directly or indirectly influence an organization's operational performance. There are three main company types:

- those competing against the organization in the pursuit of its objectives;
- those supplying raw materials, goods, and services, and those that add value as distributors, dealers, and retailers, further down the marketing channel (which organizations have the potential to influence the performance of the organization directly by adding value through production, assembly, and distribution of products prior to reaching the end user); and
- those with the potential to influence the performance of the organization *indirectly* in the pursuit of its objectives (which organizations are often agencies supplying services such as consultancy, financial services, or marketing research or communication).

Analysis of the performance environment is undertaken so that organizations can adapt to better positions than those of their stakeholders and competitors. These adjustments are made as circumstances develop and/or in anticipation of environmental and performance conditions. The performance environment encompasses not only competitors, but also suppliers and other organizations such as distributors.

Knowledge about the performance arena allows organizations to choose how and where to operate and compete, given limited resources. Knowledge allows adaption and development in complex and increasingly turbulent markets. Conditions vary from industry to industry. Some are full of potential and growth opportunities, such as Fairtrade food, low-cost air travel, and the online travel and gaming industries, whilst others are in decline or at best stagnating, for example high street music stores and car manufacturing. Rivalry may be on an international, national, regional, or local basis. The source and strength of competitive forces will vary, so that a strong organization operating in an 'unattractive' industry may have difficulty in achieving an acceptable performance. Weaker organizations, however, operating in 'attractive' environments may record consistently good performances.

Analysing Industries

An industry is composed of various firms that market similar offerings. According to Porter (1979), we should review the 'competitive' environment within an industry to identify the major competitive forces in order to assess their impact upon an organization's present and future competitive positions.

There are a number of variables that help to determine how attractive an industry is and which shape the longer-term profitability for the different companies that make up the industry. Think of industries such as shipbuilding, cars, coal, and steel, in which levels of profitability have been weak and hence unattractive to prospective new entrants. Now think of industries such as new media, oil, banking, and supermarkets, in which levels of profitability have been astonishingly high. The competitive pressures in all of these markets vary quite considerably, but there are enough similarities to establish an analytical framework to gauge the nature and intensity of competition. Porter suggests that competition in an industry is a composite of five main competitive forces—that is, the level of threat that new competitors will enter the market, the threat posed by substitute products, and the bargaining power of both buyers and suppliers, which in turn affect the fifth force, the intensity of rivalry between the current competitors. Porter called these variables the 'Five Forces of Competitive Industry Analysis' (see Figure 2.5).

Generally, the more intense the rivalry between the industry players, the lower will be their overall performance. Conversely, the lower the rivalry, the greater will be the performance of the industry players. Porter's model is useful because it exposes the competitive forces in operation in an industry and can lead to an assessment of the strength of each of the forces. The collective impact determines what competition is like in the market. As a general rule, the stronger the competitive forces, the lower the profitability in a market. An organization needs to determine a competitive approach that allows it to influence the industry's competitive rules, to protect it from competitive forces as much as possible, and to give it a strong position from which to compete.

New Entrants

Industries are seldom static. Companies and brands enter and exit industries all of the time. Consider the UK music retailing industry: it has witnessed the entrance of iTunes competing head-on with industry stalwarts, HMV, for example. In the book-retailing market, Amazon (and its e-reader, Kindle) have revolutionized how people buy and read books, with many people no longer visiting physical bookshops or buying physical copies of books, impacting on retailers such as Waterstones in the UK and Dillons in the US.

When examining an industry, we should consider whether economies of scale are required to operate successfully within it. For example, motor manufacturing in Sweden requires significant investment in plant and machinery. Unfortunately, since Swedish labour costs are high and foreign direct investment incentives (such as government development grants) are not as sufficiently strong, major Swedish car manufacturers have got into difficulties and

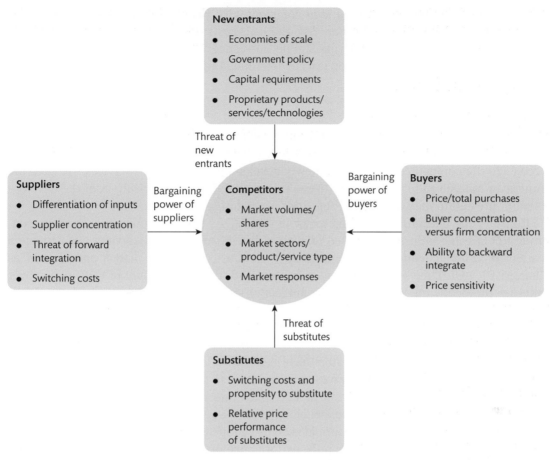

Figure 2.5

Industry analysis: Porter's Five Forces

Source: Adapted from Porter (1979). Reproduced with the kind permission of Harvard Business School Publishing.

either moved part of their manufacturing to China (Volvo) or collapsed (Saab). New entrants may be restricted through government and regulatory policy, or they may well be frozen out of an industry because of the capital requirements necessary to set up business. For example, in the oil and gas industry, huge sums of capital are required not only to fund exploration activities, but also to fund the extraction and refining operations.

Companies may be locked out of a market because companies within that market are operating using proprietary products/services or technologies, as in the pharmaceutical industry in which patents protect companies' investments in new medicines. The cost of a typical new patented drug in 2011 was around US$1.3 billion (Tufts CSDD, 2011) and can take around twelve years (Anon., 2001). Few companies can compete in such a market, since the set-up and ongoing R&D costs are very large, and pharmaceutical companies are increasingly looking to set up risk-sharing agreements. In 2009, pharmaceutical industry giants Pfizer and

GlaxoSmithKline agreed to set up a joint company, ViiV Healthcare, to develop and market their HIV/AIDS drugs in a bid to share risk and R&D costs (Ruddick, 2009). AstraZeneca has partnered with US firm, Bristol-Myers Squibb, for cancer drugs and with diagnostics company, Dako Denmark A/S, to develop tests to determine the most appropriate drugs for cancer patients (Reade, 2010).

Substitutes

In any industry, there are usually substitute products and services that perform the same function or meet similar customer needs. Levitt (1960) warned that many companies fail to recognize the competitive threat from newly developing products and services. He cites the American railroad industry's refusal to see the competitive threat arising from the development of the automobile and airline industries in the transport sector.

Consider the telecommunications sector in the UK. As telecommunications markets continue to converge with the increased take-up of broadband Internet services, we can see a variety of different companies operating in the same competitive market space, such as Orange, BT, AOL Time Warner, and many others. With the development of VOIP (voice over Internet protocol), an Internet telecommunication voice transmission standard, fixed-line telecommunications is already a commodity and firms operating in the area now look to develop value-added services such as online TV (content on demand), interactive gaming, and web-conferencing services.

Many countries' fixed-line operators have held on to large numbers of their subscribers even though much cheaper alternatives have appeared in the market (such as cable–Internet fusion telephone plans incorporating mobile, fixed-line telephone, online access, and TV packages). Consumers consider the switching costs associated with shifting from their original provider to another, which in turn affects their propensity to substitute that offering for a new one. They consider the relative price performance of one over the other. For example, if we decide that we wish to travel from Amsterdam to Geneva, we can fly from Schiphol airport to Genève Aéroport, take the train, or drive (or hire a car and drive if we don't have one). We would consider the relative price differences, and we would also factor into the decision how comfortable and convenient these different journeys were before we make our choice. In analysing our place within an industry, we should consider what alternative offerings, which also meet our customers' needs, exist in the marketplace.

Buyers

Companies should ask themselves how much of their sales go to one individual company. This is an important question because if one buying company purchases a large volume of product from a supplier, as car manufacturers do from steel suppliers, it is likely to be able to demand price concessions (price/total purchases) when there are lots of competing suppliers in the marketplace relative to the proportion of buyers (buyer concentration versus firm concentration). Buyers may also decide to increase their bargaining power through **backward integration**. For example, a company is backward integrated when it moves into manufacturing the products/services that it previously bought from suppliers. Another factor impacting upon a buyer's bargaining power is how price-sensitive that particular company is (see Chapter 8). Dependent on their own trading circumstances, some companies may be more price-sensitive than others. If they are more price-sensitive and there are lots of competing suppliers, a business can collapse. Most companies try to enhance other factors associated with an offering (such as customer experience) to try to reduce a client company's price-sensitivity. When analysing an industry, we should understand the bargaining power that buyers have with their suppliers, since this can impact upon the price charged and the volumes sold or total revenue earned.

Suppliers

In analysing an industry, we should determine how suppliers operate within that industry and the extent of their bargaining power. For example, if few suppliers operate within an industry with a large number of competitors, the suppliers have the stronger bargaining advantage. Conversely, in an industry in which there many suppliers with few competing companies, the buying companies have the bargaining advantage. We should also consider whether or not the suppliers provide unique components/products/services that may enhance their bargaining situation. In some industries, suppliers increase their market dominance by forward integrating (for example, a toy manufacturer setting up a retail outlet to sell its own products). **Forward integration** not only allows a company to control its own supply chain better, but also allows it to sell at lower prices. If companies face high switching costs—economic, resource, and time costs associated with using another supplier—then their suppliers have stronger bargaining power as a result.

Competitors

To analyse an industry, we should understand which companies operate within that particular industry. For example, in the UK cosmetics sector, the market leading cosmetic manufacturers include Avon, Estée Lauder, L'Oréal (UK), Procter & Gamble, Unilever, and large retailers such as Boots, The Body Shop, and Superdrug Stores. In undertaking a competitor analysis, we outline each company's structure (details of the main holding company, the individual business unit, any changes in ownership), details of current and future developments (from websites), and the company's latest financial results. We would be interested in calculating the market volumes and shares for each competitor, since market share is a key indication of company profitability and return on investment (Buzzell et al., 1975).

In analysing the competitors within an industry, we are interested in different competitor offerings in different market sectors. Clark and Montgomery (1999) call this process of identification of competitors the 'supply-based approach', because it considers those firms that supply the same sorts of offerings as your own firm. However, they identify another approach to competitor identification, which they term the 'demand-based approach', identifying competitors based on customer attitudes and behaviour. Firms perceived to have similar offerings are regarded as competitors.

We are also interested in measuring market responses to any new strategy developments that our company initiates. Research indicates that many companies do not consider their competitors' strategies except occasionally in relation to pricing strategy, perhaps because they—wrongly—do not feel it to be worth the effort (Montgomery et al., 2005). Generally, managers also tend to name relatively few competitors and should focus more on competitors as determined by customer requirements (Clark and Montgomery, 1999).

Research Insight 2.2

To take your learning further, you might wish to read the following influential paper:

Porter, M. E. (1979) 'How competitive forces shape strategy', *Harvard Business Review*, 57(2): 137–45.

This paper was Porter's first public presentation of his ideas about industry analysis. They were subsequently reproduced in his book *Competitive Strategy: Techniques for Analysing Industries and Competitors*, published the following year by The Free Press of New York, and which has become the seminal work on industry analysis.

@ Visit the **Online Resource Centre** to read the abstract and access the full paper.

■ Understanding the Internal Environment

An analysis of the internal environment of an organization is concerned with understanding and evaluating the capabilities and potential of the products, systems, human, marketing, and financial resources. An analysis of an organization's resources should not focus on the relative strength and weakness of a particular resource, but look at the absolute nature of the resource itself.

Product Portfolio Analysis

When managing a collection or portfolio of products, we should appreciate that understanding the performance of an individual product can often fail to give the appropriate insight. What is really important is an understanding about the relative performance of offerings. By creating a balance of old, mature, established, growing, and very new offerings, there is a better chance of delivering profits now and at some point in the future, when the current offerings cease to be attractive and profitable. One of the popular methods for assessing the variety of businesses/offerings that an organization has involves the creation of a two-dimensional graphical picture of the comparative strategic positions. This technique is referred to as a 'product portfolio', or 'portfolio matrix'.

The Boston Consulting Group (BCG) developed the original idea and its matrix—the **Boston box**, shown in Figure 2.6—is based on two key variables: market growth and relative market share (that is, market share as a percentage of the share of the product's largest competitor, expressed as a fraction). Thus a relative share of 0.8 means that the product achieves 80 per cent of the sales of the market leader's sales volume (or value, depending on which measure is used). This is not the strongest competitive position, but not a weak position either. A relative market share of 1 means that the company shares market leadership with a

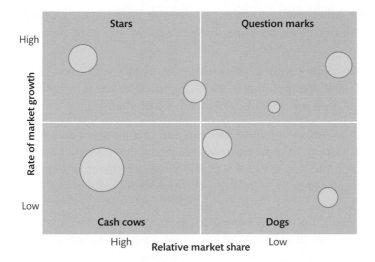

Figure 2.6

The Boston Box

Source: Reprinted from B. Hedley, 'Strategy and the business portfolio', *Long Range Planning*, 10, 1, 12. © 1977, with permission from Elsevier.

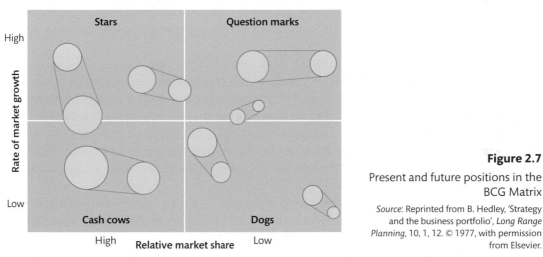

Figure 2.7

Present and future positions in the BCG Matrix

Source: Reprinted from B. Hedley, 'Strategy and the business portfolio', *Long Range Planning*, 10, 1, 12. © 1977, with permission from Elsevier.

competitor with an equal share. A relative market share of 2 means that the company has twice the market share of the nearest competitor.

In Figure 2.7, the vertical axis refers to the rate of market growth and the horizontal axis refers to a product's market strength, as measured by relative market share. The size of the circles represents the sales revenue generated by the product. Relative market share is generally regarded as high when you are the market leader (that is, the relative market share is 1 or greater). Determining whether or not market growth rate is high or low is more problematic and depends on the industry. In some industries, a market growth rate of 5 per cent might be regarded as high, whereas in others this might be 10 per cent. The benchmark between high and low is often taken to be 10 per cent.

- *Question marks* are products that exist in growing markets, but have low market share. As a result, there is negative cash flow and they are unprofitable.
- *Stars* are most probably market leaders, but their growth has to be financed through fairly heavy levels of investment.

- *Cash cows* exist in fairly stable, low-growth markets and require little ongoing investment. Their very high market share draws both positive cash flows and high levels of profitability.

- *Dogs* experience low growth, low market share, and generate negative cash flows. These indicators suggest that many of them are operating in declining markets and they have no real long-term future. Divestment need not occur just because of low share.

In 2007, Procter & Gamble decided to leave the paper business, and this involved selling off Bounty, its kitchen roll brand, and Charmin, its toilet tissue brand. It sold the business because of falling performance and because it did not see how it could achieve number one or two position in the different paper markets. Instead, it sold the business to its main rivals, SCA (Godsell, 2007).

From a reverse perspective, in 2009, Coca-Cola bought a £30 million stake in Innocent Drinks, in an attempt to give it access to the UK smoothie market—a market that, prior to 2008 (and the recession), had grown rapidly over the previous ten years and in which Coca-Cola had no presence whatsoever. By buying a minority stake in Innocent, Coca-Cola bypassed the set-up costs of developing its own 'question mark' smoothie product, and gained a market presence at a modest cost.

Portfolio analysis draws attention to the cash flow and investment characteristics of each of a firm's products, and indicates how financial resources can be manoeuvred to attain optimal strategic performance over the long term. Excess cash generated by cash cows should be utilized to develop question marks and stars, which are unable to support themselves. This enables stars to become cash cows and self-supporting. Dogs should be retained only as long as they contribute to positive cash flow, and do not restrict the use of assets and resources elsewhere in the business. Once they do so, they should be divested or ejected from the portfolio.

By plotting all of a company's offerings onto the grid, it is easy to appreciate just how well balanced the portfolio of offerings is. An unbalanced portfolio would be one that has too many offerings clustered in one or two quadrants. Where offerings are distributed equally, or at least are not clustered in any one area, and where market shares and cash flows equate with their market position, the portfolio is said to be financially healthy and well balanced. By analysing the portfolio in this way, it becomes possible to project possible strategies and their outcomes. Portfolio analysis is an important precursor activity to the development of new offerings (see Chapter 7).

Portfolio Issues

Portfolio analysis is an important guide to strategic development because it forces answers to questions such as:

- how fast will the market grow?
- what will be our market share?
- what investment will be required?
- how can a balanced portfolio be created from this point?

Some of these questions are considered in Market Insight 2.4.

Market Insight 2.4

AstraZeneca's Drug Problem

In 2012, the Anglo-Swedish pharmaceutical firm, AstraZeneca (AZ), announced that it was to cut 7,300 jobs in the UK, despite global sales of US$33.6 billion and profits of around US$8.1 billion in 2011. The problem is the huge cost of developing drugs today and that medicines have now been developed for so many medical problems. Pharmaceutical companies are therefore having to focus on more complex clinical areas to develop new drugs. The cost of failure can also be high, with AstraZeneca writing off £281 million in development costs when it discontinued research on Motavizumab, a respiratory anti-virus drug, in 2010 and US$241 million in development costs when it discontinued research on Olaparib, an ovarian cancer drug, and TC-5214, an antidepressant, in 2011.

A further problem stems from the fact that some of its key brands will soon come to the end of their patent protection. Once drugs go ex-patent (which typically offers twenty years of legal protection from competition), other companies can enter the market and produce 'generics', selling the drug at a much cheaper price (since they only have to cover the production costs and not the research and development costs). AZ's top-selling drugs, Crestor and Seroquel, both with sales over US$5 billion, come off patent in 2016 and 2012, whilst its heartburn drug, Nexium, comes off patent in the US in 2014.

When drugs are developed, they typically have to pass through three phases of clinical trials before they can be registered and launched onto the relevant market. AZ's drug portfolio currently includes products in the cardiovascular, gastrointestinal, infection, neuroscience, oncology, and respiratory and inflammation therapy areas. However, whilst it has drug development projects in all of these therapy areas in various trial phases, its overall number of drug development projects has dropped in the last three years as it tries to target projects more efficiently. Given the enormous costs associated with drug development, unsurprisingly AZ and other pharmaceutical companies are looking at ways in which they can share the risk of drug development with their competitors, universities and other research partners.

Sources: AstraZeneca (2010; 2012); Gallagher (2012)

1 **How should AstraZeneca maintain sales of its branded prescription drugs when they go off patent in the light of competition from generics?**

2 **Given the increasing cost of drug development, how else could AstraZeneca develop its portfolio of drugs to enable it to remain competitive?**

3 **How do the opportunities for prescription drug companies in emerging markets differ from the market opportunities in Western markets?**

However, the questions posed and the answers generated through use of the Boston Box do not produce marketing strategies in themselves. As with all analytical tools and methodologies, the BCG provides strategic indicators, not solutions. Management must then make decisions based upon their judgement. The Boston Box has been criticized for providing rigid solutions to portfolio evaluation when exceptions to the rule might exist: for example, proposing that 'cash cow' products should not be invested in, when a company may rely solely on its 'cash cow' products to provide profits and not necessarily have new products/services in the pipeline to replace them. Equally, the Boston Box proposes that 'dog' products should be divested, when in fact they may actually be returning a profit to the company. Finding the necessary and objective data to plot the positions of products or strategic business units (SBUs) on the two axes of relative market share and market growth rate can also be problematic: reliable industry data may not actually always be available. Finally, it is not always easy to determine what market we are concerned with: for example, if we consider the car market, do we include electric vehicles as well as diesel and petrol-powered vehicles?

Chapter Summary

To consolidate your learning, the key points from this chapter can be summarized as follows.

■ **Define the global marketing environment**

The global marketing environment incorporates the external environment, the performance environment, and the internal environment. The external environment incorporates macro-environmental factors that are largely uncontrollable and which an organization generally cannot influence. The performance environment incorporates key factors within an industry that impact upon strategic decision-making. The internal environment is controllable and is the principal means, through its resource base, by which an organization influences its strategy. The external environment consists of the political, economic, socio-cultural, technological, legal, and ecological influences, and organizations have relatively little influence on each of these. The performance environment consists of the competitors, suppliers, and indirect service providers who shape the way in which an organization achieves its objectives. Here, organizations have a much stronger level of influence. The internal environment concerns the resources, processes, and policies with which an organization manages to achieve its goals. Organizations can directly influence these elements.

■ **Explain PESTLE analysis and show how it is used to understand the external environment**

We considered the various components of the external marketing environment in detail using the PESTLE acronym, which includes the political, economic, socio-cultural, technological, legal, and ecological factors. It is important to note that some of these factors are more important than others in any particular industry. We use the acronym to identify possible macro-environmental impacts upon any particular organization at a given time.

■ **Explain the environmental scanning process**

Environmental scanning involves gathering data on customers, competitors (prices, new products), on company resources and capabilities (competitors' R&D capabilities, competitor's advertising spend), suppliers of labour and funding, and on international markets (including competitor intentions, customer needs, and market peculiarities). Problems associated with environmental scanning include the failure of management to grasp change, to collect the right data, and to take advantage of appropriate opportunities identified.

■ **Analyse the performance environment using an appropriate model**

The most common technique used to analyse the performance environment is Porter's Five Forces Model of Competitive Analysis. He concludes that the more intense the rivalry between the industry players, the lower will be their overall performance, and the lower the rivalry, the greater will be the performance of the industry players. Porter's Five Forces comprise: (1) suppliers; (2) buyers; (3) new entrants; (4) competitors; and (5) substitutes.

■ **Understand the importance of analysing an organization's internal environment, and identify the key resources and capabilities**

An organization's principal resources relate to its portfolio of offerings that it carries and the financial resources at its disposal. We use portfolio analysis, specifically the Boston Box, to help us to determine whether offerings are stars, dogs, question marks, or cash cows, each category of which provides differing levels of cash flow and resource requirements to develop.

Review Questions

1 What does the acronym PESTLE stand for?

2 What key information should be sought in the environmental scanning process?

3 How might changes in the global environment affect marketing strategy?

4 What are Porter's Five Forces?

5 What is portfolio analysis and why is it useful?

Scan this image to go online and access the chapter's multiple-choice questions, web links, Internet activities, and more!

Worksheet Summary

Visit the **Online Resource Centre** and complete Worksheet 2.1. This will help you to learn how the PESTLE framework, Five Forces model, and BCG Matrix can be used to analyse the marketing environment. It will also help you to understand how the internal, external, and performance environments interact.

References

Advertising Standards Authority (ASA) (2011) 'ASA Adjudication on L'Oreal (UK) Ltd', available online at http://www.asa.org.uk/ASA-action/Adjudications/2011/7/LOreal-(UK)-Ltd/SHP_ADJ_149640.aspx [accessed 26 February 2012].

Aguilar, F. Y. (1967) *Scanning the Business Environment*, New York: Macmillan.

Albright, K. S. (2004) 'Environmental scanning: radar for success', *Information Management Journal*, May–June: 38–45.

Anon. (2001) 'Cost of developing drugs found to rise', *Wall Street Journal*, 3 December.

Anon. (2010) 'US embassy cables: Shell says "we have people in all relevant Nigerian ministries"', *The Guardian*, 8 December, available online at http://www.guardian.co.uk/world/us-embassy-cables-documents/230356/print [accessed 19 February 2012].

Anon. (2012) 'Where's the party? How the Communist Party is trying to expand its influence in the private sector', *The Economist*, 28 January, available online at http://www.economist.com/node/21543575 [accessed 19 February 2012].

AstraZeneca (2010) *Annual Report 2010*, available online at http://www.astrazeneca-annualreports.com/2010/ [accessed 20 February 2012].

AstraZeneca (2012) *Investor Relations General Presentation*, available online at http://www.astrazeneca.com/cs/Satellite?blobcol=urldata&blobheader=application%2Fpdf&blobheadername1=Content-Disposition&blobheadername2=MDT-Type&blobheadervalue1=inline%3B+filename%3DDownload.pdf&blobheadervalue2=abinary%3B+charset%3DUTF-8&blobkey=id&blobtable=MungoBlobs&blobwhere=1285632630062&ssbinary=true [accessed 20 February 2012].

Baines, P. and Viney, H. (2010) 'An unloved relationship? Dynamic capabilities and political-market strategy: a research agenda', *Journal of Public Affairs*, 10(1): 258–64.

BBC News (2006) 'Supermarkets covet Polish spend', 10 September, available online at http://news.bbc.co.uk/1/hi/business/5332024.stm [accessed 26 February 2012].

BBC News (2012) 'WikiLeaks suspect Bradley Manning "should be tried"', 12 January, available online at http://www.bbc.co.uk/news/world-16539409 [accessed 19 February 2012].

Beal, R. M. (2000) 'Competing effectively: environmental scanning, competitive strategy, and organisational performance in small manufacturing firms', *Journal of Small Business Administration*, Jan: 27–47.

Buzzell, R. D., Gale, B. T., and Sultan, R. G. M. (1975) 'Market share: a key to profitability', *Harvard Business Review*, Jan–Feb: 97–106.

Chandy, R. K., Prabhu, J. C., and Antia, K. D. (2003) 'What will the future bring? Dominance. technology expectations and radical innovation', *Journal of Marketing*, 67(July): 1–18.

Clark, B. H. and Montgomery, D. B. (1999) 'Managerial identification of competitors', *Journal of Marketing*, July: 67–83.

Costa, M. (2010) 'Pink pound's value rises in mainstream markets', *Marketing Week*, 4 November, available online at http://www.marketingweek.co.uk/pink-pounds-value-rises-in-mainstream-markets/3020077.article [accessed 29 April 2012].

Fairtrade Foundation (2012) 'Global survey shows UK leads the way on Fairtrade', available online at http://www.fairtrade.org.uk/press_office/press_releases_and_statements/october/global_survey_shows_uk_leads_the_way_on_fairtrade.aspx [accessed 26 February 2012].

Forrester Consulting (2009) *The Total Economic Impact of Innocentive Challenges: Single Company Case Study*, Report prepared for InnoCentive, Cambridge, MA: Forrester Consulting.

Gallagher, J. (2012) 'Is AstraZeneca a sign of wider pharmaceutical woes?', *BBC News*, 2 February, available online at http://www.bbc.co.uk/news/health-16851703 [accessed 20 February 2012].

Godsell, M. (2007) 'Not number one, not interested', *Marketing*, 21 March, p. 18.

Harris, P., Gardner, H., and Vetter, N. (1999) '"Goods over God": lobbying and political marketing—a case study of the campaign by the Shopping Hours Reform Council to change Sunday trading laws in Britain', in B. I. Newman (ed.) *Handbook of Political Marketing*, London: Sage Publications, pp. 607–21.

Hedley, B. (1977) 'Strategy and the business portfolio', *Long Range Planning*, 10(1): 12.

Hillman, A., Keim, G. D., and Schuler, D. (2004) 'Corporate political activity: a review and research agenda', *Journal of Management*, 30(6): 837–57.

Howe, J. (2006) 'The rise of crowdsourcing', *Wired*, 14 June, available at: http://www.wired.com/wired/archive/14.06/crowds.html [accessed 17 April 2010].

Kewley, S. (2002) 'Japanese lobbying in the EU', in R. Pedler (ed.) *European Union Lobbying*, Basingstoke: Palgrave Press, pp. 171–200.

Levitt, T. (1960) 'Marketing myopia', *Harvard Business Review*, July–Aug: 45–56.

Lim, J.-S., Sharkey, T. W., and Kim, K. I. (1996) 'Competitive environmental scanning and export involvement: an initial enquiry', *International Marketing Review*, 13(1): 65–80.

May, R. C., Stewart, W. H. Jr, and Sweo, R. (2000) 'Environmental scanning behaviour in a transitional economy: evidence from Russia', *Academy of Management Journal*, 43(3): 403–27.

Melewar, T. C., Mui, H., Gupta, S., and Knight, J. (2008) 'The impact of the current expansion of the European Union on international marketing strategies on Norwegian multinational farmed salmon producers', *Marketing Intelligence and Planning*, 26(4): 405–15.

Millward Brown (2010) 'Brandz™ Top 100 Most Powerful Brands', *Millward Brown Optimor*, available online at http://c1547732.cdn.cloudfiles.rackspacecloud.com/BrandZ_Top100_2010.pdf [accessed 18 February 2012].

Milmo, D. (2011) 'Fairtrade's annual sales defy recession to pass £1bn', *The Guardian*, 28 February, available online at http://www.guardian.co.uk/business/2011/feb/28/fairtrade-sales-rise-despite-recession [accessed 28 April 2012].

Molson Coors (2011) 'Molson Coors (UK and Ireland) targets women with launch of Animeé', Molson Coors Press Release, available online at http://www.molsoncoors.com/en/News/United%20Kingdom/Corporate/2011/July/18/Molson%20Coors%20UK%20and%20Ireland%20targets%20women%20with%20launch%20of%20Animee.aspx [accessed 20 February 2012].

Montgomery, D. B., Moore, M. C., and Urbany, J. E. (2005) 'Reasoning about competitive reactions: evidence from executives', *Marketing Science*, 24(1): 138–49.

Neate, R. (2008) 'Vodka overtakes Scotch after Polish influx', *The Telegraph*, 12 June, available online at http://www.telegraph.co.uk/news/uknews/2119735/Vodka-overtakes-Scotch-after-Polish-influx.html [accessed 26 February 2012].

Ngamkroeckjoti, C. and Speece, M. (2008) 'Technology turbulence and environmental scanning in Thai food new product development', *Asia Pacific Journal of Marketing and Logistics*, 20(4): 413–32.

Nwajiaku-Dahou, K. (2010) 'WikiLeaks Shell "revelations" are old news in Nigeria', *The Guardian*, 10 December, available online at http://www.guardian.co.uk/commentisfree/2010/dec/10/wikileaks-shell-revelations-nigeria/print [accessed 19 February 2012].

Office for National Statistics (ONS) (2011) 'Polish-born people resident in the UK 2001-2010', available online at http://www.ons.gov.uk/ons/rel/migration1/migration-statistics-quarterly-report/august-2011/polish-people-in-the-uk.html [accessed 18 February 2012].

Orsato, R. J. (2006) 'Competitive environmental strategies: when does it pay to be green?', *California Management Review*, 48(2): 127–43.

Porter, M. (1979) 'How competitive forces shape strategy', *Harvard Business Review*, Mar–Apr: 86–93.

Rao, P. M. (2005) 'Sustaining competitive advantage in a high-technology environment: a strategic marketing perspective', *Advances in Competitiveness Research*, 13(1): 33–47.

Reade, L. (2010) 'Pharma giants collaborate in risk-sharing strategy: risky business', 9 February, available online at http://www.icis.com/Articles/2010/02/15/9333163/pharma-giants-collaborate-in-risk-sharing-strategy.html [accessed 26 February 2012].

Ruddick, G. (2009) 'Glaxo–Pfizer tie-up opens new era in AIDS battle', *The Telegraph*, 31 October, available online at http://www.telegraph.co.uk/finance/newsbysector/pharmaceuticalsandchemicals/6474678/Glaxo-Pfizer-tie-up-opens-new-era-in-Aids-battle.html [accessed 26 February 2012].

Sclater, I. (2005) 'The digital dimension', *The Marketer*, May: 22–3.

Shell (2011) 'Shell in Nigeria: Our economic contribution', available online at http://www-static.shell.com/static/nga/downloads/pdfs/briefing_notes/economic_contribution.pdf [accessed 19 February 2012].

Sweney, M. (2011) 'L'Oréal's Julia Roberts and Christy Turlington ad campaigns banned', *The Guardian*, 27 July, available online at http://www.guardian.co.uk/media/2011/jul/27/loreal-julia-roberts-ad-banned [accessed 26 February 2012].

Taylor, J. (2010) 'A new lager that's clearly for ladies', *Metro*, 15 April, p. 35.

Tufts Centre for the Study of Drug Development (Tufts CSDD) (2011) 'Drug developers are aggressively changing the way they do R&D', 5 January, available online at http://csdd.tufts.edu/news/complete_story/pr_outlook_2011 [accessed 26 February 2012].

United Nations Population Division (UNPD) (2011) *World Population Prospects: The 2010 Revision*, available online at http://esa.un.org/unpd/wpp/ [accessed 18 February 2012].

Whitla, P. (2009) 'Crowdsourcing and its application in marketing activities', *Contemporary Management Research*, 5(1): 15–28.

Wilson, R. W. (1977) 'The effect of technological environment and product rivalry on R&D effort and licensing of inventions', *Review of Economics and Statistics*, 59(2): 171–9.

for sale

3

Understanding Customer Behaviour

After reading this chapter, you will be able to:

- explain the consumer acquisition process;

- understand the processes involved in human perception, learning, memory, and motivation in consumer decisions;

- explain how reference groups influence consumer behaviour; and

- describe the main processes and stages associated with organizational buying and purchasing.

Simon Harrop for BRAND sense agency

BRAND sense agency helps clients to build brands that enjoy deeper emotional connections with their consumers through both communications and the customer experience, to arrive at a holistic understanding of the brand's sensory impact. We talk to Simon Harrop, chief executive officer, to find out more.

Imagine that you're walking through a supermarket, surrounded by products in aisles and point-of-sale material all vying for your attention, when you suddenly become aware of the smell of bread, which captures your senses and sends you off in a hurry to the supermarket's boulangerie. If smell has such power in a supermarket, could it be used for advertising or to enhance the customer experience in other ways? In such a vision- and sound-cluttered promotional world, could other senses be used instead?

BRAND sense agency was set up because of a belief that brands and marketers rely too heavily on vision and words to communicate and engage with consumers. Our intuition and experience was confirmed when we carried out one of the largest ever studies into the relationship between brands and consumers across all of the senses. There is a serious imbalance between how, as humans, we experience brands and how marketers seek to communicate brand propositions. Our mission is to address this imbalance, to make marketing more effective, and to build a business that we enjoy in the process!

Consumer behaviour is the sum of our rational and conscious relationship with the products or services that we buy, but also the emotional and non-conscious influences. Consumer behaviour is also the sum of experience, intention, perception, and conception of all that we buy. In the modern world, with so much choice and so much information to process, we are increasingly relying on habit and non-conscious associations to make our choices.

A sensory approach involves breaking down the key elements of the emotional relationship with brands in a category and identifying differentiated emotional space that a particular brand in that category can own. We then link this emotional space to key sensory attributes. When these attributes are aligned to this emotional space, you have a strong brand. If there is dissonance between experience and brand expectation, we work with our clients to create a development programme to bring these elements into line. This has a positive influence on consumer perception and behaviour.

Our research highlighted the fact that consumers value all senses in their relationship with brand fairly much in balance. However, for certain brands in particular categories, some senses will clearly be more important than others, such as smell for shampoo. It is our contention that a multi-sensory approach should take a holistic view across each sense. In practice, most brands are already considering words and pictures, as we have seen, so most of our work involves helping with smell, taste, sound, and, to a certain extent, touch.

When BRAND sense agency was approached by a major Colombian bank, a bank that was beset with problems in developing a differentiated proposition from other banks in the marketplace, particularly in the interior and exterior design of the branches, it wanted to make a

Courtesy of BrandSENSE's sensory marketing approach, this bank smells almost as good as it looks!

difference, not with the common approach to branding, but with a multi-sensory approach, emphasizing sound and smell as well as sight. Colombian banks had all tended to offer the same financial service products and even looked the same.

1 If you were trying to create a multi-sensory brand communication approach to help the Colombian bank to differentiate itself in the marketplace through sight, sound, and smell, what would you do?

▪ Introduction

What selection process did you go through when deciding which university course you were going to study? How do you decide which restaurant to go to, or which film to see? How would you decide which specification of tablet to buy for your company? An understanding of customer behaviour is important because it allows us to empathize with our customers. World-class companies understand their customers' needs/wants and behaviours profoundly. In this chapter, we explore business and consumer **buyer** behaviour. We consider **cognitions** (thoughts), perceptions (how we see things), and learning (how we memorize techniques and knowledge). As buyers, we are always perceiving and learning. Learning about offerings is no different from learning generally. Consider, if you work for a company, how you would find out about the costs of hotels for an event that you might be organizing (such as a product launch). We don't simply know prices and product performances intuitively; we have to learn about them.

In this chapter, we explore one of the most exciting areas of marketing: customers' motivations to purchase/acquire. We discuss opinions, **attitudes**, and values, to explain how we are persuaded by **reference groups**—that is, groups influencing our decision-making. Fast-moving consumer goods (FMCG) companies constantly bombard us with images of celebrity endorsers, who act as reference groups for many offerings. But buyers in companies can act in this way: for many years, IBM, the computer company, traded on its quality reputation and the idea that 'no one ever got sacked for buying IBM'. This chapter seeks to provide an insight into customer behaviour, an understanding of which is the cornerstone of good marketing practice. We first consider consumer behaviour, before considering business-to-business (B2B) buyer behaviour later in the chapter.

Consumer Buying Behaviour

What is going on in consumers' minds, individually, when they decide whether or not to buy—or, in the case of a not-for-profit consumer, acquire—a particular offering? We first need to understand how offerings move from producers to consumers. For example, consider luxury-brand Hermes' controversial crocodile skin handbags, retailing for more than €35,000 (Shears, 2009). In a simplified process, the skin is sold by a crocodile farmer to the manufacturer, who dries, cures, and tans it, before stitching it and sending it on to the major brand owner, who stocks and retails it. At any of these stages, a different supply chain partner could be involved (see Chapter 11 for more on this topic). There are a variety of transactions—that is, the individual relationships between various buyers and sellers as the raw materials are transformed into an offering—and **transvections**—that is, the sequence of transactions seen from the seller's perspective all the way through the supply chain

process (Alderson and Martin, 1965). Understanding transactions and transvections is important, because it helps us to understand how propositions are developed as they move from suppliers through companies to users. Next, we consider the end-user component of the buyer–seller relationship, the perspective of the consumer buyer, and how they acquire offerings.

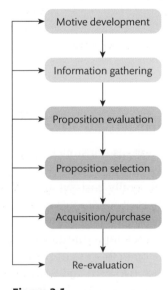

Figure 3.1

The consumer acquisition process

The Consumer Acquisition Process

The consumer acquisition process consists of six distinct stages (see Figure 3.1). The model highlights the importance and distinctiveness of proposition selection and re-evaluation phases in the process. In Figure 3.1, the buying process is iterative, because each stage can lead back to any of the previous stages in the process or move forward to the next stage in the process.

Motive Development

First, consumers decide that they need to acquire an offering. This involves the initial recognition that some sort of problem needs solving. To solve our buying problem, we must first become aware of it. So a lady might decide to buy new swimwear for a holiday, or because she's grown tired of what she had before, or because she thinks it's out of fashion, or to cheer herself up.

Research Insight 3.1

To take your learning further, you might wish to read the following influential book:

Howard, J. A., and Sheth, J. N. (1969) *The Theory of Buyer Behavior*, **New York: John Wiley and Sons.**

Howard and Sheth's theory of the buyer behaviour process provided original and powerful insights into the psychology of the buying process by considering how learning theory can be applied to customer behaviour. The buyer behaviour process consists of stimulus inputs (such as price, quality, service, and social settings), which feed into a perceptual process in which the inputs are received and considered, and which then interact with a person's attitudes and motives and existing choice criteria. This may or may not lead to purchase intention, and other outputs, including changes in attention given to the product, the extent to which the consumer understands what the brand stands for (brand comprehension), and the consumer's attitude towards the brand (whether they like it or not).

@ Visit the **Online Resource Centre** to read the abstract and to access the full paper.

Information Gathering

Next, as consumers, we look for alternative ways of solving our problems. With the swimwear buyer, she might ask herself where she bought her bikini before, how much bikinis generally cost, what retail outlets sell bikinis, and where they are located. She might also ask herself where her friends normally buy bikinis, what kinds of bikini are fashionable at the moment, perhaps which retailers offer discounts, and which store staff treat her best. Her search for a solution may be active—that is, an **overt search**—or passive—in other words, she is open to ways of solving her problem, but she is not actively looking for information to help her (Howard and Sheth, 1969). The search for information may be internal—that is, she may consider what she already knows and the products that she might buy to solve her problem— or external—that is, she feels that she doesn't know enough about her problem, so she seeks advice or supplementary information to help her to decide.

Proposition Evaluation

Once we feel that we have all of the information that we need to decide, we evaluate the proposition. But first we determine the criteria used to rank various offerings. These might be rational (such as cost) or irrational (for example, based on desire). For example, the swim-wear buyer might ask herself which shop is the best value for money or which is the most fashionable retailer. A consumer is said to have an **evoked set of products** when they come to evaluate which particular offerings they consider to solve their particular problem. An evoked set for bikini consumers might include M&S, H&M, Next, or Amazon. A more affluent buyer might visit Victoria's Secret, Agent Provocateur, or Harrods.

Proposition Selection

The proposition that we eventually select is the one that we evaluate as fitting our needs best. However, we might decide on a particular proposition away from where we buy/acquire it. For example, the swimwear buyer might check the stock of a shop online and make her selection there, but when she turns up at the retailer to try it on, the bikini she wants is not available and so she decides to buy an alternative. Proposition selection is a separate stage in the acquisition process, distinct from evaluation, because there are times when we must re-evaluate what we buy/acquire because what we want is not available.

Acquisition/Purchase

Once selection takes place, different approaches to acquisition might exist. For example, the swimwear buyer might make a routine purchase: a bikini from a shop that she's always shopped at regularly. Because the purchase is regular, she will not become particularly involved in the decision-making process. She simply buys the proposition again that she has bought previously unless new circumstances arise. The purchase may be special, conducted on a one-off or infrequent basis, such as a bikini for a honeymoon in the Maldives. In this case, the swimwear buyer will need to become more involved in the decision-making process, to ensure that she understands what she is buying and that she is happy that it satisfies her needs. With infrequent (and large) purchases, the marketer should try to ease the pain of payment, for example by extending credit. The store's policy on returns (that is, whether it allows this or not) may also have an impact on whether or not our consumer actually buys swimwear from a particular retailer.

Re-evaluation

The theory of **cognitive dissonance** (Festinger, 1957) suggests that we are motivated to re-evaluate our beliefs, attitudes, opinions, or values if our position at one point in time is not the same as the position that we hold at an earlier period due to some intervening event, circumstance, or action. This difference in evaluations is psychologically uncomfortable, causing anxiety. For example, we may feel foolish or regretful about a purchasing decision, so we may be motivated to reduce our anxiety by redefining our beliefs, attitudes, opinions, or values to make them consistent with our circumstances. We might actively avoid situations and information that increase our feeling of dissonance. The bikini buyer might be unhappy with her purchase because, although she liked it online, when she tried it on at home, it didn't flatter her figure.

Cognitive dissonance has significant application in marketing. The dissonance may be particularly acute in a purchase with high **involvement**, such as a car, a house, or a high-value investment product. (See Market Insight 3.1 for Volvo's approach to minimizing cognitive dissonance.)

The buying process is iterative. At the re-evaluation phase of the acquisition process, the re-evaluation can lead us back to any of the previous phases in the acquisition process as a result of experiencing cognitive dissonance.

Dissonant cognition? Sounds like a nasty medical problem, but post-purchase anxiety is common with first-time housebuyers

Source: © iStockphoto LP 2010

Volvo Deals for Anxious Buyers

In 2010, car manufacturer Volvo, headquartered in Gothenburg, Sweden, sold 37,400 new cars in Britain, taking a 1.8 per cent share of the market, behind more popular UK brands such as Ford, Vauxhall, Volkswagen, Peugeot, Audi, and Honda. Sales were up 0.5 per cent between 2007 and 2010 despite the difficult trading environment. Since 2007, the car market has suffered as a result of the **credit crunch** and declining consumer confidence.

Vehicle manufacturers and dealership sales personnel understand the anxiety that car buyers might feel when purchasing new cars. The buyer's key consideration is ensuring that he or she obtains value for money and doesn't feel as though he or she has been 'ripped off'. The problem is acute when customers are buying new cars, because new cars are more expensive than second-hand cars and lose 20–30 per cent of their value in depreciation from the moment they leave the showroom. Of course, there are benefits: new cars look better, incorporate the latest design features, and have reduced maintenance costs.

Car dealers work hard to reinforce the decision made by new car buyers by sending customers newsletters and offering efficient (or free three-year warranty) after-sales service to ensure that there are no, or at least fewer, maintenance problems. In many cases, new vehicles are sold with free insurance, '0% finance' deals, or 'buy now, pay later' schemes, all of which are designed to reduce the cognitive dissonance that many car buyers feel after their purchase. In addition, websites are designed to allow customers to customize their cars and to book test drives.

At Volvo, on selected models, including the V60, the deal is sweetened by offering 0% financing to ease customers' pain of purchase. But other, more popular, car manufacturers offer different attractive promotions. Will this therefore be enough to increase Volvo's UK market share?

Sources: Mintel (2010), http://www.volvocars.com/uk

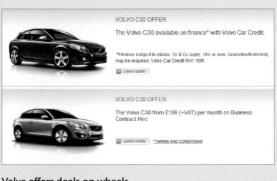

VOLVO C30 OFFER

The Volvo C30 available on finance* with Volvo Car Credit.

*Finance subject to status. Ts & Cs apply. 18s or over. Guarantee/indemnity may be required. Volvo Car Credit RH1 1SR

LEARN MORE

VOLVO C30 OFFER

The Volvo C30 from £199 (+VAT) per month on Business Contract Hire

LEARN MORE *TERMS AND CONDITIONS

Volvo offers deals on wheels

Source: © 1998–2008 Volvo Car Corporation

1 What else could Volvo do to reduce customers' cognitive dissonance?

2 In difficult economic times, would cognitive dissonance increase or decrease?

3 Consider a time when you purchased an offering that left you feeling anxious. What was it and why did it make you feel anxious?

The Psychology of Consumer Behaviour

Often, consumers misunderstand messages because they have not received, comprehended, or remembered those messages or because the messages were unclear. Consumer understanding depends on how effectively the message is transmitted and received. In this section, we consider how messages are perceived and remembered.

In any one day, consumers receive thousands of messages. Consider a typical working woman in Amsterdam, Holland, awoken by her clock radio, blaring out adverts for the local shopping centre. While she eats her breakfast, she might encounter advertisements on her television. She perceives magazine advertisements in, say, *De Telegraaf* or *Metro*, and when she opens her post, she sees mail from charities (such as Samenwerkende Hulporganisaties, SHO) and financial service organizations (perhaps ING Bank). On her way to the tram, she encounters billboards advertising, among other things, L'Oréal products. When she finally arrives at work, she has been subjected to hundreds of auditory, visual, and audio-visual marketing messages. When she retires to bed in the evening, she could have received thousands of marketing messages. Considering that consumers also receive word-of-mouth messages, we begin to realize just how sophisticated human **perception**, learning, and memory processes must be to filter, and store, relevant messages.

Perceptions

The American Marketing Association (AMA, 2012) defines perceptions as 'the cognitive impression that is formed of "reality" which in turn influences the individual's actions and behaviour toward that object'. If we pay attention to all of the messages that we receive, rather than filter through only those that we find meaningful, we would overload, like a computer when it crashes. The process of screening meaningful from non-meaningful information is called **selective exposure** (Dubois, 2000). Consumers are interested in certain relevant offerings at any particular moment: men would not normally be interested in adverts for women's handbags unless they were to want to buy one as a present; young people are not usually interested in advertising messages for pensions; if you were to want to book a flight, you would become interested in airline companies' and travel agents' advertisements; and washing machine adverts become interesting if you need a washing machine! The messages that we choose to ignore and forget are removed from our perceptual processes; the brain selectively processes information. In this way, we avoid exposure to some messages, but seek out others. We might selectively expose ourselves to certain media messages through the media that we choose to read, watch or use (only browsing certain newspapers, websites, or TV programmes, for example). As marketers, it is important to determine which media channels customers actually use.

The personal importance that someone attaches to a given communication is called 'involvement'. It explains a person's receptivity to communications. Marketers are interested in people's receptivity because we are interested in changing or altering customer perceptions. Figure 3.2 illustrates a variety of common products and how involved US consumers generally are with them in terms of considering them rationally or emotionally (see Ratchford, 1987).

A particular product's position is an average of all consumers and might not represent a particular individual's decision-making, however. So the purchase of life insurance can be generally regarded as being in the high-involvement/thinking quadrant. This product's positioning suggests the need for more informative advertising/promotion. An expensive watch, residing in the high-involvement/feeling quadrant, suggests an emotional advertising approach. Products in the low-involvement/thinking quadrant, such as bleach, suggest using advertising/promotion to create and reinforce habitual buying. Finally, products in the low-involvement/feeling quadrant, such as women's magazines, should be promoted on the basis

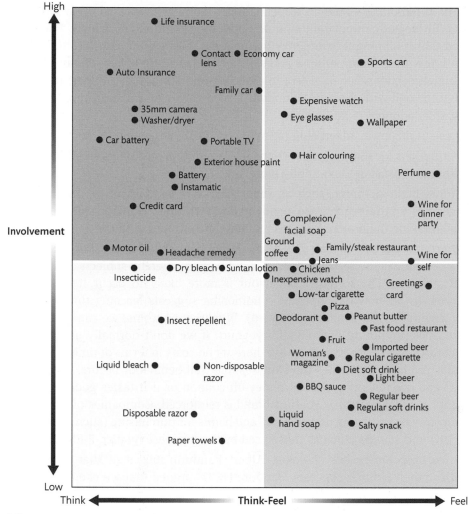

Figure 3.2

Involvement/think–feel dimension plot for common products

Source: Adapted from Ratchford (1987)

of personal satisfaction (Ratchford, 1987). However, recent research by Wood (2012) suggests that brands should all be pursuing emotional advertising approaches rather than message-based approaches, because the former are more effective.

Learning and Memory

Consumers continually learn about new product and service characteristics, their relative performance, and new trends by learning. Learning is the process by which we acquire new knowledge and skills, attitudes, and values, through study and experience, or by modelling others' behaviour (such as parents, friends). There are various theories of human learning, which include **classical conditioning**, **operant conditioning**, and **social learning theory**, as follows.

- *Classical conditioning*—Russian Nobel Laureate Ivan Pavlov carried out a series of experiments with dogs, manipulating stimuli before the presentation of food. Using a bell, he realized that if he rang it before serving food, the dogs would associate the sound of the bell with the presentation of food and salivate. He called this phenomenon 'classical conditioning'. It occurs when we learn to associate one thing with another: in this case, the sound of the bell with the arrival of food. The classical conditioning approach to learning is frequently adopted in marketing:
  - the use of jingles in advertising (such as 'ooh Danone!' or Intel's 'sonic' logo);
  - supermarkets locating bakery sections in-store so that customers smell warm bread and feel hungry, causing them to buy more; and
  - perfume manufacturers (such as Dior) place free samples of products in sachets in magazines, so that readers see an advert and associate the image that they see with the smell, making them more likely to purchase the product in future.
- *Operant conditioning*—Skinner (1954) pioneered the behaviourist school of learning, stating that learning is the result of operant conditioning whereby subjects act on an environmental stimulus. The resulting behaviour is more likely to occur if this behaviour is reinforced. In other words, operant conditioning suggests learning through behavioural reinforcement (by punishment or reward). In marketing terms, we can consider a typical in-store sales promotion—perhaps for yoghurt. If we don't normally use this brand, but we're curious, we might try it, because there are no costs in terms of time, effort, or money. The sales promotion provides the stimulus, the trial behaviour occurs, and if we like the yoghurt and are rewarded with a money-off coupon or if it tastes good, our purchasing behaviour for that particular yoghurt brand is reinforced. Companies often reinforce consumer loyalty by providing reward cards and points for purchasing (such as the Nectar card in the UK) and stamps (such as those used by the Japanese retailer, 7-Eleven).
- *Social learning theory*—Psychologist Albert Bandura suggested that humans are less animalistic than Skinner suggests. Bandura (1977) argued that we can delay gratification and dispense our own rewards or punishment. Humans have a choice over how to react to stimuli, since we do not blindly follow our instinctual drives. We can reflect on our own actions and change our future behaviour. We can therefore also learn from how others respond to situations. Bandura called this 'modelling'. The implications for marketing are profound: for adolescents, role models include both parents and famous athletes and celebrities, but of these groups parents are more influential (Martin and Bush, 2000).

What happens once consumers have learnt information? How do they retain it in their memories and what stops them from forgetting? Consumers do not necessarily have the same experiences and knowledge of particular offerings. Knowledge develops with familiarity, repetition of marketing messages, and consumer's acquisition of information about an offering. Marketing messages need to be repeated, because people forget them over time—particularly specific arguments or messages, more so than the general substance or conclusion of the message (Bettinghaus and Cody, 1994). Memorization can be enhanced by using symbols (such as corporate logos and signs). Shapes, creatures, and people can all carry significant meanings, as seen in trademarks and logos. Various airlines have adopted symbols as logos: for example, the kangaroo of Australian airline Qantas, the Intel symbol, the Olympic movement's 'five rings' symbol, Apple's bitten apple logo, and the Nike 'Swoosh'.

Memories store perceptions, experiences, and knowledge in a highly complex system (Bettman, 1979), which can be affected by a number of factors, including:

- **recognition** and recall—less frequently used words in advertising are recognized more and recalled less;
- the importance of context—memorization is strongly associated with the context of the stimulus, so information available in memory will be inaccessible in the wrong context;
- object coding and storage—we store information in the form that it is presented to us, either by object (brand) or dimension (product/service attribute);
- load processing—we find it more difficult to process information into our short- and long-term memories when presented with lots of information at once;
- input mode—short-term recall of sound input is stronger than short-term recall of visual input when the two compete for attention, such as in television and Internet advertising; and
- repetition—recall and recognition of marketing messages/information increase the more a consumer is exposed to them, although later exposures add increasingly less to memory performance.

Often, consumers' knowledge of offerings is incomplete or inaccurate (Alba and Hutchinson, 2000).

Interestingly, provision of in-store point-of-purchase (POP) information is more successful than general advertising (Bettman, 1979). This is why brand manufacturers frequently conduct product trials in-store, offering consumers the opportunity to try a product without expending time, money, and effort in purchasing the item.

Motivation

There is still debate about whether customers are primarily motivated by rational (Howard and Sheth, 1969) or irrational motives. Holbrook et al. (1986) started to consider irrational motives when they suggested that our wants could be latent, passive, or active, and were related to both intrinsic and extrinsic reasons, as follows.

- *Latent*—Needs are hidden, our subject is unaware of his or her need.
- *Passive*—The costs of acquisition exceed the expected satisfaction derived from acquisition.
- *Active*—The subject is aware of his or her needs and expects perceived benefits to exceed the likely costs of acquisition.

According to Holbrook et al. (1986), when our needs are active, they can arise either through **habit** or through a process of choosing a brand called **picking**. Picking is the process of deliberative selection of an offering from amongst a repertoire of acceptable alternatives, even though the consumer believes the alternatives to be essentially identical in their ability to satisfy his or her need. It can be motivated by intrinsic and/or extrinsic evaluations: intrinsic evaluation occurs because a consumer likes an offering, perhaps because of anticipated pleasure from using it; an extrinsic evaluation might occur because a friend mentioned that the offering was great. Extrinsic evaluations can also entail explicit cost–benefit analyses.

Theory of Planned Behaviour (TPB)

Understanding motivations helps us to understand why people behave as they do. The theory of planned behaviour (TPB) outlines how behaviour is brought about by an intention to act in a certain way. This intention to act is affected by the attitude that we have towards a particular behaviour, encompassing the degree to which we have a favourable or unfavourable evaluation or appraisal of the behaviour in question. Intention to act is also affected by a subjective norm, which is perceived social pressure to perform or not perform a particular behaviour. Finally, intention to act is also affected by perceived behavioural control, which refers to the perceived ease or difficulty that we have of performing a particular behaviour, based on a reflection on our past experience and future obstacles.

Figure 3.3 illustrates the theory. For example, if we consider cigarette use, we may well have different attitudes towards smoking based on our geographic location—whether we live in China rather than in New Zealand, for example. Equally, we will also consider the opinions that significant others have towards smoking cigarettes. An advert launched by the UK National Health Service (NHS) aimed to encourage smoking cessation by promoting how smoking causes anxiety in smokers' children, who fear that their parents will die. TPB considers whether we believe we have the capacity to bring about the desired behaviour. For example, we might think that we can't give up smoking because we need a cigarette to calm our nerves ('My job is stressful'). As a social marketer trying to encourage smoking cessation, we could either: a) try to alter subjects' attitudes towards smoking; b) change their views on how others see them as smokers; or c) change their perceptions of how they perceive their own ability to give up.

Alternatively, we could change the context in which subjects make their decisions, to make it easier for them to avoid undertaking their behaviour. Recently, there has been recognition that we can change people's behaviour not by appealing to their rationality, but by changing the context in which they undertake their behaviour and 'nudging' them towards new actions. This approach is called 'behavioral economics' and is increasingly being used by governments around the world to influence their citizens' behaviour and by market research companies to understand consumers. In Denmark, to increase the number of organ donors, the government requires people to make a choice about donation when they apply for their driving licence, when they can perceive risk both to themselves and others (Anon., 2012).

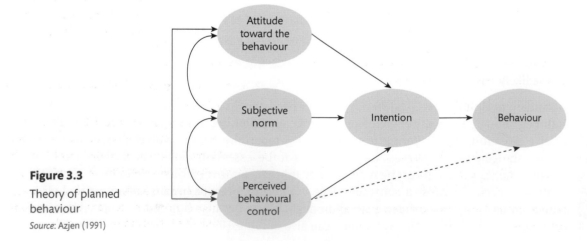

Figure 3.3

Theory of planned behaviour

Source: Azjen (1991)

Market Insight 3.2 offers a discussion of **behavioural economics** in the context of binge-drinking.

Market Insight 3.2

Drinking Irresponsibly: 'Just One More'

Market research companies are increasingly using behavioural economics to supplement existing research approaches to better understand the context of customer decision-making in addition to the psychological motivations of customers. Research by BrainJuicer Labs in the UK tackles the social problem of binge-drinking, now a major problem in the UK, and thought to cost the NHS £2.7 billion per year (expected to rise to £3.7 billion by 2015), and up to £55 billion per year for the whole economy if we include road accidents and crime.

Behavioural economics suggests that identifying a behavioural solution to such a problem lies not in rationally convincing consumers to drink less, but in managing the situational influences on drinking to ensure that they subconsciously consume less. Undertaking a literature review of behavioural economics and related disciplines led the BrainJuicer team to ascertain four key factors influencing binge-drinking:

- personal factors (emotions, habits);
- social influences (peer influence, mimicry, and reciprocity);
- local environment influences (physical, visual, auditory); and
- choice environment (the options available to people and how these are presented).

The company then recruited participants from a mix of employees and members of a market research panel to take part in a mass ethnographic research game.

The logo for Brainjuicer, the innovative market research agency—now why do I feel thirsty?

Participants were assigned to one of four detective teams, each named after a famous detective, and asked to visit pubs and observe people drinking. The Miss Marple team considered personal factors; the Poirot team, social influences; the Sherlock Holmes team, local environmental influences; and the Columbo team considered choice environment factors when binge-drinking.

What the teams found is that binge-drinking could be reduced in several ways, including by:

- introducing more seating and tables in pubs (people standing tend to drink faster and more);
- reducing the amount of loud, fast music;
- bartenders offering smaller alcohol measures rather than large measures by default and free water;
- making soft drinks and smaller bottles of beer more visible by displaying them at the front rather than the back of the bar;
- providing visual cues that may prime healthy behaviour (such as posters of athletes);
- discouraging round-buying (that is, when one person buys everybody's drinks in turn), which can precipitate faster drinking; and
- encouraging mixed-sex customer groups.

What is fascinating about the research is that these factors could potentially substantially reduce binge-drinking. The problem is: what is the incentive for a pub to introduce such measures, since reducing binge-drinking also reduces revenue?

Sources: Anon. (2011a); Wood et al. (2012)

1 Why do you think people drink faster when buying drinks in rounds?

2 If you are not from the UK, what is the culture of drinking in your country? If you do come from the UK, what other factors have you noticed about UK drinking culture that encourages binge-drinking?

3 The UK government is likely to introduce a higher tax per unit of alcohol to discourage binge-drinking. Do you think this is likely to be successful?

The Importance of Social Contexts

Although our personality impacts upon how we choose to think and consume products, the opinions, attitudes, and values of others also affect how we consume. We consider each of these three psychological constructs next.

Opinions, Attitudes, and Values

Opinions are cognitive—that is, based on our thoughts—and can be described as quick responses given to opinion poll questions about current issues or instant responses to questions from friends. They are held with limited conviction, because we have often not formed or fully developed an underlying attitude on an issue. An opinion might be what we think of the latest advertising campaign, for example, for a high-profile brand.

Attitudes are what psychologists call **affective**, in that they are linked to our emotional states by comparison, and they are held with a greater degree of conviction, over a longer duration, and are more likely to influence behaviour.

Values are **conative**—that is, they are linked to our motivations and behaviour—and are held even more strongly than attitudes and underpin our attitudinal and behavioural systems. Values tend to be linked to our consciences, developed through the familial socialization process, through cultures and subcultures, and through our religious influences, and are frequently formed in early childhood.

It is important to recognize that, although we sometimes have a specific attitude towards something, we do not always follow it in terms of our behaviour. In other words, we may want to be more fashionable in our dress sense, but we do not bother trying new styles!

go online

Visit the **Online Resource Centre** and follow the web link to the VALs™ survey to identify into which consumer segment you fall.

Group Influence

Consumers learn through imitation (that is, social learning). We've learned, for example, by observing and copying our parents and friends. As consumers, we may consider our opinions, attitudes, values, and behaviour patterns in relation to those of our reference groups. 'Reference groups' are those groups:

> that the individual tends to use as an anchor point for evaluating his/her own beliefs and attitudes. A reference group may be positive; i.e. the individual patterns his or her own beliefs and behaviour to be congruent with those of the group, or it may be negative.
>
> (AMA, 2012)

However, if a consumer feels that his or her freedom to choose is being threatened, he or she may react against this intervention. So a consumer whose decision alternative is blocked, partially or wholly, will become increasingly motivated to go against that specific decision alternative through rebellious behaviour (Clee and Wicklund, 1980): for example, the 'tween-age' daughter (aged between 10 and 12) who is told by her father not to buy short skirts might continue to do so. This form of negative group influence occurs because of **psychological reactance**.

With reference to how we perceive and use products and services, consumers' assumptions about an individual's behaviour, based on identified group membership, become automated if they are frequently and consistently made (Bargh and Chartrand, 1999). This represents a form of social learning. For example, a Swedish male consumer might continue to purchase Abba-branded herring because this was the brand that his parents ate at the breakfast table, while a French female might drink Orangina religiously because that is what her parents provided for her as a child. The link between a consumer and a particular reference group depends on how closely the consumer associates with the particular reference group. When we do associate closely, the attachment to the brand is also often assumed: for example, consumers identifying with the skateboarding genre might wear Vans trainers because the skateboarding crowd generally wear Vans trainers.

Orangina: *zut alors*! The French can't get enough of this tasty drink

Source: Orangina Schweppes International

Message receipt is also affected by peer group pressure, through word of mouth, whether intended or not. Members of groups tend to conform to a group norm, enhancing the self-image of the recipient and increasing the feeling of group identity and belonging. Consumers therefore may have their own cultures and subcultures, which impact upon how a particular marketing message may be received. Some marketing messages might incorporate **celebrity endorsement** appeals, through popular culture role models, who have influence over the target consumer group. (See Market Insight 3.3 for an example of a celebrity endorsement campaign.) Chupa Chups, the Spanish lollipop brand, the logo of which was originally developed by Spanish surrealist painter Salvador Dali, was endorsed by Madonna, taking it from a children's sweet to the latest adult fashion accessory; sales doubled in the early 1990s when the coach of FC Barcelona, Johan Cruyff, was seen on the sidelines in TV images sucking Chupa Chups in his bid to give up smoking (Anon., 2011b). Word-of-mouth communication is also powerful because we trust our friends' and colleagues' opinions. About 81 per cent of word-of-mouth takes place person to person, 10 per cent by phone, and only about 9 per cent online, according to research (Mitchell, 2011).

Market Insight 3.3

IKEA: Mattresses Fit for a Princess

Most Europeans are familiar with the Hans Christian Andersen fairy tale 'The Princess and the Pea'. The story has it that a prince, keen to marry a princess, is never quite certain that those whom he meets are *real* princesses. On a dark and stormy night, a bedraggled, but beautiful, young woman arrives at the palace, seeking shelter and claiming to be a princess. The prince's mother swiftly devises a test: the 'princess' will sleep atop a pile of twenty mattresses and twenty feather beds—and if her skin is so sensitive that she still feels the single hard pea placed beneath them all, then her royalty will be proven. The princess, of course, emerges from her room after a sleepless night, declaring herself bruised black and blue. She and the prince marry, and (naturally) live happily ever after.

Market Insight 3.3 (continued)

Fast forward from the fairytale past to the present, and IKEA has sourced its very own princess, Princess Xenia of Saxony, in a new campaign by London advertising agency Mother to promote its mattresses. Reputed to be a sensitive sleeper, Princess Xenia's ideal mattress turns out to be the Sultan Hjelmas, providing extra back support. Interestingly, research by a team at Sweden's Karolinska Institute indicates that people who are sleep-deprived are rated as less attractive and less healthy by their peers. The aim of the IKEA campaign is therefore to suggest that customers can look like royalty after getting a good night's rest on IKEA mattresses. If it's good enough for Princess Xenia, it must be good enough for the rest of us—now where's that handsome prince?

Source: Anon. (2010); Wikipedia (2012); http://www.ikea.com; http://www.motherlondon.com/creative/ikea-sleep-like-a-princess

1 **Do you think that Princess Xenia of Saxony's endorsement of IKEA will be effective?**

2 **From who else might IKEA have sought an endorsement? How successful would such a campaign be?**

3 **Think of another celebrity endorsement campaign of which you're aware. Who is the brand, who is the endorser, and do you think that this campaign was/will be effective?**

Meet Princess Xenia
Gabriela Florence
Sophie Iris of Saxony

At IKEA, we wanted to put our mattress guide to the test, so we tracked down the most sensitive sleeper we could think of. Meet Princess Xenia of Saxony, she sleeps on her back and struggles to keep warm at night. We knew if our mattress guide could help her find the right mattress, it could help everyone sleep like a princess.

IKEA®

Princess Xenia could not make up her mind which IKEA mattress to choose, so she took them all!

Source: Courtesy of IKEA. Photographer: Jo Metson Scott.

Social Grade

'Social grade' refers to a system of classification of consumers based on their socio-economic grouping. 'Social grade' was originally developed for the National Readership Survey (NRS) in the 1950s. Social grade is a means of classifying the population by the type of work that they do, based on the occupation of the chief income earner (the member of the household with the largest income). NRS Ltd, the company behind the NRS, continues to provide social grade population estimates, obtaining these from NRS interviews with a representative sample of some 36,000 adults every year (see Table 3.1). There is a widely held belief that consumers make purchases based on their socio-economic position within society, which holds true only to a degree.

The NRS classification approach is widely used by market research agencies in the UK because of its simplicity. Social grade provides an effective demographic tool for advertising

Table 3.1 Social grading scale

Social grade	Social status	Occupational status	Population estimate, Great Britain, age 15+ (1981) (%)	Population estimate, Great Britain, age 15+ (2011) (%)
A	Upper middle class	Professionals, chief executives, and senior managers with a large number of dependent staff	2.9	4.6
B	Middle class	Intermediate, managerial, administrative, or professional	13.6	21.6
C1	Lower middle class	Supervisory, clerical and non-manual administrative, lower managerial or early professional (e.g. junior white-collar workers based in offices)	22.7	27.9
C2	Skilled working class	Skilled manual workers	31.8	21.8
D	Working class	Semi- and unskilled manual workers	19.1	15.5
E	Those at lowest levels of subsistence	Unemployed and casual workers, pensioners or widowers with no income other than that provided by the state	9.9	8.6

Source: National Readership Survey. Reproduced with the kind permission of the National Readership Survey.

planning, and it is still extensively used by advertisers, advertising agencies, and media owners. As Table 3.1 shows, more and more people in the UK now work in office-based environments (ABC1) rather than in manual or unskilled professions (C2DE). As a result, the social-class approach to segmentation is becoming less capable of discriminating between different group behaviours (see Chapter 6).

Lifestyles

Marketers increasingly target consumers on the basis of lifestyle. The AMA defines lifestyle as 'the manner in which the individual copes and deals with his/her psychological and physical environment on a day-to-day basis' (AMA, 2012). In order to generate clusters of consumers according to different lifestyle types, marketers typically ask consumers questions around their activities, interests, and opinions (AIO), and then cluster them according to their responses (at which we look in more detail in Chapter 6). The general idea is that if marketers fit around a consumer's lifestyle, consumers are more likely to benefit from, and appreciate, the proposition offered.

◼ Organizational Buying Behaviour

The buying processes undertaken by organizations differ in a number of ways from those used by consumers. These differences reflect the potential high financial value associated with these transactions, the product complexity, the relatively large value of individual orders, and the nature of the risk and uncertainty. As a result, organizations have developed particular processes and procedures that often involve a large number of people. What is central, however, is that the group of people involved in organizational purchasing processes is referred to as a **decision-making unit (DMU)**, that the types of purchases they make are classified as **buyclasses**, all of which are made in various **buyphases**. We discuss each of these processes later in this section.

Research Insight 3.2

To take your learning further, you might wish to read the following influential paper:

Johnson, W. J., and Lewin, J. E. (1996) 'Organizational buying behavior: toward an integrative framework', *Journal of Business Research*, 35(Jan): 1–15.

This paper is important because it includes critical contributions by the leading researchers in the area of buyer behaviour including the work of Robinson et al. (1967), Webster and Wind (1972), and Sheth (1973). It concludes by developing a model of buying behaviour drawing on a number of constructs developed since these three leading models were published.

@ Visit the **Online Resource Centre** to read the abstract and to access the full paper.

Only by appreciating the particular behaviour, purchasing systems, people, and policies used by an organization can suitable marketing and selling strategies be implemented. In this section, we consider some of the key issues associated with the way in which organizations purchase the offerings necessary to achieve their corporate goals.

Two definitions of organizational buyer behaviour reveal important aspects of this subject. First, Webster and Wind (1972) defined organizational buying as 'the decision making process by which formal organizations establish the need for purchased products and services and identify, evaluate and choose among alternative brands and suppliers'. This adopts a buying organization's perspective and highlights the important point that organizational buying behaviour involves ongoing processes rather than a single, static, one-off event. There are a number of stages, or phases, associated with product procurement, each of which often requires a key decision to be made. In that sense, organizational buying behaviour is similar to consumer buying behaviour.

A second definition, by Parkinson and Baker (1994: 6, cited by Ulkuniemi, 2003), states that organizational buying behaviour concerns 'the purchase of a product or service to satisfy organizational rather than individual goals'. Organizational buying behaviour is therefore about three key issues:

1 the functions and processes through which buyers move when purchasing offerings for use in business markets;

2 strategy, when purchasing is designed to assist value creation and competitive advantage, and to influence supply chain activities; and

3 the network of relationships of which an organization is a part when purchasing. The placement of orders and contracts between organizations can confirm a current trading relationship, initiate a new set of relationships, or may even signal the demise of a relationship.

Organizational buying behaviour is not solely about the purchase of offerings from other companies. In addition to this, it is concerned with the strategic development of the organization, with creating value, and with the management of inter-organizational relationships. Hollyoake (2009) argues that business marketing is increasingly about managing buyers' experiences and interactions. This involves creating expectations, often referred to as the 'brand promise', and then delivering products and services against these promises. It is important that a customer's evaluation of his or her experience be ahead of what was expected. Hollyoake develops these ideas to consider 'ease of doing business' as a measure of the supplier–customer relationship and to discover the key dimensions of the customer experience. He suggests that experiences are founded on four pillars: 1) trust; 2) interdependence; 3) integrity; and 4) communication.

Grönroos (2009) develops the principles on expectations into a new perspective of business marketing, referred to as 'promise management'. These ideas are rooted in what Grönroos sees as the purpose of contemporary marketing—namely, marketing as value creation. Firms are involved in developing and delivering value propositions (promises). These propositions of value can be realized only once an offering is consumed and that consumption can only be undertaken by customers. Therefore value creation is experienced only by customers as value fulfilment.

Decision-Making Units: Characteristics

Although organizations designate a buyer as responsible for purchasing a range of products and services, often a range of people are involved in the purchasing process. The purchasing process is the means by which an organization creates value. This group of people is referred to as either the DMU or the **buying centre** (see also Chapter 6). In many circumstances, they are informal groupings of people who come together to contribute to the decision-making process. Decision-making units vary in composition and size according to the nature of each individual purchasing task. Webster and Wind (1972) identified a number of people who undertake different roles within a buying centre (see Figure 3.4), as follows.

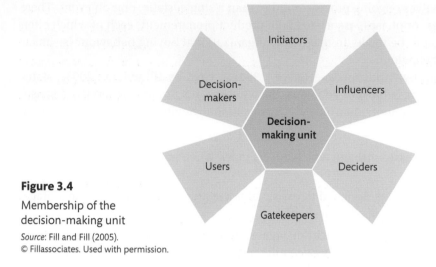

Figure 3.4

Membership of the decision-making unit

Source: Fill and Fill (2005).
© Fillassociates. Used with permission.

- **Initiators** start the process by requesting an item to be purchased. They may also assume other roles within the DMU or wider organization.

- **Users** literally use the product once it has been acquired and they also evaluate its performance. Users might initiate the purchase process and be involved in the specification process. Their role is continuous, although it may vary from the highly involved to the peripheral.

- **Influencers** often set the technical specifications for the proposed purchase and assist the evaluation of alternative offerings by potential suppliers. These may be consultants hired to complete a particular project. For example, an office furniture manufacturer would regard office managers as key decision-makers, but understand that specifiers, such as office designers and architects, influence the office manager's decision regarding furniture decisions.

- **Deciders** make purchasing decisions and are the most difficult to identify because they may not have formal authority to make the purchase decision, yet they are sufficiently influential internally that their decision carries the most weight. In repeat buying activities, the buyer may also be the decider. However, it is normal practice for a senior manager to authorize expenditure decisions involving sums over a certain financial limit.

- **Buyers** (purchasing/procurement managers) select suppliers and manage the process whereby the required products are purchased. Buyers may not decide which product is to be purchased, but they influence the framework within which the decision is made. They will formally undertake the process whereby products and services are purchased once a decision has been made to procure them. They will therefore assume the roles of both an initiator and a buyer.

- **Gatekeepers** have the potential to control the type and flow of information to the organization and the members of the DMU. These gatekeepers may be assistants, technical personnel, secretaries, or telephone switchboard operators.

The size and form of the buying centre is not static. It can vary according to the complexity of the product being considered and the degree of risk that each decision is perceived to carry for the organization. Different roles are required and adopted as the nature of the buying task changes with each new purchase situation (Bonoma, 1982). All of these roles might be undertaken by one individual. It is vital for seller organizations to identify members of the buying centre, and to target and refine their messages to meet the needs of each member of the buying centre. Membership of the DMU is usually far from fixed, and this fluidity can pose problems for selling organizations because it is difficult to identify who are the key personnel. The behaviour of DMU members is also largely determined by the interpersonal relationships of the members of the centre.

The B2B Acquisition Process

Organizational buying decisions vary in terms of the nature of the offering, the frequency and the relative value of the purchases made, their strategic impact, and the type of relationship in existence with suppliers. Robinson et al. (1967) suggest that there are three main types of buying situation, each of which possesses specific characteristics. They term these 'buy-classes' (see Table 3.2) and they include the following.

- **New task**—In this scenario, the organization is buying for the first time. The risk is inevitably large, because there is little collective experience of the offering or of the relevant suppliers. As a result, there are normally a large number of decision participants. Each participant requires a lot of information, and a relatively long period of time is needed for the information to be assimilated and a decision made.

- **Modified rebuy**—Having purchased an offering already, uncertainty is reduced, but not eliminated, so the organization may request through its buyer(s) that certain modifications be made to future purchases, such as adjustments to the specification of the product, further negotiation on price levels, or perhaps an arrangement for alternative delivery patterns or different service levels. Fewer people are involved in the decision-making process than in the new task situation.

Table 3.2 Main characteristics of the buyclasses

Buyclass	Degree of familiarity with the problem	Information requirements	Alternative solutions
New task	The problem is fresh to the decision-makers	A great deal of information is required	Alternative solutions are unknown, all are considered new
Modified rebuy	The requirement is not new, but is different from previous situations	More information is required, but past experience is of use	Buying decision needs new solutions
Straight rebuy	The problem is identical to previous experiences	Little or no information is required	Alternative solutions not sought or required

Source: Fill (2009), Pearson Education Limited. Reproduced with the kind permission of Pearson Education Limited.

- **Straight rebuy**—In this situation, the purchasing department reorders on a routine basis, very often working from an approved list of suppliers. These may be products that an organization consumes in order to keep operating (such as office stationery), or may be low-value materials used within the operational, value-added part of the organization (manufacturing processes). No other people are involved with the exercise until different suppliers attempt to change the decision-making environment. For example, a new supplier may interrupt the procedure with a potentially better offer; this may stimulate the emergence of a modified rebuy situation.

Straight rebuy presents classic conditions for the use of automatic reordering systems. Costs can be reduced, managerial time redirected to other projects, and the relationship between buyer and seller embedded within a stronger framework. One possible difficulty is that both parties perceive the system to be a significant exit barrier should conditions change, and this may deter flexibility or restrict opportunities to develop the same or other relationships. By using electronic purchasing systems at the straight rebuy stage, organizations can empower employees to make purchases, although control still resides with purchasing managers. The benefits are that employees are more involved, the purchasing process is speeded up, costs are reduced, and purchasing managers can spend more time with other higher priority activities.

go online

Visit the **Online Resource Centre** and follow the web link to Electronic Commerce Europe, the biggest online trade network in the world, for more information on the use of electronic B2B purchasing.

Buyphases

Organizational buyer behaviour consists of a series of sequential activities through which organizations proceed when making purchasing decisions. Robinson et al. (1967) referred to these as 'buying stages', or 'buyphases'. The following sequence of buyphases is particular to the new task situation. Many of these buyphases are ignored or compressed according to the complexity of the offering, and when either a modified rebuy or straight rebuy situation is encountered.

Need/Problem Recognition
The need/recognition phase is about the identification of a gap between the benefits that an organization is experiencing now and the benefits that it would like to obtain. For example, when a new offering is to be produced, there is an obvious gap between having the necessary materials and components, and being out of stock and unable to build. The first decision therefore is about how to close this gap and there are two broad options: outsourcing the whole or parts of the production process; or building or making the objects oneself. The rest of this section is based on a build decision being taken.

Product Specification
As a result of identifying a problem and the size of the gap, influencers and users can determine the desired characteristics of the product needed to resolve the problem. This may take

the form of either a general functional description, or a more detailed analysis and the creation of a detailed technical specification for a particular proposition. What sort of engine is required for a new airplane? What thrust is it expected to achieve? How much will it cost to service? This phase is an important part of the buying process because, if it is executed properly, it will narrow the supplier search and save on associated costs. The results of the functional and detailed specifications are often combined within a purchase order specification.

Supplier and Product Search

At this stage, the buyer actively seeks suppliers who can supply the necessary product(s). There are two main issues at this point: first, will the product match the specification and the required performance standards? Second, will the potential supplier meet the other organizational requirements, such as experience, reputation, accreditation, and credit rating? In most circumstances, organizations review the market and their internal sources of information, and arrive at a decision based on rational criteria. Organizations work, wherever possible, to reduce uncertainty and risk. By working with others who are known, those of whom the organization has direct experience, and those who can be trusted, risk and uncertainty can be reduced substantially.

Evaluation of Proposals

Depending on the complexity and value of the potential order(s), the proposal is a vital part of the process and should be prepared professionally. The proposals from the shortlisted organizations are reviewed in the context of two main criteria: 1) the purchase order specification; and 2) an evaluation of the supplying organization. If the potential supplier is already a part of the network (a 'preferred supplier'), then little search and review time is needed. If the proposed supplier is not part of the network, a review may be necessary to establish whether it will be appropriate (in terms of price, delivery, and service) and whether there is the potential for a long-term relationship or whether this is a single purchase that is unlikely to be repeated.

Supplier Selection

The DMU will normally undertake a supplier analysis and use a variety of decision criteria, according to the particular type of item sought. This selection process takes place in the light of proposals evaluation. A further useful perspective is to view supplier organizations as a continuum, from reliance on a single source to the use of a wide variety of suppliers for the same offering. Many organizations balance supplier risk by purchasing from several suppliers at the same time or from members of a panel in rotation. The major disadvantage is that this approach can fail to drive costs as low as possible, because the discounts derived from volume sales are not achieved. The advantage to the buying centre is that a relatively small investment is required and little risk is entailed in following such a strategy. At the other end of the continuum are organizations that use only a single supplier. All purchases are made from the single source until circumstances change to such a degree that the buyer's needs are no longer satisfied. An increasing number of organizations are choosing to enter alliances with a limited number or even single-source suppliers. The objective is to build a long-term buyer–supplier relationship, to work together to build quality, and to help to achieve each other's goals.

Evaluation

The order is written against the selected supplier, which is then monitored and evaluated against criteria such as responsiveness to enquiries, modifications to the specification, and timing of deliveries. When the product is delivered, it may reach the stated specification, but fail to satisfy the original need. In this case, the specification needs to be rewritten before any future orders are placed. Developments in the environment can impact on organizational buyers, and change both the nature of decisions and the way in which they are made. For example, the decision to purchase new plant and machinery requires consideration of the future cash flows generated by the capital item. Many people will be involved in the decision, and the time necessary for consultation may mean that other parts of the decision-making process are completed simultaneously.

The Role of Purchasing in Organizations

All organizations buy a variety of products and services in order to operate normally and achieve their performance targets. So far, we have set out general principles, types, and categories associated with organizational buying. However, the way in which organizations buy products and services varies considerably and does not always fit neatly with the categories presented earlier. Professional purchasing is, for many organizations, an integral part of their overall operations and strategic orientation (Ryals and Rogers, 2006; Pressey et al., 2007). In the past, the goal for procurement has been to play off one supplier against another and, as a result, to reduce costs and improve short-term profits (see Market Insight 3.4). Purchasing departments used to be regarded as an isolated function within organizations—a necessary, but uninteresting, aspect of organizational performance. That perspective changed towards the end of the twentieth century. Now, organizations reduce the number of their suppliers, sometimes to only one, and **strategic procurement** (as it is known) is used to negotiate with suppliers on a cooperative basis, to help to build long-term relationships. Purchasing has become an integral part of an organization's operations.

The reason for this change was because research showed that business performance improves when organizations adopt a collaborative, rather than adversarial, approach to purchasing and account management (Swinder and Seshadri, 2001). However, several other issues have changed the role of purchasing—namely, customer sophistication, increasing competition, and various strategic issues.

- *Customer sophistication*—As a result of increasing customer sophistication, organizations try to differentiate their offerings and become more specialized. Organizational purchasing has to follow this movement and become more specialized, otherwise organizations become increasingly ineffective in meeting customer needs.

- *Increasing competition*—With increasing competition, margins have been eroded. Consequently, more attention has been given to internal costs and operations. By influencing purchasing costs and managerial costs associated with dealing with multiple suppliers, the profitability of the organization can be directly impacted. As a result, purchasing polices, processes, and procedures within organizations have increased in importance.

- *Strategic issues*—There are several strategic issues related to the purchasing activities undertaken by organizations, including the following.

- *The 'make or buy' decision*—Should organizations make and/or assemble products for resale, or outsource or buy in particular products, parts, services, or sub-assemblies and concentrate on what is referred to as core activities or competences?

- *The growth of the purchasing function*—The benefits that arise through closer cooperation with suppliers, and the increasing influence of buyer–seller relationships and 'joint value creation' have inevitably led to a tighter, more professional, and integrated purchasing function.

- *The integration of the purchasing function*—New IT systems have raised the level of possible integration of purchasing and operations to the extent that the competitive strength of the organization can be enhanced (Hemsworth et al., 2008).

Svahn and Westerlund (2009) identify six main purchasing strategies used by organizations.

- *Price minimizer*—This purchasing strategy refers to a buyer's efficiency orientation where the main purchasing goal is to seek the lowest price for the product. To help to achieve this, the buyer actively promotes competition among several potential suppliers.

- *Bargainer*—This purchasing strategy focuses on a dyadic buyer–seller relationship. Here, the buyer's strategy is to achieve operational efficiency through long-term collaboration with a selected supplier (Anderson and Narus, 1999).

- *Clockwiser*—This purchasing strategy refers to network relationships that function predictably and precisely, just as a clock works. Again, the goal is strict efficiency, achieved through the vigilant integration of production-based integrated control systems and IT, and the careful coordination of the value activities performed by each supply network partner (Glenn and Wheeler, 2004).

- *Adaptator*—This purchasing strategy focuses on adapting the manufacturing processes between the exchange parties. This can arise during the purchase of one major offering when the seller is required to accommodate its proposition to the particular needs of the buyer.

- *Projector*—This purchasing strategy occurs between buyers and sellers who are development partners. This can occur during projects when partners develop their products and services in close collaboration, after which the joint-development project is completed and the parties continue the development work independently. As an example of this strategy, we could explore the collaboration between Nokia and Skype. These major players in the information and communication technology (ICT) industry joined their development efforts in order to develop a radically novel type of mobile phone that utilizes the Voice over Internet Protocol (VoIP) service (the free call system created by Skype).

- *Updator*—This purchasing strategy is based on collaboration in research and development. Here, collaboration between partners is continuous and the nature of the relationship is not a dyad, but a supply network. This collaboration is intentional, as demonstrated by the collaboration between Rolls Royce and Boeing in the development of the Dreamliner. These major players in the aerospace industry joined forces in order to develop a novel type of airplane that is larger and more efficient than other planes currently in existence.

Market Insight 3.4

Ryanair Casts Its Buying Net Wide

With rising oil prices, declining disposable income and increased security costs, few major airlines are doing well. Some are going through periods of consolidation (for example, the merger of the UK's British Airways and Spain's Iberia into International Airlines Group (IAG) in 2011); others have gone bust (such as Alitalia in 2009). American Airlines declared itself bankrupt in 2011 in a bid to renegotiate its labour contracts and other liabilities. It then announced 13,000 job cuts in early 2012.

One airline that is doing rather well, however, is the low-cost, 'no frills' Ryanair. It anticipates increasing passenger numbers from around 70 million in 2011 to 130 million over the next decade, and is consequently looking to buy as many as 200–300 aircraft. The chief executive officer, Michael O'Leary, states that he will buy aircrafts only at cheap prices. Currently, he has an all-Boeing fleet; if he were to buy from other suppliers, his operating costs would increase. He is hedging his bets at the moment, however, and is deep in negotiations with Boeing of the US, Irkut of Russia, and Comac of China. Suppliers should perhaps be wary of entering too far into negotiations with him though, as Airbus previously found out to its cost in 2002 when, after detailed negotiations, O'Leary picked Boeing.

Is Ryanair's exploration of Chinese and Russian planes simply a negotiation strategy to attempt to get Boeing to lower its prices? And will the strategy work?

Sources: Kenney (2011); Parker (2011a; 2011b); BBC News (2012)

1 Which of the Svahn and Westerlund (2009) six purchasing strategies do you think Ryanair is adopting?

2 Do you think this approach to purchasing is likely to foster long-term supplier collaboration? Why (not)?

3 Visit http://www.boeing.co.uk. Exactly what products and services does it offer to airline customers?

Chapter Summary

To consolidate your learning, the key points from this chapter can be summarized as follows.

■ **Explain the consumer acquisition process**

Consumer buying behaviour has both rational and irrational components, although rational theories have dominated the marketing literature until now. Although there are a variety of models of consumer buying behaviour, the consumer acquisition model is perhaps the simplest to understand, stressing the way in which the consumer goes through six key stages in the acquisition process, including motive development, information gathering, product evaluation, product selection, acquisition, and re-evaluation.

- **Understand the processes involved in human perception, learning, memory, and motivation in consumer decisions**

  The human perception, learning, and memory processes involved in consumer choice are complex. Marketers should ensure that, when designing advertising, when developing distribution strategies, when designing new goods and services, and other marketing tactics, they (repeatedly) explain this information to consumers in order for them to engage with the information and then subsequently retain it, if it is to influence their buying decisions.

- **Explain how reference groups influence consumer behaviour**

  Reference groups, including such role models as parents, entertainers, and athletes, have an important socializing influence on our consumption behaviour, particularly in adolescence. However, where we live, what social class we come from, what lifestyle we lead, and in what stage of the life cycle we are all have an impact on our behaviour as consumers. Celebrity endorsers are particularly powerful influencers in this regard, because fame is becoming an increasingly attractive quality to many modern consumers.

- **Describe the main processes and stages associated with organizational buying and purchasing**

  Organizational buying behaviour can be understood to be a group buying activity in which a number of people with differing roles make purchasing decisions that affect the organization and the achievement of its objectives. Buying decisions can be categorized in terms of different types of decision (buyclasses) and different stages (buyphases).

Review Questions

1 What is the process through which consumers go when buying an offering?
2 How are the psychological concepts of perception, learning, and memory relevant to our understanding of consumer choice?
3 What is celebrity endorsement?
4 Name four of the different types of person that make up a decision-making unit (DMU).
5 What is the process through which companies go when buying a particular proposition?

Scan this image to go online and access the chapter's multiple-choice questions, web links, Internet activities and more!

Worksheet Summary

Visit the **Online Resource Centre** and complete Worksheet 3.1. This will help you to learn about consumer behaviour related to the National Readership Survey's social grading system (A, B, C1, C2, D, and E).

References

Alba, J. W. and Hutchinson, J. W. (2000) 'Knowledge calibration: what consumers know and what they think they know', *Journal of Consumer Research*, 27: 123–56.

Alderson, W. and Martin, M. W. (1965) 'Toward a formal theory of transactions and transvections', *Journal of Marketing Research*, 2(May): 117–27.

American Marketing Association (AMA) (2012) *Dictionary of Marketing Terms*, available online at http://www.marketingpower.com [accessed 1 April 2012].

Anderson, J. and Narus, J. A. (1999) *Business Market Management: Understanding, Creating, and Delivering Value*, Upper Saddle River, NJ, Prentice-Hall.

Anon. (2010) 'Sleep beauty no fable', *The Sydney Morning Herald*, 21 December, available online at http://www.smh.com.au/lifestyle/beauty/sleeping-beauty-no-fable-20101221-193qt.html [accessed 6 April 2012].

Anon. (2011a) 'Alcohol abuse to cost NHS an extra £1bn by 2015', *Metro*, 13 February, available online at http://www.metro.co.uk/news/855387-alcohol-abuse-to-cost-nhs-an-extra-1billion-by-2015 [accessed 6 April 2012].

Anon. (2011b) 'Chupa Chups: celebrity fans, who include Madonna, have helped make the brand the world's best selling lollipop', *Marketing*, 23 November, p. 16.

Anon. (2012) 'Nudge nudge, think think', *The Economist*, 24 March, available online at http://www.economist.com/node/21551032 [accessed 6 April 2012].

Azjen, I. (1991) 'The theory of planned behaviour', *Organisational Behaviour and Human Decision Processes*, 50: 179–211.

Bandura, A. (1977) *Social Learning Theory*, Englewood Cliffs, NJ: Prentice-Hall.

Bargh, J. A. and Chartrand, T. L. (1999) 'The unbearable automaticity of being', *American Psychologist*, 57(7): 462–79.

BBC News (2012) 'American Airlines announces 13,000 job cuts', 1 February, available online at http://www.bbc.co.uk/news/business-16847278 [accessed 6 April 2012].

Bettinghaus, E. P. and Cody, M. J. (1994) *Persuasive Communication*, 5th edn, London: Harcourt Brace.

Bettman, J. R. (1979) 'Memory factors in consumer choice: a review', *Journal of Marketing*, 43(Spring): 37–53.

Bonoma, T. V. (1982) 'Major sales: who really does the buying?', *Harvard Business Review*, 60(3): 111–18.

Clee, M. A. and Wicklund, R. A. (1980) 'Consumer behaviour and psychological reactance', *Journal of Consumer Research*, 6: 389–405.

Dubois, B. (2000) *Understanding the Consumer: A European Perspective*, London: FT/Prentice-Hall.

Festinger, L. (1957) *A Theory of Cognitive Dissonance*, Palo Alto, CA: Stanford University Press.

Fill, C. (2009) *Marketing Communications: Interactivity, Communities and Content*, 5th edn, Harlow: Pearson Education Limited.

Fill, C. and Fill, K. E. (2005) *Business Marketing: Relationships, Systems and Communications*, Harlow: FT/Prentice Hall.

Glenn, R. R. and Wheeler, A. R. (2004) 'A new framework for supply chain manager selection: three hurdles to competitive advantage', *Journal of Marketing Channels*, 11(4): 89–103.

Grönroos, C. (2009) 'Marketing as promise management: regaining customer management for marketing', *Journal of Business & Industrial Marketing*, 24(5/6): 351–59.

Hemsworth, D., Sánchez-Rodríguez, C., and Bidgood, B. (2008) 'A structural model of the impact of quality management practices and purchasing-related information systems on purchasing performance: a TQM perspective', *Total Quality Management and Business Excellence*, 19(1/2): 151–64.

Holbrook, M. B., Lehmann, D. R., and O'Shaughnessy, J. (1986) 'Using versus choosing: the relationship of the consumption experience to reasons for purchasing', *European Journal of Marketing*, 20(8): 49–62.

Hollyoake, M. (2009) 'The four pillars: developing a bonded business-to-business customer experience', *Database Marketing & Customer Strategy Management*, 16(2): 132–58.

Howard, J. A. and Sheth, J. N. (1969) *The Theory of Buyer Behavior*, New York: John Wiley and Sons.

Johnson, W. J. and Lewin, J. E. (1996) 'Organizational buying behavior: toward an integrative framework', *Journal of Business Research*, 35(Jan): 1–15.

Kenney, C. (2011) 'Why airlines keep going bankrupt', *Planet Money*, 16 December, available online at http://www.npr.org/blogs/money/2011/12/16/143765367/why-airlines-keep-going-bankrupt [accessed 6 April 2012].

Martin, C. A. and Bush, A. J. (2000) 'Do role models influence teenagers' purchase intentions and behavior?', *Journal of Consumer Marketing*, 17(5): 441–54.

Mintel (2010) 'Car Buying: UK', March, London: Mintel International Group Ltd, available online at http://www.mintel.com [accessed 1 April 2012].

Mitchell, A. (2011) Word-of-mouth is over-hyped', *Marketing*, 5 October, pp. 28–9.

Parker, A. (2011a) 'Ryanair chief looks for blue Sky beyond Boeing contract', *Financial Times*, 24 October, p. 16.

Parker, A. (2011b) 'Ryanair eyes new growth phase', *Financial Times*, 24 October, p. 15.

Parkinson, S. T. and Baker, M. J. (1994) *Organizational Buying Behavior: Purchasing and Marketing Management Implications*, London: Macmillan Press.

Pressey, A., Tzokas, N., and Winklhofer, H. (2007) 'Strategic purchasing and the evaluation of "problem" key supply relationships: what do key suppliers need to know?', *Journal of Business & Industrial Marketing*, 22(5): 282–94.

Ratchford, B. T. (1987) 'New insights about the FCB grid', *Journal of Advertising Research*, 27(4): 24–38.

Robinson, P. J., Faris, C. W., and Wind, Y. (1967) *Industrial Buying and Creative Marketing*, Boston, MA: Allyn & Bacon.

Ryals, L. J. and Rogers, B. (2006) 'Holding up the mirror: the impact of strategic procurement practices on account management', *Business Horizons*, 49: 41–50.

Shears, R. (2009) 'Crocs of gold: they claim to be appalled by fur, so why do stars flaunt €35,000 designer bags that exploit the brutal trade in crocodile skin?', *Daily Mail*, 11 July, p. 50.

Sheth, J. N. (1973) 'A model of industrial buyer behavior', *Journal of Marketing*, 37(Oct): 50–6.

Skinner, B. F. (1954) 'The science of learning and the art of teaching', *Harvard Educational Review*, 24: 88–97.

Svahn, S. and Westerlund, M. (2009) 'Purchasing strategies in supply relationships', *Journal of Business & Industrial Marketing*, 24(3/4): 173–81.

Swinder, J. and Seshadri, S. (2001) 'The influence of purchasing strategies on performance', *Journal of Business and Industrial Marketing*, 16(4): 294–306.

Ulkuniemi, P. (2003) 'Purchasing software components at the dawn of market', available online at http://herkules.oulu.fi/isbn9514272188/ [accessed 6 April 2012].

Webster, F. E. and Wind, Y. (1972) *Organizational Buying Behaviour*, Englewood Cliffs, NJ: Prentice Hall.

Wikipedia (2012) 'The Princess and the Pea', available online at http://en.wikipedia.org/wiki/The_Princess_and_the_Pea [accessed 6 April 2012].

Wood, O. (2012) 'How emotional tugs trump rational pushes: the time has come to abandon a 100-year-old advertising model', *Journal of Advertising Research*, 52(1): 31–9.

Wood, O., Samson, A., Harrison, P., and Batchelor, A. (2012) 'Calling times on binge-drinking: behavioural economics uncovers the hidden influences behind binge-drinking', Paper presented to the Market Research Society Annual Conference, 20–21 March, London.

4

Marketing Research

- Learning outcomes

After reading this chapter, you will be able to:

- define the terms 'market research' and 'marketing research';

- explain the use of marketing information systems;

- explain the role of marketing research and the range of approaches used;

- recognize the importance of ethics and the adoption of a code of conduct when undertaking marketing research; and

- describe the problems arising when conducting international marketing research.

Claire Spencer for i to i research

The i to i research agency conducted market research to help the London Organising Committee of the Olympic Games (LOCOG) to win public support during the bid process for London to hold the Games in 2012. We spoke to Claire Spencer, chief executive officer, to find out more.

Since the creation of the Olympic Movement in 1894, Britain has been a strong protagonist, playing host to the Games in 1908 and 1948, and sending hundreds of British Olympians to compete. In the intervening years, Britain made two unsuccessful bids before London was nominated Official Candidate City for the 2012 Games in May 2004. In 2004 and 2005, the London organization produced a compelling case for London to host the 2012 Olympic Games in what Mike Lee, director of communications, called the 'most competitive ever bidding procedure mounted by the IOC'.

It was crucial that the London 2012 team convinced the 117-strong International Olympic Committee (IOC) voting members that London had the potential to deliver on the five selection criteria: i) the best Olympic Plan; ii) low-risk delivery; iii) an enthusiastic country; iv) clear benefits of holding the Games in London; v) a professional, likeable, and trustworthy team. In order to persuade the 117 IOC members that London met the five selection criteria, the London 2012 organization embarked on a large-scale communications programme both internationally and within the UK.

However, London was challenged with one particular selection criterion: the Games had to be held by an 'enthusiastic country', which, quite frankly, it had not been. Compared to the level of public support for the

i to i research
brand communications evaluation

The i to i research logo

Games in competing cities (Paris, Moscow, New York, and Madrid), London's enthusiasm was low. With public support hovering around the 60–70 per cent mark, there was always the question: what did the other 30–40 per cent think? LOCOG felt that there was a need to commission marketing research to help it to develop a communication campaign to generate a more enthusiastic public, partly by encouraging the public to register their support for the bid by petition. Specifically, the research would need to aid evaluation of LOCOG's communication campaign in terms of: 1) whether the right messages were being communicated to engender support and registration for London to host the Games; and 2) which part of the campaign was working/not working in terms of, for example, advertising (which media), and PR (which stories).

1 **If you were creating the research programme for the bid team of the LOCOG to help it to improve London's support for the bid, how would you design the research programme?**

■ Introduction

What is the most persuasive advertisement that you've seen recently? How do companies make such useful products? Most of us take it for granted that great companies make great products, using their intuition, and that is why they are great. But, more often than not, companies develop goods and services through rigorous research programmes designed to identify customers' constantly changing needs. These goods and services don't design themselves: they are made in the light of the knowledge that market research can bring to our understanding of customers' needs and wants. We start this chapter with an outline of the origins of market research beginning at the start of the twentieth century. Along with advertising, market research is one of the key sub-disciplines of marketing practice and a fundamental component of the marketing philosophy.

We have chosen to call this chapter 'Marketing research' rather than 'Market research', because whereas market research is conducted to understand markets—customers, competitors, and industries—marketing research is conducted to determine the impact of marketing strategies and tactics on customers, competitors, and industries. Marketing research includes market research. In this chapter, we provide a definition of what 'marketing research' is, before proceeding to outline the research process, including how and why it is conducted and commissioned. In this chapter, we discuss **marketing information systems** and the rise in the use of digital technology in marketing research. Finally, we discuss the problems and challenges of conducting international marketing research, a complex field because of the need to ensure that data obtained from one country is comparable to that from another if it is to be used properly in organizational decision-making.

The exact genesis of market research is unknown, but the first systematic data-collection exercise appears to have been the census of the Chinese people around AD 2. In Britain, the first serious survey was by William the Conqueror, who commissioned the Domesday Book in AD 1085 to discover the extent of land and resources to determine suitable tax rates. However, the first official census of people, rather than land, took place in Britain in AD 1801 (Anon., 1989). Techniques used in these examples to collect large-scale demographic information have informed the techniques used later to understand consumer tastes. The first marketing research department is difficult to determine, but one former Procter & Gamble (P&G) executive suggests that it was the economic research department established at P&G to 'help anticipate fluctuations in the commodity market'. It was from this department that Dr Paul Smelser went on to establish the company's first market research department in 1924 (Stevens, 2003). But 'serious research into consumer tastes, habits and buying patterns took off in the years following World War I' (Arvidsson, 2004). One of the best-known figures in the development of marketing research was George Gallup (1901–84), the American public opinion analyst who invented the Gallup opinion poll and founded the American Institute for Public Opinion in 1936 (Anon., 1989). His work used statistics to measure reader interest in magazine and newspaper advertisements. Another pioneer was Arthur Charles Nielsen, Sr, who established A. C. Nielsen in Chicago, Illinois, in 1923—a large international company best known for its broadcast measurement systems for television audience ratings (Nielsen, 2007).

■ Definitions of Marketing Research

Marketing research is used to obtain information that provides the management of an organization with sufficient insight to make informed decisions on future activities. It follows the philosophical premise of marketing that, to be successful, an organization must understand the motivations, desires, and behaviour of its customers and consumers. However, there is sometimes confusion between the terms 'market research' and 'marketing research'. The International Chamber of Commerce (ICC)/European Society for Opinion and Market Research (ESOMAR) multipart definition of 'marketing research' stresses that:

> Marketing research is a key element within the total field of marketing information. It links the consumer, customer and the public to the marketer through information which is used to identify and define marketing opportunities and problems; generate, refine and evaluate marketing actions; improve understanding of marketing as a process and of the ways in which specific marketing activities can be made more effective. Marketing research specifies the information required to address these issues; designs the method for collecting information; manages and implements the data-collection process; analyses the results; and communicates the findings and their implications.
>
> (ESOMAR, 1995)

This definition of marketing research has also been adopted, with modifications, by the American Marketing Association (AMA, 2009), which adds that marketing research is used to monitor marketing performance.

The Market Research Society (MRS), in the UK, defines 'market research' as:

> The collection and analysis of data from a sample or census of individuals or organisations relating to their characteristics, behaviour, attitudes, opinions or possessions. It includes all forms of market, opinion and social research such as consumer and industrial surveys, psychological investigations, qualitative interviews and group discussions, observational, ethnographic and panel studies.
>
> (MRS, 2010)

So market research is work undertaken to determine either structural characteristics of the industry of concern (for example, demand, market share, market volumes, customer characteristics, and segmentation), whereas marketing research is work undertaken to understand how to make specific marketing strategy decisions, such as for pricing, sales forecasting, product testing, and promotion (Chisnall, 1992). Even though marketing research is the foundational element of modern marketing practice, market research is valued by some companies more than others as dependent on the market or marketing information needed.

Visit the **Online Resource Centre** and follow the web links to the MRS and ESOMAR to learn more about these professional marketing associations.

go online

■ Marketing Information Systems

Marketing information systems (MkISs) are very important for the conduct of marketing research. The purpose of using marketing information is to provide us with timely information on a continuous basis, to support our decision-making. But what kind of information do we actually need as marketers? Typically, we might have the following information needs:

- aggregated marketing information in quarterly, annual summaries;
- aggregated marketing information around product/markets (such as sales data);
- analytical information for decision models (SWOT, segmentation analyses);
- internally focused marketing information (sales, costs, marketing performance indicators);
- externally focused marketing information (for example, macro and industry trends);
- historical information (sales, profitability, market trends);
- future-oriented marketing information (environmental scanning information);
- quantitative marketing information (such as costs, profit, market share); and
- qualitative marketing information (for example, buyer behaviour, competitor strategy information) (Ashill and Jobber, 2001).

Such information could be provided on both a continuous and an ad hoc basis. Continuous information on industry trends can be gleaned from secondary data sources such as Mintel reports. However, the market research manager needs to remember both to buy the reports and to input the data into a suitable MkIS. Other information may be obtained on an ad hoc basis through commissioning specialist market research projects, such as for pricing or segmentation research. This also needs to be fed into the MkIS to provide the company with an up-to-date picture of its marketing environment and customer base. The qualitative information related to competitor strategy might be gleaned from sales reports or reports from overseas agents, for example.

The key difficulty for the marketing manager is to obtain and customize the MkIS to fit the company's specific needs (because the needs will probably change according to its industry), and to ensure that the data is input on a timely and continuous basis.

Axelrod (1970) suggests adherence to the following fourteen basic rules for building a MkIS.

1 Get top management involved.
2 Set the objective for the system carefully.
3 Figure out what decisions your MkIS will influence.
4 Communicate the benefits of the system to users.
5 Hire and motivate the right people.
6 Free the MkIS from accounting domination.
7 Develop the system on a gradual and systematic basis.
8 Run a new MkIS in parallel with existing procedures.
9 Provide results from the system to users quickly after its initiation.

10 Provide information on a fast turnaround basis.

11 Tie the MkIS in with existing data-collection procedures.

12 Balance the work of the MkIS between development and operations.

13 Feed valid meaningful data into the system, not useless information.

14 Design a security system to ensure that different groups get different access to the information.

More recently, there has been a strong trend towards using customer relationship management (CRM) systems to mine customer data, particularly when undertaking research into characterizing customer groups and their product/service usage. Britain's largest supermarket group Tesco, has long used dunnhumby—a customer analytics agency—to analyse its customer and point-of-sale (POS) data. dunnhumby processes around 5 billion items of information per week for Tesco (McCawley, 2006), or about 156 items of information per week for every household in Britain. Each customer has a unique profile of past-purchase transactions linked to lifestyle data derived from his or her address details. This information allows Tesco to determine the importance and use of price promotions, the degree of promotional cherry-picking (that is, buying a product only when it's on special offer), the portfolio of products that a customer purchases, how much he or she spends on groceries, and other issues using a process that it calls 'basket analysis' (Humby, 2007). In this situation, data has become a strategic asset to the firm, allowing Tesco to differentiate itself from competitors through highly effective loyalty marketing programmes designed to reward customers for shopping at Tesco stores.

■ Commissioning Market Research

In order to commission market research, the client must determine whether or not he or she wants to commission an agency, a consultant, a field and tabulation agency, or a data preparation and analysis agency (which, unlike field and tab, will not undertake the fieldwork). Typically, a consultant might be used for a small job that does not require extensive fieldwork; a field and tab agency, when the organization can design its own research, but not undertake the data collection; a data preparation and analysis agency, when it can both design and collect the data, but does not have the expertise to analyse it; and a **full-service agency**, when it does not have the expertise to design the research and to collect or analyse the data.

Agencies are usually shortlisted according to some criteria and then asked to make a presentation of their services. The criteria used to evaluate the agencies' suitability, once they have submitted a proposal, might include:

● the agency's reputation;

● the agency's perceived expertise;

● whether the study offers value for money;

● the time taken to complete the study; and

● the likelihood that the research design will provide insights into the **management problem**.

Shortlisted agencies are given a preliminary outline of the client's needs in a **research brief**, and asked to provide proposals on research methodology, timing, and costs. After this, the client will select an agency to do the market research work required.

The Marketing Research Brief

The research brief is a formal document prepared by a client organization submitted to the marketing research agency. When marketing research is conducted in-house, the department manager who requires the research prepares a brief for the marketing research manager. The brief should outline a management problem to be investigated (see Market Insight 4.1 for an example).

The typical contents of a research brief might comprise the following.

- *Background summary*—This provides a brief introduction, including details about the company and its products and/or services.
- *The management problem*—This is a clear statement of why the research should be undertaken and what business decisions are dependent upon its outcome.
- *The marketing research questions*—The manager should compile a detailed list of the information necessary in order to make the decisions sought.
- *The intended scope of the research*—This will include the areas to be covered, and which industries, type of customer, etc. The brief should give an indication of when the information is required and explain why that date is important (pricing research might, for example, be required for a sales forecast meeting).
- *Tendering procedures*—The client organization should outline how agencies are to be selected as a result of the tendering process. Specific information may be required, such as CVs from agency personnel to be involved in the study and referee contact addresses. The number of copies of the report required and preferences with regard to layout are usually also outlined.

Market Insight 4.1

Private Jet Service Insight: The Brief

Hank Sopel is the managing director of TaxiJet, a start-up private jet company, operating out of London Luton airport. He has managed to obtain around £30 million of private equity and investor funding to launch a new private jet airline service, principally operating from the UK to Europe at the customer's choice of time and locations (inbound and outbound). However, before he launches, he wants to know much more about the type of service that his potential customers want so that he can:

- understand how current private jet users and European business-class flyers use existing airline services at present and their purchasing motives;
- understand how he should develop his promotional approach to generate awareness of the new service to existing private jet users and potential switcher clients prepared to upgrade from flying European business class with commercial scheduled airlines; and
- determine how to custom-design the service to meet potential clients' needs in terms of both private individuals and business users.

Private jet: the ultimate flying experience
Source: © iStockphoto LP 2010

An important feature of the new service is that the private jets that Hank intends to use are based on a new breed of very light jets (VLJs), typified by the Cessna Citation Mustang, which are cheaper to purchase, maintain, and operate, not least because they fly at a higher altitude, use less fuel, and are made of lighter material. These jets, however, are smaller than many existing private jets, providing seating for only six persons (including two pilots), with a flying range of up to three hours, potentially taking clients to most parts of Europe, reaching up to Turkey in the East and Moscow in Russia.

Because of the lower costs of operation and the smaller size of the plane, there is a feeling that this new breed of jet could open the market up for private jet travel, positioning it somewhere just above first class (in flexibility, comfort, and convenience) and around

business class (in terms of in-flight services, such as meals and entertainment) when compared to existing scheduled airline services, and potentially taking private jet travel beyond the remit of only wealthy corporate leaders. Hank also recognizes that the economic situation in the UK is not strong, given the unwelcome media attention focusing on the use of private jets by companies in financial difficulties (such as General Motors in the US).

He wants to understand more about his potential clients' purchasing motives in the current market environment. Despite the economic difficulties, there is still a profitable market for private jet use, especially among high net worth individuals travelling for business and leisure purposes. He also wants to know whether there is a need for other specific add-on services, including limousines to and from London, for example.

Sopel invites in representatives of Dynamic Research Limited (DRL) and spends two hours briefing them, before asking them to prepare a proposal.

Source: Market Research Society (MRS). Reproduced with kind permission.

1 Do you think that this brief has clear research objectives? Why (not)?

2 Does the research brief indicate or imply that a specific methodology should be used? If so, which method does it imply?

3 Do you think the research objectives are feasible? Why (not)?

■ The Marketing Research Process

There are a number of basic stages in the process that should guide any marketing research project. These are outlined in Figure 4.1. The first, and most crucial, stage of the process involves problem definition and setting the information needs of the decision-makers.

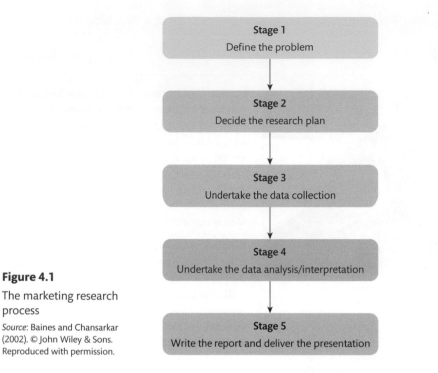

Figure 4.1

The marketing research process

Source: Baines and Chansarkar (2002). © John Wiley & Sons. Reproduced with permission.

Stage 1: Problem Definition

This process occurs when an organization provides a marketing research brief defining the management problem. An example might be the Carrefour supermarket chain, explaining that sales are not as strong as expected in one of its new stores in the Czech Republic (a symptom of a problem) and that management is wondering whether or not this is as result of the emergence of a new competitor supermarket nearby. (This problem is shown in Figure 4.2.)

The marketing researcher then needs to translate the management problem into a marketing research question. To do this, the market researcher talks to the staff commissioning the study to shed further light on the situation. This leads to the development of a marketing research question. This question may include a number of sub-questions for further exploration. A possible, very general, marketing research question and a number of more specific sub-questions are shown in Figure 4.3.

Sometimes, the management problem is clear. The organization needs a customer profile, an industry profile, an understanding of buyer behaviour, or to test advertising concepts for its next TV advertising campaign and so on. The more clearly the commissioning organization defines the management problem, the easier it will be to design the research to provide

Figure 4.2

Example of a management problem

Management probelem

Sales at the new store have not met management expectations, possibly as a result of the emergence of a new competitor

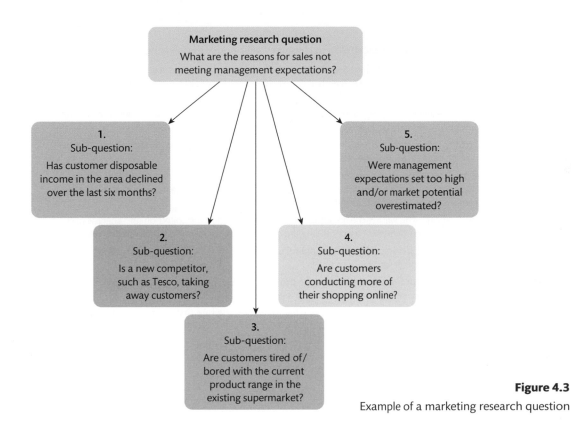

Figure 4.3

Example of a marketing research question

insight to aid management decision-making. Once the agency has discussed the brief with the client, the agency provides a detailed outline of how it intends to investigate the problem. This document is called the **research proposal**. Figure 4.4 briefly outlines a typical marketing research proposal.

Visit the **Online Resource Centre** to see an example of a research proposal for TaxiJet, the start-up airline company at which we looked in Market Insight 4.1, and to learn more about how to write a research proposal.

go online

Stage 2: Decide the Research Plan

At this stage, we decide whether or not to undertake primary or secondary research or both. Often, we might undertake an initial phase of secondary research to see whether someone has considered the same research question that we now encounter. So, if we had recently bought a new cinema and wanted to know the types of person that lived in the local area, we could consult secondary data sources, which would tell us more about the characteristics of people living in the area (such as gender, age, population size). However, if we were to want to know what types of film they prefer, we might resort to a survey of a **sample** of the population.

Primary versus Secondary Research
Primary research is research conducted for the first time, involving the collection of data primarily for the purpose of a particular project. 'Secondary data' is second-hand data, collected

The basic structure and contents of a typical research proposal should include the following.

- **Executive summary**   This is a brief summary of the research project including the major outcomes and findings; it is rarely more than one page in length. It allows the reader to obtain a summary of the main points of the project without having to read the full report.

- **Background to the research**   This offers an outline of the problem or situation and the issues surrounding it. This section demonstrates the researcher's understanding of the management problem.

- **Research objectives**   This outlines the objectives of the research project, including the data to be generated and how this will be used to address the management problem.

- **Research design**   This comprises a clear, non-technical description of the research type adopted and the specific techniques to be used to gather the required information. This will include details on data-collection instruments, sampling procedures, and analytical techniques.

- **Personnel specification**   This will list the details of the people involved in the collection and analysis of the data, providing a named liaison person and outlining the company's credibility in undertaking the work.

- **Time schedule**   This will offer an outline of the time requirements, with dates for the various stages to completion and presentation of results.

- **Costs**   A detailed analysis of the costs involved in the project is usually included for large projects; for smaller projects, this will comprise simply a total cost for the project.

- **References**   Typically, three references are listed so that a client can be sure that an agency has the requisite capability to do the job in hand.

Figure 4.4

A marketing research proposal outline

for some other purpose. **Secondary research**, known also as **desk research**, involves gaining access to the results or outcomes of previous research projects. This method can be a cheaper and more efficient process of data collection.

We can do a large amount of secondary research for free by searching the Internet. Other sources of secondary data include:

- government sources, such as export databases, government statistical offices, social trend databases, and other resources;

- the Internet, including sources identified using search engines, blogs, and discussion groups;

- company internal records, including information housed in a marketing information/CRM system or published sales reports, marketing plans, and research reports previously commissioned;

- professional bodies and trade associations, which frequently have databases available for research purposes, online, which may include industry magazine articles and research reports; and

- market research companies (such as Mintel, Euromonitor, and ICC Keynote), which frequently undertake research into industry sectors or specific product groups, and can be highly specialized.

go online

Visit the **Online Resource Centre** and follow the web links to learn more about these market research organizations.

In practice, most research projects involve a combination of secondary and primary research, with a desk research phase occurring at the beginning to ensure that a company is not wasting its money on research that has already been conducted. Once this initial insight is gleaned, we determine whether or not to commission a primary data study. Assuming that primary research needs to be undertaken, researchers usually design their research by considering what type of research to employ. Marketing directors need to have some understanding of the different types of study that can be conducted, because this has an impact on the type of data and information to be collected to help to provide insight to their management problem.

Categories of Research Design

Generally speaking, we define three categories of research design: exploratory, descriptive, and causal. These categories specify the approach adopted for collection and analysis of the data necessary to identify a management problem.

1 **Exploratory research** is used when little is known about a particular management problem and to discover the general nature of the questions that might relate to it. Exploratory designs enable the development of hypotheses. We tend to adopt qualitative methods, such as **focus groups**, **in-depth interviews**, **projective techniques**, and **observational studies**. Exploratory research also makes use of secondary data, non-probability (subjective) samples, case analyses, and subjective evaluation of the resultant data.

2 **Descriptive research** focuses on accurately describing the variables being considered. It uses quantitative methods, particularly surveys (on- and offline), for example in consumer profile studies, product usage studies, price surveys, attitude surveys, sales analyses, and media research.

3 **Causal research** is used when there is a need to determine whether one variable causes an effect in another variable. For example, if we were interested in determining whether temperature increases cause Coca-Cola sales to increase, we might use this method. Studies into the determination of advertising effectiveness and customer attitude changes are other examples. The difficulty arises in determining whether or not the sales effect was caused by the price increase or some other unmeasured variable.

Qualitative versus Quantitative Research

At the beginning of a research project, we might consider whether to use **qualitative research** or **quantitative research**, or some combination of the two. The two main forms of research are outlined in Figure 4.5, along with the techniques associated with each main form of research. Whereas quantitative research techniques, such as surveys, emphasize theory testing, qualitative techniques are used to identify meaning and understanding. The client, or the in-house marketing research manager, may have specific budget constraints or an idea of which particular approach he or she wishes to adopt. However, the choice really depends on the circumstances of the research project and its objectives.

Quantitative research methods, such as a survey, are designed to elicit responses to predetermined, standardized questions from a large number of participants. This involves collecting information from many people, and quantifying the responses as frequencies or percentages and descriptive statistics. Other quantitative research methods include mass

Causal modelling and structural equation modelling	Experiments	Surveys and other multivariate techniques	Mystery shopping studies	Case studies	In-depth interviews	Focus groups	Ethnographic studies	Semiotic studies

Quantitative research techniques   Qualitative research techniques

⟵——⟶

Figure 4.5

A continuum of research techniques

observation techniques and experiments. Experiments are designed to determine cause-and-effect relationships, particularly in psychological studies. **Mystery shopping** is a common research technique, used particularly in retailing (on- and offline), in which consumers are recruited by researchers to act as anonymous buyers and use forms to evaluate customer satisfaction, service quality, and the customer's own evaluation of their experiences. In contrast, qualitative research techniques are typically used to identify the basic factors contextualizing the management problem. The most common forms of qualitative research are discussion groups and in-depth interviews. Projective techniques can also be used in both forms. Qualitative research techniques attempt to uncover the underlying motivations behind consumers' opinions, attitudes, perceptions, and behaviour. Consequently, they adopt unstructured methods to elicit information from participants.

In the market research industry, the most familiar qualitative techniques are in-depth interviews, focus groups, and **consumer juries**. The objective is to uncover feelings, attitudes, memories, and interpretations. They can range in form from an informal conversation to highly structured interviews. They might be used to seek an interviewee's perspective on a new campaign or to develop customer profiles covering a wide range of needs and preferences. Focus groups, or **group discussions**, have been used extensively in the marketing communications industry for many years. They normally consist of a small number of target consumers brought together to discuss elements from the initial concept stage to post-production stage. At the concept stage, the target sample is presented with rough outlines or **storyboards** giving an idea of the campaign(s) under consideration. A professional moderator aims to understand the thoughts, feelings, and attitudes of the group towards a product or service, media, or message. Consumer juries consist of a collection of target consumers who are asked to rank in order ideas or concepts put to them and to explain their choices. In addition to these common qualitative techniques, there is growing use of more cultural qualitative techniques, such as **semiotics** and ethnography (see Market Insight 4.2), drawing upon techniques borrowed from linguistic philosophy, cultural anthropology, and the systematic study of signs and codes (Goulding, 2002). These techniques have formed the basis of many national and international television campaigns and brand repositioning exercises, for organizations such as BT, Tesco, and Coca-Cola.

Ethnographic studies, which are informed by participant observation and interview methods, are being increasingly used, especially with digital and social technologies provid-

In 2012, a consumer jury of over 1.6 million people voted via a BT-run Facebook page for Jane, the main character in BT's national television advertising campaign, to become pregnant.

Source: Copyright BT.

ing increasing opportunities for the study of our digital social selves and social networks (see Market Insight 4.3).

Semiotic research, in contrast, is aimed at understanding consumer culture, which, instead of interviewing or observing people, analyses the content of advertisements and other texts to identify the meaning of the signs and symbols contained.

Qualitative techniques generally involve a small number of participants. The emphasis is on obtaining rich, detailed information from a small group of people rather than short, specific answers from a large group of participants. The major characteristics of qualitative and quantitative marketing research techniques are outlined in Table 4.1. Case studies can be qualitative or quantitative depending on the number of case studies used and the purpose of the research. For example, Colgate-Palmolive might well research the product life cycle of a particular toothpaste brand in Pakistan, India, Turkey, and the United Arab Emirates (UAE) before launching a new brand in India.

Qualitative research is used to uncover underlying motivations for people's behaviour, attitudes, opinions, and perceptions, but because the research approach uses small samples, the results derived are not generalizable to the wider population of interest. They are used to generate only insights.

Quantitative research techniques are used to obtain representative samples to enable generalizability and are based on larger participant samples than qualitative research; the samples are selected either randomly or to match the population. One disadvantage of quantitative research is that we typically predetermine the answers, so there is a chance that participants do not fully express their true opinions.

The Museum of Me

Ethnography is the participant observation of people within their own social cultural habitats. With the rise in social networking sites such as Facebook, we are seeing increased use of ethnography to study these digital communities. To provide a snapshot of what an ethnographer observes, Intel has launched a new Facebook application that is regarded as the world's first viral, consumer-driven digital ethnography tool: the 'Museum of Me'. The application compiles all of your content from your Facebook profile, allowing users to create and explore a visual archive of their social life. This raises both opportunities and ethical considerations for researchers, and provides an indication of how much information consumers will share if you make it an engaging experience, as well as an example of how technology can be used to build deep and rich virtual ethnographic profiles. Once created, the user can view virtual rooms showing information that he or she has regularly shared with his or her Facebook friends in the form of pictures, personal photos, videos, status updates, and wall posts. At the end of the tour, a visual representation of the user's digital social Facebook network is displayed. For market researchers, this provides an opportunity to engage consumers not only as participants, but as partners in a digital ethnographic

Museum of Me: it's all about you!
Source: Intel

tracking study for the creation of digital profiles for segmentation and market understanding.

Sources: Reisinger (2011); Murphy (2011); http://www.intel.com/museumofme/r/index.htm

1 **How would an ethnographic study of Facebook help us to understand social network users?**

2 **What do you think could be the marketing implications of data generated from watching a group of Facebook users?**

3 **What do you think are the ethics of watching the digital social interactions of people for research purposes?**

Designing the Research Project

When we know what type of research to conduct and whether or not we need secondary data to understand the management problem, we should consider:

- who to question and how (the sampling plan and procedures to be used);
- what methods to use (for example, discussion groups or an experiment);
- which types of question are required (open questions for qualitative research or closed questions for a survey); and
- how the data should be analysed and interpreted (that is, which approach to data analysis).

Research methods describe the techniques and procedures that we adopt to obtain the necessary information.

Table 4.1 Qualitative and quantitative research methods compared

Characteristic	Qualitative	Quantitative
Purpose	To identify and understand underlying motivations, memories, attitudes, opinions, perceptions, and behaviours	To determine the representativeness of the sample to the population, i.e. how similar is the sample to the population?
Size of sample	Involves a small number of participants, typically fewer than 30	Involves a large number of participants, more than 30
Type of information generated	Provides detailed information	Provides narrowly defined descriptive information
Degree of structuring	Uses an unstructured approach, typically using open questions	Uses a structured questioning process and frequently closed, multiple, fixed-response questions
Type of data analysis	Uses a non-statistical word (content-based) analysis, e.g. the NVivo qualitative analysis software	Statistical analysis, e.g. using **SPSS** software
Sampling approach	Uses **non-probability sampling** methods	Uses **probability sampling** techniques

Figure 4.6 indicates the key components that we need to consider when designing both qualitative and quantitative research projects. The design of marketing research projects involves determining how each of these components interrelates with the others. The components comprise:

- research objectives;
- the sampling method;
- the interviewing method to be used;
- the research type and methods undertaken;
- the question and questionnaire design; and
- data analysis.

Each of these components impacts on the others. When designing research projects, we must first determine the type of approach to use for a given management problem (for example, exploratory, descriptive, or causal); then we will determine which techniques are most capable of producing the desired data at the least cost and in the minimum time period. Generally, certain types of research (exploratory, descriptive, causal) use certain methods and techniques.

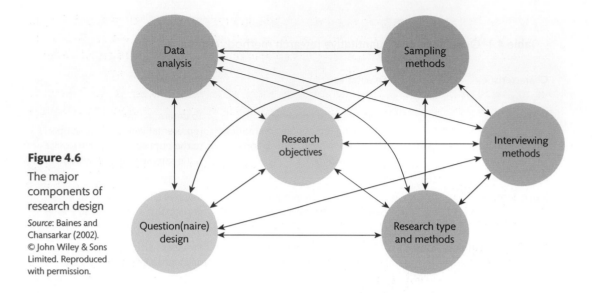

Figure 4.6

The major components of research design

Source: Baines and Chansarkar (2002). © John Wiley & Sons Limited. Reproduced with permission.

For example, exploratory research studies use qualitative research methods, non-probability sampling methods, and non-statistical data analysis methods. Descriptive research projects usually adopt survey interviews using quota or random sampling methods and statistical analysis techniques. Causal researchers use experimental research designs using convenience or probability sampling methods and statistical data analysis procedures.

Stage 3: Sampling and Data Collection

This stage involves the conduct of the fieldwork and the collection of the required data. At this stage, we send out questionnaires, or run the focus group sessions, or conduct telephone surveys, depending on the research design decisions. The procedures undertaken when conducting the fieldwork might relate to how to ask the questions of the participants—whether by telephone, mail, or in person—and how to select an appropriate sample, how to pre-code the answers to a questionnaire (quantitative research), or how to code the answers arising out of open-ended questions (particularly with qualitative research).

The market research manager might be concerned about whether or not to conduct the research in-house or commission a field and tab agency. Other issues concern how to ensure high data quality. When market research companies undertake shopping mall intercept interviews, they usually re-contact a proportion of the participants to check their answers to ensure that the interviews have been conducted properly.

In qualitative research, samples are often selected using non-probability sampling methods such as convenience or judgement. In quantitative research, we might use either probability or non-probability methods.

- *Probability methods* include:
  - **simple random sampling**, in which the population elements are accorded a number and a sample is selected by generating random numbers that correspond to the individual population elements;

- **systematic random sampling**, in which population elements are known and the first sample unit is selected using random number generation, but after which each of the succeeding sample units is then selected systematically on the basis of an nth number, where n is determined by dividing the population size by the sample size;
- **stratified random sampling**, in which a specific characteristic(s) is used (such as gender or age) to design homogeneous sub-groups from which a representative sample is then drawn.
- *Non-probability methods* include:
  - **quota sampling**, in which criteria such as gender, ethnicity, or some other customer characteristic are used to restrict the sample, but the selection of the sample unit is left to the judgement of the researcher;
  - **convenience sampling**, in which no such restrictions are placed on the selection of the participants and anybody can be selected;
  - **snowball sampling**, in which participants are selected from rare populations (for example, high-performance car buyers), initially from responses to newspaper adverts and then further identified using referrals from the initial participants (thereby 'snowballing' the sample).

The Internet and digital technologies have had a strong effect on marketing research, and will continue to do so into the future. In 2011, ESOMAR reported that online research now accounts for 22 per cent of all quantitative and 6 per cent of all qualitative research activities (ESOMAR, 2011). There has been explosive growth in the last decade in quantitative online research methods. Quantitative online market research has doubled in the last five years to become the most popular worldwide data collection method, according to ESOMAR (2010), and accounts for nearly a third of all market research by value. Many companies have switched their telephone and personal interviewing research approaches to use online and mobile methods. With respect to mobile technologies, in Europe, according to Eurobarometer, fewer than 70 per cent of Europeans now use a landline. The number of mobile-only homes ranges from fewer than 10 per cent in Sweden, Germany, and the Netherlands, to 66 per cent in Finland and 75 per cent in the Czech Republic (Mareck, 2010). The mobile phone has become a standard tool of communication with multiple features, for voice, digital services, email, photos, videos, and even navigation. This has strong implications for the conduct of telephone interviewing, such as the representation of landline telephone lists for sampling, and is enabling researchers to collect a wide range of very rich data serviced through a myriad of mobile applications.

With online research specifically, panels of participants are often used to limit self-selection bias inherent in online survey research, with two types of **panel study** used (Miles, 2004).

- **Access panels** provide samples for survey-style information and are made up of targets who have been invited by email to take part with a link to the web survey, an example of which includes the online pollster YouGov.
- **Proprietary panels** are set up or commissioned by a client firm and are usually made up of that company's customers. To encourage participation in these surveys, the researchers often use incentives such as the chance to win a prize.

But there are pros and cons involved with undertaking online research, as shown in Table 4.2. (For more on online research, see Bradley, 2010.)

Table 4.2 Advantages and disadvantages on online research

The pros of online research	The cons of online research
1 Clients and analysts can see results being compiled in real time.	1 Online panels' demographic profile can differ from that of the general population.
2 Online surveys save time and money compared with face-to-face interviews.	2 If questionnaires take longer than 20 minutes to fill in, quality can suffer and they may go uncompleted.
3 Consumers welcome surveys that they can fill in when they want to and often need no incentive to do so.	3 Poor recruitment and badly managed panels can damage the data.
4 A more relaxed environment leads to better-quality, honest, and reasoned responses.	4 Technical problems, such as browser incompatibility, can mean that panellists give up.
5 Panellist background data allows immediate access to key target audiences unrestricted by geography.	5 Programming costs are higher than for offline questionnaires.

Source: Miles (2004: 40). Reproduced with the kind permission of Haymarket Media Group Limited.

go online

Visit the **Online Resource Centre** and complete Internet Activity 4.2 to learn more about the Market Research World, a useful source of online research resources.

Research Insight 4.1

To take your learning further, you might wish to read the following influential papers:

Comley, P. and Beaumont, J. (2011) 'Online research: Methods, benefits and issues—Part 1', *Journal of Direct, Data and Digital Marketing Practice*, 12(4): 315–27; 'Online research: Methods, benefits and issues—Part 2', *Journal of Direct, Data and Digital Marketing Practice*, 13(1): 25–39

These articles review the development of online research methods over the last ten years. They describe how online market research has now become a de facto methodology for many organizations, and consider the key growth drivers, benefits, and issues of online access panels, online surveys, river sampling, client panels and databases, website visitor surveys, and developments in qualitative online market research.

Visit the **Online Resource Centre** to read the abstract and to access the full paper.

Stage 4: Data Analysis and Interpretation

This stage of the market research process comprises data input, analysis, and interpretation. How the data is input usually depends on the type of data collected. Qualitative data, which is usually alpha-numeric—that is, a combination of alphabetical and numerical characters— is often entered into word-processed documents as interview transcripts from audio or video-tape, or entered directly into computer software applications (for example, NVivo) as video or sound files for content analysis. Quantitative data analysis uses statistical analysis packages (such as SPSS). In these cases, data are usually numeric and are first entered into spreadsheet packages (for example, Microsoft Excel) or entered directly into the statistical computer application itself. Online questionnaires are particularly useful in this regard, because the data is automatically entered into a database, saving significant periods of data input time and ensuring a higher level of data quality. If **computer-assisted personal interviewing (CAPI)** or **computer-assisted telephone interviewing (CATI)** methods are used, analysis can also occur instantaneously as the interviews are undertaken. **Computer-assisted web interviewing (CAWI)** techniques allow the researcher to read the questions from a computer screen and directly enter the responses of the participants. Using the Internet, CAWI techniques can also include the playback of video and audio files.

Market research methods are used to aid managerial decision-making; therefore the data obtained needs to be valid and reliable. **Validity** and **reliability** are important concepts in quantitative market research. They aid researchers in understanding the extent to which the data obtained from the study represent reality and 'truth'. Quantitative research methods rely on the degree to which the data elicited is able to be reproduced in a later study (that is, reliability) and the extent to which the data generated is bias-free (that is, valid). Validity is defined as the extent to which a measurement is a true reflection of the underlying variable or construct that it is attempting to measure (Parasuraman, 1991). One way of measuring validity is the use of the researcher's subjective judgement to ascertain whether or not an instrument is measuring what it is supposed to measure (content validity). For example, a question asked about job satisfaction does not necessarily infer loyalty to the organization.

Reliability is defined as 'a criterion for evaluating measurement scales; it represents how consistent or stable the ratings generated by a scale are' (Parasuraman, 1991: 443). Reliability is affected by concepts of time, analytical bias, and questioning error. We can also distinguish between two types of reliability: internal and external reliability (Bryman, 1989). To determine how reliable the data is, we conduct the study again over two or more time periods to evaluate the consistency of the data. This is known as the 'test–retest' method and measures external reliability. Another method used involves dividing the responses into two random sets and testing both sets independently using **t-tests** or **z-tests**. This illustrates internal reliability. The two different sets of results are then correlated. This method is known as 'split-half reliability testing'. These methods are more suited to testing the reliability of rating scales than data generated from qualitative research procedures. The results of a quantitative marketing research project are reliable if we conduct a similar research project within a short time period and the same or similar results are obtained in the second study. For example, if the marketing department of a travel agency chain were to interview 500 of its customers and discover that 25 per cent are in favour of a particular resort (for example, a particular Greek island), then repeat the study the following year and discover that only 10 per cent of the sample are interested in the same resort, then the results of the first study could be said to be unreliable in comparison and the procurement department should not base its purchase of package holidays purely on the previous year's finding.

In qualitative research, concepts of validity and reliability are generally less important, because the data is not used to imply representativeness. Qualitative data is more about the generation of ideas and the formulation of hypotheses. Validity may be assured by sending out transcripts to participants and/or clients for checking, to ensure that what they have said in in-depth interviews or focus groups was properly reproduced for analysis. When the analyst reads the data from a critical perspective to determine whether or not this fits with his or her expectations, this constitutes what is termed a '**face validity** test'. Reliability is often achieved by checking that similar statements are made by the range of participants, across and within the interview transcripts. Interviewees' transcripts are checked to assess whether or not the same participant, or other participants, have made the discussion point. Such detailed content analysis tends to be conducted using computer applications (such as NVivo).

Stage 5: Report Preparation and Presentation

The final stage of a research project involves reporting the results and presenting the findings to the external or in-house client. The results should be presented free from bias. Marketing research data are of little use unless they can be translated into a format that is meaningful to the manager or client who initially demanded the data. Presentations are often attended by senior people within the commissioning organization, who may or may not have been involved in commissioning the work. Usually, agencies and consultants write their reports using a basic prewritten template, which corresponds to a 'house style', although the content placed within that template is obviously different for each individual project. With so much data and information available to marketing practitioners, the presentation of such complex data in a meaningful way has been a barrier to its usefulness. In Market Insight 4.3, we discuss the rise in the use of infographics—a device used to aid the presentation of complex market and marketing information.

Market Insight 4.3

Infographics: Making Art out of Science

Presenting complex information in a meaningful way is a key objective of marketing research practitioners. With the rise in information technology and advanced graphics programs, there has been a rise in popularity of the use of the scientific art form the 'infographic', a conjunction of information and graphic. Infographics are visual devices intended to communicate complex information quickly and clearly. The characteristic of a good infographic is its ability to display complex information in a succinct, creative, visual, organized, transparent, and relevant manner. It is, however, important to consider their accuracy and to be cautious with their use. Users of infographics should think before they link and marketers should ensure that all of the facts in their infographics are correct. Among the most common devices used in an infographic are horizontal bar, vertical column, and round or oval pie charts, which can summarize a lot of statistical information. In addition to presenting data, infographics can be used to show how a system works: for an organizational chart, the lines of authority, or a systems flowchart that shows sequential movement.

With their roots in print, by the year 2000, the use of Adobe Flash-based animations on the web had allowed the creation and sharing of the infographic art form to rise in popularity and in many forms. In 2002, they were used in television: the two Norwegian musicians comprising the band Röyksopp issued a music video for their song 'Remind Me' that was completely made from animated infographics; in 2004, a television commercial for the French energy company Areva used similar animated infographics. Both of these videos and their high visibility have helped the corporate world to recognize the value in using this form of visual language to describe complex information efficiently.

For more recent examples of infographics, visit http://infographipedia.com/

Sources: Newsom and Haynes (2004); McArdle (2011); http://infographipedia.com/

1 **How do you think an organization such as Tesco and dunnhumby (see 'Marketing Information Systems') could use an infographic to present data to its board about the Tesco ClubCard scheme?**

2 **Visit http://infographipedia.com/, select an infographic, and analyse its content. What type of data or information is it reporting?**

3 **What do you think the research limitations are of presenting data and information as an infographic?**

■ Market and Advertisement Testing

Marketing research is used to reveal attitudes, to a campaign, brand, or some other aspect of the exchange process; market testing, by comparison, measures actual behaviour. There is a difference, because attitudes do not always determine action (see Chapter 3). For example, a consumer may respond very positively to the launch of a new, top-of-the-range TV in surveys, but family circumstances or lack of funds may mean that the TV is never purchased. Market testing studies use **test markets** to carry out controlled experiments in specific TV or radio regions, where specific adverts can be shown, before exposing the 'new feature' (product, service, campaign, distribution, etc.) to a full national, or even international, launch. Depending on the feature involved, another region or the rest of the market may act as the **control group** against which results can be measured. As an example, films are often test-screened before they are released. Because they represent multimillion-dollar enterprises in their own right, getting them right is an important consideration.

Marketing research is frequently used to test advertisements, whether these are in print, online, or broadcast via radio or TV (see also Chapter 10). The research company Millward Brown International is particularly well known for this type of research. There are a variety of methods used to test adverts. Typically, quantitative research is undertaken to test customer attitudes before and after exposure to the advertisement to see whether or not the advert has had a positive impact. In addition, research occurring after exposure to the advert would also test the extent to which audiences can either recognize a particular advert (for example, by showing customers a copy of a TV advert still, a print advert, or a photo online) or recall an advert without being shown a picture (we call this 'aided' and 'unaided' recall). Qualitative research is also used to identify and test specific themes that might be used in the adverts, and to test storyboards and **cuts** of adverts (before they are properly produced). More recently, revolutionary advances in technology allow us to evaluate visual imagery more objectively, without relying on the opinion of the participant. (For a useful discussion of audience and advertising research, see Bradley, 2010.)

■ Marketing Research and Ethics

Marketing research is based on the willing cooperation of individuals or organizations that provide the answers to our questions, for example by filling in questionnaires, scanning home shopping, or by attending focus groups. Marketing research should be carried out in an objective, unobtrusive, and honest manner. Researchers are concerned about the public's increased unwillingness to participate in marketing research and the problem of recruiting suitable interviewers. The apathy among interviewees is probably associated with the growing, perhaps excessive, amount of research conducted, particularly through intrusive telephone interviewing, which is increasing, and door-to-door type survey interviewing, which is declining. Marketing research is increasingly conducted online. This has created its own set of ethical concerns: how can we verify that someone online is who he or she says that he or she is? Is it acceptable to observe and analyse customer blogs and social networking site conversations? Market Insight 4.4 shows an example of the analysis of Twitter information captured during the London riots in 2011: is this ethical?

Generally, marketing research neither attempts to induce sales of a product or service nor influence customer attitudes, intentions, or behaviours. The MRS Key Principles (MRS, 2010: 4) outline the following imperatives to which researchers must adhere.

1 Ensure that participation in their activities is based on voluntary informed consent.
2 Be straightforward and honest in all their professional and business relationships.
3 Be transparent as to the subject and purpose of data collection.
4 Respect the confidentiality of information collected in their professional activities.
5 Respect the rights and well-being of all individuals.
6 Ensure that their participants are not harmed or adversely affected by their professional activities.
7 Balance the needs of individuals, clients, and their professional activities.
8 Exercise independent professional judgement in the design, conduct, and reporting of their professional activities.
9 Ensure that their professional activities are conducted by persons with appropriate training, qualifications, and experience.
10 Protect the reputation and integrity of the profession.

The MRS Code of Conduct—which is based on the ESOMAR Code—is binding on all members of the MRS. The general public and other interested parties are entitled to assurances that no information collected in a research survey will be used to identify them, or be disclosed to a third party without their consent. In that respect, data in European countries is also subject to an EU Data Protection Directive. Participants must be informed as to the purpose of the research and the length of time for which they will be involved in it. Research findings must also be reported accurately and not used to mislead in any way. In conducting marketing research, researchers have responsibility for themselves, their clients, and the participants from whom the information is being gathered.

The results of marketing research studies should remain confidential unless agreed by the client and agency, and the agency should provide detailed accounts of the methods employed to carry out the research project where this is requested by the client.

Market Insight 4.4

Twitter under Siege

In August 2011, London was 'under siege' as a result of a sequence of riots. Politicians and media alike attributed the rise and organization of the London riots to social media activity, with a call for 'switching off' social networks during civil unrest. However collection and analysis of Twitter usage data, one of the social networks at the heart of the controversy, reported usage trends to the contrary.

Twitter, the microblogging social network site (SNS), was launched in 2006. The site affords the ability to share posts called 'tweets', consisting of up to 140 characters, which are displayed on user accounts in reverse chronological order. Users can subscribe to other users' posts without the need for them to subscribe reciprocally. It has gained the attention of mainstream media, scholars, and the general public for its increasing worldwide popularity and use in everyday life, Twitter was one of the social networking sites mentioned by David Cameron in his emergency parliamentary address at the height of the London riots. However, preliminary analysis of how Twitter was used during the unrest presents a more complex picture, showing little immediate evidence that the service was used to orchestrate disorder.

In a bid to understand Twitter usage, and to report on its use during and after the riots in a series of news articles, *The Guardian* invested resources in collecting, analysing,

and drawing insight from a unique database of more than 2.5 million tweets containing keywords, phrases, and hashtags linked to England's riots. The database collected tweets sent between midnight on 6 August and 8 pm on 17 August 2011. Timing trend analysis of network usage drawn from this data questions the assumption that Twitter played a widespread role in inciting violence.

Twitter activity in twelve riot locations shows that the majority of surging social media traffic occurs *after* the first verified reports of incidents in an area, and was mainly used to react to riots and looting. Twitter was used far more by those seeking to follow fast-moving events than those seeking to incite trouble later in the week. Twitter usage trends showed that it may even have helped to spread warnings of rioting locations, with reports of stores closing early and police presence building in the area hours ahead of the outbreak. The usage analysis also revealed how extensively Twitter was used to coordinate a movement by citizens to clean the streets after the disorder. More than 206,000 tweets, 8 per cent of the total, related to attempts to clean up the debris left by four nights of rioting and looting.

In summary, usage trend analysis of more than 2.5 million Twitter messages relating to the riots has cast doubt on the rationale behind government proposals to ban people from social networks or to shut down such sites in times of civil unrest.

Sources: Sagolla (2009); Arceneaux and Weiss (2010); Ball and Lewis (2011); Twitter Inc. (2012a; 2012b)

Crowdsourcing via Twitter: a mob of cleaners who clean up after a mob of vandals

Source: Photographer: Paul Ellis

1 Do you think it is ethical for *The Guardian* or other organizations to collect, analyse, and report on user tweets from Twitter?

2 What do you think some of the ethical considerations could be around the reporting of trends observed in how people use social networking sites?

3 Read the MRS Key Principles. Is the collection and reporting of tweets in accordance with these Principles?

go online

Visit the **Online Resource Centre** and complete Internet Activity 4.1 to learn more about the Marketing Research Code of Practice and the Social Media Research Guidelines adopted by ESOMAR.

■ International Marketing Research

Marketing researchers often find it challenging to understand how culture operates in international markets and therefore how it affects research design. Complexity in the international business environment (see also Chapters 2 and 5) makes international marketing research more complex, because it affects the research process and design. The main decision is whether or not to customize international marketing research to each of the separate countries in a study, using differing scales and sampling methods, or to try to use one single method for all countries, adopting an international **sampling frame**. In many ways, this debate mirrors the standardization–customization dilemma that is common in international marketing generally.

International researchers try to ensure that comparable data is collected despite differences in sampling frames, technological developments, and availability of interviewers. Western approaches to marketing research, data collection, and culture might be inappropriate in some research environments because of variations in economic development and consumption patterns. How comparable are the data related to the consumption of McDonald's products collected through personal interviews in the UAE, telephone interviews in France, and shopping mall intercept questionnaires in Sweden? Similarly, we could ask the question: is the use of Unilever's Timotei shampoo by consumers in Latvia satisfying the same consumer needs as those of consumers in the UK? Ensuring comparability of data in research studies of multiple markets is not simple. Concepts could be regarded differently; the same products and services could have different functions; language may be used differently; even within

Table 4.3 Types of semantic equivalence in international marketing research

Type of equivalence	Explanation	Example
Conceptual equivalence	When interpretation of behaviour, or objects, is similar across countries, conceptual equivalence exists.	Conceptual equivalence should be considered when defining the research problem, in wording the questionnaire, and determining the sample unit, for example, there would be less need to investigate 'brand loyalty' in a country where competition is restricted and product choice limited.
Functional equivalence	Functional equivalence relates to whether a concept has a similar function in different countries.	Using a bicycle in India, where it might be used for transport to and from work, or France, where it might be used for shopping, is a different concept from purchasing a bike in Norway, where it might be used for mountain biking. Functional differences can be determined using focus groups before finalizing the research design by ensuring that the constructs used in the research measure what they are supposed to measure.
Translation equivalence	Translation equivalence is an important aspect of the international research process. Words in some languages have no real equivalent in other languages.	The meaning associated with different words is important in questionnaire design, since words can connote a different meaning from that intended when directly translated into another language. To avoid translation errors of these kinds, the researcher can adopt one of the following two methods. 1 *Back translation*—A translator fluent in the language in which the questionnaire is to be translated is used and then another translator, whose native language is the original language, is used to translate back again. Differences in wording can be identified and resolved. 2 *Parallel translation*—a questionnaire is translated using a different translator fluent in the language into which the questionnaire is to be translated, as well as from, until a final version is agreed upon.

Source: Malhotra (1999: 814)

a country, products and services might be measured differently, the samples (the people who consume a particular product or service) might be different, and the data-collection methods adopted may be different because of different country infrastructures. This is where equivalence is important. Table 4.3 outlines three types of equivalence: **conceptual equivalence**; **functional equivalence**; and **translation equivalence**. All these types of equivalence impact

Table 4.4 Types of measurement and data collection equivalence

Type of equivalence	Explanation	Example
Measurement equivalence	This measures the extent to which measurement scales are comparable across countries.	Surveys are conducted in the US using imperial systems of measurement, whilst the metric system is used in Europe.
		Clothing sizes adopt different measurement systems in Europe, North America, or South-East Asia.
		Multi-item scales present challenges for international researchers, because dissatisfaction might not be expressed in the same way in one country compared to another.
		Some cultures are more open in expressing opinions or describing their behaviour than others.
Sampling equivalence	Determining the appropriate sample to question may provide difficulties when conducting international marketing research projects.	The respondent profile for the same survey could vary from country to country, e.g. different classification systems are used for censorship of films shown at the cinema in France from those used in the UK.
Data collection equivalence	When conducting research studies in different countries, it may be appropriate to adopt different data collection strategies.	Typically, data collection methods include (e)mail, personal (or CAPI), or telephone (or CATI).

For the Data collection equivalence example, the following bulleted list appears:

- *Mail or email*—Used more where literacy or Internet access is high and where the (e)mail system operates efficiently. Sampling frames are compiled from electoral registers, although it is now illegal in some countries to use these lists. European survey respondents can be targeted efficiently and accurately as international sampling frames do exist.
- *Telephone/CATI*—In many countries, telephone penetration may be limited and CATI software, using **random digit dialling**, more limited still. Telephone penetration is around 95 per cent in America, although European average figure lower after introduction of new eastern economies.
- *Personal interviews/CAPI*—Used most widely in European countries favouring the door-to-door and shopping mall intercept variants. Shopping mall intercept interviews are not appropriate in Arabic countries, where women are not to be approached in the street. Here, comparability is achieved using door-to-door interviews. In countries where it is rude to disagree openly with someone, e.g. China, it's best to use in-depth interviews.

on the semantics (that is, meaning) of words used in different countries, such as that used when developing the wording for questionnaires or in focus groups. Getting the language right is important, because it affects how participants perceive the questions and structure their answers.

When designing international research programmes, it is important to consider how the meaning of words is different and how the data need to be collected. Different cultures have different ways of measuring concepts. They also live their lives differently, meaning that it may be necessary to collect the same or similar data in a different way. Table 4.4 outlines how measurement, sampling, and data collection equivalence impacts on international research.

As we can see in Table 4.4, achieving comparability of data when conducting international surveys is difficult. Usually, the more countries included in an international study, the more likely it is that errors will be introduced, and that the results and findings will be inaccurate and liable to misinterpretation. International research requires local and international input, so the extent to which one can internationalize certain operations of the research process depends on the objectives of the research.

With international projects, the key decision is to determine how much to centralize and how much to delegate work to local agencies. There is, throughout this process, ample opportunity for misunderstandings, errors, and lack of cultural sensitivity. To proceed effectively, the central agency should identify a number of trusted local market research providers on a variety of continents. Typically, an international agency will have a network of trusted affiliates who provide such a service and are monitored on a continual basis.

Research Insight 4.2

To take your learning further, you might wish to read the following influential paper:

Craig, C. S. and Douglas, S. P. (2001) 'Conducting international marketing research in the twenty-first century', *International Marketing Review*, 18(1): 80–90.

This article indicates how international marketing research practice should adapt to support firms in the twenty-first century in four key areas. First, international marketing research must focus on market growth opportunities outside industrialized nations. Second, researchers need to develop the capability to conduct and coordinate research in these diverse research environments. Third, there is a need to develop new creative approaches to probe cultural underpinnings in these countries. Finally, there is a need to incorporate technological changes, including the Internet, into the process of conducting and disseminating international research.

Visit the **Online Resource Centre** to read the abstract and to access the full paper.

Chapter Summary

To consolidate your learning, the key points from this chapter can be summarized as follows.

■ **Define the terms 'market research' and 'marketing research'**

'Market research' is work undertaken to determine structural characteristics of the industry of concern (such as demand, market share, market volumes, customer characteristics, and segmentation), whereas 'marketing research' is work undertaken to understand how to make specific marketing strategy decisions, such as pricing, sales forecasting, product testing, and promotion.

■ **Explain the use of marketing information systems**

Marketing information systems (MkISs) and customer relationship management (CRM) information systems are commonly used in companies to collect, store, and analyse data, in order to generate and disseminate marketing intelligence, and to generate effective marketing programmes. Increasingly, companies are recognizing the importance of mining customer data and the competitive advantages that such strong customer understanding can bring.

■ **Explain the role of marketing research and the range of approaches used**

Marketing research plays an important role in the decision-making process of a business and tends to contribute through ad hoc studies, as well as continuous data collection, through industry reports and from secondary data sources, as well as through competitive intelligence either commissioned through agencies or conducted internally, with data gathered informally through sales forces, customers, and suppliers.

■ **Recognize the importance of ethics and the adoption of a code of conduct when undertaking marketing research**

Ethics is an important consideration in marketing research because consumers and customers provide personal information about themselves. Their privacy needs to be protected through the strict observance of a professional code of ethics and the relevant laws in the country in which the research is conducted.

■ **Describe the problems arising when conducting international marketing research**

International market research is complex because of the differences in language, culture, infrastructure, and other factors that intervene in the data-collection process and make obtaining comparable, equivalent data more difficult. International marketing research is also more complex because it is difficult to obtain semantic equivalence—that is, because concepts mean different things in different countries. Similarly, obtaining equivalence in measurement, sampling, and data collection can be difficult because of local variations. International research requires a strong mix of central coordination with local input to be effective.

Review Questions

1 What are the origins of market research?
2 How do we define 'market research' and 'marketing research'?
3 What are the main different types of research that are conducted in marketing?
4 Why is a code of conduct important when conducting marketing research?
5 What is the concept of equivalence in relation to obtaining comparable data from different countries?

Scan this image to go online and access the chapter's multiple-choice questions, web links, Internet activities, and more!

Worksheet Summary

Visit the **Online Resource Centre** and complete Worksheet 4.1. This will help you to learn how to define a marketing research problem for a low-price airline, design a research plan, and then select the most appropriate method for data collection.

References

American Marketing Association (AMA) (2009) 'Dictionary of Marketing Terms: Marketing Research', available online at http://www.marketingpower.com [accessed 15 November 2009].

Anon. (1989) *The Hutchinson Concise Encyclopaedia*, 2nd edn, London: BCA.

Arceneaux, N. and Weiss, A. S. (2010) 'Seems stupid until you try it: press coverage of Twitter, 2006–09', *New Media & Society*, 12(8): 1262–79.

Arvidsson, A. (2004) 'On the "pre-history of the panoptic sort": mobility in market research', *Surveillance and Society*, 4(1): 456–74.

Ashill, N. J. and Jobber, D. (2001) 'Defining the information needs of senior marketing executives: an exploratory study', *Qualitative Market Research: An International Journal*, 4(1): 52–60.

Axelrod, J. N. (1970) '14 Rules for building an MIS', *Journal of Advertising Research*, 10(3): 3–12.

Baines, P. and Chansarkar, B. (2002) *Introducing Marketing Research*, Chichester: John Wiley and Sons.

Ball, J. and Lewis, P. (2011) 'Riots database of 2.5m tweets reveals complex picture of interaction', *The Guardian*, 24 August, available online at http://www.guardian.co.uk/uk/2011/aug/24/riots-database-twitter-interaction?intcmp=239 [accessed 13 December 2011].

Bradley, N. (2010) *Marketing Research: Tools and Techniques*, 2nd edn, Oxford: Oxford University Press.

Bryman, A. (1989) *Research Methods and Organisation Studies*, London: Unwin Hyman.

Chisnall, P. M. (1992) *Marketing Research*, 4th edn, Maidenhead: McGraw-Hill.

Comley, P. and Beaumont, J. (2011a) 'Online research: Methods, benefits and issues—Part 1', *Journal of Direct, Data and Digital Marketing Practice*, 12(4): 315–27.

Comley, P. and Beaumont, J. (2011b) 'Online research: Methods, benefits and issues—Part 2', *Journal of Direct, Data and Digital Marketing Practice*, 13(1): 25–39.

Craig, C. S. and Douglas, S. P. (2001) 'Conducting international marketing research in the twenty-first century', *International Marketing Review*, 18(1): 80–90.

European Society for Opinion and Marketing Research (ESOMAR) (1995) *ICC/ESOMAR International Code of Marketing and Social Research Practice*, 6, available online at http://www.esomar.org [accessed 17 June 2007].

European Society for Opinion and Marketing Research (ESOMAR)(2010) *Global Market Research Report 2010*, available to buy online at http://www.esomar.org [accessed 11 April 2012].

European Society for Opinion and Marketing Research (ESOMAR) (2011) *Global Market Research Report 2011*, available to buy online at http://www.esomar.org [accessed 11 April 2012].

Goulding, C. (2002) *Grounded Theory*, London: Sage Publications.

Humby, C. (2007) 'R is for relevance: an antidote to CRM hype', Paper presented to the Return on Marketing Investment (ROMI) Club, 15 May, Cranfield University.

Malhotra, N. K. (1999) *Marketing Research: An Applied Approach*, 3rd edn, Englewood Cliffs, NJ: Prentice-Hall.

Mareck, M. (2010) 'Using mobile phones for research', *Research World*, May: 43–4.

Market Research Society (MRS) (2010) *MRS Code of Conduct*, available online at http://www.mrs.org.uk/standards/codeconduct.htm [accessed 10 April 2010].

McArdle, M. (2011) 'Ending the infographic plague', *The Atlantic*, 23 December, available online at http://www.theatlantic.com/business/archive/2011/12/ending-the-infographic-plague/250474/ [accessed 2 January 2011].

McCawley, I. (2006) 'Analysis: dunnhumby—department of Tesco', *Marketing Week*, 8 June, p. 13.

Miles, L. (2004) 'Online, on tap', *Marketing*, 16 June, pp. 39–40.

Murphy, L. (2011) 'The new netnography: Intel launches the Museum of Me', *Greenbook Blog*, 3 June, available online at http://www.greenbookblog.org/ [accessed 8 October 2011].

Newsom, D. and Haynes, J. (2004) *Public Relations Writing: Form and Style*, 7th edn, Boston, MA: Wadsworth.

Nielsen (2007) 'Our history', available online at http://uk.nielsen.com/company/history.shtml [accessed 15 November 2009].

Parasuraman, A. (1991) *Marketing Research*, 2nd edn, Wokingham: Addison-Wesley.

Reisinger, D. (2011) 'Intel's Facebook "Museum of Me" is a must-try', *CNET Blog*, 2 June, available online at http://news.cnet.com/8301-13506_3-20068257-17/intels-facebook-museum-of-me-is-a-must-try/ [accessed 8 October 2011].

Sagolla, D. (2009) *140 Characters: A Style Guide for the Short Form*, Hoboken, NJ: John Wiley and Sons.

Stevens, R. E. (2003) 'Views from the hills: Genesis II—the second beginning', available online at http://shopperscientist.com/archive/views/index.html [accessed 2 December 2007].

Twitter Inc. (2012a) 'FAQs about following: what is following?', available online at http://support.twitter.com/groups/31-twitter-basics/topics/108-finding-following-people/articles/14019-faqs-about-following [accessed 8 October 2011].

Twitter Inc. (2012b) 'Twitter via SMS FAQ', available online at http://support.twitter.com/articles/14014-twitter-via-sms-faq?tw_p=twt [accessed 8 October 2011].

Part 2

Principles of Marketing Management

5

Marketing Strategy

Learning outcomes

After reading this chapter, you will be able to:

- describe the strategic planning context and process;

- explain the key influences that impact on and shape marketing strategy;

- develop a SWOT analysis and explain how it can help strategic marketing decision-making;

- explain how understanding competitors can assist when developing a marketing strategy;

- identify the characteristics of strategic marketing goals and explain the nature of the associated growth strategies;

- understand the principles of marketing metrics, and how these can contribute to the implementation and control of the marketing planning process; and

- outline the key elements of a marketing plan.

Dan Germain for Innocent Drinks

Innocent Drinks markets its smoothies in a highly innovative way. What strategies will it use to market its new water/juice drinks? We speak to Dan Germain, head of creative at Innocent, to find out more.

Innocent Drinks makes smoothies—drinks made from pure whole crushed fruit, with no preservatives, colouring, or nasty additives. They're sold in little bottles and big cartons, all of which feature trademark Innocent fun and games on the back of the pack. Innocent effectively developed a whole new drinks sector—one that many experts at the start said could not be done. Innocent now has 77.5 per cent market share (http://www.innocentdrinks.co.uk).

In 1999, Innocent's three co-founders had a great product and lots of enthusiasm, but no experience of running a business, no customers, and no turnover. To help us to get started, we made a few smoothies and sold them at a small music festival. We asked our customers to place their empty cups in a 'Yes' or 'No' bin to vote whether the three of us should give up our jobs and make smoothies full-time. At the end of the weekend, the 'Yes' bin was full and so we quit our jobs the next day, spent several months finding the necessary finance, and started a company that is now doubling its profits every year.

It hasn't all been plain sailing: initially, distributors refused to stock our drinks. Innocent's response was to load up a van and take the drinks to delicatessens and health food shops in Notting Hill. As a form of introduction, we said: 'We're a local juice company that's just started up. Here are four boxes for free: stick them on your shelves, and if they sell, give us a ring.' Out of the fifty shops reached, forty-five wanted more. We then went back to the distributors, told them the story about the delis, and gave them a pallet for free. Now, 2 million smoothies a week are sold—a big change from those early days (http://www.innocentdrinks.co.uk).

However, with growth and success, questions arose about how we should develop the company and the Innocent brand. There are lots of opportunities to move into a number of health-related sectors. The strong ethical and health credentials associated with the brand provide opportunities for development, but these beliefs can constrain and limit the scope of the areas into which we can move. For example, one area with great potential is drinks made from fruit juice and spring water.

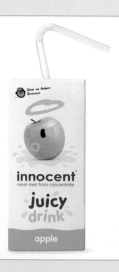

Innocent's fruit juice, as 'good' as its smoothies
Source: Innocent Drinks

1 But there are plenty of these types of product already in the market, so what challenges might Innocent-branded water/fruit juice face in order to be successful and what impact would such a product have on the Innocent brand?

Introduction

Have you ever thought about how organizations organize themselves so that they can make sales, achieve profits, and keep all of their stakeholders satisfied? As you can imagine, this does not happen accidentally and a great deal of thought, discussion, planning, and action needs to occur. This involves getting answers to questions such as: in which markets should we be operating? What resources are necessary for us to be successful in these markets? Who are our key competitors and what strategies are they using? How can we develop and sustain advantage over these competitors? And what is happening in the wider world that might affect our organization? These questions refer to issues that represent the strategic context in which organizations operate. These contextual issues can be considered in terms of four main elements—namely, the organization (and its resources, skills, and capabilities), the target customers, a firm's competitors, and the wider environment. These are set out in Figure 5.1.

Samsung's strategic context is shaped by its communications expertise and leading-edge technology skills, customers who expect a stream of added-value communication-related products, and Apple, the market leader in the mobile phone handset market. In addition, the wider environment is becoming politically more sensitive to climatic change issues, terrorism anxieties, social change, the repercussions of the economic crisis, and surges in technological development. By understanding and managing these four elements, it is possible to develop a coherent strategic marketing plan through which products or services have a greater chance of success than they would if no analysis or planning were undertaken. For a marketing strategy to be developed successfully, it is first necessary to understand an organization's strategic context, and then to fit the marketing strategy so that it matches the strategic context. Many organizations articulate their strategic context and their intended performance in the markets that they have targeted, in terms of a framework that defines their vision, mission, values, **organizational goals**, and organizational strategy.

The vision sets out an organization's future. It is a statement about what an organization wants to become. It should give shape and direction to an organization's future. A vision should stretch an organization in terms of its current position and performance, yet at the

Figure 5.1

The four elements of the strategic context

same time it should help employees to feel involved and motivated to be part of the organization's future. According to its website, Samsung Electronics' vision for the current decade is to 'Inspire the world, create the future'. As part of this vision, Samsung plans to drive US$400 billion in revenue and become one of the world's top five brands by 2020.

The mission represents what the organization wishes to achieve in the long term. It should be a broad statement of intention that sets out an organization's purpose and direction. It should be oriented to particular markets and customers served. A mission applies to all parts of an organization and, in that sense, serves to bind the many parts of an organization together. However, above all else, the mission should provide a reference point for its managers and employees. The mission should help managers to make decisions concerning which opportunities to pursue and which to ignore. It should aid investment and development decision-making. See Table 5.1 for examples of different mission statements.

Mission statements are sometimes prepared as a public relations (PR) exercise, or are so generic that they fail to provide sufficient guidelines or inspiration. Some are simply not realistic and are to be avoided: to expect an airport such as Adelaide or Hong Kong to become the largest airport in the world is totally infeasible. Good mission statements are market-oriented not product-oriented. For example, the product-oriented approach 'We make and sell lorries and trucks' is too general, and runs the risk of becoming outdated and redundant. By focusing on the needs of the customers that the organization is seeking to serve, the mission can be

Table 5.1 A selection of mission statements

Organization	Mission statement
Tesco	'To create value for customers to earn their lifetime loyalty . . .'
Coca-Cola	'To refresh the world . . . To inspire moments of optimism and happiness . . . To create value and make a difference . . .'
SAS	'We provide best value for time and money to Nordic travellers whatever the purpose of their journey.'
Oxfam	'Oxfam works with others to overcome poverty and suffering.'
IBM	'At IBM, we strive to lead in the invention, development, and manufacture of the industry's most advanced information technologies, including computer systems, software, storage systems, and microelectronics. We translate these advanced technologies into value for our customers through our professional solutions, services, and consulting businesses worldwide.'
JCB	'Our mission is to grow our company by providing innovative, strong, and high performance products and solutions to meet our global customers' needs.'

more realistic and have a much longer lifespan. So 'We transport your products quickly and safely to your customers', or 'Logistical solutions for your company' provides a market-oriented approach to the mission statement. Similarly, rather than 'Amazon.com sells books, Kindles, and DVDs' (product approach), it is much better to say that Amazon.com 'strives to be Earth's most customer-centric company where people can find and discover virtually everything they want to buy online'. Similarly, Haier, the leading Chinese manufacturer, does not make home appliances; it makes 'lives more convenient and comfortable through innovative appliances'.

Visit the **Online Resource Centre** and complete Internet Activity 5.1 to learn more about the use of mission and vision statements by differing organizations, and their implications for marketing activities.

go online

An organization's values must be in line with its vision and mission, if only because they define how people should behave with each other in the organization and because they help to shape how the goals will be achieved. **Organizational values** define the acceptable interpersonal and operating standards of behaviour. They govern and guide the behaviour of individuals within the organization. Organizations that identify and develop a clear, concise, and shared meaning of values and beliefs shape the organizational culture and provide direction, so that all participants can understand and contribute.

Market Insight 5.1

The Value of Values

IKEA claims that, for many years, its values have affected the way in which it works: 'These values are as important at an IKEA store in Ireland as they are in a photo studio in Sweden or a distribution centre in China.'

Humbleness and willpower
We respect each other, our customers and our suppliers. Using our willpower means we get things done.

Leadership by example
Our managers try to set a good example, and expect the same of IKEA co-workers.

Daring to be different
We question old solutions and, if we have a better idea, we are willing to change.

Togetherness and enthusiasm
Together, we have the power to solve seemingly unsolvable problems. We do it all the time.

Cost-consciousness
Low prices are impossible without low costs, so we proudly achieve good results with small resources.

Constant desire for renewal
Change is good. We know that adapting to customer demands with innovative solutions saves money and contributes to a better everyday life at home.

Accept and delegate responsibility
We promote co-workers with potential and stimulate them to surpass their expectations. Sure, people make mistakes. But they learn from them!

Consistency in their values is mirrored by IKEA's consistency in store design throughout the world.
Source: © IKEA

Market Insight 5.1

However, few organizations set out how their values are derived. IBM is an exception. In an open statement, Samuel J. Palmisano, chairman, president, and chief executive officer, recalls the way in which IBM's current values originated. He refers to the importance and time spent thinking, debating, and determining IBM's fundamentals. He states that, in a time of great change, IBM needed to affirm reasons for being, setting out how the company is different to others, and what should drive individual employee behaviour.

He says:

> Importantly, we needed to find a way to engage everyone in the company and get them to speak up on these important issues. Given the realities of a smart, global, independent-minded, 21st-century workforce like ours, I don't believe something as vital and personal as values could be dictated from the top.

So, for a three-day period, all 319,000 IBMers around the world were invited to engage in an open 'values jam' on the global intranet. Following much open debate, honesty, and involvement, the employees determined the following values:

- 'dedication to every client's success';
- 'innovation that matters, for our company and for the world';
- 'trust and personal responsibility in all relationships'.

The statement concluded:

> To me, it's also just common sense. In today's world, where everyone is so interconnected and interdependent, it is simply essential that we work for each other's success. If we're going to solve the biggest, thorniest and most widespread problems in business and society, we have to innovate in ways that truly matter. And we have to do all this by taking personal responsibility for all of our relationships—with clients, colleagues, partners, investors and the public at large. This is IBM's mission as an enterprise, and a goal toward which we hope to work with many others, in our industry and beyond.

Sources: Based on http://www.ikea.com/; http://www.ibm.com/ibm/values/us/

1 How do these two sets of values differ?

2 What might be the impact on employees of a set of seven rather than three values?

3 Find a third set of values, this time from a not-for-profit organization, and compare these with those of IKEA or IBM.

Organizational values are important because they can help to guide and constrain not only behaviour, but also the recruitment and selection decisions. Without them, individuals tend to pursue behaviours that are in line with their own individual value systems, which may lead to inappropriate behaviours and a failure to achieve the overall goals. However, it should be remembered that values per se do not drive a business; as Williams (2010) informs us, they drive the people within the business. For values to be of value and to have meaning, they must be internalized by the people in the organization.

Organizational goals at the strategic level represent what should be achieved, the outcomes of the organization's various activities. These may be articulated in terms of profit, market share, share value, return on investment, or numbers of customers served. In some cases, the long term may not be a viable period and a short-term focus is absolutely essential. For example, should an organization's financial position become precarious, then it may be necessary to focus on short-term cash strategies in order to remain solvent and so to remove any threat arising from a takeover or administrators being called in prior to bankruptcy.

Organization or **corporate strategy** is the means by which the resources of the organization are matched with the needs of the environment in which the organization decides to operate. Corporate strategy involves bringing together the human resources, logistics, production, operations, marketing, IT, and financial parts of an organization into a coherent strategic plan that supports, reinforces, and helps to accomplish the organizational goals in the most effective and efficient way. In this chapter, we are concerned with the composition of the marketing strategy that should support and reinforce the corporate strategy.

In some very large organizations, the planning process is made complicated and difficult because the organization operates in a number of significantly different markets. In these cases, the organization creates **strategic business units (SBUs)**. Each SBU assumes the role of a separate company, and creates its own strategies and plans in order to achieve its corporate goals and contribution to the overall organization. So the Indian company Tata operates through seven SBUs—namely, Information Technology and Communications, Engineering, Materials, Services, Energy, Consumer Products, and Chemicals; each of these Tata companies operates independently. Royal Philips Electronics uses four SBUs: Domestic Appliances and Personal Care; Lighting; Medical Systems; and Consumer Electronics. Each of these represents a significantly different market, each with its own characteristics, customer needs, and competitors.

According to McDonald (2002: 37), who is referred to by many as the global guru of marketing planning, the strategic marketing planning process consists of a series of logical steps through which we have to work in order to arrive at a marketing plan. These steps can be aggregated into four phases. The first phase is concerned with setting the right mission and corporate goals. The second involves reviewing the current situation or context in which the organization is operating. The third phase is used to formulate strategy, and the final phase considers the allocation of resources necessary to implement and monitor the plan.

So, at a broad level, the strategic marketing planning process is as follows.

1 At the corporate level, the organization sets out its overall vision, mission, and values.

2 Measurable corporate goals are established that apply to the whole organization.

3 A series of analyses and audits are undertaken to understand the external situation in which the organization intends to operate and the resources available to be used.

4 Strategies are formulated and probable outcomes estimated.

5 Depending on the size of the organization, the range of businesses (SBUs) and/or products is determined, and resources are allocated to help and support each one.

6 Each business and/or product then develops detailed functional and competitive strategies and plans, such as a marketing strategy and plan.

7 The plan is implemented, and the results measured and used to feed into the next planning cycle.

What arises from this is that marketing strategy and planning should support and contribute to the overall company strategy. However, it should also be understood that marketing strategy and planning can occur at the business, product, or market level.

Research Insight 5.1

To take your learning further, you might wish to read the following influential paper:

Mintzberg, H. (1987) 'The strategy concept: five Ps for strategy', *California Management Review,* **30(1): 11–26.**

Mintzberg's paper made an important contribution because it argued that strategy should not be regarded only as a linear, sequential planning process. Mintzberg shows that strategy can also be interpreted as a plan ploy, a pattern, a perspective, and a position.

 Visit the **Online Resource Centre** to read the abstract and to access the full paper.

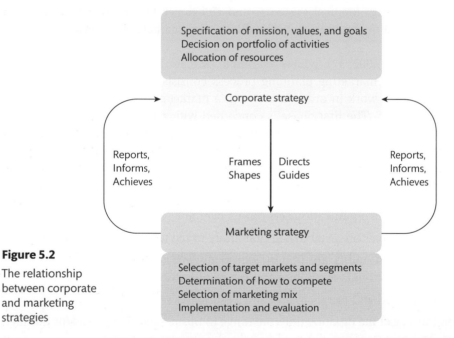

Figure 5.2

The relationship between corporate and marketing strategies

■ Influences on Strategic Marketing Planning

The development of a strategic marketing plan is a complex and involved process. It does not occur in the linear, logical steps suggested in the 'Introduction', but certain key aspects can be identified. These aspects concern three broad activities that are necessary when considering the development of marketing strategy and will form the framework through which we examine this topic. These three elements are shown in Figure 5.3.

Figure 5.3
Three key activities of marketing strategy development

The first activity is to develop knowledge and understanding of the marketplace (see Market Insight 5.2), and is referred to as **strategic market analysis**. The second activity is to determine what the marketing strategy should achieve—in other words, what are the 'strategic marketing goals' that need to be accomplished. The third activity concerns how the goals are to be achieved. This relates directly to 'strategic marketing action'—that is, how the strategies are to be developed as plans and how these plans are to be implemented. These three activities form the basis of this chapter and are considered in turn.

Strategic Market Analysis

The starting point of the marketing strategy process is the development of knowledge and understanding about the target market(s) that have been identified as part of the corporate strategy. Different people in the organization will have varying levels of market knowledge and expertise: some of it accurate and up to date; some of it out of date and inaccurate. It is crucial that all people involved in the strategy process are well informed with accurate, pertinent, and up-to-date information.

In Chapter 2, we saw how PESTLE and environmental scanning processes can be used to understand and make sense of the external environment in which organizations operate. We also considered Porter's (1985) 'Five Forces' model to understand industry dynamics and how firms should compete strategically if they are to be successful in the performance environment. We gained an insight into the importance of understanding the internal environment, and how a firm's resources need to complement the external and performance environments. The task now is to assimilate this information, to bring it together in a form that can be easily understood, and in this respect consideration is given to **SWOT analysis**.

However, before these tools can be used, analysis of the performance environment—most notably, our competitors, and the industry's key suppliers and distributors—is required.

Analysing Competitors

The importance of understanding competitors cannot be overstated. Noble et al. (2002) found that organizations that pay particular attention to their competitors generally perform better than those who do not. In order to undertake an analysis of a firm's competitors, five key questions must be answered, as follows.

- Who are our competitors?
- What are their strengths and weaknesses?
- What are their strategic goals?
- Which strategies are they following?
- How are they likely to respond?

Who Are Our Competitors?

Competitors are those firms that offer products and services that attempt to meet the same market need as our own. There are several ways in which a need might be met, but essentially two approaches can be identified: firms need to be aware of their direct and indirect competitors. Direct competitors are those that offer the same target market similar products and services, such as easyJet, Flybe, and Ryanair. Direct competitors may also offer a product in the same category, but target different segments: for example, Haagen-Dazs, Walls, and Green and Black's offer a range of ice cream products for different target markets. Indirect competitors are those that address the same target market, but offer a different product or service to satisfy the market need, such as HMV, Sony, and Apple's iPod.

Green & Black's ice cream, targeting the ethical consumer

Source: Courtesy of Green & Blacks

By understanding who the main competitors are, it becomes possible to make judgements about the nature and likely intensity of the competition along with who might represent a key threat. This also provides a view about how a firm's own marketing strategy should evolve. For example, the strategy of a market leader that identifies little competition will be different from that of a small firm trying to establish a small market share. The former may try to dominate the whole market, whereas the latter may attack the leader or find a small, underserviced segment, called a **niche market**, and start to make it its own market.

What Are Their Strengths and Weaknesses?

Getting information about a competitor's range of products, and their sales volumes and value, their profitability, prices, and discount structures, the nature of their relationships with suppliers and distributors, their communications campaigns and special offers, are all important. In some circumstances, getting information about new products that are either in development or about to be launched can be critical.

In addition to these marketing elements, however, it is important to obtain information about a whole range of other factors, not only their marketing activities. These factors include their production and manufacturing capabilities, their technical, management, and financial resources, and their processes, distribution channels, and relative success in meeting customer and market needs.

As this information accumulates and is updated through time, it is necessary to use the information in order to understand what a competitor's strengths and weaknesses might be, and either to avoid the areas in which competitors are strong or exploit their weaknesses. The overall task is to determine what **competitive advantage** a competitor might have and whether this advantage can be sustained, imitated, or undermined. (Ideas about competitive advantage are explored in greater detail later in 'Strategic Market Action'.)

What Are Their Strategic Goals?

Contrary to what is often written in the popular press, profit is not the single, overriding strategic goal for most organizations. Firms develop a range of goals, encompassing ambitions such as achieving a certain market share (which is quite common), market leadership, industry recognition for technological prowess or high-quality performance, or market reputation for innovation, environmental concern, or ethical trading.

Developing a full understanding of a competitor's strategic goals is not an easy task and this can usually only be inferred from a competitor's actions. Some firms try to recruit senior executives from their competitors in order to get real insight into their strategic intentions. Although this happens quite frequently, it is not an ethical way of operating, and organizations can impose severe legal and financial constraints on employees in terms of for whom they can work if they leave and the timescale within which they are not allowed to work in the industry.

Which Strategies Are They Following?

Once a competitor's goals are understood, it becomes easier to predict what its marketing strategies are likely to be. These strategies can be considered through two main factors: competitive scope; and positioning.

Competitive scope refers to the breadth of the market addressed. Is the competitor attempting to service the whole of a market, particular segments, or a single **niche** segment? If it is servicing a niche market, one of the key questions to be asked is: will it want to stay and dominate the niche, or is it simply using it as a trial, before springboarding into other market segments?

Brands can be positioned in markets according to the particular attributes and benefits that a brand offers: cameras might be positioned according to their technical features, whereas cosmetics are often positioned on style and fashion, frequently with campaigns led by brand ambassadors who are considered to personify the brand values. Once this is understood, it is possible to follow the marketing mix elements that are aligned to support the positioning strategy. Some brands are based on price and a low-cost strategy. This approach requires a focus on reducing costs and expenses rather than investing in heavy levels of marketing communications and/or product **research and development (R&D)**. (We will consider low-cost strategies in further detail later in 'Generic Strategies'.)

How Are They Likely to Respond?

Understanding the strategies of competitors helps to inform whether they are intent on outright attack or defence, and how they might react to particular strategies initiated by others. For example, a price cut might be met with a similar reduction, a larger reduction, or none at all; changes in the levels of investment in advertising might produce a similar range of responses.

Some market leaders believe that an aggressive response to a challenger's actions is important; otherwise, their leadership position might be undermined. There are, of course, a range of responses that firms may use, reflecting organizational objectives, leadership styles, industry norms, and new strategies born of new owners.

Suppliers and Distributors

So far, analysis of the performance environment has tended to concentrate on the nature and characteristics of a firm's competitive behaviour. This is, of course, important, but Porter (1985) also realized that suppliers can influence competition and he built this into his 'Five Forces' model. However, since Porter published his work, there have been several significant supply-side developments—most notably, the development of outsourcing. 'Outsourcing' concerns the transfer of non-core activities to an external organization that specializes in the activity or operation. For example, transport and delivery services are not core activities to most companies, although they constitute an important part of the value they offer their customers. In Japan, the Hitachi Transport System, a third-party logistics (3PL) service, is used by companies as an outsourced provider to transport their goods. Many suppliers have therefore become an integral part of a firm's capabilities. Rather than act aggressively, they are more likely to be cooperative and work in support of the firm that has outsourced the work to them.

Similar changes have occurred downstream in terms of a manufacturer's marketing channel. Now, it is common to find high levels of integration between a manufacturer and their distributors, dealers, and retailers (see also Chapter 11). Account needs to be taken of the strength of these relationships and consideration needs to be given to how market performance might be strengthened or weakened by the capabilities of the channel intermediary. Suppliers and distributors have become central to the way in which firms can develop specific competitive advantages. It is therefore important that analysis of the performance environment incorporates a review of those organizations that are key suppliers and distributors to the firm under analysis.

Market Insight 5.2

Coca-Cola's Many Strategic Pillars

In 2010, Coca-Cola sold 25.5 billion unit cases of drinks across its 500 brands and grew volumes by 5 per cent. Some might say that this performance was exceptional in a recession affected economic climate. Coca-Cola currently sells 1.7 billion drinks every day, but the vision is to double its revenue by 2020, and that represents an annual turnover of £123.4 billion. To do this means growing many of their current brands, which include Coke, Fanta, Sprite, and Powerade, and this entails developing strategies that embrace internal and external environments.

Part of its strategy, according to Coca-Cola chairman and chief executive Muhtar Kent, involves the company avoiding some of the mistakes that it has made in the past. These include nearly going out of business in 1923 when sugar prices skyrocketed and then again when the government rationed sugar in 1940. Other difficulties concerned the launch and sudden retraction of 'new' Coke, the Belgium schoolchildren who fell ill after allegedly drinking Coca-Cola products, and a court case in which some Coca-Cola employees accused Coca-Cola of racial discrimination. Many of these challenges are regarded by Coca-Cola management as a result of their own arrogance and failure to listen and work with partners as effectively as they should.

Another part of their strategy requires that Coca-Cola develops closer working relationships with its strategic partners, retail customers, and consumers. Such collaboration is necessary so that Coca-Cola earns their trust. Indeed, the current strategy has involved bringing everyone together, including all bottlers and partners, to focus on the brand.

However, Coca-Cola's strategy is predicated on the knowledge that there are six particular events in the world that have the potential to reshape the industry fundamentally, changes that dwarf the events in the 2000–10. The company recognized that the pace of global socio-economic change would impact heavily on the business and that Coca-Cola needed to start operating differently if it was to thrive. These six global trends have acted as a basis around which the Coca-Cola vision has been developed.

- *A growing middle class* It is estimated that there will be between 800 million and a billion people entering the middle classes between 2010 and 2020. This is regarded as the greatest economic shift in history. Over 60 per cent of this new wealth will come from emerging nations.
- *Mass urbanization* Many populations are moving from rural to urban environments. For the next several years, an urban population the size of New York will be created every 90–100 days.
- *Economic rebalancing* Rather than two economic superpowers, there will be a massive rebalancing of economic might, partly a result of the growing middle classes. This includes the 'BRIC' countries (Brazil, Russia, India, and China), but Indonesia, Turkey, Morocco, Vietnam, Chile, and Mexico are also likely to grow disproportionately.
- *The new generation* A sophisticated, engaged, and well-communicated youth generation is on the rise.
- *Rising prices* There is an increasing scarcity of resources, which leads to volatility in energy prices.
- *New consumers* Consumers have revised their priorities, their values, and their expectations, leading to a new focus on the meaning of the word 'value'.

Sources: Choueke (2011); http://www.coca-cola.com

1 How might the mistakes made in the past inform marketing strategy for the next ten years?

2 Why do you think Coca-Cola makes no mention of competitors as a platform around which to build its own strategy?

3 How might the six pillars shape Coca-Cola's future marketing strategy?

SWOT Analysis

Perhaps the most common analytical tool is SWOT analysis. 'SWOT' stands for 'strengths', 'weaknesses', 'opportunities', and 'threats'. Essentially, it is a series of checklists derived from the marketing audit and the PESTLE analysis (see Chapter 2), and is presented as *internal* strengths and weaknesses, and *external* opportunities or threats.

- Strengths and weaknesses relate to the internal resources and capabilities of the organization, as perceived by customers (Piercy, 2002).

- A *strength* is something that an organization is good at doing, or something that gives it particular credibility and market advantage.

- A *weakness* is something that an organization lacks or performs in an inferior way in comparison to others.

- Opportunities and threats are externally oriented issues that can potentially influence the performance of an organization or product. Information about these elements is normally generated through PESTLE analysis.

  - An *opportunity* is the potential to advance the organization by the development and satisfaction of an unfulfilled market need.

  - A *threat* is something that, at some time in the future, may destabilize and/or reduce the potential performance of the organization.

SWOT analysis is a tool used to determine an overall view of an organization's strategic position. It highlights the need for a strategy to produce a strong fit between the internal capability (strengths and weaknesses) and the external situation (opportunities and threats). SWOT helps an organization to sort through the information generated in the audit; it serves to identify the key issues, and then prompts thought about converting weaknesses into strengths and threats into opportunities—in other words, generating conversion strategies. For example, some companies have developed and run call centres for their own internal use, but saw opportunities to use their strength to run call centres for other companies. It is also said that, a few years ago, one major computer company used its call centre only during the day; an opportunity was spotted to run the call centre at night, routing calls for a nationwide pizza company.

SWOT in inexperienced hands often leads to long lists of items. Although the SWOT process may lead to the generation of these lists, the analyst should be attempting to identify the *key* strengths and weaknesses and the *key* opportunities and threats. These key elements should impact on strategy; if they don't, then they should not be in the analysis. A strength is not a strength if it does not have strategic implications.

Once the three or four elements of each part of the SWOT matrix have been derived, then a number of pertinent questions need to be asked.

1 Does the organization do something far better than its rivals? If it does, this is known as a 'competitive advantage' (or a 'distinctive competence', or 'differential advantage'), and this can lead to a competitive edge.

2 Which of the organization's weaknesses does the strategy need to correct and is it competitively vulnerable?

3 Which opportunities can be pursued, and are there the necessary resources and capabilities to exploit them?

4 Which strategies are necessary to defend against the key threats?

Figure 5.4 depicts a SWOT grid for a small digital media agency. The outcome of a successful SWOT analysis is a series of decisions that help to develop and formulate strategy and goals.

Note that there are no more than four items in any one category—not a list of ten or more items. It is important to prioritize and to make a judgement about what is really key, rather than only an interesting point. The actions that follow the identification of the key issues should be based around matching opportunities with strengths and weaknesses with threats.

Strengths	Weaknesses
Quick to respond to changes in the marketing environment	Too much work from a few clients and at non-premium rates
Flat management encourages fast decision making	Little project-management skills
Use of contractors enables flexibility—lowers employment costs/finance and improves customers' perception of expertise	High office and finance costs
	Low customer base

Opportunities	Threats
Emerging markets such as Professional Services (e.g. dentists, lawyers, surveyors)	Larger media houses buying business
New distribution channels	Speed of technological advances
Tax incentives to encourage eCommerce	Contractors have low levels of loyalty

Figure 5.4

A SWOT analysis for a small digital media agency

In this example, it may be possible to diversify into professional services, a niche market (an opportunity), using particular contractors who have knowledge and relevant expertise (a strength).

Weaknesses need to be addressed, not avoided. Some can be converted into strengths; others, into opportunities. In this example, entering the professional services market would probably increase the number of customers and enable premium rates to be earned.

Threats need to be nullified. By building relationships with key contractors (suppliers) and selected larger media houses, for example, these threats might be dissipated—and even developed into strengths.

■ Strategic Marketing Goals

The purpose of strategic market analysis is to help managers to understand the nature of the industry, the way in which firms behave competitively within the industry, and how competition is generally undertaken. From this information, it becomes easier to determine exactly what the marketing strategy should actually achieve—in other words, what the strategic marketing goals should be.

There are several types of strategic objective, but four main ones are considered here briefly—namely, niche, **hold**, **harvest**, and **divest** goals. The section that follows does, however, consider a further objective: growth. Figure 5.5 sets out the content for this section.

- *Niche* objectives are often the most suitable when firms operate in a market dominated by a major competitor and when their financial resources are limited. A niche can either be a small segment, or even a small part of a segment. Niche markets often arise because it is not economic for the leading competitors to enter this segment simply because these customers have special needs and the leading firm does not want to devote resources in this way.

Figure 5.5

Five dimensions of
strategic marketing goals

To be successful in niche markets, it is important to have a strongly differentiated product offering supported by a high level of service. The Australian government identified several niche markets when exploring ways in which it could develop its tourism business. It identified sports, cycling seniors, culture and the arts, backpackers, health, people with disabilities, caravanning and camping, food, wine, and agri-tourism as potential niche markets.

Strewth! Tourism Australia would have us all turning turtle

Source: © Tourism Australia

- *Hold* objectives are concerned with defence. They are designed to prevent and fend off attack from aggressive competitors. Market leaders are the most likely to adopt a holding strategy, because they are prone to attack from new entrants and their closest rivals as they strive for the most market share. Market leadership is important, because it generally drives positive cash flows, confers privileges such as strong bargaining positions with suppliers, and enhances image and reputation. Holding strategies can take a number of forms, varying from 'doing nothing' in order to maintain market equilibrium, to implementing a counter-offensive defence, to withdrawing from a market completely.

- *Harvesting* objectives are often employed in mature markets as firms/products enter a decline phase. The goals are to maximize short-term profits and to stimulate a positive cash flow. By stripping out most of the marketing communications and R&D, it becomes possible to generate cash that can be used elsewhere. These funds can be used to generate new products, to support 'stars', or to turn 'question marks' into 'dogs' if it is realized that there will not be a long-term profit stream (see Chapter 2).

- *Divest* objectives are sometimes necessary when products continue to incur losses and to generate negative cash flows. Divestment can follow on naturally from a harvesting strategy. Typically, low-share products in declining markets are prime candidates to be divested. Divestment may be actioned by selling off the product should a suitable buyer be available, or simply by withdrawing from the market. For example, Procter & Gamble divested the Sunny Delight brand of orange drink, General Motors sold off Saab to sports car manufacturer Spyker (Madslien, 2010), Ford sold off Jaguar to the Indian company Tata, and Volvo to the Chinese company Zhejiang Geely Holding Group.

Growth

The vast majority of organizations consider growth to be a primary objective (see Market Insight 5.3). However, there are different forms of growth and care needs to be taken to ensure that the right growth goals are selected. Growth can be intensive, by concentrating activities on markets and/or products that are familiar; it can be integrated when an organization continues to work with the same products and same markets, but starts to perform some of the activities in the value chain that were previously undertaken by others. Growth by **diversification** refers to developments outside the current chain of value-adding activities. This type of growth brings new value chain activities because the firm is operating with new products and in new markets.

The idea that growth is allied to product–market relationships is important and Ansoff (1957) proposed that organizations should first consider whether new or established products are to be delivered in new or established markets. Considering the 'Ansoff matrix' (or the 'product/market matrix'), shown in Figure 5.6, is an important first step in deciding what the marketing strategy should be. The matrix provides a useful framework for considering the relationship between strategic direction and market opportunities. This matrix provides four broad strategic options to organizations, depending on whether the product and/or the market are considered new to the organization.

The matrix illustrates that the element of risk increases the further the strategy moves away from known quantities, an existing product, and/or an existing market. So product development

	Present products	New products
Present markets	Market penetration	Product development
New markets	Market development	Diversification

Figure 5.6

Ansoff's matrix

Source: Adapted from Ansoff (1957)

(requiring a new product) and **market development** (a new market) typically involve a greater risk than penetration (existing product and existing market), with diversification (new product and new market) carrying the greatest risk of all. Although four types of opportunity are presented, some organizations can pursue more than one type of opportunity simultaneously. Market Insight 5.4 applies this framework to a real-life example.

A market development strategy involves increasing sales by selling existing products in new markets, either by gaining new customers domestically or entering new markets internationally. So we are trying to sell more of the same things to different people. We might target different geographical markets at home or abroad, or target different groups of people, such as a different demographic profile from our current customers. For example, Guaranty Trust Bank started in Nigeria in 1990 in retail banking, but then developed markets throughout West Africa, before recently entering the UK corporate banking market. Other examples include the use of military equipment for consumer purposes (such as miniature cameras in mobile phones originated from espionage) and, more controversially, the selling of cigarettes to women in the early 1930s–40s. We currently see **franchise** chains such as McDonald's expanding into new geographical locations domestically by targeting new audiences through differing distribution outlets such as McCafe and airport eateries. These are good examples of developing new markets domestically for an existing product.

A riskier strategy is entering a new international market with an existing product. To build brand awareness and to minimize risk, organizations rely on the reputation of their brands in domestic markets. The entry of the Japanese, European, and American auto industry into China and India during the last decade is a good example of international market development. Here, we see players such as Ford, Honda, Toyota, etc., trying to transfer their reputation in well-established Western markets to gain early footage in rapidly developing markets. Other examples include Cadbury Schweppes selling existing brands of chocolate bars in Africa, and McDonald's expanding its franchise and entering foreign markets such as China, Russia, and Brazil.

Cadbury's Dairy Milk: organic, responsible, and now available at the Olympic Games!

Source: © 2010 Cadbury

One of the main decisions is: 'Do we pursue new audiences in our domestic market or enter new international markets?' Some of the main differences between domestic and international marketing include language, culture, the complexity of research and decision-making, market knowledge, and the stability of the marketing environment. For example, international markets are often seen as more unstable than domestic markets as a result of their sensitivity to fluctuations in currency rates, immigration patterns, and political and trade relations. Furthermore, development in international markets requires a higher degree of investment from the organization and a greater understanding of the changing nature of world markets (see Chapter 4).

Market Insight 5.3

Strategic Phone Manoeuvres

The need to develop flexible business strategies in the mobile phone market is a reflection of several environmental conditions. The market is young and constantly changing as new technologies emerge on a regular basis, as new partnerships between handset suppliers and the various owners of operating systems are forged, and as customers preferences change.

For example, the Finnish mobile company Nokia, at the time the largest handset manufacturer, announced in 2011 that, as part of its revised business strategy, it was to collaborate with Microsoft. The goal was to develop a smartphone based on Windows Phone software as its primary smartphone platform. This would enable it to compete more effectively with Google and Apple smartphones, to which it had lost considerable business in the previous couple of years. By combining resources, Nokia hoped to drive innovation by integrating its application and content store into the Microsoft Marketplace.

In addition, the strategy involved internal changes, one of which was to replace its group executive board with the Nokia Leadership Team, and to operate two new distinct business units: Smart Devices and Mobile Phones.

Later in 2011, Microsoft UK brought together its entire product portfolio, including business software and Bing, its search engine, into a single marketing team. This signified a strategy that was moving away from a traditional product marketing approach, to one (it was reported) that was more about listening to customers about the technology experiences that they value.

Scott Dodds, general manager of business strategy and marketing at Microsoft UK, commented: 'The future of our business depends on our ability to deeply understand the challenges of our customers and partners and to show them the real value of our broad product and service portfolio.'

HTC, the world's fourth biggest smartphone maker, made a major strategic move when it switched its corporate strategy. Formerly, it was a white-label manufacturer making handsets for others; it became a primary manufacturer for Google's Android operating system. The strategy appeared to work in 2010 and for the first two quarters of 2011. HTC marketed a series of nearly identical phones using the names 'ChaCha', 'Salsa', 'Incredible', 'Legend', 'Titan', 'Rhyme', 'Sensation', 'Radar', 'Explorer', and 'Evo' amongst many others. However, HTC's financial results turned for the worse later in 2011. This led to suggestions that HTC's strategy of swamping too many market sectors with too many phones failed to provide a sustainable point of **differentiation** and, as a result, had no competitive advantage relative to the other devices in the market.

See also Market Insight 1.1 for a discussion of the smartphone market.

Sources: Based on Baker (2011); Chapman (2011); O'Reilly (2011; 2012)

1 If you were marketing director at HTC, how would you establish competitive advantage?

2 Which type of growth strategy has HTC been pursuing?

3 Prepare notes outlining how growth based on technical excellence and innovation can accommodate customer needs.

Strategic Market Action

Having analysed the industry and the main competitors, performed a SWOT analysis and determined suitable strategic marketing goals, the final set of marketing strategy activities concerns the identification of the most appropriate way of achieving the goals and then putting the plan into action—that is, the implementation phase.

There is no proven formula or toolkit that managers can use simply because of the vast array of internal and external environmental factors. What they can draw upon is experience and a range of strategies that they know are more likely to be successful than others. In the following sections, we consider ideas about competitive advantage, generic strategies, competitive positioning, strategic intent, and marketing planning and implementation, as presented in Figure 5.7.

Competitive Advantage

Competitive advantage is achieved when an organization has a significant and sustainable edge over its competitors in attracting buyers. Advantage can also be secured by coping with the competitive forces better than its rivals. Advantage can be developed in many different ways. Some organizations have an advantage simply because they are the best-known organization or brand in the market; some achieve it by producing the best-quality product or having attributes that other products do not have. For example, some pharmaceutical brands have an advantage while patent protection exists. As soon as the patent expires and competitors can produce generic versions of the drug, the advantage is lost. Some organizations have the lowest price, whereas others provide the best support and service in the industry. However, whatever the advantage, the superiority has to be sustainable through time.

The conditions necessary for the achievement of sustainable competitive advantage (SCA) are, according to Porter (1985), as follows.

1 The customer consistently perceives a positive difference between the products and services offered by a company and its competitors.

2 The perceived difference results from the company's relatively greater capability.

Figure 5.7

Strategic marketing action

3 The perceived difference persists for a reasonable period of time. (SCA is durable only as long as it is not easily imitated.)

Generic Strategies

If the importance of achieving a competitive advantage is accepted, then it is necessary to understand how strategies can lead to the development of sustainable competitive advantages. Porter (1985) proposed that there are two essential routes to achieving above-average performance: to become the lowest-cost producer, or to differentiate the product/service to a degree that it is of superior value to the customer. These strategies can be implemented in either broad (mass) or narrow (focused) markets. Porter suggested that these give rise to three generic strategies: overall **cost leadership**; differentiation; and focus strategies.

- *Cost leadership* does not mean a lower price, although lower prices are often used to attract customers. By having the lowest cost structure, an organization can offer standard products at acceptable levels of quality, yet still generate above-average profit margins. If attacked by a competitor using lower prices, the low-cost leader has a far bigger cushion than its competitors. It should be appreciated that charging a lower price than its rivals is not the critical point. The competitive advantage is derived from how the organization exploits its cost–price ratio. By reinvesting the profit, for example by improving product quality, investing more in product development, or building extra capacity, long-run superiority is more likely to be achieved.

- A *differentiation* strategy requires that all value chain activities are geared to the creation of products that are valued by, and which satisfy, the needs of particular broad segments. By identifying particular customer groups, each of which has a discrete set of needs, a product can be differentiated from its competitors. The fashion brand Zara differentiated itself by reformulating its value chain so that it became the fastest high-street brand to design, produce, distribute, and make fashion clothing available in its shops.

  Customers are sometimes prepared to pay a higher price, a price premium, for products that deliver superior or extra value. For example, the Starbucks coffee brand is strongly differentiated and valued, because consumers are willing to pay higher prices to enjoy the Starbucks experience. However, differentiation can be achieved by low prices, as evidenced through the success of low-cost airlines Ryanair and easyJet.

  Products can be differentiated using a variety of criteria; indeed, each element of the marketing mix is capable of providing the means for successful, long-term differentiation. Differentiation can lead to greater levels of brand loyalty. For example, in contrast to low-cost Lidl, Waitrose provides a strongly differentiated supermarket service.

- *Focus strategies* are used by organizations to seek gaps in broad market segments or to find gaps in competitors' product ranges. In other words, focus strategies help to seek out unfulfilled market needs. The focused operator then concentrates all value chain activities on a narrow range of products and services.

  Focus strategies can be oriented towards being the lowest-cost producer for the particular segment or towards offering a differentiated product for which the narrow target segment is willing to pay a higher price. This means that there are two options for a company wishing to follow a **focus strategy**—low cost and differentiation—both of which occur within a

Waitrose supermarkets: that bit different!

Source: © 2012 Waitrose

particular, narrow, segment. The difference between a broad differentiator and a focused differentiator is that the former bases its strategy on attributes valued across a number of markets, whereas the latter seeks to meet the needs of particular segments within a market.

Porter argues that, to achieve competitive advantage, organizations must achieve one of these three generic strategies. To fail to be explicit, strategically, results in organizations being 'stuck in the middle'. This means that they achieve below-average returns and have no competitive advantage. It has been observed, however, that some organizations have been able to pursue low-cost and differentiated strategies simultaneously. For example, an organization that develops a large market share through differentiation and by creating very strong brands may well become the cost leader as well. Porter's contribution is very important—but these generic strategies should not be treated as though they are set in stone. It is, however, a useful approach and one that has contributed to our understanding about the way in which markets operate.

Competitive Positioning

Having collected industry information, analysed competitors, and considered our resources, perhaps the single most important aspect of developing marketing strategy is to decide how to compete in the selected target markets. Two key decisions arise: what position do we want in the market (which is considered here), and what will be our strategic intent? This is examined in the following section.

Table 5.2 Types of market position	
Position	**Explanation**
Market leader	The market leader has the single largest share of the market. Market leadership is important, because it is these products and brands that can shape the nature of competition in the market, and set out standards relating to price, quality, speed of innovation, and communications, as well as influence the key distribution channels. For example, Tesco was an ordinary mid-ranking supermarket in the 1980s, but has since grown to become the leading UK supermarket.
Market challengers	Products that aspire to the leadership position are referred to as market challengers. These may be positioned as number two, three, or even four in the market. They actively seek market share and use aggressive strategies to take share from all of their rivals. For example, Sainsbury's and Asda are the two main market challengers in the UK supermarket sector.
Market followers	These firms have low market shares and do not have the resources to be serious competitors. They pose no threat to the market leader or challengers, and often adopt 'me too' strategies when the market leader takes an initiative. If we extend the examples within the supermarket sector, then Morrison's might be deemed as a market follower.
Market nichers	Nichers are specialists. They select small segments within target markets that the larger companies do not want to exploit. They develop specialized marketing mixes designed to meet the needs of their customers. They are threatened by economic downturns when customers either cease buying that type of product or buy more competitively priced products. They are also vulnerable to changes in customer tastes and competitor innovation.

The position that a product adopts in a market is a general reflection of its market share. Four positions can be identified—market leader; challenger; follower; and nicher—and each has particular characteristics, as set out in Table 5.2.

There are two main reasons for considering the competitive positions adopted by companies. The first is to understand the way in which the various firms are positioned in the market, and, from that, to deduce the strategies that they are likely to follow and their most probable strategies when attacked by others. The other reason is to understand where the company is currently positioned and to decide where it wants to be positioned at some point in the future. This will shape the nature and quantity of the resources to be required, and the strategies to be pursued.

Implementation

The implementation of any marketing plan is incomplete without methods to control and evaluate its performance. It is vitally important to monitor the results of the programme as it unfolds, not only when it is completed. Therefore measures need to be stated in the plan about how the results of the programme will be recorded and disseminated. Recording the performance of a marketing plan against targets enables managers to make adjustments should the plan not perform as expected, perhaps as a result of unforeseen market events.

For ease of explanation, the marketing planning process has been depicted as a linear, sequential series of management activities. This certainly helps to simplify understanding about how strategy can be developed and it also serves to show how various activities are linked together. However, it should be recognized that strategy development and planning, whether at corporate, business, or functional levels, is not linear, does not evolve in preset ways, and is not always subject to a regular, predetermined pattern of evolution. Indeed, politics, finance, and interpersonal conflicts all help to shape the nature of an organization's marketing strategy.

Marketing implementation is a fundamental process in marketing because it is the action phase of the strategic marketing process. Whereas many of the concepts in this text help us to design marketing programmes, the implementation phase is about actually doing it—and with action comes unpredictability.

The implementation of any marketing plan is far from straightforward, because a variety of problems can arise. However, there are certain elements that impact on the implementation of most strategic marketing plans, and these are considered here.

- The structure and type of marketing function and the degree to which a marketing orientation prevails across the organization.
- The degree of team-working among co-workers associated with the implementation process. These can be internal (employees) and external (consultants, agencies or outsourced customer service representatives).
- The controls used to measure the effectiveness of the implementation process. These are referred to as marketing metrics.

The Structures and Types of Marketing Organization

How we organize ourselves to undertake marketing has an impact on how efficient and how effective we are. In addition, the way in which we organize the marketing function has an impact on how our colleagues in other professional disciplines view us and our effectiveness. According to a Chartered Institute of Marketing (CIM) survey, only 10 per cent of boardroom time is spent discussing marketing issues, whereas the number of chief executive officers (CEOs) with a marketing background appears to be falling (CIM, 2009a).

go online

Visit the **Online Resource Centre** and follow the web link to the CIM to learn more about the role of marketing in organizations.

Despite the fact that brands account for 28 per cent of companies' total intangible value on average, according to Brand Finance, boards of directors are not required to report to investors what they are doing with their most key assets, their brands. However, as Jack (2010) reports, investors appear to be more interested in how companies manage their brands. In addition, some financial analysts are beginning to accept that marketing and brand equity issues need to be taken more seriously.

So it seems that marketing professionals are either less effective than their professional colleagues or they are underrated. The question is: how should marketers organize a more effective function with their organization?

A further problem is that marketers do not always control all of the elements of the marketing mix that are assumed to be under their control. For example, as O'Malley and Patterson (1998) indicate, marketers seldom control pricing, distribution, product development, and even promotion (which is often outsourced to agencies), although they may exercise influence over all of these activities and more. In addition, marketing may not necessarily be organized as a separate department, but the ethos and influence of marketing philosophy may still be apparent and impact on an organization's decision-making (Harris and Ogbonna, 2003).

Marketing is present in all aspects of an organization, because all departments have some role to play with respect to creating, delivering, and satisfying customers. For example, employees in the R&D department designing new products to meet poorly serviced existing customer needs are performing a marketing role. Similarly, members of the procurement department buying components for a new product or service must purchase components of specific quality and at a certain cost that will meet customer needs. In fact, we can go through all departments of a company and find that, in each department, there is a marketing role to be played to some extent. In other words, marketing should be regarded as something that is distributed throughout an organization and all employees should be considered to be part-time marketers (Gummesson, 1990). Marketing is not something that only people in the marketing department undertake.

Types of Marketing Organization

Marketers have not always been able to highlight easily the performance of their departments against the return on investment made in paying marketing salaries and budgets by senior management. As a result, organizations have developed different ways of organizing their sales and marketing functions.

- In some organizations, marketing and sales are separate departments reporting to the manager in charge of a particular SBU. In this situation, it is the job of the manager to coordinate the different departmental inputs into a coherent and complementary set of strategies.

- In other organizations, each sales and marketing department reports to an SBU manager, who then reports to a corporate headquarters. Corporate headquarters also has a corporate marketing group, which will tend to handle the marketing for the group as a whole (for example, corporate identity, group market research).

- In some organizations, communications are treated as a separate department as well, adding to the variety of ways in which organizations are configured.

Marketing organizations have changed in recent years. There is now an increased emphasis on key account management, in which senior marketing personnel serve important accounts or customer segments, sometimes through cross-functional teams involving sales, marketing, and-supply chain management personnel, particularly in sales and operations planning (S&OP) meetings, in which detailed supply and demand plans are considered and reconciled (such as at AstraZeneca, the pharmaceutical giant). When firms are operating in more than one country, the role of the country manager has been reduced. As companies have globalized (for example, Nike) and their efforts spread across countries, senior managers now tend to operate across whole continental regions (such as Europe, the Middle East, or Africa). In addition, product managers have lost their role as the primary marketing coordinator of sales, marketing, R&D, manufacturing, and other functions. This role has shifted to key account managers or category managers (as in Procter & Gamble), who oversee whole brand categories rather than individual products.

In addition, there has been an increasing shift towards outsourcing marketing activities. For example, advertising and market research have traditionally been outsourced to agencies by large multinational and many medium-sized firms. Recently, there has been an increasing shift towards outsourcing sales activities (for example, in health insurance), data warehousing (among car and electrical goods manufacturers), and customer data analytics (supermarkets and financial services).

Team-Working

Whether customer service or marketing communications initiatives are outsourced or not, marketers have to be strong team players (see Chapter 1), especially as more and more departments take over functions that were once most closely associated with marketing, such as pricing and product development (Bristow and Frankwick, 2001).

Marketers are typically organizers of other people's efforts. For example, they may liaise with an in-house market research manager to determine the research plan for the year ahead for a particular product, or they may work with the advertising agency account planner and his or her team to formulate an integrated marketing communications campaign. If they are involved in pricing and budgeting, it is frequently as a result of discussions with an executive from the finance department rather than the outcome of undertaking the detailed costing work in their own capacity. Marketing personnel may have conversations with sales personnel over how to support the sales functions' objectives, but they do not get personally involved in selling. Similarly, marketing personnel should have an input into distribution of goods and services, particularly where service design might form a competitive advantage, but they would not actually undertake a service redesign exercise by themselves; this usually falls to the operations or supply chain management department instead. In less well-funded organizations, such as small to medium-sized enterprises (SMEs), marketing executives may pick up some of these tasks themselves, perhaps undertaking market research and marketing communications activities in-house, to offset costs.

Marketing is an activity concerned with creating customer value and concerns most departments in an organization. Yet, despite the long-recognized central importance of the customer (Levitt, 1960), marketers are all too often organized into silos as a line function, a department, rather than as a cross-departmental staff function, like human resources (HR) or IT (Sheth and Sisodia, 2006). This is still the case despite the fact that 'there is now increasing recognition that cross-functional working relationships have a key role to play in the successful implementation of marketing decisions' (Chimhanzi, 2002).

In order to develop marketing's influence in a team setting, organizations must commit to the following.

- They must develop joint reward systems, which work across departments and reduce inter-departmental conflict (Chimhanzi, 2002). Successful marketing teams are appropriately rewarded; so it is important that salespeople are evaluated and compensated not only for achieving sales volume targets, but also for their contribution to the implementation of marketing programmes more generally, which may have wider objectives than short-term sales revenue increases (Strahle et al., 1996).

- They must communicate the value of the marketing department to other teams—firms that are market-oriented, for example, tend to show greater profitability (Wong and Saunders, 1993).

- Through their senior managers, they must encourage the informal integration of departments and greater inter-functional coordination (Day, 1994).

Working successfully in teams requires participants to use a range of interpersonal skills from a variety of project management-related and marketing-related skill sets. However, of the many reasons for marketing strategies and plans to underperform, two stand out: internal politics and budgeting.

Internal Politics and Negotiation

Part of the task of introducing a new marketing strategy into an organization is the process of persuading colleagues that the marketing strategy is the right strategy to adopt and implement. Sometimes, marketing colleagues resist efforts to implement strategy. However, there has been a movement away from forms of organization that stress central coordination and multilevel hierarchies towards more flexible organizational forms, in which numerous organizations are tied together in cooperative supply chains (Achrol and Kotler, 1999).

Whether we are operating in networks of organizations or as part of a central marketing department within a company, it is important to overcome resistance to strategy implementation. Resistance to marketing implementation is known as **counter-implementation**. It is defined as encompassing:

> a variety of different resistant behaviours that are motivated by anxiety on behalf of those tasked with or involved in the implementation process. Such behaviour may be motivated intentionally or unintentionally, but all may reduce the effectiveness of strategic implementation efforts.
>
> (Thomas, 2002)

Budgeting

Managing a budget is an important aspect of a marketing manager's job. A marketing budget should indicate how much is to be spent, or perhaps invested, on marketing activities, when these activities should start, and when they should finish. There are no hard-and-fast rules on how much should be allocated to marketing spend, but there is a general view that many companies lack a formal and proper budgeting process.

A marketing budget may be between 5 per cent and 7 per cent of sales revenues (excluding salaries), but exactly how much is spent on marketing activities is dependent on the particular industry, each firm, and the overall economic climate. For example, the strongest companies to emerge from the previous recession were found to have invested 9 per cent more in their marketing budgets than their least successful competitors (CIM, 2009b). However, empirical work by Srinivasan et al. (2011) suggests that investment in both R&D and advertising during a recession should be based on the actual conditions facing the firm. They provide a model, to which they refer as a 'contingency approach', enabling firms to determine for themselves whether and how such investments should be made.

As might be expected, there are some broad differences in the pattern in which large and small firms, and those operating in consumer and business-to-business (B2B), invest in communications in periods of relative stability. Large companies in consumer markets tend to invest more heavily on most elements of the communication mix. Business-to-business and smaller organizations, unsurprisingly, tend to invest the larger part of their budgets on less-expensive activities, including direct mail, email, telephone marketing, and lead generation. Their involvement in social media is relatively limited, although a few B2B companies are actively involved in social media.

Developing New Programmable Space

Herman Miller (HM) is a major office furniture designer and manufacturer. Since 1923, the company has been renowned for selling high-quality, ergonomically designed, office chairs, desks, and storage facilities to major private companies, governments, and other leading organizations around the world. However, in 2000, the company began to consider the future, and soon reached the conclusion that growth in white-collar workers was going to slow and so the demand for office furniture was also likely to fall. This represented a major threat to the company, because its strategy was built around these main markets.

A new team of seven people was created. The team comprised a mix of leading technologists, architects and engineers, some with no experience of the business. They were required to innovate, to identify new markets, and to guide HM to undeveloped areas of commercial potential. The team worked in relative isolation from other HM employees and outside contractors and experts.

The result was a raft of innovations, many of which served to redefine office interiors and the company itself. One of these was the launch of a new company called Convia. Essentially, Convia offers an intelligent modular electrical system with a programmable data network, which is installed in a ceiling. It also provides an assembly that allows for the suspension of office interior devices. The result was a new market, one based on 'programmable workspace'.

The value in this new approach can be seen in terms of the property development market. Buildings and offices can be reconfigured without disposing of wires, conduits, and other embedded materials. For facilities management companies, energy and light management issues can be managed more effectively. For users, space can be personalized, so that the levels of heat, light, and sound can be adjusted with a simple mouse click. HM now offered programmable workspace solutions and was the first to do so.

The company repositioned itself as a researcher, designer, manufacturer, and distributor of innovative office furniture. HM develop solutions for organizations so that they provide great places for people to learn and work. HM moved from a company that sold furniture to one that provides buildings with intelligent infrastructure and enables people to better manage their working environments.

Sources: Adapted from Birchard (2010); http://www.hermanmiller.co.uk/

Herman Miller: where even the chairs are intelligent
Source: Courtesy of Herman Miller

1 **Identify the issues that HM might have experienced implementing this strategy.**

2 **To what extent is HM's response really strategic?**

3 **Consider HM's scenario within the framework of the Ansoff matrix. What other strategic options could the company have followed?**

Marketing Metrics

There is increased acceptance of the need to determine efficiency and effectiveness in organizational marketing efforts. In the past, marketing control has been achieved through the annual marketing plan, analysis of company profitability, some measures of efficiency (for example, number of employees as a proportion of revenue or in retailing, net profit per square foot of retail space), or in terms of market share or some other strategic measure. However, in the past, these measures have been focused towards financial or HR measures. More recently, there has been a considerable shift in thinking towards the need for customer-based measurements (Kaplan and Norton, 1992). There has been a move towards setting key performance indicators (KPIs), which companies set and measure their progress towards in order to determine whether or not they have improved or maintained their performance over a given period of time.

Research Insight 5.2

To take your learning further, you might wish to read the following influential paper:

Kaplan, R. S., and Norton, D. P. (1992) 'The balanced scorecard: measures that drive performance', *Harvard Business Review,* Jan–Feb: 71–9.

This seminal, much-quoted article outlines how companies should move beyond financial measures of performance to measures of performance incorporating financial, internal, innovation, and learning, and customer perspectives, seeking to answer questions such as: how do we look to shareholders? At what must we excel? Can we continue to improve and create value? And how do customers see us? The paper sparked a revolution in company performance measurement practice.

@ Visit the **Online Resource Centre** to read the abstract and to access the full paper.

Research indicates that British companies are now using a variety of marketing metrics as KPIs in marketing. Ten particular metrics were identified in a telephone study of 200 UK marketing and finance senior executives (Ambler et al., 2004), as listed and explained in Table 5.3.

However, Clark and Ambler (2011), reporting on a review of the use of KPIs, conclude that:

> there is no list of metrics that is right for every organization. No list is theoretically correct. Organizations need to determine what works in practice. Any relevant metric—that is, any metric that makes sense and has predicted performance—should be at least considered.
>
> (Clark and Ambler, 2011: 21)

Table 5.3 The ten most popular key performance indicators (KPIs)

Metric	Explanation
Profit/ profitability	This is the main KPI. 'Profit' broadly refers to how much cash there is left in the business when all expenses are subtracted from all of the revenues generated. It represents what is left over either for distribution to the shareholders of the business, whether that be a private or public business, or for reinvestment in the business.
Sales	For some companies, sales value or volume is an even more important KPI than profitability. This is an incorrect priority, because profitability is key for business survival. Sales value is determined by measuring how many units of a product or service are sold multiplied by the average unit price; sales volume is calculated by determining how many units of a product or service have been sold.
Gross margin	The performance of many companies is measured on the gross profit margins that they can achieve relative to the industry standard. For example, the gross profit margin for supermarkets in the UK is around 5–8 per cent, whereas in the US gross profit margins are considerably lower, at around 2–5 per cent.
Awareness	The extent to which the target market knows or has heard of your brand is an attractive performance measure. The majority of companies use brand awareness, but unfortunately this helps us to understand only how hard the marketing communications are working; it says little about the marketing strategy because creating awareness may not necessarily build sales.
Market share	Market share, for profit-oriented companies, is a principal measure of market performance. When measured relative to the performance of the market leader, the figure gives an indication of the company's overall level of competitiveness. A company's market share is determined by measuring a company's sales revenues, as a proportion of the total sales revenues in that industry.
Number of new products	Innovation and the rate at which a company brings new products to the market is becoming an increasingly important performance metric for many companies. As product life cycles decrease and the speed of product imitation increases, developing new products can be crucial. In itself, however, this is an insufficient measure of marketing strategy success.
Relative price	The price of a company's offering can be indicative of how much it is valued in the marketplace. A company that can charge a price premium, vis-à-vis its competitors, is said to have a 'competitive advantage'. Relative price is determined by measuring the price of company A's offering against the price of the market-leading company, or nearest competitor, if company A is the market leader.

Table 5.3 (continued)

Metric	Explanation
Customer satisfaction	By striving to reach the highest levels of customer satisfaction (or delight), companies seek to ensure that they retain their customers and that they will attract new ones. However, there is a danger that too much cost is sunk into generating customer satisfaction and that these costs eat too much of the profits. As a stand-alone measure, customer satisfaction is incomplete.
Distribution/ availability	In some industries, such as film distribution, the extent to which an offering is distributed is crucial if the opportunity to maximize revenues is to be realized. For many businesses, distribution is critical, so that customers can readily purchase a company's product/ services. For this reason, companies often set up sophisticated systems designed to link their customers' purchasing needs with their own purchasing and distribution needs.
Number of customer complaints	Most businesses seek to minimize the number of complaints about their product or service. This can be achieved through staff training, product testing, research, and setting appropriate expectations. Taken as one of a series of KPIs, the number of complaints can be considered insightful into a company's progress.

Marketing Planning

So far in this chapter, we have considered the key activities associated with the strategic marketing planning process—essentially one of analysis, goals, and action. In order for organizations to be able to develop, implement, and control these activities at a product and brand level, marketing plans are derived. This final section of the chapter considers the characteristics of the marketing planning process, identifies the key activities, and considers some of the issues associated with the process.

Marketing planning is a sequential process involving a series of activities leading to the setting of marketing objectives and the formulation of plans for achieving them (McDonald, 2002). A marketing plan is the key output from the overall strategic marketing planning process. It details a company's or brand's intended marketing activity.

Marketing plans can be developed for periods of one, two, to five years, and anything up to twenty-five years. However, too many organizations regard marketing plans as a development of the annual round of setting sales targets that are then extrapolated into quasi-marketing plans. This is not helpful, because it fails to account for the marketplace, customer needs, and resources. It is important that the strategic appraisal and evaluation phase of the planning process be undertaken first. This should cover between a three-year and five-year period, and should provide a strategic insight into the markets, competitors, and the organization's resources that shape the direction and nature of the way in which the firm has decided to compete. Once agreed, these should then be updated on an annual basis and modified to meet changing internal and external conditions. Only once the strategic marketing plan has been developed should detailed operational or functional marketing plans, covering a one-year period, be developed (McDonald, 2002). This makes marketing planning a continuous process, not something that is undertaken once a year, or worse, just when a product is launched.

A marketing plan designed to support a particular product consists of a series of activities that should be undertaken sequentially. These are presented in Table 5.4.

Table 5.4 Key activities within a marketing plan

Activity	Explanation
Executive summary	This is a brief, one-page summary of key points and outcomes.
Overall objectives	Reference should be made to the organization's overall mission and corporate goals—the elements that underpin the strategy.
Product/market background	This comprises a short summary of the product and/or market to clarify understanding about target markets, sales history, market trends, main competitors, and the organization's own product portfolio.
Marketing analysis	This provides insight into the market, customers, and the competition. It should consider segment needs, current strategies, and key financial data. The marketing audit and SWOT analysis are used to support this section.
Marketing strategies	This section should be used to state the market(s) to be targeted, the basis on which the firm will compete, the competitive advantages to be used, and the way in which the product is to be positioned in the market.
Marketing goals	Here, the desired outcomes of the strategy should be expressed in terms of the volume of expected sales, the value of sales and market share gains, levels of product awareness, availability, profitability, and customer satisfaction.
Marketing programmes	A marketing mix for each target market segment has to be developed, along with a specification of who is responsible for the various activities and actions, and the resources that are to be made available.
Implementation	This section sets out the: • way in which the marketing plan is to be controlled and evaluated; • financial scope of the plan; and • operational implications in terms of human resources, research, and development, and system and process needs.
Supporting documentation	Marketing plans should contain relevant supporting documentation too bulky to be included in the plan itself, but necessary for reference and detail, e.g. the full PESTLE and SWOT analyses, marketing research data, and other market reports and information, plus key correspondence.

Many of the corporate-level goals and strategies, and internal and external environmental analyses, that are established within the strategic marketing planning process can be replicated within each of the marketing plans written for individual products, product lines, markets, or even SBUs. As a general rule, only detail concerning products, competitors, and related support resources need change prior to the formulation of individual marketing mixes and their implementation, within functional-level marketing plans.

The strategic marketing planning process starts with a consideration of the organization's goals and resources, and an analysis of the market and environmental context in which the organization seeks to achieve its goals. It culminates in a detailed plan, which, when implemented, is measured to determine how well the organization performs against the marketing plan.

Chapter Summary

To consolidate your learning, the key points from this chapter can be summarized as follows.

- **Describe the strategic planning context and process**

  The strategic planning process commences at corporate level. Here, the organization sets out its overall mission, purpose, and values. These are then converted into measurable goals that apply to the whole organization. Then, depending upon the size of the organization, the range of strategic business units (SBUs) and/or products is determined, and resources allocated to help and support each one. Each SBU and/or product develops detailed functional and competitive strategies and plans, such as a marketing strategy and plan.

- **Explain the key influences that impact on and shape marketing strategy**

  There are three key influences on marketing strategy: strategic market analysis, which is concerned with developing knowledge and understanding about the marketplace; strategic marketing goals, which are about what the strategy is intended to achieve; and strategic marketing action, which is about how the strategies are to be implemented.

- **Develop a SWOT analysis and set out how it can help strategic marketing decision-making**

  SWOT analysis is a tool used to determine an overall view of the strategic position, and highlights the need for a strategy to produce a strong fit between the internal capability (strengths and weaknesses) and the external situation (opportunities and threats). SWOT analysis serves to identify the key issues, and then prompts thought about converting weaknesses into strengths and threats into opportunities.

- **Explain how understanding competitors can assist the development of marketing strategy**

  An analysis of a firm's competitors involves answers to five key questions: who are our competitors? What are their strengths and weaknesses? What are their strategic goals? Which strategies are they following? How are they likely to respond?

- **Identify the characteristics of strategic marketing goals and explain the nature of the associated growth strategies**

  There are several types of strategic objective, but the four main ones are niche, hold, harvest, and divest goals. However, the vast majority of organizations also consider growth to be a primary objective. Although there are different forms of growth, intensive, integrated, or diversified are generally accepted as the main forms.

- **Understand the principles of marketing metrics, and how these can contribute to the implementation and control of the strategic marketing planning process**

  There is increasing recognition of the importance of using marketing metrics in the control mechanism of the implementation phase of a marketing programme. Many companies now use some variant of the balanced scorecard (Kaplan and Norton, 1992). Recent research has highlighted widespread use of marketing metrics in firms, including metrics in the following areas: profit/profitability; sales value and volume; gross margin; awareness; market share; number of new products; relative price; number of customer complaints; consumer satisfaction; distribution/availability; total number of customers; marketing spend; perceived quality/esteem; customer loyalty/retention; and relative perceived quality (Ambler et al., 2004).

- **Outline the key elements of a marketing plan**

  The following represent the key elements associated with the structure of a marketing plan: overall objectives; product/market background; market analysis; marketing strategy and goals; marketing programmes; implementation, evaluation, and control. Although depicted as a linear process, many organizations either do not follow this process or do not include all of these elements, or undertake many of these elements simultaneously.

Review Questions

1. What is the difference between a 'vision' and a 'mission'?
2. Make brief notes outlining the strategic planning process.
3. Identify the key characteristics of SWOT analysis. What actions should be taken once the SWOT grid is prepared?
4. Porter (1985) argues that firms can differentiate themselves in one of two main ways. What are they and how do they work?
5. List the various parts of a marketing plan.

Scan this image to go online and access the chapter's multiple-choice questions, web links, Internet activities, and more!

Worksheet Summary

Visit the **Online Resource Centre** and complete Worksheet 5.1. This will help you to learn about the differences between internal strength and weakness; external threats and opportunities, and how to conduct a SWOT analysis for Sony (that is, the PS4) in the games console market.

References

Achrol, R. S. and Kotler, P. (1999) 'Marketing in the network economy', *Journal of Marketing*, 63: 146–63.

Ambler, T. (2000) 'Marketing metrics', *Business Strategy Review*, 11(2): 59–66.

Ambler, T., Kokkinaki, F., and Puntoni, S. (2004) 'Assessing marketing performance: reasons for metrics selection', *Journal of Marketing Management*, 20: 475–98.

Ansoff, I. H. (1957) 'Strategies for diversification', *Harvard Business Review*, 35(2): 113–24.

Baker, R. (2011) 'Nokia to partner with Microsoft under new structure', *Marketing Week*, available online at http://www.marketingweek.co.uk/sectors/telecoms-and-it/nokia-to-partner-with-microsoft-under-new-structure/3023364.article [accessed 22 January 2012].

Birchard, B. (2010) 'Herman Miller's design for growth', *Strategy+Business*, 25 May, available online at http://www.strategy-business.com/article/10206?gko=9695a [accessed 5 July 2010].

Bristow, D. N. and Frankwick, G. L. (2001) 'Product managers influence tactics in marketing strategy development and implementation', *Journal of Strategic Marketing*, 2: 211–27.

Chapman, M. (2011) 'Nokia fights back with Microsoft smartphones', *Marketing*, 26 October, available online at http://www.brandrepublic.com/news/1100666/Nokia-fights-back-Microsoft-smartphones/?DCMP=ILC-SEARCH [accessed 22 January 2012].

Chartered Institute of Marketing (CIM) (2009a) *White Paper: The Future of Marketing*, available online at http://www.cim.co.uk/filestore/resources/agendapapers/futureofmarketing.pdf [accessed 6 April 2010].

Chartered Institute of Marketing (CIM) (2009b) *White Paper: Keep Calm and Carry on Marketing—Marketing in a Recession*, available online at http://www.cim.co.uk/filestore/resources/agendapapers/keepcalm.pdf [accessed 6 April 2010].

Chimhanzi, J. (2002) 'The impact of marketing/HR interactions on marketing strategy implementation', *European Journal of Marketing*, 38(1–2): 73–98.

Choueke, M. (2011) 'Behind closed doors at the world's most famous brand', *Marketing Week*, 26 May, available online at http://www.marketingweek.co.uk/analysis/cover-stories/behind-closed-doors-at-the-world's-most-famous-brand/3026712.article [accessed 21 January 2012].

Clark, B. and Ambler, T. (2011) 'Marketing metrics portfolio', *Marketing Management*, Fall: 16–21.

Day, G. S. (1994) 'The capabilities of market-driven organisations', *Journal of Marketing*, 58(3): 37–52.

Gummesson, E. (1990) 'Marketing orientation revisited: the crucial role of the part-time marketer', *European Journal of Marketing*, 25(2): 60–75.

Harris, L. C. and Ogbonna, E. (2003) 'The organisation of marketing: a study of decentralised, devolved and dispersed marketing activity', *Journal of Management Studies*, 40(2): 483–512.

Jack, L. (2010) 'Building a bridge between marketing and boardroom', *Marketing Week*, 25 February, available online at http://www.marketingweek.co.uk/in-depth-analysis/cover-stories/building-a-bridge-between-marketing-and-boardroom/3010326.article [accessed 5 April 2010].

Kaplan, R. S. and Norton, D. P. (1992) 'The balanced scorecard: measures that drive performance', *Harvard Business Review*, Jan–Feb: 71–9.

Levitt, T. (1960) 'Marketing myopia', *Harvard Business Review*, July–Aug: 45–56.

Madslien, J. (2010) 'Spyker boss outlines Saab plans', available online at http://www.news.bbc.co.uk/1/hi/business/8512224.stm [accessed 25 March 2010].

McDonald, M. (2002) *Marketing Plans and How to Make Them*, 5th edn, Oxford: Butterworth-Heinemann.

Mintzberg, H. (1987) 'The strategy concept: five Ps for strategy', *California Management Review*, 30(1): 11–26.

Noble, C. H., Sinha, R. K., and Kumar, A. (2002) 'Market orientation and alternative strategic orientations: a longitudinal assessment of performance implications', *Journal of Marketing*, 66(4): 25–40.

O'Malley, L. and Patterson, M. (1998) 'Vanishing point: the mix management paradigm reviewed', *Journal of Marketing Management*, 14(8): 829–51.

O'Reilly, L. (2011) 'Microsoft appoints UK CMO', *Marketing Week*, 11 October, available online at http://www.marketingweek.co.uk/sectors/telecoms-and-it/microsoft-appoints-uk-cmo/3030881.article [accessed 22 January 2012].

O'Reilly, L. (2012) 'HTC needs to turn up the volume on its "Quietly Brilliant" strategy', *Marketing Week*, 6 January, available online at http://www.marketingweek.co.uk/sectors/telecoms-and-it/htc-needs-to-turn-up-the-volume-on-its-'quietly-brilliant'-strategy/3033082.article [accessed 22 January 2012].

Piercy, N. (2002) *Market-Led Strategic Change: Transforming the Process of Going to Market*, Oxford: Butterworth-Heinemann.

Porter, M. E. (1985) *The Competitive Advantage: Creating and Sustaining Superior Performance*, New York: Free Press.

Sheth, S. N. and Sisodia, R. S. (2006) *Does Marketing Need Reform? Fresh Perspectives on the Future*, New York: M. E. Sharpe.

Srinivasan, R., Lilien, G. L., and Sridhar, S. (2011) 'Should firms spend more on research and development and advertising during recessions?', *Journal of Marketing*, 49(75): 49–65.

Strahle, W. M., Spiro, R. L., and Acito, F. (1996) 'Marketing and sales: strategic alignment and functional implementation', *Journal of Personal Selling and Sales Management*, 16(1): 1–20.

Thomas, L. C. (2002) 'The nature and dynamic of counter-implementation in strategic marketing: a propositional inventory', *Journal of Strategic Marketing*, 10: 189–204.

Williams, R. (2010) 'What do corporate values really mean?', *Psychology Today*, 7 February, available online at http://www.psychologytoday.com/blog/wired-success/201002/what-do-corporate-values-really-mean [accessed 7 February 2012].

Wong, V. and Saunders, J. (1993) 'Business orientations and corporate success', *Journal of Strategic Marketing*, 1: 20–40.

6

Market Segmentation and Positioning

Learning outcomes

After reading this chapter, you will be able to:

- describe the principles of market segmentation and the segmentation, targeting, and positioning (STP) process;

- explain the characteristics and differences between market segmentation and product differentiation;

- explain how market segmentation can be undertaken in both consumer and business-to-business markets;

- describe different targeting strategies; and

- explain the concept of positioning and illustrate how the use of perceptual maps can assist the positioning process.

Elaine Rosscraig for Stagecoach

Stagecoach Group Plc operates bus services across the UK. How does it know who its customers are and where they want to access its services? We speak to Elaine Rosscraig to find out more.

Stagecoach UK Bus is part of the Stagecoach Group Plc and one of the largest bus operators in the UK, operating both express and local bus services across the country. The company also operates a comprehensive network of intercity operations under the Megabus brand. We connect communities in over a hundred towns and cities in the UK, operating a fleet of around 7,000 buses. We carry over 2 million customers every day on our network, which stretches from Devon to the north of Inverness. So how do we identify who our customers are and where they may wish to access our services? Well, that's a very important question.

At Stagecoach, we have developed our segmentation, targeting, and positioning (STP) strategy using primary research. The results of the primary research have helped us to identify our key market segments, which we have compiled into three groups based on their use of bus services. These groups may be categorized as: 'user'; 'lapsed user'; and 'non-user'.

An important target market for Stagecoach is the non-user segment. The customers contained within this segment demonstrate a propensity to switch the mode of transport to bus. We estimate that about 30 per cent of existing non-bus users in the UK have a propensity to switch the mode of transport that they are regularly using, given the appropriate incentives. In addition, it is essential that Stagecoach addresses the perceived barriers associated with bus travel among this group.

Through profiling our customers using geodemographic criteria, we have further identified micro-demographic segments within each of the local areas that we serve, to whom specific barriers to bus use are an issue. This information has formed the basis of our segmentation strategy and how we subsequently tailor our communication with each of these prospect customer groups.

The major issue that we need to consider is how public transport is perceived by these target segments. Public transport in general has a negative reputation in the UK. This is the result historically of limited customer communication, inadequate staff training, and poor customer relations within the industry.

Customer perception of Stagecoach is linked directly to the journey experience and customer satisfaction.

Stagecoach, the bus company
Source: http://www.stagecoachbus.com/

In order of priority, the following aspects of our service contribute to customer satisfaction: reliability/punctuality; staff attitude; comfort during the journey; cleanliness of the vehicle (interior and exterior); space for bags/pushchairs; and value for money.

1 Given the primary research findings to date and the market segments identified, what would you recommend Stagecoach should do to target and position its brand to the differing market segments to encourage customers to switch their mode of transport to Stagecoach's bus services?

■ Introduction

Ever wondered why we don't target everyone with our marketing activities or how market segments are identified? Think about universities: how do you think they identify with which students to communicate about degree programmes? What criteria do they use? What about international and domestic student groups: is this difference important for the marketing of higher education services to prospective students?

In this chapter, we consider how organizations decide on which segments of a market to focus on in their marketing efforts. This process is referred to as **market segmentation** and is an integral part of marketing strategy. After defining market segmentation, this chapter explores the differences between market segmentation and **product differentiation**. We also consider techniques and issues concerning market segmentation within consumer and business-to-business (B2B) markets. The method by which whole markets are subdivided into different segments is referred to as the **STP process** and it is around this process that this chapter is structured.

■ The STP Process

'STP' refers to three activities: segmentation, targeting, and positioning (see Figure 6.1). Marketers segment markets and identify attractive segments to target (that is, on whom to focus and why), identify new product opportunities, develop suitable positioning and **communication** strategies (that is, what message to communicate), and allocate resources to prioritize marketing activities (that is, how much should they spend and where). The use of the STP process has grown because of the increasing prevalence of mature markets, greater diversity in customer needs, and the ability to reach specialized, niche segments.

The key benefits of the STP process include:

- enhancing a company's competitive position, providing direction and focus for marketing strategies, including targeted advertising, new product development, and brand differentiation

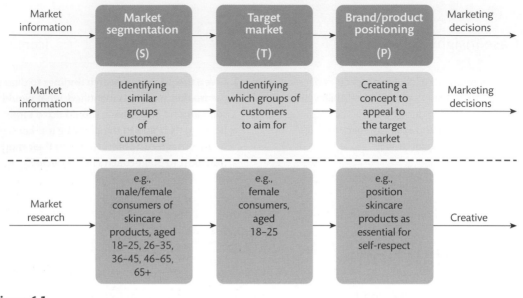

Figure 6.1
The STP process

—for example, Coca-Cola identified that Diet Coke (also marketed as Coca-Cola Lite) was regarded as 'girly' and 'feminine' by male consumers, so it developed a new product, Coke Zero, targeted at the health-conscious male segment of the soft drinks market;

- examining and identifying market growth opportunities through identification of new customers, growth segments, or product uses—for example, Lucozade changed its original marketing strategy under which it was positioned for people who were ill and rebranded it as an energy drink; and

- effective and efficient matching of company resources to target market segments that promise the greatest return on marketing investment (ROMI)—for example, HSBC uses data-informed segmentation strategies to target direct marketing messages and rewards to customers that it characterizes as offering long-term value to the company.

■ The Concept of Market Segmentation

Market segmentation is the division of a mass market into identifiable and distinct groups or segments, each of which has common characteristics and needs, and displays similar responses to marketing actions. There is widespread agreement that segmentation forms an important foundation for successful marketing strategies and activities (Wind, 1978; Hooley and Saunders, 1993). The purpose of market segmentation is to ensure that the elements of marketing activities are designed to meet particular needs of different customer groups.

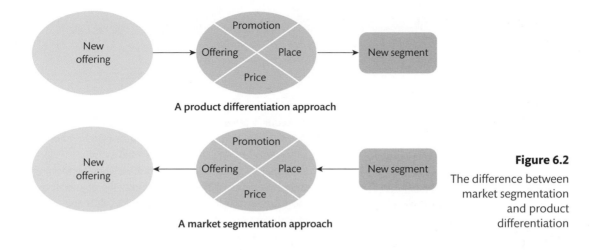

Figure 6.2

The difference between market segmentation and product differentiation

Because companies have finite resources, it is not feasible to produce all possible products, for all of the people, all of the time. The best that can be aimed for is to provide selected offerings for selected groups of people, most of the time. This enables the most effective use of an organization's scarce resources.

Market segmentation is related to product differentiation. If you aim at different market segments, you might adapt different variations of your offering to satisfy those segments. Equally, if you adapt different versions of your offering, this may appeal to different market segments. The former is market segmentation (a focus on market segments); the latter is product differentiation (a focus on the product offering). For example, G-Star RAW (or G-Star) is a Dutch designer clothing company that produces fashionable and high-quality urban clothing. G-Star specializes in making clothing using raw denim, an unwashed, untreated denim, with designs influenced by vintage military clothing, which appeals to youth student market segments. The difference between product differentiation and market segmentation is illustrated in Figure 6.2.

Market segmentation was first proposed as an alternative market development technique in markets in which there are relatively few competitors selling an identical product—that is, imperfectly competitive markets. In markets in which there are lots of competitors selling identical products, market segmentation and product differentiation produce similar results, because product differentiation approaches meet market segment needs more closely. With increasing proliferation of tastes in modern society, many consumers have an increased disposable income. As a result, marketers often seek to design product offerings around consumer demand (market segments) rather than around their own production needs (product differentiation). An industry in which we see a lot of product differentiation is medical innovation, in which the market for the product might not realize its need or have alternatives to satisfy it, which is instead met by innovation in production processes (see Market Insight 6.1).

The Silent Epidemic

Coeliac disease is known as a silent epidemic. It is the most prevalent autoimmune disease in the world, affecting about 1 per cent of the global population. It occurs in genetically predisposed individuals as a result of an abnormal immune response to gluten, the storage protein of wheat. Our understanding of the disease has much evolved in recent years and finding gluten-free food is much easier today than it used to be. However, the diagnostic process for testing for coeliac disease remains relatively complex, long, and tedious. As a result, it is a vastly undiagnosed disease. It is estimated that only about 1 in 5,000 patients suffering from the disease is diagnosed. It is this diverse mode of presentation of symptoms and complex testing procedures that makes the diagnosis difficult to make. The total market for the treatment of coeliac disease, including therapeutic applications, is estimated to reach US$8 billion by 2019.

In 2010, a family-driven business, based in Valais, Switzerland, was awarded the Frost & Sullivan European Product Differentiation Excellence Award for its innovation in point-of-care testing for coeliac disease. Augurix was established in 2006 and is focused on developing innovations in point-of-care testing, one of the major trends shaping the future of medical diagnostics. The company has developed the Simtomax® test. It is the only known point-of-care test for screening coeliac disease that reaches lab-accurate results. The test replicates existing expensive laboratory diagnostic procedures, using a fraction of the blood sample normally required, and it delivers results in 10 minutes with equivalent reliability. The intended use of Simtomax® is to exclude coeliac disease when performing large screening or differential diagnosis, thereby moving more quickly towards therapy. It provides clear and unambiguous results within 10 minutes, requires no training or equipment, and can be stored at room temperature. This diagnostic test significantly reduces the medical costs and use of healthcare services, and has effectively addressed the urgent market need for a rapid and simple test for coeliac disease.

In 2010, the Simtomax® test received the 'CE' mark, allowing for product commercialization in the European Union; it is already available in Switzerland, Italy and France, offering a clear economic advantage over the traditional laboratory techniques.

Sources: http://www.augurix.com/; http://www.frost.com/

1 Augurix won an award for 'excellence in product differentiation'. Explain how the company has used a product differentiation approach.

2 Why was market segmentation not used as a suitable strategy for Augurix?

3 Choose a health-related product that you have in your bathroom cabinet (such as headache tablets, plasters, cough syrup) and identify the likely segments to which it appeals.

▪ The Process of Market Segmentation

The market segmentation process is often problematic because an offering can have multiple applications (Griffith and Pol, 1994). There are also increasing customer variability and problems associated with the identification of the key differences between groups of customers. To aid the process, there are two main approaches to segmenting markets. The first adopts the view that the market consists of customers that are essentially the same, so the task is to

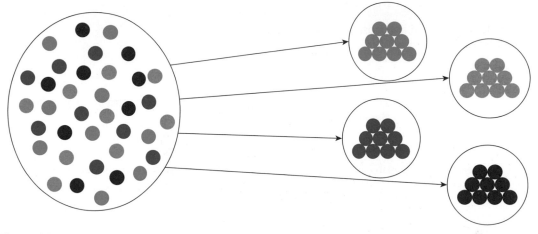

Figure 6.3

Segment heterogeneity and member homogeneity

Note: Other segmentation researchers have distinguished between a priori or post hoc segmentation methods following a six- or seven-stage process of development, as outlined in Table 6.1.

identify groups that share particular differences. This is the **breakdown method**. The second approach considers a market to consist of customers that are all different, so the task is to find similarities. This is known as the **build-up method**.

The breakdown approach is the most established and is the main method used for segmenting consumer markets. The build-up approach seeks to move from the individual level at which all customers are different to a more general level of analysis based on the identification of similarities (Freytag and Clarke, 2001). The build-up method is customer-oriented, seeking to determine common customer needs. The aim of both methods is to identify market segments in which identifiable differences exist between segments (segment heterogeneity) and similarities exist between members within each segment (member homogeneity). This is displayed in Figure 6.3.

Other segmentation researchers have distinguished between **a priori segmentation** or **post hoc segmentation** methods, following a six-stage or seven-stage process of development, as outlined in Table 6.1.

In **business markets**, segmentation should reflect the relationship needs of the parties involved and not be based solely on the traditional consumer market approach, such as the breakdown method. Through the use of both approaches, a more accurate, in-depth, and potentially more profitable view of industrial markets can be achieved (Crittenden et al., 2002). However, problems remain concerning the practical application and implementation of B2B segmentation. Managers often report that although the analytical processes are reasonably clear, it is not apparent how they should 'choose and evaluate between the market segments obtained (Naudé and Cheng, 2003).

Segmentation theory has developed during a period when transactional marketing was the principal approach to marketing, rather than the relational approaches prevalent in today's service-dominated environment. Under the transactional approach, the allocation of resources to achieve the designated marketing mix goals was of key importance. However, customers who make up the various segments have needs that may change and, consequently, those

Table 6.1 A priori and post hoc segmentation approaches

Stage	A priori	Post hoc
1	Selection of the base (a priori) for segmentation (e.g. **demographics** socio-economics)	Sample design—mostly using quota or random sampling approaches
2	Selection of segment descriptors (including hypotheses on the possible link between these descriptors and the basis for segmentation)	Identification of suitable statistical methods of analysis
3	Sample design—mostly using stratified sampling approaches and occasionally quota sampling	Data collection
4	Data collection	Data analysis—formation of distinct segments using multivariate statistical methods (e.g. cluster analysis, CHAID)
5	Formation of the segments based on a sorting of respondents into categories	Establishment of the profile of the segments using multivariate statistical methods (e.g. factor analysis) and selection of segment descriptors (based on the key aspects of the profile for each segment)
6	Establishment of the profile of the segments using multivariate statistical methods (e.g. multiple discriminant analysis, multiple regression analysis)	Translation of the findings about the segment's estimated size and profile into specific marketing strategies, including the selection of target segments and the design or modification of specific marketing strategy
7	Translation of the findings about the segment's estimated size and profile into specific marketing strategies, including the selection of target segment(s) and the design or modification of specific marketing strategy	N/A

Note: N/A, stage not applicable
Source: Adapted from Wind (1978) and Green (1979)

customers may no longer remain members of the particular segment to which they originally belonged (Freytag and Clarke, 2001). Consequently, market segmentation programmes must use current customer data. The segmentation process will therefore vary according to prevailing conditions in the marketplace and the changing needs of the parties involved.

Research Insight 6.1

To take your learning further, you might wish to read the following influential paper:

Beane, T. P. and Ennis, D. M. (1987) 'Market segmentation: a review', *European Journal of Marketing*, 21(5): 20–42.

Beane and Ennis' article provides a useful insight into the main bases for market segmentation, and the strengths and weaknesses of the key statistical methods that we use to analyse customer data to develop segmentation models. The article suggests that there are many ways in which to segment a market and that it is important to exercise creativity when doing so.

@ Visit the **Online Resource Centre** to read the abstract and to access the full paper.

Market Segmentation in Consumer Markets

To segment consumer markets, we use market information collected based on certain key customer-related, product-related, or situation-related criteria (variables). These are classified as **segmentation bases** and include profile ('Who are my market and where are they?'), behavioural ('Where, when, and how does my market behave?'), and psychological criteria ('Why does my market behave in that way?'). These differing types of segmentation base are depicted in Figure 6.4. A fourth segmentation criterion that can be added is contact data, a customer's name and full contact details beyond their postcode (for example, postal address, email, and mobile and home telephone number). Contact data are useful for tactical-level marketing activities such as addressable direct marketing.

Table 6.2 illustrates the key criteria used for consumer market segmentation.

When selecting different bases for segmentation, the trade-off between data acquisition costs and the ability of the data to indicate predictable customer choice behaviour needs to be considered. As depicted in Figure 6.5, demographic and geodemographic data are relatively easy to measure and obtain; however, these bases suffer from low levels of accurate consumer behaviour predictability. In contrast, behavioural data—that is, what a customer does, their product usage, purchase history, and media usage—although more costly to acquire, provides a more accurate base on which to predict future behaviour. So the brand of toothpaste that you purchased on the last three occasions is more than likely going to be the brand of toothpaste that you purchase next time. However, this is also influenced by a customer's susceptibility to marketing communications, such as sales promotions (media usage and response behaviour) and market environment.

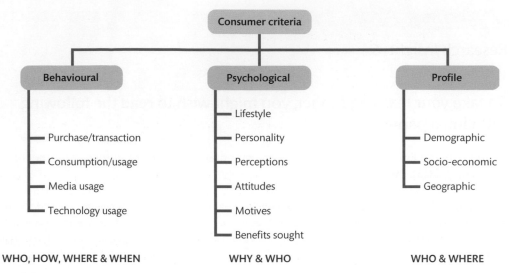

Figure 6.4

Segmentation criteria for consumer markets

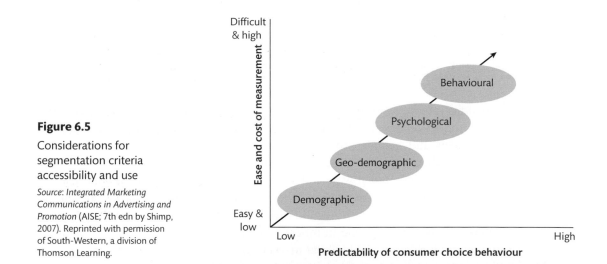

Figure 6.5

Considerations for segmentation criteria accessibility and use

Source: Integrated Marketing Communications in Advertising and Promotion (AISE; 7th edn by Shimp, 2007). Reprinted with permission of South-Western, a division of Thomson Learning.

Profile Criteria

A core customer-related method of segmenting consumer goods and service markets is the use of profile criteria to determine who the market is and where they are. To do this, we use demographic methods (age, gender, race), socio-economics (determined by social class or income levels), and geographic location (by postal code systems). For example, a utility company might segment households based on geographical area to assess brand penetration in certain regions, or a financial investment fund might segment the market based on age, employment, income, and asset net worth to identify attractive market segments for a new investment portfolio. These are all examples of segmentation based on profile criteria.

Table 6.2 Segmenting criteria for consumer markets

Base type	Segmentation criterion	Explanation
Profile	Demographic	Key variables concern age, sex, occupation, level of education, religion, social class, and income characteristics.
	Lifestage	Based on the principle that people need different products and services at different stages in their lives (e.g. childhood, adulthood, young couples, retired).
	Geographic	The needs of potential customers in one geographic area are often different from those in another area, as a result of climate, custom, or tradition.
	Geodemographic	There is a relationship between the type of housing and location in which people live and their purchasing behaviours.
Psychological	Psychographic (lifestyles)	Analysing consumers' activities, interests, and opinions, we can understand individual lifestyles and patterns of behaviour that affect their buying behaviour and decision-making processes. We can also identify similar product and/or **media usage** patterns.
	Benefits sought	The motivations that customers have for making purchases provide an insight into the benefits that they seek from product use.
Behavioural	Purchase/ transaction	Data about customer purchases and transactions provides scope for analysing who buys what, when, how often, how much they spend, and through what transactional channel they purchase.
	Product usage	Segments can be derived on the basis of customer usage of the product offering, brand, or product category. This may be in the form of usage frequency, time of usage, and usage situations.
	Media usage	What media channels are used, by whom, when, where, and for how long provides useful insight into the reach potential for certain market segments through differing media channels, and also insight into their media lifestyle.

Demographic

Demographic variables relate to age, gender, family size and life cycle, generation (for example, 'baby boomers', 'Generation Y', 'Millennials'), income, occupation, education, ethnicity, nationality, religion, and social class. They indicate the profile of a consumer, and are particularly useful in assisting marketing communications and media planning, not least because media selection criteria are developed around these variables.

Age is a common way of segmenting markets and is often the first way in which a market is delineated. Children are targeted for confectionery and toys because their needs and tastes are very different from those of older people. For example, Yoplait Dairy Crest (YDC) launched Petits Filous Plus probiotic yogurt drinks to extend the brand and to increase its appeal among 4–9-year-olds and their parents.

Gender differences have also spawned a raft of products targeted at women, including beauty products and fragrances (for example, Clinique, Chanel), magazines (such as *Glamour*, *Cleo*, *Cosmopolitan*), hairdressing (Pantene, Clairol), and clothes (H&M, Zara). Products targeted at men include magazines (such as *FHM*, *GQ*), grooming products (hair gel and styling mousse), and beverages (Heineken, Carlsberg). Some brands develop products targeted at both men and women, for example fragrances (such as Calvin Klein) and watches (such as Tag Heuer). Increasingly, marketers recognize the importance of segments that have not traditionally been targeted by certain product categories, including insurance products designed for women, such as First for Women Insurance (FFW) in South Africa and Sheila's Wheels in the UK, and beauty products for men, such as L'Oréal's men's range.

Heineken: promotes itself as the beer for blokes

Source: © 2011 Copyright HEINEKEN International

Income or socio-economic status is another important demographic variable because it determines whether a consumer will be able to afford a product. This comprises information about consumer personal income, household income, employment status, disposable income, and asset net worth. Many companies target affluent consumers (for example, Chanel, DKNY, Bentley) offering high-end exclusive product offerings. Targeting low-income earners can also be profitable. German discount supermarkets such as Aldi and Lidl have made a considerable market impact by developing an offering for low-income market segments.

Life cycle

Lifestage analysis is based on the principle that people have varying amounts of disposable income and different needs at different stages in their lives. Adolescents need different products from a single, 26-year-old person, who in turn needs different products from a 26-year-old who is married and has young children. For example, in the UK, Tesco, ASDA Wal-Mart, and Sainsbury's have all invested in the development of product lines targeted at singles with high disposable incomes and busy lifestyles, in the form of their 'meal for one' ranges, in contrast with the 'family value' brands and 'multipacks' targeted at families. As families grow and children leave home, so the needs of the parents change and their disposable income increases. Holidays (such as Disneyland Paris) and automobiles (for example, people carriers) are key product categories that are influenced by the lifestage of the market.

Historically, the family life cycle consisted of nine categories through which individuals and households would progress: single bachelor; newly married; married with children under the age of 6; married with children over the age of 6; older married couples with dependent children; empty nest household with or without employment; and solitary survivor in work or retired. However, since this classification was developed, society has changed, and continues to change in terms of values, beliefs, and family life cycle. A more modern lifecycle classification is the Target Group Index (TGI) Lifestage Segmentation Product, which classifies twelve lifestage groups based on age, marital status, household composition, and children (for example, if they have children and the child's age). These groups are presented in Table 6.3.

Visit the **Online Resource Centre** and follow the web link Kantar Media to learn more about the TGI.

go online

Geographics

This approach is useful when there are clear locational differences in tastes, consumption, and preferences. For example, what do you put on your toast in the morning: Vegemite, Marmite, jam, or jelly? Or perhaps you don't eat toast at all and prefer cold meats or rice dishes for your morning meal? Whereas the British often celebrate Christmas with turkey dishes, many Swedes eat fish. These consumption patterns provide an indication of preferences according to differing geographical regions. Markets can be considered by country or region, by size of city or town, by postcode, or by population density, such as urban, suburban, or rural. For example, it is often said that American beer drinkers prefer lighter beers compared with their UK counterparts, whereas German beer drinkers prefer a much stronger drink. In contrast, Australians prefer colder, more carbonated, beer than the British or the Americans. In addition to product selection and consumption, geographical segmentation is important for retail location, advertising and media selection, and recruitment.

Geodemographics

The marriage of geographics and demographics variables has become an indispensable tool for market analysis. Fusing census data with demographic information, especially socio-economic

Table 6.3 Kantar Media: TGI lifestage segmentation groups

Lifestage group	Demographic description	% of adults
Fledglings	15–34, not married/living as couple and have no son or daughter, living with own parents	10
Flown the nest	15–34, not married/living as couple, do not live with relations	4
Nest builders	15–34, married/living as couple, do not live with son/daughter	5
Playschool parents	Live with son/daughter and youngest child aged 0–4	13
Primary school parents	Live with son/daughter and youngest child aged 5–9	7
Secondary school parents	Live with son/daughter and youngest child aged 10–15	8
Mid-life independents	35–54, not married/living as couple, do not live with relations	4
Unconstrained couples	35–54, married/living as couple, do not live with son/daughter	7
Hotel parents	Live with son/daughter and have no child aged 0–15	10
Senior sole decision-makers	55+ not married/living as couple and live alone	10
Empty nesters	55+, married/living as couple, and do not live with son/daughter	19
Non-standard families	Not married/living as couple, live with relations, do not live with son/daughter, and do not live with parents if aged 15–34	3
Unclassified	Not in any group	0.28

Note: Figures do not add up to 100 per cent as a result of rounding.
Source: Reproduced with the kind permission of Kantar Media.

data, can lead to a rich mixture of information about who lives where and what they are like. Consumers can be classified by where they live, which is often dependent on their stage in life and their lifestyle.

Visit the **Online Resource Centre** and complete Internet Activity 6.1 to learn more about how we use databases compiled with geodemographic data to profile market segments effectively.

go online

Two of the best-known UK geodemographic systems are ACORN and MOSAIC. ACORN—A Classification of Residential Neighbourhoods—demonstrates how postcode areas are broken down into five lifestyle categories, seventeen groups, and fifty-six types. The lifestyle categories include wealthy achievers, urban prosperity, comfortably off, moderate means, and hard pressed. Marketers use this information to improve their understanding of customers and target markets, and to determine where to locate operations, field sales forces, retail outlets, and so on. ACORN can also be used to determine where to send direct marketing material, and where to host billboard and other advertising campaigns. In total, ACORN categorizes all of Britain's 1.9 million UK postcodes, using over 125 demographic statistics within England, Scotland, Wales, and Northern Ireland, and 287 lifestyle variables. The classification technique operates on the principle that people living in similar areas have the same needs and lifestyles.

go online

Visit the **Online Resource Centre** and follow the web link to CACI to learn more about the ACORN system.

MOSAIC is a **geodemographic segmentation** system developed by Experian and marketed in many countries worldwide. MOSAIC was originally constructed for the UK using the 1990 census, and is updated annually and overhauled after each census. The resulting UK segmentation system consists of 141 Mosaic person types aggregated into sixty-seven household types and fifteen groups, to create a three-tier classification. MOSAIC is based on the premise of assigning lifestyle groups to differing geographic catchment areas.

go online

Visit the **Online Resource Centre** and follow the web link to Experian to learn more about the MOSAIC system.

Psychological Criteria

Psychological criteria used for segmenting consumer markets include attitudes and perceptions (for example, negative feelings about fast food), **psychographics** or the lifestyles of customers (such as the 'extrovert', the 'fashion conscious', the 'high achiever'), and the types of benefit sought by customers from their consumption choices.

Psychographics

Psychographic approaches rely on the analysis of consumers' activities, interests, and opinions to understand consumers' individual lifestyles and patterns of behaviour. A traditional form of lifestyle segmentation is AIO, based on customer activities, interests, and opinions. These provide useful insight into what makes people tick. Taylor Nelson Sofres (TNS) developed a UK lifestyle typology that comprised the following types of lifestyle category: 'belonger'; 'survivor'; 'experimentalist'; 'conspicuous consumer'; 'social resistor'; 'self-explorer'; and the 'aimless'.

The Accor Hotel Group has used value-based segmentation to develop its brand. The Dorint-Novotel was repositioned to attract those who value personal efficiency. This involved changing the service offering by introducing efficiency-related facilities such as automated checkouts, car hire facility, 24-hour food, and wireless computing. The Dorint-Sofitel brand was repositioned by introducing fine art for the walls, real fires, fine wines, live piano in the reception, libraries, and more experienced concierge staff. This was designed to appeal to those who valued classical styling, customization, and passion (Howaldt and Mitchell, 2007). Market Insight 6.2 discusses market segmentation based on demographic and psychographic criteria.

The Consumer Doppelgänger: What Has Age Got to Do With It?

Have you ever noticed that some mothers and daughters have similar tastes in clothing? According to research, style is determined by how old you feel, not how old you are, explaining a so-called 'consumer doppelgänger' phenomenon. This suggests that mothers and daughters have more in common than their looks, and that this is far more profound than simply buying the same product or brand. Temple University marketing professor Ayalla Ruvio explains this behaviour as motivated by intentionally wanting to have the same identity. Much past consumer research has tended to focus on the unconscious influence of role models and celebrities on adolescents, and the influence of children on family purchases such as groceries; this emerging research broadens the existing mimicry literature by uncovering the factors that lead mothers to intentionally copy or 'doppelgäng' their daughters' style. The phenomenon is akin to reverse socialization: the children, instead of learning style and social cues from their parents, are actually the ones influencing the adults' behaviour. As it turns out, mothers and daughters have a mutual tendency to mimic each other's purchases when they regard the other as an expert in a particular domain—in this case, fashion and youth culture.

The research identified mothers' mimicking tendencies as markedly stronger than their daughters', but since many mothers have full-time jobs and take care of their children and homes, they don't have time to monitor what is fashionable, so they copy their daughters as a shortcut. Teenage girls, on the other hand, would rather copy celebrities than their mums, and adolescent girls tended to copy a celebrity's look intentionally, particularly when the chosen celebrity matches the adolescent's perceived age. Reference group appeals have always been powerful, but celebrities are perhaps the most powerful reference group. The implications for advertisers and retailers are plentiful. In terms of age segmentation, consumers should be classified based on their cognitive age, not their chronological age, since this is what influences purchase decisions.

Jessie J, whose face and legs endorse House of Holland for Pretty Polly tights
Source: Getty

Sources: Thompson et al. (2006); Gavish et al. (2011); Krauss Whitbourne (2011)

1 **Which segmentation criteria should be used to segment the market for women's clothing?**

2 **How should the family life cycle and psychographic criteria be used to segment the market for women's clothing?**

3 **How could a clothing company's segmentation strategy differ if it were targeting teenagers and mothers for women's wear?**

Benefits Sought

Rather than provide offerings based on design and style, the 'benefits sought' approach is based on the principle that we should provide customers with exactly what they want, based on the benefits that they derive from use. Major airlines often segment on the basis of the benefits that passengers seek from transport by differentiating between the first class passenger (given extra luxury benefits in their travel experience), the business class passenger (who gets some of the luxury of the first class passenger), and the economy class passenger (who gets none of the luxury of the experience, but enjoys the same flight). This segmentation approach is useful with respect to new and emerging technologies. Marketers can identify the key benefits and motivations of electronic technology adoption and use. For example, the benefits of convenience, accessibility, and handset durability dominate mobile handset adoption for blue-collar trade workers; teenagers seek novelty through gaming applications (apps), camera pixel resolution, and the latest trends in handset design; office workers seek smartphone multifunctionality.

Behavioural Criteria

Product-related methods of segmenting consumer goods and service markets include using behavioural methods (such as product usage, purchase, and ownership) as bases for segmentation. Observing consumers as they use products or consume services is an important source of ideas for new uses or good/service design and development. Purchase, ownership, and usage are three very different behavioural constructs that we can use to help us to profile and segment consumer markets.

Usage

A company may segment a market based on how often a customer uses its offerings, categorizing these into high, medium, and low users. **Product usage segmentation** allows the development of service specifications or marketing mixes for each user group. For example, heavy users of public transport might be targeted differently from heavy users of private vehicles for car pooling activities. Consumer product use can be investigated from three perspectives.

1 *Social interaction*—This perspective considers the symbolic aspects of usage and the social meanings attached to the consumption of socially conspicuous products, such as a car or a house (Belk et al., 1982; Solomon, 1983). For example, in 2011, Greenpeace launched a guerilla advertising campaign against Europe's biggest car maker Volkswagen, targeting current and future owners, highlighting Volkswagen's alleged poor environmental record.

VW darkside campaign
Source: Sandison/Greenpeace

2 *Experiential consumption*—This perspective considers emotional and sensory experiences that derive from usage, especially emotions such as satisfaction, 'fantasies, feelings and fun' (Holbrook and Hirschman, 1982). For example, Apple is the most valuable company in the world, in large part because Steve Jobs innately understood the importance of emotion and the value of having fans and advocates of Apple products.

3 *Functional utilization*—This perspective considers the functional usage of products and their attributes in different situations (Srivastava et al., 1978; McAlister and Pessemier, 1982), such as how and when cameras are used, how often, and in what contexts.

Transaction and Purchase

The development of electronic point-of-sale (EPOS) computing systems, standardized product codes/article numbers in Europe and the US, and integrated purchasing systems (web, in-store, telephone) has facilitated a rapid growth in the collection of consumer transactional data. This provides an additional consumer characteristic upon which to base market segmentation. These systems allow retailers to track who buys what, when, for how much, in what quantities, and with what incentives (for example, sales promotions). Companies now have the ability to monitor purchase patterns in a variety of geographical regions, at different times or seasons of the year, for various good/service lines and increasingly for differing market segments.

Transactional and purchase information is very useful for marketers to assess who are their most profitable customers. Analysing the recency, frequency, and monetary (RFM) value of purchases, marketers can identify the most profitable market segments. Transactional data is a record of behaviours and might provide some insight into useful purchase trends, but these will not provide deep insight into the underlying reasons for purchase and consumption trends.

Market Insight 6.3 shows an example of the combined use of social media usage, geographic, and mobile data to profile and target consumers through Foursquare.

Market Insight 6.3

Foursquare on Loyalty

Attracting and retaining consumers is very important and now, with developments in social media, it can be done for free, or for very little cost, using one of the many mobile loyalty social platforms now available. Foursquare is a mobile loyalty application that was created in 2009 and is gaining more popularity by the day. By January 2012, the community consisted of around 15 million people worldwide, with over 1.5 billion check-ins and over 600,000 businesses using the Merchant Platform.

The basis of the Foursquare mobile loyalty programme relies on two parts: the consumer's ability to input information into the programme; and the merchant's ability to offer rewards not only to new customers, but also to those who continually use their services.

After downloading the Foursquare mobile loyalty app to a mobile phone, consumers then enter information about where they are. This is called a 'check-in'. Once checked in at a certain venue, they can share this information with their friends via Facebook and Twitter. They also have the option of redeeming specials, writing reviews and reading other reviews, inviting friends, exploring other venues in the area, creating lists, and even following other people's lists (such as a list of 'Top ten restaurants in the area'). Furthermore, consumers are offered the option of recommending certain venues and observing trends.

On the merchant side, once registered with Foursquare, a business is able to use the mobile loyalty programme as a platform from which to engage consumers in a variety of different ways. For example, the venue may add a 'loyalty special' for those who check in with their mobile phone more than five times, or a 'newbie special' for first-time check-ins if the objective is to create new

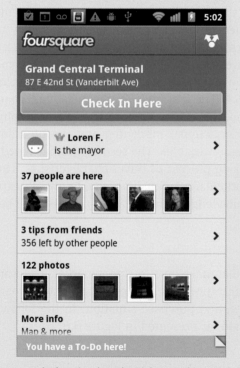

Foursquare: the location-based social networking service

Source: © foursquare 2012

business. Another innovative way in which to get the most from Foursquare is to offer 'last minute specials' on a day that business is slow. Check-in services seem to be present a robust way for retailers to segment out their customer base based on geography and behaviour.

As check-ins become more mainstream, the potential for targeted segmentation is growing with the following implications.

- *Loyalty*—Businesses are able to create robust customer loyalty programmes based on frequency of patronage, and to micro-segment and offer individualized rewards at a much cheaper cost than traditional loyalty programmes.
- *Brand awareness*—The sharing of check-ins on social media sites such as Twitter or Facebook is invaluable: it represents the ability to reach a more targeted audience via a medium (word of mouth) that is arguably more powerful than traditional advertising.
- *Promotion driving traffic*—Businesses are able to promote as needed to drive traffic on an individual level—with no need to dilute the brand by promoting to the entire customer base.

The Foursquare mobile loyalty platform is so much more than simply another customer loyalty reward programme or social network. For many customers, this type of marketing brings a new and innovative way in which to shop and be entertained wherever you are.

1 Why do you think retailers would use Foursquare to target customers?

2 How do you think customers could be segmented based on the data and information that Foursquare provides merchants?

3 Think of your own mobile phone use behaviour. What characteristics do you think a business on Foursquare might use to segment people like you?

Media Usage

The logic of segmenting markets on the basis of frequency of readership, viewership, or patronage of **media vehicles** is well established for print, broadcast, and digital-based network technologies (for example, Internet usage, mobile usage). Segmenting users on the basis of their media usage provides input when evaluating the efficiency and effectiveness of media. Furthermore, differences in frequency may lead to differences in response to repeated passive ad exposures, the competing ads of other sponsors, and prior ad exposure. Frequency of media usage has been the predominant measure of media usage experience. However, Olney et al. (1991) also identified viewing time as an important dependent variable in a model of advertising effects. Holbrook and Gardner (1993) have also argued that duration time is a critical outcome measure of consumption experiences and may be a useful behavioural indicator of experiential versus goal-directed orientations.

■ Segmentation in Business Markets

Business-to-business market segmentation is the identification of 'a group of present or potential customers with some common characteristic which is relevant in explaining (and predicting) their response to a supplier's marketing stimuli' (Wind and Cardozo, 1974). Unfortunately, B2B market segmentation has not been as well researched as consumer market segmentation (Bonoma and Shapiro, 1983). There are two main groups of interrelated variables used to segment B2B markets, as presented in Table 6.4. The first involves organizational characteristics, such as organizational size and location, sometimes referred to as **firmographics**. Those seeking to segment markets in which transactional marketing and the breakdown approach dominate should expect to start with these variables. The second group is based on the characteristics surrounding the decision-making process of buyer characteristics. Those organizations seeking to establish and develop particular relationships would normally expect to start with these variables, and build up their knowledge of their market and customer base.

Organizational Characteristics

These factors concern the buying organizations that make up a business market. There are a number of criteria that can be used to cluster organizations, including size, geography, market served, value, location, industry type, usage rate, and purchase situation. In the following sections, we discuss the main three categories used, as presented in Figure 6.6.

Organizational Size

Using **organizational size segmentation**, we can identify particular buying requirements. Large organizations may have particular delivery or design needs based on volume demand. For example, supermarkets such as France's Carrefour and Britain's Tesco pride themselves on purchasing goods in large quantities to enable them to offer cheaper goods. The size of the organization may have an impact on the usage rates of a good or service, so organizational size is likely to be linked to whether an organization is a heavy, medium, or low buyer of a company's offerings.

Table 6.4 Segmentation bases used in business markets

Base type	Segmentation base	Explanation
Organizational characteristics	Organizational size	Grouping organizations by their relative size (MNCs, international, large, SMEs) enables the identification of design, delivery, usage rates or order size, and other purchasing characteristics.
	Geographic location	Often, the needs of potential customers in one geographic area are different from those in another area.
	Industry type (SIC codes)	**Standard industrial classifications (SIC codes)** are used to identify and categorize all types of industry and business.
Buyer characteristics	**Decision-making unit (DMU) structure**	Attitudes, policies, and purchasing strategies used by organizations allow organizations to be clustered.
	Choice criteria	The types of good/service bought and the specifications that companies use when selecting and ordering goods, services and equipment form the basis for clustering customers and segmenting business markets.
	Purchase situation	Segmenting buyers on the way in which a buying company structures its purchasing procedures, the type of buying situation, and whether buyers are in an early or late stage in the purchase decision process.

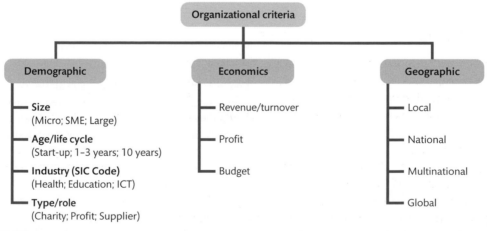

Figure 6.6

Segmentation by organizational characteristics

Note: ICT, information communication technology; SME, small and medium-sized enterprise

Geographical Location

Targeting by geographical location is one of the commoner methods used to segment B2B markets, and is often used by new or small organizations attempting to establish themselves. This approach is particularly useful because it allows sales territories to be drawn up around particular locations that salespersons can service easily. Such territories may be based on European regions, such as Scotland, England, and Wales, Scandinavia, Western Europe and Eastern Europe, and the Mediterranean. Alternatively, they may be based on specific regions within a country. In Eastern Europe, for example, sales territories may be based on individual nations (Poland, the Czech Republic, Romania, and Hungary). However, this approach is increasingly less useful as the Internet and associated websites increase the channels for distribution and communicating product and service offerings.

SIC Codes

Standard Industrial Classification (SIC) codes—that is, codes used to classify business establishments by the type of economic activity that they conduct—are often used to get an indication of the size of a particular market. They are easily accessible and standardized across most Western countries, such as the UK, Europe, and the US. However, some marketers have argued that SIC codes contain categories that are too broad to be useful. Consequently, SIC codes have received limited application, although they do provide 'some preliminary indication of the industrial segments in [a] market' (Naudé and Cheng, 2003).

go online

Visit the **Online Resource Centre** and complete Internet Activity 6.2 to learn more about how we use SIC codes to segment business markets.

Market Insight 6.4 provides an example of how an SME used organizational characteristics and usage benefits to segment and cluster its business customers.

Market Insight 6.4

B2B Safety Pilz!

In B2B markets, segmentation is often used to win a competitive advantage and is linked strongly with a strategy to achieve a sustainable differentiated position. The Pilz brand has stood for safety in automation for over sixty years. In 2009, Pilz was named as one of Germany's hundred most innovative SMEs. As a leading, innovative automation technology company, Pilz is an expert in the safety of human, machine, and the environment. Characterized by its versatile range of applications, the organization provides worldwide, customer-oriented solutions in automation safety in all areas of mechanical engineering, be it the automotive, food, and woodworking industries to airports, theatre, and roller coasters.

Currently employing more than 1,500 staff worldwide, Pilz operates internationally as a technology leader in safe automation technology; with a head office in Germany, Pilz is represented by twenty-six subsidiaries and branch offices on all continents. Given its many and varied customer markets and bespoke customer solution offerings, Pilz segments its business customers by: industry type (for example, packaging, airport), solution application (such as conveyor system), usage benefits (flexibility, price), and geography (for example, Germany, Asia). Pilz business customers form small clusters based

---

on similar needs in business application and usage benefits from Pilz customized offerings, as follows.

- Cluster 1: Conveyor System—for example, Airport Schiphol
- Cluster 2: Robotic Interpolation—for example, fast-moving consumer goods (FMCGs) such as chocolate manufacturer Nestlé
- Cluster 3: Energy Supply—for example, IBM Deutschland GmbH
- Cluster 4: Manufacture—for example, Dunlop Tyres

To differentiate itself, Pilz positions itself to its customers on three core elements, as follows.

- *Total customer orientation*—Pilz lives by and works alongside its customers, and real close customer proximity is evident at all levels and in all areas to instill confidence through individual consultation, flexibility, and reliable service.

- *Technology leadership*—Pilz is a world market leader through technology, oriented towards current market requirements and market leadership in key areas of safe automation, securing its leadership in research and technology.
- *Overall solutions*—Pilz is a solution supplier for safe automation, providing both individual and overall solutions, from innovative products to comprehensive services.

Sources: Anon. (2009b); Falson (2009); http://www.pilz.com

1 What is the purpose of segmentation in B2B or industrial marketing?

2 What criteria or bases does Pilz use to segment its business markets?

3 What are the key elements that Pilz uses to differentiate itself from its competitors?

Customer Characteristics

These factors concern the characteristics of buyers within the organizations that make up a business market. There are a number of criteria that can be used to cluster organizations in this way, including by decision-making unit (DMU), by purchasing strategy, and by relationship type, attitude to risk, choice criteria, and purchase situation.

Decision-Making Unit

An organization's DMU (see Chapter 3) may have specific requirements that influence its purchase decisions in a particular market, such as policy factors, purchasing strategies, a level of importance attached to these types of purchase, or attitudes towards vendors and towards risk. These characteristics may help to segregate groups of organizations for particular marketing programmes.

Some organizations establish policies that govern purchasing decisions. For example, a business may require specific delivery cycles to support manufacturing plans. Increasingly, organizations require that certain quality standards are met by their suppliers and that they are members of particular quality standards organizations (such as the ISO 9000 series).

Segmentation might be based on the closeness and level of interdependence already existing between organizations. Organizational attitude towards risk and the degree to which an organization is willing to experiment through the acquisition of new industrial products can vary. This variance is partly a reflection of the prevailing culture and philosophy, leadership, and managerial style, and can also be used as the basis for segmentation. The starting point of any B2B segmentation is a good database or customer relationship management (CRM) system. It should contain customer addresses, contact details, and detailed purchase and transaction history. Ideally, it will also include the details of those buyers present in the customer company's DMU structure.

Choice Criteria

Business markets can be segmented on the basis of the specifications of proposition that they choose. For example, a computer manufacturer may segment the business market for computers on the basis of those requiring computers with strong graphical capabilities (for example, educational establishments, publishing houses) and computers with strong processing capabilities (such as scientific establishments), or mobile and wireless functionality (perhaps tablets). Companies do not necessarily need to target multiple segments; they might simply target a single segment, as Haagen-Dazs has done in the super-premium ice cream market.

Purchase Situation

There are three questions associated with **purchase situation segmentation** that need to be considered. These are as follows.

1 What is the structure of the buying organization's purchasing procedures? Centralized, decentralized, flexible, or inflexible?

2 What type of buying situation is present? New task (that is, buying for the first time), modified rebuy (that is, not buying for the first time, but buying something with different specifications from previously), or straight rebuy (that is, buying the same thing again)?

3 What stage in the purchase decision process have target organizations reached? Are they buyers in early or late stages, and are they experienced or new?

For example, a large services project management consultancy company such as Serco in the UK might segment the market for project management services into public and private services. The focus might be on fulfilling large government contracts that are put out to tender—that is, when a group of selected buyers are offered the opportunity to bid for an exclusive franchise to deliver agreed services for a defined period of time. The service provider with the best bid is then selected accordingly by the tendering organization, using its own, sometimes secret and unpublished, choice criteria and an exclusive contract is written for the winning supplier.

Typically, in segmenting business markets, a service provider may use a mix of macro- and micro-industrial market segmentation approaches, by defining the customers whom a company wants to target using a macro-approach, such as SIC code or geographic region, and then further segmenting using the choice criteria based on which the customers select a company. In other words, multi-stage market segmentation approaches can be adopted.

■ Target Markets

The second important part of the STP process is to determine which, if any, of the segments uncovered should be targeted and made the focus of a comprehensive marketing programme.

Ultimately, managerial discretion and judgement determines which markets are selected and exploited, and which are ignored. Kotler (1984) suggested that, for market segmentation to be effective, all segments must be:

- *distinct*—that is, each segment must clearly differ from other segments, in which case different marketing mixes will be necessary;
- *accessible*—buyers must be able to be reached through appropriate promotional programmes and distribution channels;
- *measurable*—the segment must be easy to identify and measure; and
- *profitable*—the segment must be sufficiently large to provide a stream of constant future revenues and profits.

This approach to the evaluation of market segments is often referred to by the mnemonic 'DAMP'. Another approach to evaluating market segments uses a rating approach for different segment attractiveness factors, such as market growth, segment profitability, segment size, competitive intensity within the segment, and the cyclical nature of the industry (for example, whether or not the business is seasonal, such as retailing, or dependent on government political cycles, as are some large-scale defence contracts). Each of these segment attractiveness factors is rated on a scale of 0–10 and loosely categorized in the high, medium, or low columns, based on either set criteria or subjective criteria, dependent on the availability of market and customer data and the approach adopted by the managers undertaking the segmentation programme (see Table 6.5).

Other examples of segment attractiveness factors might include segment stability (that is, stability of the segment's needs over time), mission fit (that is, the extent to which dealing

Table 6.5 Examples of segment attractiveness factors

Segment attractiveness factor	Rating		
	High (10–7)	Medium (6–4)	Low (3–0)
Growth	+2.5%	+2.5% to −2.0%	<2.0%
Profitability	>15%	10–15%	<10%
Size	<£5m	£1m–£5m	<£1m
Competitive intensity	Low	Medium	High
Cyclicality	Low	Medium	High

Source: McDonald and Dunbar (2004). Reproduced with permission. © Elsevier.

Table 6.6 Example of a segment attractiveness evaluation matrix

Segment attractiveness factors	Weight	Segment 1		Segment 2		Segment 3	
		Score	Total	Score	Total	Score	Total
Growth	225	2.6	1.55	5	1.25	10	2.5
Profitability	225	2.9	2.25	4	1.05	58	2.0
Size	215	2.6	0.95	5	0.95	57	1.05
Competitive intensity	215	2.5	0.75	6	0.95	56	0.9
Cyclicality	220	2.5	0.55	8	1.65	55	15
Total	100	5.9		5.65		7.45	

Source: McDonald and Dunbar (2004). Reproduced with permission. © Elsevier.

with a particular segment fits the mission of your company, perhaps for political or historical reasons), and a whole host of other possibilities. Once the attractiveness factors have been determined, we can then weight the importance of each factor and rate each segment on each factor using the classifications in Table 6.5. This generates a segment attractiveness evaluation matrix, as shown in Table 6.6.

Decisions need to be made about whether a single product is to be offered to a range of segments, whether a range of products should be offered to multiple segments or a single segment, or whether one product should be offered to a single segment. Whatever the decision, a marketing strategy should be developed to meet the needs of the segment, and to reflect an organization's capability with respect to its competitive strategy and available resources.

Targeting Approaches

Once identified, an organization should select its preferred approach to target marketing. Four differing approaches can be considered (see also Figure 6.7).

- *The* **undifferentiated approach**—There is no delineation between market segments and instead the market is viewed as one mass market with one marketing strategy for the entire market. Although very expensive, this approach is selected in markets in which there is limited segment differentiation. The 2012 Olympics, for example, marketed at a world market or certain government services.

Figure 6.7
Target marketing approaches

- *The* **differentiated targeting strategy**—There are several market segments to target, each being attractive to the marketing organization. To exploit market segments, a marketing strategy is developed for each segment. For example, Hewlett Packard has developed its product range and marketing strategy to target the following user segments of computing equipment: home office users; small and medium-sized businesses; large businesses; and health, education, and government departments. A disadvantage of this approach is the loss of economies of scale resulting from the resources required to meet the needs of many market segments.

- *A* **concentrated marketing strategy**—Where there are only a few market segments, this approach (also known as a **niche marketing strategy**) is often adopted by firms that either have limited resources to fund their marketing strategy or wish to adopt a very exclusive strategy in the market. Aston Martin, the iconic British manufacturer of sports cars, uses this approach to target high net worth individuals interested in stylish, expensive, high-performance cars. This approach is also used by SMEs and micro-sized organizations, mainly as a result of their limited resources. For example, a local plumber may focus on the local residential market.

- *A* **customized targeting strategy**—Marketing strategy is developed for each customer as opposed to each market segment. This approach predominates in B2B markets (for example, marketing research or advertising services) or consumer markets with high-value, highly customized products (such as a custom-made car). For example, a manufacturer of industrial electronics for assembly lines might target and customize its product differently for Nissan, Unilever, and Levi's, given the differing requirements in assembly line processes for the manufacture of automobiles, foodstuffs, and clothing.

■ Segmentation Limitations

Market segmentation is a useful process for organizations to aggregate customer needs into distinct groups, but it has been criticized for the following reasons.

- The process approximates offerings to the needs of customer groups, rather than individuals, so there is a chance that customers' needs are not fully met. **Customer relationship**

marketing processes and software increasingly allow companies to develop customized approaches for individual customers.

- There is insufficient consideration of how market segmentation is linked to competitive advantage (see Hunt and Arnett, 2004). The product differentiation concept is linked to the need to develop competing offerings, but market segmentation does not stress the need to segment on the basis of differentiating the offering from competitors.

- It is unclear how valuable segmentation is to the manager. Suitable processes and models to measure the effectiveness of market segmentation processes are not yet available.

The processes involved in the target marketing process are not as precise as many authors imply. Dibb et al. (2001) suggest that segmentation plans in B2B markets often fail because businesses fail to overcome barriers encountered when implementing their plans, including the following.

- *Infrastructure barriers*—Culture, structure, and the availability of resources may prevent the segmentation process from ever starting. For example, there may be a lack of financial resource or political will to collect the market data necessary for a segmentation programme, or an organizational culture might be rigidly product-oriented.

- *Process issues*—A lack of experience, guidance, and expertise can hamper how segmentation is undertaken and managed. Typically, market research agencies and in-house market research teams use market data and statistical software packages to undertake this task. However, because the different statistical methods provide different results, care must be taken in determining which method to use and how to interpret these results when they are produced.

- *Implementation barriers*—Once a new segmentation model is determined, how do organizations move towards a new segmentation model? This may require a move away from a business model based on products (for example, engine sizes for fleet buyers) towards one based on customer needs. There is frequently insufficient information and practical guidance for managers to enable segmentation strategies successfully (Goller et al., 2002).

■ Positioning

Having segmented the market, determined the size and potential of market segments, and selected specific target markets, the third part of the STP process is to position a brand within the mind of the target market(s). Positioning is the means by which goods and services can be differentiated from one another and so give consumers a reason to buy. It encompasses two fundamental elements. The first concerns the physical attributes, the functionality, and that capability that a brand offers, such as a car's engine specification, its design, and carbon emissions. The second positioning element concerns the way in which a brand is communicated and how consumers perceive the brand relative to other competing brands in the marketplace. This element of communication is vitally important, because it is 'not what you do to a product, it is what you do to the mind of a prospect' (Ries and Trout, 1972) that determines how a brand is really positioned in a market.

Positioning concerns a product's attributes and design—that is, how the product is communicated, and the way in which these elements are fused together in the minds of customers. It is not only the physical nature of the product that is important for positioning and it is not only communication that leads to successful positioning. Claims (through communication) that a shampoo will remove dandruff will be rejected if the product itself fails to deliver. Positioning, therefore, is about how customers judge a product's value relative to competitors, its ability to deliver against the promises made, and the potential that customers have to derive value from the offering. To develop a sustainable position, we must understand the market in which the product is to compete and the way in which other brands are competing.

At a simple level, positioning takes place during the target market selection process. Strategic groups are the various clusters of brands that compete directly against each other. For example, in the car market, Tata, Toyota, and Mercedes each have brands that compete against each other in the high-end luxury car market. This strategic group consists of Jaguar, Lexus, and the Mercedes S-Class, among others. The specification and design of these cars are based on the attributes that customers in this segment deem to be important and for which they are prepared to pay. However, designing a car that includes key attributes alone is not sufficient; successful positioning of each of these car brands is also important in order that customers can perceive how each brand is different and understand the value that each represents.

Key to this process is identifying those attributes considered to be important by consumers. These attributes may be tangible (for example, the gearbox, transmission system, seating, and interior design) and intangible (the reputation, prestige, and allure that a brand generates). By understanding what customers consider to be the ideal standard or level that each attribute needs to attain and how they rate the attributes of each brand in relation to the ideal level, and each other, it becomes possible to see how a brand's attributes can be adapted and communicated to become more competitive.

Perceptual Mapping

Understanding the complexity associated with the different attributes and brands can be made easier by developing a visual representation of each market, known as a 'perceptual map'. These maps are used to determine how various brands are perceived, according to the key attributes that customers value. **Perceptual mapping** therefore represents a geometric comparison of how competing products are perceived (Sinclair and Stalling, 1990).

One thing to note is that the closer products/brands are clustered together on a perceptual map, the greater the competition. The further apart the positions, the greater the opportunity for new brands to enter the market, simply because the competition is less intense. For example, in the UK new car market, there are numerous brands in the marketplace all competing with each other across differing core attributes, such as whether or not the car is needed for business purposes, is needed for carrying more than three people, is needed for carrying large items on a roof rack, or needs a large boot and so on. To show how the differing brands are positioned relative to each other using scores on the above attributes for each car brand, we can measure and map the brand positioning. Figure 6.8 shows the positioning of each of the main car brands in relation to the main product attributes, but also indicates four clusters of car buyers in the UK new car buyers market.

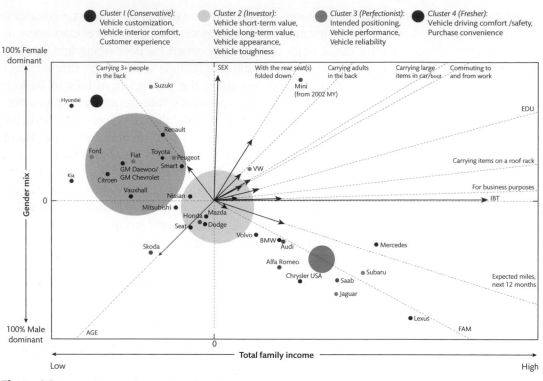

Figure 6.8

Perceptual map for UK new car buyers market

Sources: Leung, K. T. (2010), 'Road vehicle state estimation using low-cost GPS/INS', Unpublished EngD thesis, Cranfield: Cranfield University.

The four clusters are 'conservatives', 'investors', 'perfectionists', and 'freshers'.

- Conservatives buy based on perceptions of vehicle customization, interior comfort, and experience.
- Investors buy based on the value and appearance of the car.
- Perfectionists buy on the basis of perceptions of vehicle performance, reliability, and the company's advertising.
- Freshers buy based on their perceptions of vehicle driving comfort and safety, and purchase convenience.

Figure 6.8 shows us many things. For example, it indicates that women prefer Mini, Suzuki, and Hyundai, whereas men prefer Lexus, Jaguar, and Saab. It also shows us that those on higher family incomes are more likely to prefer Lexus, Mercedes, and Subaru.

Perceptual mapping can provide significant insight into how a market operates. For example, it provides marketers with an insight into how their brands are perceived and it also provides a view about how their competitors' brands are perceived. In addition to this, substitute products can be uncovered based on their closeness to each other (Day et al., 1979). All of the data reveals strengths and weaknesses that, in turn, can assist strategic decisions about how to differentiate on the attributes that matter to customers and how to compete more effectively in the target market. This is the principal value of perceptual mapping.

Positioning and Repositioning

Understanding how brands are positioned provides important inputs not only to the way in which a brand performs, but also to the marketing communications used to support a brand (see Chapters 7 and 10). Through communications, and especially advertising, information can be conveyed about each attribute and, in doing so, can adjust the perceptions that customers have of the brand. Marketing communications can be used in one of two main ways to position brands—namely, to position a brand either functionally or expressively (symbolically), as explained in Table 6.7. Functionally positioned brands emphasize the features and benefits,

Table 6.7 Product positioning strategies

Position	Strategy	Explanation
Functional	Product features	Brand positioned on the basis of the attributes, features, or benefits relative to the competition, e.g. 'Volvos are safe'; 'Weetabix contains all of the vitamins needed for the day'; and 'Red Bull provides energy'.
	Price quality	Price can be a strong communicator of quality, typified by the lager Stella Artois, which is positioned in the UK as 'reassuringly expensive'. A high price can denote high quality; conversely, a low price can also denote low quality.
	Use	By informing when or how a product can be used, we can create a position in the minds of the buyers, e.g. Kellogg's repositions its products to be consumed throughout the day, not only at breakfast; After Eight mint chocolates clearly indicate when they should be eaten.
Expressive	User	By identifying the target user, messages can be communicated clearly to the right audience. So, Flora margarine was for men, and then it became 'for all the family'. Some hotels position themselves as places for weekend breaks, as leisure centres, or as conference centres.
	Benefit	Positions can be established by proclaiming the benefits that usage confers on those that consume. The benefit of using Sensodyne toothpaste is that it enables users to drink hot and cold beverages without the pain associated with sensitive teeth and gums.
	Heritage	Heritage and tradition are sometimes used to symbolize quality, experience, and knowledge. Kronenbourg 1664, 'Established since 1803', and the use of coats of arms by many universities to represent depth of experience are designed to convey trust, permanence, and longevity.

whereas expressive brands emphasize the ego, social, and hedonic satisfactions that a brand can bring. Both approaches make a promise. With regard to haircare, for example, this is a promise to deliver cleaner, shinier, and healthier hair (functional), or hair with which we are confident because we want to be seen and admired, or because it is important that we feel more self-assured (expressive).

Technology, customer tastes, and competitors' new products are some of the reasons why markets change. If the position adopted by a brand is strong, if it was the first to claim the position and the position is being continually reinforced with clear, simple messages, then there may be little need to alter the position originally adopted. However, most marketers need to be alert and be prepared to reposition their brands, because the relative positions occupied by brands, in the minds of customers, will be challenged and shifted around on a frequent basis. However, repositioning is difficult to accomplish, because of the entrenched perceptions and attitudes held by buyers towards brands and the vast (media) resources required to make the changes.

Repositioning is a task that revolves around a product and the way in which it is communicated. The following four ways outline how to approach repositioning a product, depending on the individual situation facing a brand. In some cases, a brand might need to be adapted before relaunch.

1 *Change the tangible attributes and then communicate the new proposition to the same market*—Regent Inns repositioned in 2007, ahead of the UK public smoking restrictions, by moving the focus of bar and restaurant brands such as Walkabout, Jongleurs, and Old Orleans to food rather than drinks, and changing lighting and seating to alter the atmosphere and ambience. The brands' logos were also refreshed (Godsell, 2007).

2 *Change the way in which a product is communicated to the original market*—Vodafone have changed its global positioning in an attempt to throw off its 'stuffy' image. This has involved changing its strap line from 'Power to you' to 'Instant connections', communicating more relational values.

3 *Change the target market and deliver the same product*—On some occasions, repositioning can be achieved through marketing communications alone, but targeted at a new market. For example, Lucozade was repositioned from a drink for sickly children, a niche market with limited volume sales growth, to an energy drink for busy, active, and sports-oriented people, achieved through heavyweight advertising campaigns.

4 *Change both the product (attributes) and the target market*—For example, the Indian company Dabur needed to develop, but had to reposition itself as an FMCG company, rather than retain its earlier position as an Ayurvedic medicine manufacturer. To do this, it had to develop new product offerings and new packaging; it dropped the umbrella branding strategy and adopted an individual branding approach. This was then communicated, using leading Bollywood actors and sports stars, to reach various new markets.

Research Insight 6.2

To take your learning further, you might wish to read the following influential book:

Ries, A. and Trout, J. (2006) *Positioning: The Battle for your Mind*, London: McGraw-Hill Professional.

Al Ries and Jack Trout's book, originally published in 1981, remains the bible of advertising strategy. They define 'positioning' not as what you do to a product to make it acceptable to potential customers, but as what you do to the mind of the prospect. Positioning requires an outside-in rather than an inside-out thinking approach.

Visit the **Online Resource Centre** to read more about the book.

Chapter Summary

To consolidate your learning, the key points from this chapter can be summarized as follows.

- **Describe the principles of market segmentation and the STP process**

  Whole markets are subdivided into different segments through the STP process. STP refers to the three activities that should be undertaken, sequentially, if segmentation is to be successful: segmentation, targeting, and positioning. Market segmentation is the division of a market into different groups of customers with distinctly similar needs and product/service requirements. The second part of the STP process determines which segments should be targeted with a comprehensive marketing programme. The third part of the STP process is to position a brand within the target market(s).

- **Explain the characteristics and differences between market segmentation and product differentiation**

  Market segmentation is related to product differentiation. Given an increasing proliferation of tastes, marketers have sought to design product and service offerings around consumer demand (market segmentation) more than around their own production needs (product differentiation).

- **Explain how market segmentation can be undertaken in both consumer and business-to-business markets**

  Data based on differing consumer, user, organizational, and market characteristics is used to segment a market. These characteristics differ for business-to-consumer (B2C) and business-to-business (B2B) markets. To segment consumer goods and service markets, market information based on certain key customer-related, product-related, or situation-related criteria (variables) is used. These are classified as segmentation bases, and include profile, behavioural, and psychological criteria. To segment business markets, two main groups of interrelated variables are used: organizational characteristics and buyer characteristics.

■ **Describe different targeting strategies**

Once identified, the organization selects its target marketing approach. Four differing approaches exist: undifferentiated (target the entire market with a single strategy); differentiated (target different segments with different strategies); concentrated or niche (target only one segment from many segments); and customized target marketing (target individual customers with individual strategies).

■ **Explain the concept of positioning and illustrate how the use of perceptual maps can assist the positioning process**

Positioning provides the means by which offerings can be differentiated from one another and give customers a reason to buy. It encompasses physical attributes—the functionality and capability that a brand offers, such as a car's engine specification, its design, and carbon emissions—and the way in which a brand is communicated and how customers perceive the brand relative to other competing brands in the marketplace. Perceptual maps are used in the positioning process to illustrate differing attributes of a selection of brands. They also illustrate the existing level of differentiation between brands, provide insight into how our brand and competing brands are perceived in the marketplace and how a market operates, and reveal how to differentiate the attributes that matter to customers in order to compete more effectively in the market.

❓ Review Questions

1 Define market segmentation and explain the STP process.

2 Identify four different ways in which markets can be segmented.

3 How do market segmentation bases differ in business-to-business and consumer markets?

4 What are the different approaches to selecting target markets?

5 Describe the principle of positioning and why it should be undertaken.

 Scan this image to go online and access the chapter's multiple-choice questions, web links, Internet activities, and more!

🗒 Worksheet Summary

Visit the **Online Resource Centre** and complete Worksheet 6.1. This will aid in learning about the STP process used to develop to whom to market, in what way, and while differentiating from the competition.

References

Anon. (2009b) 'What's new in automation?' *Engineer*, 294(7777): 32.

Beane, T. P. and Ennis, D. M. (1987) 'Market segmentation: a review', *European Journal of Marketing*, 21(5): 20–42.

Belk, R. W., Bahn, K. D., and Mayer, R. N. (1982) 'Developmental recognition of consumption symbolism', *Journal of Consumer Research*, 9(June): 4–17.

Bonoma, T. V. and Shapiro, B. P. (1983) *Segmenting the Industrial Market*, Lexington, MA: Lexington Books.

Crittenden, V. L., Crittenden, W. F., and Muzyka, D. F. (2002) 'Segmenting the business-to-business marketplace by product attributes and the decision process', *Journal of Strategic Marketing*, 10: 3–20.

Day, G., Shocker, A. D., and Srivastava, R. K. (1979) 'Customer-orientated approaches to identifying product markets', *Journal of Marketing*, 43(4): 8–19.

Dibb, S., Simpkin, L., Pride, W. M., and Ferrell, D. C. (2001) *Marketing Concepts and Strategies*, Cambridge, MA: Houghton Mifflin.

Falson, S. (2009) 'Safety matters', *Process & Control Engineering (PACE)*, 62(10): 13–15.

Freytag, P. V. and Clarke, A. H. (2001) 'Business to business segmentation', *Industrial Marketing Management*, 30(6): 473–86.

Gavish, Y., Shoham, A., and Ruvio, A. (2011) 'A qualitative study of mother–adolescent daughter–vicarious role model consumption interactions', *Journal of Consumer Marketing*, 27(1): 43–56.

Godsell, M. (2007) 'Branding: Regent Inns rethinks brands', *Marketing*, 25 April, available online at http://www.brandrepublic.com/News/652827/Branding-Regent-Inns-rethinks-brands/ [accessed 3 February 2010].

Goller, S., Hogg, A., and Kalafatis, S. P. (2002) 'A new research agenda for business segmentation', *European Journal of Marketing*, 36(1–2): 252–71.

Green, P. E. (1979) 'A new approach to market segmentation', *Business Horizons*, Feb: 61–73.

Griffith, R. L. and Pol, L. A. (1994) 'Segmenting industrial market', *Industrial Marketing Management*, 23: 39–46.

Holbrook, M. B. and Gardner, M. P. (1993) 'An approach to investigating the emotional determinants of consumption durations: why do people consume what they consume for as long as they consume it?', *Journal of Consumer Psychology*, 2(2): 123–42.

Holbrook, M. B. and Hirschman, E. C. (1982) 'The experiential aspects of consumer behaviour: consumer fantasies, feelings and fun', *Journal of Consumer Research*, 9: 132–40.

Hooley, G. J. and Saunders, J. A. (1993) *Competitive Positioning: The Key to Market Success*, Englewood Cliffs, NJ: Prentice Hall.

Howaldt, K. and Mitchell, A. (2007) 'Can segmentation ever deliver the goods?', *Market Leader*, 36: 54–8.

Hunt, S. D. and Arnett, D. B. (2004) 'Market segmentation strategy, competitive advantage and public policy: grounding segmentation strategy in resource-advantage theory', *Australasian Marketing Journal*, 12(1): 7–25.

Kotler, P. (1984) *Marketing Management*, Int'l edn, Upper Saddle River, NJ: Prentice Hall.

Krauss Whitbourne, S. (2011) 'Resist the temptation to look like your kids', *Psychology Today*, 1 August, available online at http://www.psychologytoday.com/blog/fulfillment-any-age/201108/resist-the-temptation-look-your-kids [accessed 14 November 2011].

Leung, K. T. (2010) 'Road vehicle state estimation using low-cost GPS/INS', Unpublished EngD thesis, Cranfield: Cranfield University.

McAlister, L. and Pessemier, E. (1982) 'Variety-seeking behaviour: an interdisciplinary review', *Journal of Consumer Research*, 9(Dec): 311–22.

McDonald, M. and Dunbar, I. (2004) *Market Segmentation: How to Do It, How to Profit from It*, Oxford: Elsevier.

Naudé, P. and Cheng, L. (2003) 'Choosing between potential friends: market segmentation in a small company', Paper presented at the Nineteenth IMP Conference, 4–6 September, Lugano, Switzerland.

Olney, T. J., Holbrook, M. B., and Batra, R. (1991) 'Consumer response to advertising: the effects of ad content, emotions, and attitude toward the ad on viewing time', *Journal of Consumer Research*, 17(Mar): 440–53.

Ries, A. and Trout, J. (1972) 'The positioning era cometh', *Advertising Age*, 24 April, pp. 35–8.

Ries, A. and Trout, J. (2006) *Positioning: The Battle for your Mind*, London: McGraw-Hill Professional.

Shimp, T. A. (2007) *Integrated Marketing Communications in Advertising and Promotion*, 7th edn, Mason, OH: Thomson South-Western.

Sinclair, S. A. and Stalling, E. C. (1990) 'Perceptual mapping: a tool for industrial marketing—a case study', *Journal of Business and Industrial Marketing*, 5(1): 55–65.

Solomon, M. R. (1983) 'The role of products as social stimuli: a symbolic interactionism perspective', *Journal of Consumer Research Conference*, 10(Dec): 319–29.

Srivastava, R. K., Shocker, A. D., and Day, G. S. (1978) 'An exploratory study of the influences of usage situations on perceptions of product markets', Paper presented at the Advances in Consumer Research Conference, Chicago, IL.

Thompson, C. J., Rindfleisch, A., and Arsel, Z. (2006) 'Emotional branding and the strategic value of the döppelganger brand image', *Journal of Marketing*, 70(Jan): 50–64.

Wind, Y. (1978) 'Issues and advances in segmentation research', *Journal of Marketing Research*, 15(Aug): 317–37.

Wind, Y. and Cardozo, R. N. (1974) 'Industrial market segmentation', *Industrial Marketing Management*, 3: 155–66.

Part 3
The Marketing Mix Principle

Products, Services, and Branding Decisions

- Learning outcomes

After reading this chapter, you will be able to:

- describe the various types and forms of offering, and explain the product life cycle;
- explain the processes and issues associated with the development of new offerings and how they are adopted by markets;
- describe the key principles of branding;
- understand the concepts of brand associations and brand personalities, and
- explain the benefits that branding offers both to customers and to organizations.

Andrew Hicks for 3M

3M is an innovative US$23 billion diversified technology company creating products aiming to make the world healthier, safer, and more productive. Well-known brands include Scotch, Post-it, Scotchgard, Thinsulate, and Scotch-Brite. We speak to Andrew Hicks, European market development manager, to find out how the company developed an innovative, new product, the Visual Attention Service (VAS).

First set up in 1902 and now employing around 75,000 people worldwide, 3M has operations in more than sixty countries. It produces thousands of innovative products for customers and its forty-five technology platforms touch nearly every aspect of modern life. The company has applied its expertise in radio-frequency identification (RFID) technology to deliver biometric passports, its healthcare knowledge to provide hospitals with infection prevention and detection solutions, and, in 2008, it launched the MPro range of pocket projectors.

3M's enduring success is built on constant innovation. To drive this, it invests heavily in research and development (R&D), spending over US$1.4 billion in 2008. It is fundamentally a science-based company, producing thousands of imaginative products, leading in scores of markets—from health care and highway safety to office products and optical films for liquid crystal display (LCD) displays. The company's success begins with our ability to apply our technologies—often in combination—to an endless array of real-world customer needs.

We are organized into seven business divisions: Consumer and Office; Electro and Communications; Health Care; Industrial and Transportation Safety; Security and Protection Services; Optical Systems; and Display and Graphics—this last a world leader in films that brighten the displays on electronic products, such as flat-panel computer monitors, cellular phones, personal digital assistants, and LCD televisions.

The Digital-out-of-Home (DooH) department within Display and Graphics was set up in 2007. It encompasses electronic display technologies, as well as software for content delivery and tools to optimize the performance of advertising messaging. DooH set up what became the 3M Visual Attention Service (3M VAS) to complement this portfolio. The service allows designers of creative messages to assess and optimize their visual impact before committing to production.

Researchers within the traffic safety business of 3M had identified that predictive attention modelling may have a commercial opportunity within the advertising industry. In the feasibility stage, the technical capability, projected costs, and potential market opportunity were assessed to determine whether to proceed with the investment required to bring the concept to market. At this stage, we undertook desk research to determine the distribution of our target market—creative agencies—by size, turnover, and specialization. Primary research with around fifteen agencies helped to determine the value that they would place on such a service and their likely throughput of images. These customers were given access to a beta version of the site to assess how they would use such a system. Combining the data sets allowed an estimate to be made of the potential usage levels. Through ethnographic research, 3M employees work-shadowed designers to understand the creative workflow and to determine where in the process 3M VAS could offer greatest value. This research informed both the market opportunity assessment and the development of the appropriate marketing communications for this audience.

Once we determined that there was a likely market for the product, we looked at the service, the business plan, and the marketing communications plan. We knew that we had to undertake a limited release of the service to allow feedback to be gained from lead users to validate the value and market opportunity. Finally, we undertook a full commercial global launch of the service, backed by advertising and promotional campaigns, and continued customer research to refine the offer.

However, because this was a new-to-the-world service and was also not a direct substitution for an existing service, there was no reference pricing in the marketplace. When potential customers were asked what they were prepared to pay, the value that they perceived varied dramatically depending on the nature of the creative work that the system was being used to assess. For example, the media space costs for a national billboard campaign for a major promotion would cost hundreds of thousands of pounds; anything that could validate the visual effectiveness of the creative design for adverts for this type of campaign, before committing the ads to print, would be extremely valuable to the advertiser. However, the number of campaigns of this type and the quantity of creative designs considered for these campaigns is relatively small. So this would be a high-cost, low-volume model.

On the other hand, thousands of designs are created every day for packaging, advertising and other marketing communications, in which the level of investment and associated risk is much lower. In these cases, 3M VAS would still be of value, but the price that could be charged would be considerably lower—a low-cost, high-volume model.

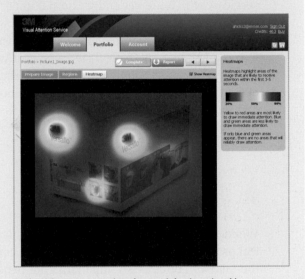

3M's VAS tests promotional material using visual heat maps

1 The question for 3M was therefore: should it launch a low-volume, high-priced product or a high-volume, low-priced product?

■ Introduction

An LG television, a train journey from Barcelona to Bucharest, a cappuccino at Costa Coffee in Adelaide, the *Dagens Nyheter* newspaper in Sweden, a copy of *Vogue* magazine in New York, and a manicure in Rio de Janeiro all have one thing in common: they are all **product** offerings.

The term 'product' in this chapter includes the tangible and intangible attributes related not only to physical goods, but also to services, ideas, people, places, experiences, and even a mix of these various elements. Anything that can be offered for use and consumption, in exchange for money or some other form of value, is referred to as a product (or an 'offering', or 'proposition').

Tangibility refers to an item's ability to be touched and whether it is capable of being stored (see also Chapter 12). For example, a bar of soap, a Rimmel lipstick, or a Vega factory conveyor belt are all tangible offerings capable of being touched and stored. A ferry trip from Sabah to Labuan in Malaysia, or a visit to hairdresser Toni and Guy, cannot be touched and are not capable of being stored. These are intangible products and are referred to as 'services'.

A customer experiences strategy is based on neither brand tangible nor intangible attributes, but refers to the memories and fantasies that individuals retain or imagine, as a result of their interaction with an offering (Tynan and McKechnie, 2009). Memories of experiences related to product usage, events, visits, or activities are internalized, unlike products and services, which are generally external to each person. Indeed, the idea that people consume emotions is emerging as an important and influential aspect of the marketing discipline. For example, the personal memories and fantasies generated as a result of a visit to a theme or leisure park such as Disneyland Paris, PortAventura in Spain, or Space World in Japan can be triggered at some point in the future. Perhaps hearing the brand name, seeing a particular event on film, or even thinking of the location might evoke these brand experiences. Pictures and videos can also be shared with friends and family through social media, which in turn help to reinforce the experience.

◼ Product Forms

When people buy offerings they are not only buying the simple functional aspect that a physical proposition offers; there are also other complexities involved in the purchase. For example, the taste of coffee is an important core benefit arising from the purchase of a jar of instant coffee granules, but in addition people are also attracted to the **packaging**, the price, the strength of the coffee, and also some of the psychosocial associations that we have learnt about a brand. The Cafédirect brand, for example, seeks to help people to understand its ties with the Fairtrade movement and, in doing so, to provide some customers a level of psychosocial satisfaction through their contribution to suppliers in developing countries.

In order to understand these different elements and benefits, we refer to three different product forms: the core, the embodied, and the augmented product forms. These are depicted in Figure 7.1 and further outlined below.

- *The core product*—This consists of the real core benefit or service. This may be a functional benefit in terms of what the product will enable you to do, or it may be an emotional benefit in terms of how the offering will make you feel. Cars provide transportation and a means of self-expression. Cameras make memories by recording a scene, person, or object through the use of digital processes or, originally, film.

- *The embodied product*—This consists of the physical good or delivered service that provides the expected benefit. It consists of many factors, such as the features and capabilities, the durability, design, packaging, and brand name. Cars are supplied with different styles, engines, seats, colours, and boot space, whereas digital cameras are offered with a variety

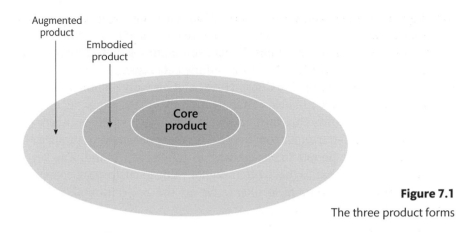

Figure 7.1

The three product forms

of picture qualities, screen sizes, pixels, zoom and telephoto features, editing, and relay facilities.

- *The augmented product*—This consists of the embodied offering plus all of those other factors that are necessary to support the purchase and any post-purchase activities, such as credit and finance, training, delivery, installation, guarantees, and the overall perception of customer service.

When these forms are brought together, it is hoped that they will provide customers with a reason to buy and to keep buying. Each individual combination or bundle of benefits constitutes added value and serves to differentiate one sports car from another sports car, one smartphone from another. Marketing strategies need to be designed around the actual and the augmented products, because it is through these that competition occurs and people are able to understand how one phone differs from another.

Understanding a brand, what it means to its core customers, and their experience of a brand is vitally important. Pepsi's battle with Coca-Cola during the 1960s and 1970s saw it gradually reduce the latter's dominant market share. The battle culminated in 1985 when Coca-Cola abandoned its original recipe and introduced 'new Coke', a sweeter formulation designed to attract Pepsi's young market. Coca-Cola's customers boycotted 'new Coke'; there was public outrage and Pepsi became market leader—but only temporarily. New Coke was soon dropped, and the original brought back and relaunched as 'classic Cola', re-establishing its credentials with its customers and retrieving number one spot in a couple of months. The problem was that Coca-Cola had not appreciated the value that the proposition as a whole represented to its primary customers. The sum of the core, embodied, and augmented product, encapsulated as the brand Coca-Cola, drew passion from its customers and was overlooked by the market researchers when searching for a means to arrest Pepsi's progress.

The development of the Internet and digital technologies has impacted on the nature of the offering and the benefits accruing from its usage. This has opened opportunities for organizations to redefine their core and actual products, often by supplementing them with 'information' about the offering, for example providing white papers or games designed to engage website visitors with the brand. Another approach has been to transform current products into digital form: for example, books onto e-readers, such as Kindle. A further approach is to change the bundle of propositions offered, sometimes achieved by presenting an online catalogue that offers a wider array than the offline catalogue.

Chaffey et al. (2009) refer to Ghosh (1998) and his early identification of the number of ways in which **digital value** can help to augment products. For example, many companies provide evidence of the awards that their products have won, whereas others parade testimonials, endorsements, and customer comments. These are designed to provide credibility, to reduce risk, and to enable people to engage with or purchase a brand. The key contribution of the Internet, in this context, is that it offers digital value to customers, sometimes as a supplement and sometimes as a complete alternative to the conventional, established core product offering.

■ Product Life Cycles

Underpinning the **product life cycle (PLC)** concept is the belief that offerings move through a sequential, predetermined pattern of development similar to the biological path that life forms follow. This pathway, the PLC, consists of five distinct stages—namely, development, introduction, growth, maturity, and decline. Sales and profits rise and fall across the various lifestages of the offering, as shown in Figure 7.2.

Offerings move through an overall cycle of different stages at different speeds. Although the life of a proposition can be extended in many ways, such as introducing new ways of

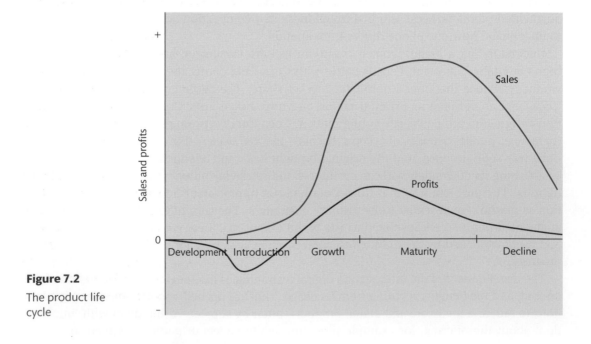

Figure 7.2

The product life cycle

using it, finding new users, and developing new attributes, the majority of products have a finite period during which management needs to maximize its return on the investment. In Sweden, mobile phones have an overall lifespan of between nine and twelve months, so it is important to extend the sales period, especially through maturity. Apple and others do this through 'app stores'. The firm offers existing iPhone customers the possibility of purchasing additional applications and games (Leistén and Nilsson, 2009).

Just as the nature and expectations of customer groups differ at each stage, so do the competitive conditions. This means that different marketing strategies, relating to the offering and its distribution, pricing, and promotion, need to be deployed at particular times so as to maximize the financial return on an offering's entire life.

The PLC does not apply to all offerings in the same way. For example, some offerings reach the end of the introduction stage and then die, as it becomes clear that there is no market to sustain them. Some follow the path into decline and then hang around, sustained by heavy advertising and sales promotions, or they get recycled back into the growth stage by repositioning activities. Others grow really quickly and then fade away rapidly. When Pot Noodle food products were first introduced, demand grew quickly, but then died off steeply at the end of the growth stage. The reason for this was that many people did not like the taste of these early products and so there was limited repeat buying.

When discussing the PLC, care must be taken to clarify what exactly is being described. The PLC concept can apply to class (computers), form (a laptop), or brand (Sony) of offering. The shape of the curve varies, with product classes having the longest cycle, because the mature stage is often extended. Product forms tend to comply most closely with the traditional cycle shape, whereas brand cycles tend to be the shortest. This is because they are subject to competitive forces and sudden change. So whereas hatchback cars (product form) enjoy a long period of success, brands such as the Ford Escort have enjoyed shorter cycles and have been replaced by cars that have more contemporary designs and features (for example, by the Ford Focus).

In principle, the PLC concept allows marketing managers to adapt strategies and tactics to meet the needs of evolving conditions and product circumstances (see Market Insight 7.1). In this sense, it is clear, simple, and predictable. However, in practice, the PLC is of limited use. For example, one problem is identifying which stage an offering has reached in the cycle. Historical sales data do not help managers to identify when an offering moves from one stage to another. This means that it is difficult to forecast sales and hence to determine the future shape of the PLC curve. The concept has also not been adapted for use with service offerings.

Contemporary marketing managers are not concerned with where their brand is within the product life cycle: there are many other more meaningful ways and metrics with which to understand the competitive strength and development of a brand, such as benchmarking. Some brands do not follow the classical S-shaped curve, but rise steeply and then fall away immediately after sales reach a crest. These shapes reflect a consumer fad—a craze for a particular piece of merchandise, typified by fashion clothing, skateboards, and toys such as the Nintendo Wii. So, great care is required when using the PLC, because its roles in commerce and when developing strategy are weak, but it is helpful generally as a way of explaining how brands develop.

PLM Developed Aircraft at Bombardier

Product lifecycle management (PLM) is a strategic approach to the management of product information in order to optimize the returns of a product. Product lifecycle management solutions are a collection of integrated software tools that are used to manage the whole process or single stages of the life cycle, or to connect different tasks. These have evolved to provide a way for all parties involved with different phases of the life cycle to collaborate with one another in order to reduce cycle costs and to reach their markets more quickly. Sometimes referred to as 'collaborative PLM', these systems seek to improve operational performance across the supply chain, from new product design through to decline and retirement.

Bombardier Aerospace is the world's third largest civil aircraft manufacturer, and leader in the design and manufacture of aviation products and services for the business, regional, and amphibious aircraft markets. Based in Montreal, Canada, Bombardier also manufactures other transportation solutions, such as railway and tram systems.

Bombardier's primary point of differentiation is its innovative capacity and that means staying ahead of the competition. Much of Bombardier's success is the result of high levels of efficiency within its design and manufacturing processes.

Bombardier's regional jet, the CRJ1000 NextGen, was designed to achieve two main goals: to provide significant operating cost advantages for clients; and to improve the passenger experience. Yet, to attain these goals and to stay ahead of the competition, Bombardier needed to cut two years from its design-to-manufacture cycle. The company already used PLM tools to streamline its design processes; it needed to use these more quickly and without disrupting its core business activities.

The solution was to outsource all aspects of its PLM systems to a specialist PLM provider (IBM), enabling Bombardier to operate even more effectively and competitively. Some of the benefits included:

- a 40 per cent increase in the efficiency of complex machining processes associated with a new wing design;
- an estimated US$30 million reduction in costs associated with deploying and maintaining PLM over five years;
- a faster time to market; and
- the elimination of the time, effort, and cost of acquiring highly specialized PLM technicians over the multiple phases of a new aircraft programme.

Sources: Based on IBM (2008); http://www.bombardier.com

1 **How would you advise Bombardier on the validity of basing strategy around the product lifecycle concept?**

2 **Identify possible PLM issues associated with building a wind farm installation.**

3 **Identify some of the issues that might arise when outsourcing.**

■ New Product Development

One of the key points that the product lifecycle concept tells us is that offerings do not last forever: their usefulness starts to diminish at some point, and eventually nearly all come to an end and die. One of management's tasks, therefore, is to be able to control the organization's range or portfolio of offerings, and to anticipate when one will become relatively tired, and when new ones are necessary in order to sustain the organization and to help it to grow.

The term 'new' products can be slightly misleading. This is because there can be a range of 'newness', both to an organization and to customers. Some new offerings might be totally new to both the organization and the market: for example, the Dyson vacuum cleaner, with its cyclone technology, revolutionized the market, previously dominated by suction-based vacuum cleaners. However, some products might only be minor adaptations that have no real impact on a market other than offering an interesting new feature, such as new colours, flavours, and pack sizes of product, and electronic facilities on CD players, digital cameras, and mobile personal players. Dyson offers its world-famous vacuum floor cleaners with a ball rather than four fixed wheels, improving manoeuvrability and providing a strong point of differentiation.

'New' offerings have to be considered, planned, developed, and introduced carefully to the market. In order to ensure a stream of new offerings, organizations have three main options:

- buy in finished products from other suppliers, perhaps from other parts of the world, or license their use for specific periods of time;

- develop offerings through collaboration with suppliers or even competitors; or

The Dyson 'bagless' vacuum cleaner revolutionized the market

Source: Dyson

- develop new offerings internally, often through research and development (R&D) departments or through adapting current products through minor design and engineering changes.

Whatever the preferred route, they all necessitate a procedure or development pattern through which they are brought to the market. It would be wrong to suggest that there should be a uniform process (Ozer, 2003), because not only are there many approaches to new product development, but also the procedures adopted by an organization reflect its attitude to risk, its culture, strategy, the product and market, and, above all else, its approach to customer relationships.

The success rate of new products is consistently poor. No more than one in ten new consumer products succeed and there are three main reasons for this, according to Drucker (1985).

1 There is no market for the product.

2 There is a market need, but the product does not meet customer requirements.

3 The product's ability to meet the market need, although satisfactory, is not adequately communicated to the target market.

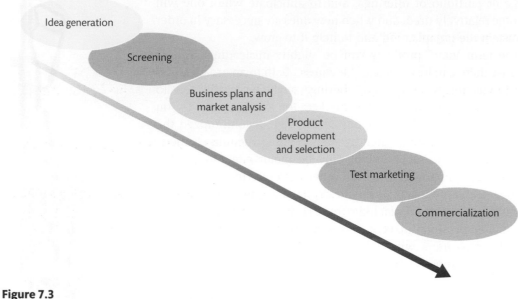

Figure 7.3

Stages within the new product development process

Successful new products are developed partly by understanding the market and partly by developing technology to meet the identified needs. Energizer batteries demonstrate this orientation with their 15-minute charger. The charger was designed to meet the needs of people who want batteries to cope with the demands of high-draining products, such as digital cameras, and who also want to reduce the recharge time. Advances in technology enabled Energizer to make its batteries last four times as long as alkaline batteries and it reduced the recharge time from eight hours to just 15 minutes (Tiltman, 2006).

The development of new products is complex and high risk, so organizations usually adopt a procedural approach. The procedure consists of several phases that enable progress to be monitored, test trials to be conducted, and the results analysed before there is any commitment to the market. The most common general new product development process (NPDP) is set out in Figure 7.3.

The NPDP presented here should be considered as a generalization and it should be understood that the various phases or episodes do not always occur in the linear sequence shown. Actions can overlap or even occur completely out of sequence, depending on the speed, complexity, and number of people or organizations involved in the NPDP. Apart from some minor issues, the process is essentially the same when developing new products for both consumer and business markets.

go online

Visit the **Online Resource Centre** and follow the web link to the Product Development and Management Association (PDMA), to learn more about the professional development, information, collaboration, and promotion of new product development and management.

Research Insight 7.1

To take your learning further, you might wish to read the following influential paper:

Kohler, T., Matzler, K., and Füller, J. (2009) 'Avatar-based innovation: using virtual worlds for real-world innovation', *Technovation*, 29(6/7): 395–407.

This interesting and topical paper considers the development of new products and services using the virtual world as the source of ideas. The paper demonstrates real cases demonstrating how, through the integration of user-generated content within various virtual worlds and an interactive new product development process, companies can tap into customers' innovative potential using the latest technology.

Visit the **Online Resource Centre** to read the abstract and to access the full paper.

Idea Generation

Ideas can be generated through customers (see Market Insight 7.2), competitors (through websites and sales literature analysis), market research data (such as reports), R&D departments, customer service employees, the sales force, project development teams, and secondary data sources such as sales records. What this means is that organizations should foster a corporate culture that encourages creativity and supports people when they bring forward new ideas for product enhancements and other improvements.

Screening

All ideas need to be assessed so that only those that meet predetermined criteria are taken forward. Key criteria include the fit between the proposed new product idea and the overall corporate strategy and objectives. Another involves the views of customers, undertaken using concept testing. Other approaches consider how the market will react to the idea and what effort the organization will need to make if the product is to be brought to the market successfully. Whatever approaches are used, screening must be a separate activity from the idea generation stage. If it is not, then creativity might be impaired.

Business Planning and Market Analysis

The development of a business plan is crucial, simply because it will indicate the potential and relative profitability of the product. In order to prepare the plan, important information about the size, shape, and dynamics of the market needs to be determined. The resultant profitability forecasts will be significant in determining how and when the product will be developed, if at all.

Product Development and Selection

In many organizations, several product ideas are considered simultaneously. It is management's task to select those that have commercial potential, and which are in the best interests of the organization and its longer-term strategy, goals, and use of resources. There is a trade-off between the need to test and reduce risk, and the need to go to market and drive income and get a return on the investment committed to the new product. This phase is expensive, so only a limited number of projects are allowed to proceed into development. Those projects that are selected for further development have prototypes and test versions developed. These are then subjected to functional performance tests, design revisions, manufacturing requirements analysis, distribution analysis, and a multitude of other testing procedures.

Test Marketing

Before committing a new product to a market, most organizations decide to test market the finished product. By piloting and testing the product under controlled, real market conditions, many of the genuine issues, as perceived by customers, can be raised and resolved, while minimizing any damage or risk to the organization and the brand. **Test marketing** can be undertaken using a particular geographical region or specific number of customer locations. The intention is to evaluate the product and the whole marketing programme under real working conditions. Test marketing, or field trialling, enables the product and marketing plan to be refined or adapted in the light of market reaction, yet before release to the whole market.

Commercialization

To commercialize a new product, a launch plan is required. This considers the needs of **distributors**, end-user customers, marketing communication agencies, and other relevant stakeholders. The objective is to schedule all those activities that are required to make the launch successful. These include communications (to inform audiences of the product's capabilities, and to position and persuade potential customers), training, and product support for all customer-facing employees.

Any perceived rigidity in this formal process should be ignored. Many new products come to market via rather different routes, at different speeds and with different levels of preparation. For example, LG's product development is closely aligned with its market research. LG found that people wanted to get their washing done in one go at the weekend, that they were concerned about the environment, and that they had little or no experience of, or desire to do, ironing. This led to the development of LG's steam washing machine. This has a large capacity drum and uses steam rather than water (as in conventional washing machines), which is good for the environment. Steam also means fewer wrinkles, so less ironing (Barda, 2009).

Network Co-Creation at Boeing

Following extensive customer research, Boeing announced on 29 March 2001 that it was to build a radically different mid-sized aircraft. Called the 'Sonic Cruiser', it offered an entirely new concept, using a delta-wing design and a range of other leading-edge technologies. The new plane would offer a 15–20 per cent increase in speed and an increased range, cutting up to three hours from ultra-long-haul routes. Throughout the concept development stages of the Sonic Cruiser, Boeing had engaged customers with its 'Working together' programme in order to define its final design characteristics.

The impact of the 9/11 attacks and the rapidly rising cost of oil had a profound impact on the airline environment, refocusing attention on efficiency and cost management in the struggle to survive. As a result, the Sonic Cruiser was officially 'shelved' two months later.

For most international airlines, the key buying criteria became efficiency, cost management, and environmental impact. There was also a real interest in working collaboratively with aircraft manufacturers such as Boeing and Airbus. As a result, in December 2002, Boeing announced the 'Dreamliner', an entirely different aircraft and value proposition from the Sonic Cruiser.

The new airplane was traditionally shaped, but designed to save airlines money. Indeed, the project was originally designated as the 7E7 ('E' for efficiency), although this was changed in 2005 to 787. Designed to use up to 20 per cent less fuel and to have an increased range, the 787 contrasted vividly with its competitor the Airbus A380. With rising fuel prices, the 787 would make huge fuel savings for airlines, especially because it is the first airliner to be built of carbon-reinforced plastic, not metal.

Based on the evident value created by early customer involvement in the Sonic Cruiser development, Boeing's innovation teams wanted to engage key customers and suppliers much earlier in the innovation cycle and with greater formality, so that they could contribute to the development and production of a more efficient aircraft. Crowdsourcing was an integral part of the project development process. 'Crowdsourcing' is a term given to the process whereby organizations deliberately invite the web community to suggest material that can be used commercially. (The difference between crowdsourcing and outsourcing is that the latter is directed at a predetermined, specific organization.)

Both customers and suppliers were involved in the Boeing 787 process. Nearly fifty of the best-in-class global suppliers were involved, with most very keen to help Boeing in the co-production of prototypes. They were also prepared to invest, collaborate, and provide resources right through to the eventual commercial production of the aircraft. The production system requires the complete participation of all subcontractors, which has set new industry standards in operations management in co-creation and co-production. Following the customers' demands to reduce operating costs, Boeing has managed to reduce predicted maintenance costs by about 30 per cent through the use of composite materials.

In 2006, Boeing launched a dedicated website, http://www.newairplane.com, to present the aircraft and to invite people to join the world design team. Since January 2005, Randy Baseliner, marketing vice president of Boeing, made weekly entries in his blog, detailing and explaining the Boeing initiatives and experiences to businesses and consumers, answering questions from the 16,000 people who visit each month, and encouraging bloggers to suggest new ideas. Boeing also supplies information to other blogs, provoking interest and providing transparency specifically for the 787 Dreamliner brand and for Boeing generally as a corporation.

However, despite the collaborative emphasis, there were problems in the supply chain, which led to a series of expensive delays, and the project stalled in 2007. Once these were overcome, there were issues concerning the design of the wing-joint assembly, which again delayed development.

The first test flight, in December 2009, was delayed over two years and the Dreamliner's first passenger flight took place in October 2011. This was a Nippon Airways four-and-a-half-hour flight from Tokyo to Hong Kong. There are orders for over 850 Boeing 787s.

Sources: Knox et al. (2007); Gates (2009); Jack (2011)

1 To what extent does the active involvement of customers and suppliers in the development process improve the project outcomes?

2 Outline three advantages of involving customers in the development of the project.

3 In what phases of the NPD process do you think co-creation can take place and why?

New Service Development

So far, the main focus of this chapter has been on the processes associated with developing new physical product offerings, without reference to services. This is partly because researchers have given much more attention to the development issues arising with products and they perceive the development of new services as either problematic or very similar to that of products. This has changed in recent years, as many Western economies have become increasingly service-oriented.

Of the few researchers in this area, Möller et al. (2008), developed ideas based on the logic that value creation is the key to the development of innovative service offerings and concepts. They distinguish three service innovation strategies: established services within competitive markets; incremental service innovation targeting value-added offerings; and radical service innovation, which aims to produce completely novel offerings.

Established services with a relatively stable value creation process are often generated under intense competitive behaviour in order to improve operational efficiency. Dell is cited as a business based on a simple concept—namely, selling computer systems direct to customers. Dell's market leadership is the result of a constant focus on delivering positive product and service experiences to customers.

Incremental service innovation describes a value creation strategy in which services are developed to provide extra value. Working together, the service provider and client can produce more effective solutions. The prime example is Google, which, in addition to providing Internet search services for individual consumers, provides search services for corporate clients, including advertisers, content publishers, and site managers. Google continually develops new service applications based on its back-end technology and the use of linked PCs that respond immediately to each query. Google's innovation has resulted in faster response times, greater scalability, and lower costs.

Radical service innovation is concerned with value creation generated through novel or unusual service concepts. This requires new technologies, offerings, or business concepts, and involves radical system-wide changes in existing value systems. MySQL, the world's leading open-source database software producer, uses this approach. By making the source code of the software freely available to everybody, the software is available to everyone to use and/or modify. However, all derivative works must be made available to the original developers. As a result, MySQL has been able to increase the number of users and developers, and subsequently offer its clients improved levels of service. This has led to increased financial performance.

Stages of Product/Service Innovation Development

It is helpful to view service innovation in the light of the product–service spectrum introduced at the start of this chapter (see also Chapter 12). Services do not always need to be seen only as an extension or add-on to a product offering; they can be a way of creating value opportunities for clients. Shelton (2009) considers service innovation in the context of four stages of solution management maturity. The early stages of innovation maturity are characterized by a product focus with a relatively small amount of services used only to augment and complement the products. The mature stages are characterized by much higher levels of service, some integrated with the products to provide solutions for customer problems.

- *Stage 1*—In this stage, services are used as after-sales product support, such as parts and repair services. Service innovation is framed around maintaining the product and ensuring that customers are satisfied with their product purchase. As a result, customers typically view the service and product business as distinct entities.

- *Stage 2*—This stage is characterized by after-sales services designed to complement the core product. Here, services should improve customer satisfaction with existing products, increase loyalty, and may generate additional purchases. Sheldon refers to Hewlett-Packard's 'PC Tune-Up', which, for a fee, provides a set of diagnostics to assess and manage customers.

- *Stage 3*—At this stage, the portfolio includes a full line of services and products designed to provide a clearly differentiated offering aimed at solving clients' lifecycle problems. Sheldon refers to Motorola's 'Total Network Care' (TNC), which provides end-to-end support services for wireless networks. Although the service organization is often consolidated into one identifiable business, products are still core to the company. End-user customers see no major perceived boundaries between products and services.

- *Stage 4*—At this, the highest end of innovation maturity, firms seek to integrate the services dimension as part of their total offer. Known as 'servitization', this involves the provision of an integrated bundle of product/service solutions for the entire life cycle of their customers, 'from cradle to grave'. These solutions are developed collaboratively with clients and therefore require a deep understanding of the customer's overall business. These firms, often market leaders, generate innovative solutions through buyer–seller collaborative processes. Solutions are developed that are of mutual value.

The Process of Adoption

The process by which individuals accept and use new products is referred to as 'adoption' (Rogers, 1983). The different stages in the **adoption process** are sequential and are characterized by

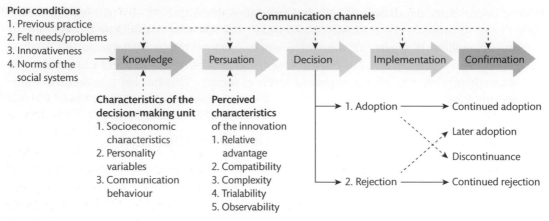

Figure 7.4

Stages in the innovation decision process of adoption

Source: Reprinted from Rogers (1983) with the permission of the Free Press. © 1962, 1971, 1983 by the Free Press.

the different factors that are involved at each stage (for example, the media used by each individual). The process starts with people gaining awareness of a product and moves through various stages of adoption before a purchase is eventually made. Figure 7.4 sets out the various stages in the process of adoption.

- In the *knowledge* stage, consumers become aware of the new product. They have little information and have yet to develop any particular attitudes towards the product. Indeed, at this stage, consumers are not interested in finding out any more information.

- The *persuasion* stage is characterized by consumers becoming aware that the innovation may be of use in solving a potential problem. Consumers become sufficiently motivated to find out more about the product's characteristics, including its features, price, and availability.

- In the *decision* stage, individuals develop an attitude toward the offering and they reach a decision about whether the innovation will meet their needs. If this is positive, they will go on to try the innovation.

- During the *implementation* stage, the innovation is tried for the first time. Sales promotions are often used as samples to allow individuals to test the product without any undue risk. Individuals accept or reject an innovation on the basis of their experience of the trial. Consider, for example, the way in which supermarkets use sampling to encourage people to try new food and drink products.

- The final *confirmation* stage is signalled when an individual successfully adopts the offering on a regular purchase basis without the help of the sales promotion or other incentives.

This model assumes that the adoption stages occur in a predictable sequence, but this cannot always be assumed to be the case. Rejection of the innovation can occur at any point, even during implementation and the very early phases of the confirmation stage. Generally, mass communications are going to be more effective in the earlier phases of the adoption process for products in which buyers are actively interested, and more interpersonal forms are more appropriate at the later stages, especially implementation and confirmation.

Diffusion Theory

Although we know that consumers may buy using both functional and emotional motives when purchasing, customers adopt new offerings at different speeds or timescales because they possess different attitudes to risk, and have differing levels of education, experience, and needs. The rate at which a market adopts an innovation is referred to as the 'process of **diffusion**' (Rogers, 1962).

According to Rogers, there are five categories of adopter, as shown in Figure 7.5.

- **Innovators**—This group, which constitutes 2.5 per cent of the buying population, is important because they have to kick-start the adoption process. These people like new ideas, and are often well educated, young, confident, and financially strong. This means that they are more likely to take risks associated with new offerings. Being an innovator in one product category, such as photography, does not mean a person will be an innovator in other categories. Innovative attitudes and behaviour can be specific to only one or two areas of interest.

- **Early adopters**—This group, comprising 13.5 per cent of the market, are characterized by a high percentage of opinion leaders. These people are very important for speeding up the adoption process. Consequently, marketing communications need to be targeted at these people, who, in turn, will stimulate word-of-mouth communications to spread information. Although early adopters prefer to let innovators take all of the risks, they enjoy being at the leading edge of innovation, tend to be younger than any other group, and are above average in education. Other than innovators, this group reads more publications and consults more salespeople than all of the others.

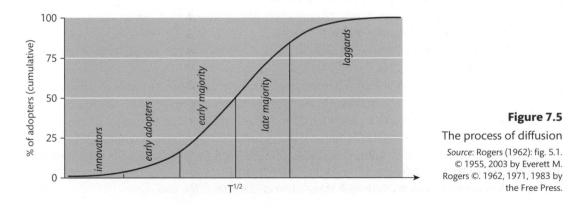

Figure 7.5

The process of diffusion

Source: Rogers (1962): fig. 5.1.
© 1955, 2003 by Everett M. Rogers ©. 1962, 1971, 1983 by the Free Press.

- **Early majority**—This group, which forms 34 per cent of the market, is more risk-averse than the previous two groups. This group requires reassurance that the offering works and has been proven in the market. They are above average in terms of age, education, social status, and income. Unlike the early adopters, they tend to wait for prices to fall and prefer more informal sources of information, and are often prompted into purchase by other people who have already purchased.

- **Late majority**—A similar size to the previous group, the late majority are sceptical of new ideas and adopt new offerings only because of social or economic factors. They read few publications and are below average in terms of education, social status, and income.

- **Laggards**—This group of people, comprising 16 per cent of the buying population, are suspicious of all new ideas and their opinions are very hard to change. Of all of the groups, laggards have the lowest income, social status, and education, and take a long time to adopt an innovation, if they ever adopt it at all.

The rate of diffusion, according to Gatignon and Robertson (1985), is a function of the speed at which sales occur, the pattern of diffusion (as expressed in the shape of the curve), and the size of the market. This means that diffusion does not occur at a constant or predictable speed: it may be fast or slow. One of the tasks of marketing communications is to speed up the process so that the return on the investment necessary to develop the innovation is achieved as quickly and as efficiently as possible.

Marketing managers need to ensure that these variables are considered when attempting to understand and predict the diffusion process. However, it is likely that a promotional campaign targeted at innovators and the early majority, and geared to stimulating word-of-mouth communications, will be more successful than if these variables are ignored.

The marketing challenge is to identify these important groups of people. Increasingly, companies are using word-of-mouth marketing techniques to promote goods and services, particularly through blogs and websites, in which instances a selection of consumers are provided with free samples and asked to write about their experiences. For example, to help to break the dominance of Samsung and LG in Korea, Electrolux identified forty influential Korean mothers, and asked them to test its brand and to then give feedback via an online retailer. To encourage trial and word-of-mouth communication, these influencers held a 'Home Show for Electrolux' with their friends. After trying it in their homes, their feedback was channelled through a home user test report (WOMMA, 2011).

■ Branding

Branding is a process by which manufacturers and retailers help to customers to differentiate between various offerings in a market. It enables customers to make associations between certain attributes or feelings and a particular brand. If this differentiation can be achieved and sustained, then a brand is considered to have a competitive advantage. It is not necessary for people to buy brands in order to enjoy and understand them. Successful brands create strong, positive, and lasting impressions through their communications, and associated psychological feelings and emotions, not only their functionality through use.

KFC's iconic 'Colonel Sanders' logo gives the restaurant a friendly face
Source: © KFC

Brand names provide information about content, taste, durability, quality, price, and performance, without requiring the buyer to undertake time-consuming comparison tests with similar offerings or other risk-reduction approaches to purchase decisions. In some categories, brands can be developed through the use of messages that are entirely emotional or image-based. Many of the 'products' in fast-moving consumer goods (FMCG) sectors, in which there is low customer involvement, use communications based largely on imagery. Other sectors, such as cars or pharmaceuticals, in which involvement tends to be high, require rational information-based messages supported by image-based messages (Boehringer, 1996). In other words, a blend of messages may well be required to achieve the objectives and goals of the campaign.

What is a Brand?

Brands are products and services that have added value. This value has been deliberately designed and presented by marketing managers in an attempt to augment their offerings with values and associations that are recognized by, and are meaningful to, their customers. Although marketing managers have to create, sustain, protect, and develop the identity of the brands for which they are responsible, it is customer perception—the images that they form of these brands, and the meaning and value that customers give to the brand—that is important. Both managers and customers are involved in the branding process.

De Chernatony and Dall'Olmo Riley (1998) identified twelve types of brand definition, but one of the commoner interpretations is that a brand is represented by a name, symbol, words, or mark that identifies and distinguishes a product or company from its competitors. However, brands consist of much more than these various elements. Brands have character—even personalities—and, in order to develop character, it is important to understand that brands are constructed of two main types of attribute: intrinsic and extrinsic.

Intrinsic attributes refer to the functional characteristics of a product, such as its shape, performance, and physical capacity. If any of these intrinsic attributes were to change, this would directly alter the product. Extrinsic attributes refer to those elements that are not intrinsic, and which, if changed, do not alter the material functioning and performance of the product itself. These include devices such as the brand name, marketing communications, packaging, price, and mechanisms that enable consumers to form associations that give meaning to the brand. Buyers often use the extrinsic attributes to help them to distinguish one brand from another, because, in certain categories, it is difficult for them to make decisions based on the intrinsic attributes alone.

Why Brand?

Brands represent opportunities for both consumers and organizations (manufacturers and retailers) to buy and to sell products and services easily, more efficiently, and relatively quickly. We will now consider the benefits from each perspective.

Consumers like brands because they:

- help people to identify their preferred products;
- reduce levels of perceived risk and, in doing so, improve the quality of the shopping experience;
- help people to gauge the level of product quality;
- reduce the amount of time spent making product-based decisions and, in turn, decrease the time spent shopping;
- provide psychological reassurance or reward, especially for products bought on an occasional basis; and
- inform consumers about the source of a product (country or company).

Branding helps customers to identify the products and services that they prefer to use in order to satisfy their needs and wants. Equally, branding helps them to avoid the brands that they dislike as a result of previous use or because of other image, associations, or other psychological reasoning.

Consumers experience a range of perceived risks when buying different products. These might be financial risks ('Can I afford this?'), social risks ('What will other people think about me wearing this dress or going to this bar?'), or functional risks ('Will this MP3 player work?'). Branding helps to reduce these risks so that buyers can proceed with a purchase without fear or uncertainty. Strong brands encapsulate a range of values that communicate safety and purchase security.

In markets unknown to a buyer or in which there is technical complexity (for example, computing, financial services), consumers use branding to make judgements about the quality of a product. This, in turn, helps consumers to save shopping time and again helps to reduce the amount of risk that they experience.

Perhaps above all other factors, branding helps consumers to develop relationships based on trust. Strong brands are normally well trusted and annual surveys often announce that Nokia, Google, and Kellogg's are some of the most trusted brands. Similarly, these surveys declare those brands that are least trusted by consumers, and very often these coincide with falling sales and reducing market share. Creating trust is important, because it enables consumers to buy with confidence.

Nokia smartphones compete in a tough market in which consumer trust and loyalty ring up profits
Source: Nokia

Many brands are deliberately imbued with human characteristics, to the point at which they are identified as having particular personalities. These **brand personalities** might be based around being seen as friendly, approachable, distant, aloof, calculating, honest, fun, or even robust or caring. Marketing communications play an important role in communicating the essence of a brand's personality. By developing positive emotional links with a brand, consumers can find reassurance through their brand purchases.

Manufacturers and retailers enjoy brands because they:

- enable premium pricing;
- help to differentiate the product from competitive offerings;
- encourage cross-selling to other brands owned by the manufacturer;
- develop customer loyalty/retention and repeat-purchase buyer behaviour;
- assist the development and use of integrated marketing communications;
- contribute to corporate identity programmes; and
- provide some legal protection.

Branding is an important way in which manufacturers can differentiate their brands in crowded marketplaces. This, in turn, enables buyers to recognize the brand quickly and to make fast, unhindered purchase decisions. One of the brand-owner's goals is to create strong brand loyalty to the extent that customers always seek out the brand, and become better prepared to accept cross-product promotions and **brand extensions**.

Perhaps one of the strongest motivations for branding is that it can allow manufacturers to set premium prices. Brands such as Andrex, Stella Artois, and L'Oréal charge a premium price—often around 20 per cent higher than the average price in their respective product categories. Premium prices allow brand managers to reinvest in brand development and, in some markets, this is important in order to remain competitive. However, it should not be assumed that the establishment of a brand will lead to automatic success. Many brands fail, sometimes because a firm fails to invest in a brand at the level required, or because management have not recognized or accepted the need to change, adapt, or reposition their brands as market preferences have moved on.

The greater the number of product-based brands, the greater the motivation for an organization to want to develop a corporate brand. Using this umbrella branding approach, organizations need invest heavily in only one brand, rather than in each and every product-based brand. This approach is not applicable to all sectors, although in business-to-business (B2B) markets in which there is product complexity, corporate branding is an effective way of communicating and focusing on a few core brand values.

Brand Associations and Personalities

As suggested earlier, brands are capable of triggering associations in the minds of consumers and these need not be based solely on a utilitarian or functional approach. These **brand associations** may sometimes enable consumers to construe a psychosocial meaning associated with a particular brand. The idea that consumers might search for brands with a personality that complements their self-concept is not new, as identified by McCracken (1986). Belk (1988) suggested that brands offer a means of self-expression, whether this is in terms of who they want to be (the 'desired self'), who they strive to be (the 'ideal self'), or who they think they should be (the 'ought self'). Brands therefore provide a means for individuals to indicate to others their preferred personality, as they relate to these 'self' concepts.

This emotional and symbolic approach is intended to provide consumers with additional reasons to engage with a brand, beyond the normal functional characteristics that a brand offers (Keller, 1998), which are so easily copied by competitors. Aaker (1997) refers to brand personality as the set of human characteristics that consumers associate with a brand. She developed the Brand Personality Scale, which consists of five main dimensions of psychosocial meaning, subsuming forty-two personality traits. These five dimensions are: sincerity (wholesome, honest, down-to-earth); excitement (exciting, imaginative, daring); competence (intelligent, confident); sophistication (charming, glamorous, smooth); and ruggedness (strong, masculine). These are depicted in Figure 7.6.

Aaker's initial research was conducted in the mid-1990s and revealed that, in the US, MTV was perceived to be best at excitement, CNN on competence, Levi's on ruggedness, Revlon on sophistication, and Campbell's on sincerity.

These psychosocial dimensions have subsequently become enshrined as dimensions of brand personality. Aaker developed a five-point framework around these dimensions in order to provide a consistent means of measurement. The framework has been used frequently and cited many times by both academics and marketing practitioners. For example, Arora and Stoner (2009) report that various studies have found that consumers choose offerings that they feel possess personalities similar to their own (Linville and Carlston, 1994; Phau and Lau, 2001). They prefer brands that project a personality that is consistent with their self-concepts. As Arora and Stoner (2009: 273) indicate, 'brand personality provides a form of identity for consumers that express symbolic meaning for themselves and for others'. Brand personality can therefore be construed as a means of creating and maintaining consumer loyalty, if only because this aspect is difficult for competitors to copy (see Market Insight 7.3).

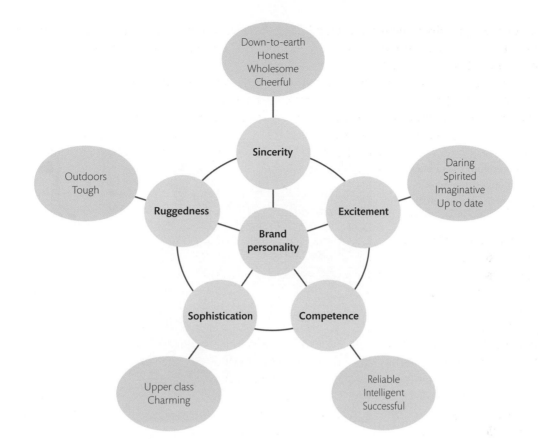

Figure 7.6

Five dimensions of psychosocial meaning

Source: Adapted from Aaker (1997)

Customers assign a level of trust to the brands that they encounter. Preferred brands signify a high level of trust and indicate that the brand promise is delivered. Marketing managers therefore need to ensure that they do not harm or reduce the perceived levels of trust in their brands. Indeed, actions should be taken to enhance trust. One way of achieving this is to use labels and logos to represent a brand's values, associations, and source. For example, all Apple products are signified, and identified by, the image of the fruit with a bite removed. Similarly, all UK meat products carry a red tractor symbol, which, according to the National Farmers Union (NFU), indicates that the meat was produced to exacting standards of food safety, kindness to animals, and environmental protection. This is intended to reassure customers about the origin and quality of the meat. A more recent symbol is that of a footprint, which refers to the carbon dioxide associated with the production and transportation of a brand. This emerged because some brands wanted a means of demonstrating the carbon savings that they had made in their supply chains. Walkers Crisps and then Tesco were the first brands to use the symbol. However, as Charles (2009) points out, one of the issues arising from the use of the carbon footprint symbol is that consumers do not understand what the figures mean. This will take time, just as the Fairtrade brand was not established overnight.

A Finnish Association with Purity

Finlandia, a premium vodka brand, targeted at younger, upmarket drinkers, was built around functional associations with the clean, clear natural environment of Finland. In an attempt to raise awareness of the brand, a campaign called 'Pure Emotion' was launched. The strategy was to be achieved by shifting the brand association to one that engaged the target consumers emotionally. The campaign was made with the support of *The Independent* newspaper, itself a source of emotion, often depicted through travel, music, and sport.

The promotion launched with advertorial content in the newspaper's *Traveller* and *Independent* magazines. Teaser ads placed on the sports pages drove readers to the promotion, online at a co-branded microsite created at http://www.independent.co.uk. This was aimed at encouraging readers/users to share videos, photos, and stories of their own 'Pure Emotion' experiences.

The microsite included three 'Pure Emotion' features, with people talking about their own emotional highs and lows in music, travel, and sport. There were also three 'user-generated Pure Emotion' galleries, featuring stories, pictures, and video from http://www.independent.co.uk users, all about emotional moments from their lives. An online competition, based around the users' uploaded Pure Emotion content, attracted 1,213 competition entries. The microsite also featured a Finlandia advertorial and a gallery of twenty front pages of *The Independent* from the past year, underlining the emotional power of newspapers.

Text links to 'Pure Emotion' were included in *The Independent*'s daily email newsletter to 80,000 subscribers

The winning photo, Finlandia's pure emotion competition

Source: Courtesy of Brown-Forman Beverages, Europe, Ltd.

and a marketing email to a 20,000-strong database. *The Independent*'s campaign was tied in with the Finlandia Vodka Pure Emotion Exhibition at Camden's Proud Gallery, showing real people's pure emotions in their own words through stories, images, and video clips. The brand also focused on its natural purity in an advertising takeover of Euston train station.

Source: Anon. (2009)

1 **Which other brands might you suggest focus on an emotional approach? Are they successful, and why?**

2 **It is argued that customers buy brands with a personality that reflects their own personalities. Name three brands that you purchase regularly. How do these reflect your personality?**

3 **Consider the personality of a brand of your choice and suggest how you might change or improve it.**

Types of Brand

There are three main types of brand: manufacturer, distributor, and generic.

Manufacturer Brands

In many markets, and especially the FMCG sector, retailers are able to influence the way in which a product is displayed and presented to customers. As a result, manufacturers try to create brand recognition and name recall through their direct marketing communications activities with end users. The goal is to help customers to identify the producer of a particular brand at the point of purchase (POP). For example, Persil, Cloetta (a Nordic chocolate and confectionery producer), Heinz, Simplot (a large private US food company), Cadbury, and Coca-Cola are strong manufacturers' brands; they are promoted heavily, and customers develop preferences based on performance, experience, communications, and availability. So, when customers are shopping, they use the images that they have of various manufacturers, combined with their own experiences, to seek out their preferred brands. Retailers that choose not to stock certain major **manufacturer brands** run the risk of losing customers.

Research Insight 7.2

To take your learning further, you might wish to read the following influential paper:

Pennington, J. R. and Ball, A. D. (2009) 'Customer branding of commodity products: The customer-developed brand', *Brand Management*, 16(7): 455–67.

In an age during which co-creation issues are prevalent, this paper provides a useful perspective on customer branding. The paper considers the process and implications of customer branding of commodity products. The authors provide numerous examples and the paper serves to counterbalance the predominantly management perspective of branding.

@ Visit the **Online Resource Centre** to read the abstract and to access the full paper.

Distributor (or Own-Label) Brands

The various organizations that make up the marketing channel often choose to create a distinct identity for themselves. The term **distributor brand**, or 'own-label brand', refers to the identities and images developed by the wholesalers, distributors, dealers, and retailers who make up the marketing channel. Wholesalers, such as Nurdin & Peacock, Alibaba, and Joosten & Bohm BV, and retailers, such as Argos, Harvey Nichols, Carrefour, Sainsbury's, IKEA, and Monsoon, have all created strong own label brands. Tesco's own-label brands Tesco Value and Tesco Finest are the largest food brands in the UK, both worth more than £1 billion, making them larger than Walker's Crisps and Coca-Cola (Berg, 2011).

This brand strategy offers many advantages to both the manufacturer, who can use excess capacity, and retailers, who can earn a higher margin than they can with manufacturers' branded goods and at the same time develop strong store images. Retailers have the additional cost of promotional initiatives, necessary in the absence of a manufacturer's support. Some manufacturers, such as Kellogg's, refuse to make products for distributors to brand, although others (Cereal Partners) are happy to supply a variety of competitors.

Occasionally, conflict emerges—especially when a distributor brand displays characteristics that are very similar to the manufacturer's market leader brand. Coca-Cola defended its brand when it was alleged that the packaging of Sainsbury's new cola drink was too similar to Coca-Cola's own established design.

Generic Brands

Generic brands are sold without any promotional materials or any means of identifying the company, with the packaging displaying only information required by law. The only form of identification is the relevant product category, such as 'plain flour'. Without having to pay for promotional support, these brands are sold at prices that are substantially below the price of normal brands. However, although briefly successful in the 1990s, their popularity has declined and manufacturers see no reason to produce these 'white carton' products. Only firms in the pharmaceutical sector use this type of brand.

Brand Strategies

Brands constitute a critical part of an organization's competitive strategy, so the development of strategies in order to manage and sustain them is really important. However, the original idea that brands provide a point of differentiation has been supplemented, not replaced, by an understanding of the relational dimension. Brands provide a way in which organizations can create and maintain relationships with customers. Brand strategies therefore need to encompass relationship issues, and to ensure that the way in which a customer relates to a brand is both appropriate and offers opportunities for cross-selling customers into other products and services in an organization's portfolio.

Brand Name

Choosing a name for a brand is a critical foundation stone because, ideally, it should enable the brand to be:

- easily recalled, spelled, and spoken;
- strategically consistent with the organization's branding policies;
- indicative of the product's major benefits and characteristics;
- distinctive;
- meaningful to the customer; and
- capable of registration and protection.

Brand names need to transfer easily across markets and, to do so successfully, it helps if customers can not only pronounce the name, but can also recall the name unaided. Sometimes, problems can arise through interpretation: for example, Traficante is an Italian brand of mineral water, but in Spanish it means 'drug dealer'; Clairol's curling iron, 'Mist Stick', had problems when launched in Germany because 'mist' is slang for manure.

One of the reasons that high-profile grocery brands are advertised so frequently is to create brand-name awareness, so that when a UK customer thinks of pet food, he or she thinks of Felix or Winalot, or a Swedish customer thinks of Mjau and Doggy. Names that are difficult to spell or are difficult to pronounce are unlikely to be accepted by customers. Short names, such as Lego, Mars, Sony, Flash, or Shell, are strong in this way.

Brand names should have some internal strategic consistency and be compatible with the organization's overall positioning. The Ford Transit, Virgin Atlantic, and Cadbury's Dairy Milk are names that reflect their parent company's policy that the company name prefixes the product brand name. Some brand names incorporate a combination of words, numbers, or initials. The portable 'sat nav' brand TomTom GO 910 and Canon's Pixma MP600 photo printer use names that do not inform about the functionality, yet use a combination of words and numbers to reflect the parent company and the product line to which they belong, and to hint of their technological content.

A brand's functional benefit can also be incorporated within a name, because this helps to convey its distinctive qualities. Deodorant brands such as Sure and Right Guard use this approach, although Lynx relies on imagery plus fragrance and dryness.

Most brands do not have sufficient financial resources to be advertised on TV or in any mainstream media; therefore it is not possible to convey brand values through imagery and brand advertising. For these brands, it is important that the name of the brand reflects the functionality of the product itself. So the brands No More Nails (a super-adhesive), Cling Film, and Snap-on-Tools all convey precisely what they do through their names. For these brands, packaging and merchandising is important in order to communicate with customers' in-store.

Increasingly, brands are being developed through the use of social media. This is essentially about people talking, either spontaneously to one another, through blogs, or through formal or informal communities, about products and brands that they have experienced in some way. The role of brand managers is to listen to these conversations and then to adapt the brands accordingly. What this suggests is that the control and identity of a brand has moved from the brand-owner to the consumer.

Finally, brands can represent considerable value to their owners, and so names need to be registered and protected for two main reasons. First, brand name protection helps organizations to prevent others from copying and counterfeiting the brand. Although copying products is now commonplace, preventing the use of the brand name helps to protect the brand-owners and enables them to maintain aspects of their brand positioning. The second reason for name registration is that the searches required when registering a name mean that the organization will not infringe the rights of others who already own the name. This can avoid costly legal arguments and delays in establishing a brand.

Branding Policies

Once a decision has been taken to brand an organization's products, an overall branding policy is required. There are three main strategies—individual, family, and corporate branding—and within these there are a number of brand combinations and variations in the way in which brands can be developed.

Individual Branding

Once referred to as a 'multi-brand' policy, individual branding requires that each product offered by an organization is branded independently of all of the others. Grocery brands offered by Unilever (such as Knorr, Cif, and Dove) and Procter & Gamble (for example, Fairy, Crest, and Head & Shoulders) typify this approach.

One of the advantages of this approach is that it is easy to target specific segments and to enter new markets with separate names. If a brand fails or becomes subject to negative media attention, the other brands are not likely to be damaged. However, there is a heavy financial cost, because each brand needs to have its own promotional programme and associated support.

Family Branding

Once referred to as a 'multiproduct brand' policy, family branding requires that all of the products use the organization's name, either entirely or in part. Microsoft, Heinz, and Kellogg's all incorporate the company name, because it is hoped that customer trust will develop across all brands. Therefore promotional investment need not be as high. This is because there will always be a halo effect across all of the brands when one is communicated and brand experience will stimulate word-of-mouth following usage. A prime example of this is Google, which has pursued a family brand strategy with Google Adwords, Google Plus, Google Maps, and Google Scholar, to name a few. What is more impressive is that Google's shattering achievements have been accomplished in such a short period and without any spend on advertising or promotional materials.

'Line family branding' is a derivative policy whereby a family branding policy is followed for all products within a single line. Bosch is a technology company operating in the automotive, industry, and home markets. Many of its products are branded Bosch, but it uses line branding for its Blaupunkt and Qualcast brands in its car entertainment and garden products divisions.

Corporate Brands

Many retail brands adopt a single umbrella brand, based on the name of the organization. This name is then used at all locations, and is a way of identifying the brand and providing a form of consistent differentiation, and form of recognition, whether on the high street or online. Major supermarkets, such as Tesco in the UK, Carrefour in France, and ASDA Wal-Mart, use this branding strategy to attract and to help to retain customers.

Corporate branding strategies are also used extensively in business markets, such as IBM, Cisco, and Caterpillar, and in consumer markets in which there is technical complexity, such as financial services. Companies such as HSBC, Prudential, and FirstDirect adopt a single name strategy. One of the advantages of this approach is that promotional investments are limited to one brand. However, the risk is similar to family branding, in that damage to one product or operational area can cause problems across the organization. For example, organizations such as Hitachi Corporation, Dell, Apple, Toshiba, Lenovo, and Fujitsu all recalled Sony batteries during the summer of 2006 on advice by Sony itself. Sony announced that it was recalling certain batteries in laptops because they could fuse, as a result of pieces of metal having been left in their cells during the manufacturing process in Japan (Allison, 2006). The recall was said to cost up to US$265 million and involved approximately 6 million batteries worldwide. The immediate impact on Sony's reputation was that it had to revise both income and profit forecasts.

Brand extensions are a way of capitalizing on the recognition, goodwill, and any positive associations of an established brand (Hem et al., 2003), and using the name to lever the brand into a new market. Mars successfully leveraged its confectionery bar into the ice cream market and, in doing so, de-seaonalized its sales by providing income in the summer when chocolate sales are normally at their lowest.

Market Insight 7.4

Brand Extensions . . . Some Right, Some Wrong

Many brands attempt to leverage their brand strength by extending into new, but associated, markets. For example, Bacardi launched a distinctly masculine, smoky-edged, and premium spiced rum brand extension called Bacardi Oakheart in 2011. This was aimed at young men who were looking for a drink that was more adventurous. It was hoped that consumers would ask for an 'Oak and Coke' when ordering.

Unilever extended its newly acquired home and personal care brand Radox into Radox Spa. This new brand was success fully developed to bring the benefits of spa relaxation into people's homes. Chocolate Weetabix was a hugely successful extension to the Weetabix brand, putting it in the top-thirty cereal brands within six months of its launch.

The Virgin brand has been successfully extended into airlines, bridal wear, holidays, financial services, mobile phones, cosmetics, gyms, and alcohol. However, Virgin Coke failed to make an impact and it is true to say that not all extensions have a strong logical connection. For example, in the Middle East, the Lal Group not only owns the supermarket chain Al Maya Lal's, but it also owns a number of retail franchises and shopping malls across the Gulf. Its move into the manufacturing and education sectors with the Lal brand is somewhat surprising.

Even more surprising are the move of toothpaste brand Colgate into frozen dinners, Cheetos developing a lip

balm, and Harley-Davidson (HD) moving into baking, with the HD icing kit, which was sold to bakeries and pastry shops to make birthday decorations! Finally, Coca-Cola even launched a line of nail polish!

Radox Spa: the indulgent bathtime brand
Source: Radox

Sources: Based on Charles (2011); Eleftheriou-Smith (2011); http://www.kippreport.com/category/in-pictures/

1 **What criteria would you advise managers to use when considering a proposed brand extension?**

2 **Find two further extensions that worked and two that failed, and determine why these outcomes occurred.**

3 **What, in your opinion, is key to a successful brand extension?**

The attractiveness of brand extension is that time and money does not need to be spent building awareness or brand values. The key role for marketing communications is to position the new extended brand in the new market and to give potential customers a reason to try it.

In the US, Brandweek and TippingSprung run an annual survey of brand extensions. In 2011, Coppertone sunglasses were named best overall brand extension, followed by Mr Clean Performance Car Washes, and Juicy Crittoure (Juice Couture's pet line) in third place. The worst brand extension was won by Burger King men's apparel.

go online

Visit the **Online Resource Centre** and follow the web links to *Brandweek* to learn more about current news in branding.

Successful brands are usually associated with a set of enduring brand values, often co-created by the brand and its loyal customers. These values provide the means through which brand extensions become possible, but understanding these values can be critical. For example, Harley-Davidson's (HD) values are essentially rugged and masculine, born out of the power and rumble associated with the motorbike. This had contributed to the development of the HD brand, but was not understood or recognized when the chain of HD shops began selling wine coolers, baby clothes, and fragrances. This alienated its very loyal customers and the inappropriate products were withdrawn. Harley-Davidson had developed a strong brand by sticking consistently to making big, classic, US motorbikes and being proud about it. By moving away from this core activity and associating itself, through brand extensions, with categories that did not reflect the strong, masculine values, the brand alienated its customers and threatened the strength of the brand itself (Anon., 2006).

Licensing the trademark of an established brand and using it to develop another brand is proving to be another popular way of using brands. In return for a fee, one company permits another to use its trademark to promote other products over a defined period of time, in a defined area. Companies such as Disney use licensing because it provides revenue at virtually no cost, and constitutes a form of marketing communications that takes the brand to new customers and markets. On the downside, brand licensing can lead to brand proliferation to the extent that the market is swamped with brand messages that fail to position the brand properly. In addition, problems with manufacturing or contractual compliance can lead to costly legal redress.

Licensing was, for a long time, a marketing activity that was the preserve of child-related toys, characters, and clothing. Now, licensing is used increasingly with adult brands, such as Gucci, Armani, Coca-Cola, and sports teams such as Manchester United, Formula One, and the Australian national cricket team.

Co-branding occurs when two established brands work together, on one product or service. The principle behind co-branding is that the combined power of the two brands generates increased consumer appeal and attraction. It also enables brands to move into markets and segments in which they would normally have great difficulty in establishing themselves. Another reason for co-branding is that it enables organizations to share resources based on their different strengths. The co-branding arrangement between Microsoft and the UK charity National Society for the Prevention of Cruelty to Children (NSPCC) gives the charity access to the financial resources of Microsoft for marketing communications to reach new donors and to raise awareness of its cause. Microsoft benefits from its association with a softer brand, one that helps to reposition Microsoft as a brand that cares.

Chapter Summary

To consolidate your learning, the key points from this chapter can be summarized as follows.

■ **Describe the various types and forms of offering and explain the product life cycle**

An offering encompasses all of the tangible and intangible attributes related not only to physical goods, but also to services, ideas, people, places, experiences, and even a mix of these various elements. Anything that can be offered for use and consumption, in exchange for money or some other form of value, is referred to as a product.

The product life cycle consists of five distinct stages: development; introduction; growth; maturity; and decline. Sales and profits rise and fall across the various lifestages of the product.

■ **Explain the processes and issues associated with the development of new products and services, and how they are adopted by markets**

The development of new products is complex and high risk, so organizations usually adopt a procedural approach. The procedure consists of several phases that enable progress to be monitored, test trials to be conducted, and the results analysed before there is any commitment to the market. The development of new services follows a similar staged process, whereby additional services are added to a core product until a point is reached at which the service and the core product are integrated into a bundled offering. The processes of adoption and diffusion explain the way in which individuals adopt new products, and the rate at which a market adopts an innovation.

■ **Describe the key principles of branding**

Brands are products and services that have added value. Brands help customers to differentiate between the various offerings and to make associations with certain attributes or feelings with a particular brand. There are three main types of brand: manufacturer; distributor; and generic.

■ **Understand the concepts of brand associations and brand personalities**

Brands are capable of triggering associations in the minds of consumers. These associations may sometimes enable consumers to construe a psychosocial meaning associated with a particular brand. This psychosocial element can be measured in terms of the associations that consumers make across five key dimensions: sincerity; excitement; competence; sophistication; and ruggedness. Brand personality provides a form of identity for consumers that expresses symbolic meaning for themselves and for others.

■ **Explain the benefits that branding offers to both customers and organizations**

Brands reduce risk and uncertainty in the buying process. They provide a snapshot of quality and positioning, helping customers to understand how one brand relates to another. As a result, branding helps consumers and organizations to buy and sell products easily, more efficiently, and relatively quickly.

Review Questions

1 Identify the three forms that make up a product.
2 Explain the product life cycle and identify the key characteristics that make up each of the stages.
3 What are the main stages associated with the new product development process?
4 Why should marketers know about the process of adoption?
5 Why is branding important to consumers and to organizations?

@ Scan this image to go online and access the chapter's multiple-choice questions, web links, Internet activities, and more!

Worksheet Summary

Visit the **Online Resource Centre** and complete Worksheet 7.1. This will help you to learn about the process of developing a new product offering and devising a suitable new brand name.

References

Aaker, J. (1997) 'Dimensions of brand personality', *Journal of Marketing Research*, 34(Aug): 347–56.

Allison, K. (2006) 'Apple recall deepens Sony battery crisis', *Financial Times*, 24 August, available online at http://www.ft.com/cms/s/c2eab782-3394-11db-981f-0000779e2340,_i_rssPage=6700d4e4-6714-11da-a650-0000779e2340.html [accessed December 2007].

Anon. (2006) 'Extension brand failures: Harley Davidson perfume', *Brand Failures Blog*, 5 November, available online at http://brandfailures.blogspot.com/2006/11/extension-brand-failures-harley.html [accessed December 2007].

Anon. (2009) 'Creative solution Finlandia', *Campaign*, 4 September, p. 24.

Arora, R. and Stoner, C. (2009) 'A mixed method approach to understanding brand personality', *Journal of Product & Brand Management*, 18(4): 272–83.

Barda, T. (2009) 'The science of appliances', *The Marketer*, May: 25–7.

Belk, R. (1988) 'Possessions and the extended self', *Journal of Consumer Research*, 15(2): 139–68.

Berg, N. (2011) 'Tesco's private label venture', *Planet Retail*, 21 June, available online at http://blog.emap.com/Natalie_Berg/2011/06/21/tescos-private-label-venture/ [accessed 29 April 2012].

Boehringer, C. (1996) 'How can you build a better brand?', *Pharmaceutical Marketing*, July: 35–6.

Chaffey, D., Mayer, R., Johnston, K., and Ellis-Chadwick, F. (2009) *Internet Marketing*, 4th edn, Harlow: FT/Prentice Hall.

Charles, G. (2009) 'Get to grips with the carbon agenda', *Marketing*, 30 September, pp. 26–7.

Charles, G. (2011) 'Bacardi readies £3m Oakheart rum launch', *Marketing Magazine*, 12 August, available online at http://www.marketingmagazine.co.uk/news/1084602/Bacardi-readies-3m-Oakheart-rum-launch/?DCMP=ILC-SEARCH [accessed 6 December 2011].

de Chernatony, L. and Dall'Olmo Riley, F. (1998) 'Defining a brand: beyond the literature with experts' interpretations', *Journal of Marketing Management*, 14: 417–43.

Drucker, P. F. (1985) 'The discipline of innovation', *Harvard Business Review*, 63(May–June): 67–72.

Eleftheriou-Smith, L.-M. (2011) 'Radox in first brand extension under Unilever ownership', *Marketing Magazine*, 21 October, available online at http://www.marketingmagazine.co.uk/news/1099920/Radox-first-brand-extension-Unilever-ownership/?DCMP=ILC-SEARCH [accessed 6 December 2011].

Gates, D. (2009) 'Dreamliner makes history with plastic, outsourcing, design—and delays', *The Seattle Times*, 11 December, available online at http://seattletimes.nwsource.com/html/businesstechnology/2010483120_787different15.html [accessed 19 December 2011].

Gatignon, H. and Robertson, T. S. (1985) 'A propositional inventory for new diffusion research', *Journal of Consumer Research*, 11(Mar): 849–67.

Ghosh, S. (1998) 'Making business sense of the Internet', *Harvard Business Review*, Mar–Apr: 127–35.

Hem, L., de Chernatony, L., and Iversen, M. (2003) 'Factors influencing successful brand extensions', *Journal of Marketing Management*, 19(7–8): 781–806.

IBM (2008) 'Bombardier Aerospace adopts a fresh approach to PLM to get its new jets in the sky faster', IBM Case Study, available online at ftp://service.boulder.ibm.com/software/solutions/pdfs/ODC03065-USEN-00.pdf [accessed 7 December 2011].

Jack, C. (2011) 'Boeing 787 (Dreamliner) wide body passenger aircraft', *Military Factory*, 26 October, 2011, available online at http://www.militaryfactory.com/aircraft/detail.asp?aircraft_id=764 [accessed 19 December 2011].

Keller, K. L. (1998) *Strategic Brand Management: Building, Measuring, and Managing Brand Equity*, Upper Saddle River, NJ: Prentice-Hall.

Knox, S., Smith, G., and Baines, P. (2007) 'Building the 7E7: NPD at Boeing', Unpublished Case Study, Cranfield: Cranfield University.

Kohler, T., Matzler, K., and Füller, J. (2009) 'Avatar-based innovation: using virtual worlds for real-world innovation', *Technovation*, 29(6/7): 395–407.

Leistén, J. and Nilsson, M. (2009) 'Crossing the chasm: launching and re-launching in the Swedish mobile phone industry', BA thesis, Jönköping International Business School, Jönköping University, available online at http://hj.diva-portal.org/smash/record.jsf?pid=diva2:158025 [accessed 19 March 2009].

Linville, P. and Carlston, D. E. (1994) 'Social cognition of the self', in P. G. Devine, D. L. Hamilton, and T. M. Ostrom (eds) *Social Cognition: Impact on Social Psychology*, San Diego, CA: Academic Press, pp. 143–93.

McCracken, G. (1986) 'Culture and consumption: a theoretical account of the structure and movement of the cultural meaning of consumer goods', *Journal of Consumer Research*, 13(June): 71–84.

Möller, K., Rajala, R., and Westerlund, M. (2008) 'Service innovation myopia? A new recipe for client/provider value creation', *California Management Review*, 50(3): 31–48.

Ozer, M. (2003) 'Process implications of the use of the Internet in new product development: a conceptual analysis', *Industrial Marketing Management*, 32(6): 517–30.

Pennington, J. R. and Ball, A. D. (2009) 'Customer branding of commodity products: the customer-developed brand', *Brand Management*, 16(7): 455–67.

Phau, I. and Lau, K. C. (2001) 'Brand personality and consumer self-expression: single or dual carriageway?', *Journal of Brand Management*, 8(6): 428–44.

Rogers, E. M. (1962) *Diffusion of Innovations*, New York: Free Press.

Rogers, E. M. (1983) *Diffusion of Innovations*, 3rd edn, New York: Free Press.

Shelton, R. (2009) 'Integrating product and service innovation', *Research Technology Management*, 52(3): 38–44.

Tiltman, D. (2006) 'In with the new', *Marketing*, 1 February, pp. 37–8.

Tynan, C. and McKechnie, S. (2009) 'Experience marketing: a review and reassessment', *Journal of Marketing Management*, 25(5–6): 501–17.

Word of Mouth Marketing Association (WOMMA) (2011) 'Offline word of mouth by influencers', 30 December, available online at http://www.womma.org/casestudy/examples/product-placement-seeding-sampling/offline-word-of-mouth-by-influ/ [accessed 25 June 2012].

8

Price Decisions

Learning outcomes

After reading this chapter, you will be able to:

- explain the relationship between price, costs, quality, and value;

- describe how consumers and customers perceive price;

- explain cost-oriented, competitor-oriented, demand-oriented, and value-oriented approaches to pricing;

- understand how to price new offerings; and

- explain how pricing operates in the business-to-business setting.

Simon Johnson for P&O Ferries

P&O Ferries operates in competition with low-cost airlines as well as low-cost ferry operators. How does it make its pricing decisions? We speak to Simon Johnson to find out more.

P&O Ferries was part of the Peninsular and Oriental Steam Navigation Company. The company was taken over in 2006 after 169 years of independence by Dubai Ports World (DPW), a large Middle Eastern ports operator, for £3.92 billion, at a 15 per cent premium above the offer from Singapore's ports operator, PSA. P&O is probably best known in the UK for its operation of ferries between the UK, Belgium, France, the Netherlands, and Spain, but it also operates container terminals and logistics operations in over a hundred ports, offering its new owner the opportunity to expand its global reach.

However, the ferry division's outlook had not been so rosy. By the end of 2004, the challenge facing our marketing team was substantial. Ferry travel was in long-term decline as a result of the competition from low-cost airlines and the reduction of duty-free incentives, which had driven the 'booze cruise' day-tripper market—people who travelled from Dover in the UK to Calais in France for cheaper wine, beers, and spirits. In addition, the popularity of France as a holiday destination for the British was in decline. Ferry travel was starting to look outmoded. Annual passenger volumes for P&O on the Dover–Calais route dropped from around 10 million in 2003 to just over 7 million by 2005.

But this wasn't all: within the ferry market itself, we faced stiff competition on key routes from a new breed of low-cost ferry operators such as Speedferries and Norfolk Line, which had resulted in significant overcapacity in the market. Rising crude oil prices, a declining advertising share of voice (as low-cost airlines spent more and more on advertising), and an ageing ferry fleet added to our woes.

The company research that we carried out among existing and lapsed passengers indicated that the low-cost airline model—of flexible, demand-based pricing and online ticket buying—had become widely understood by, and acceptable to, customers. To survive, we felt that P&O needed to do something similar with its own pricing approach. Research identified two key customer groups: the ferry *loyalists* who had stuck with the company despite intense competition; and the *convertibles*, who could be persuaded to shift back to ferry travel, having lapsed. We made the decision to develop a campaign with the key objective of delivering more customers, more cost-effectively, online. Advertising messages that seemed to resonate were that travelling by ferry was more relaxing and less hassle than travelling by air, and customers wanted a simplified pricing structure, demonstrating greater value for money.

P&O's *Pride of Canterbury*

1 If you were developing the ticket pricing policy, how would you design it to clearly demonstrate value for money?

Introduction

When did you last buy something that you thought was really expensive? Did you wonder if others would think it was expensive too? Just when is a **price** expensive and when is it not? How do companies actually set prices? What procedures do they use? Do companies use different pricing approaches when they launch new products/services? These are just some of the questions that we set out to consider in this chapter.

In this chapter, we provide an insight into how customers respond to price changes, what economists call the **price elasticity** of demand. We consider pricing decisions in relation to developing differentiated or low-cost approaches and the pricing of services. As a topic, pricing is perhaps the most difficult component of the marketing mix to understand because the price of an offering is linked to the cost of all of the many and various elements that come together to make it. The marketing manager seldom controls costs and prices of a particular offering, and usually refers to the accounting department, or marketing controller, to set prices.

We provide an indication of how to set prices for new offerings and how to change prices for existing offerings. We consider pricing approaches in both consumer and business-to-business (B2B) markets, and we briefly discuss online pricing (for example, on the increasingly popular comparison websites).

The Concept of Pricing and Cost

Pricing

Price is a complex component of the marketing mix. The term 'price' has come to encompass both 'the amount of money expected, required, or given in payment for something [and] an unwelcome experience or action undergone or done as a condition of achieving an objective' (Anon., 2012). In marketing terms, we consider price to be the amount that the customer has to pay or exchange to receive a good or service. For example, when purchasing a KFC Zinger Burger® meal (incorporating a chicken sandwich, small fries, and a drink), the price exchanged for the meal might be, say, US$7.49, £4.99, 399 rupees, or 49 yuan, depending on where you live. The £4.99 element is the price, the assigned numerical monetary worth of the meal. However, this notion of pricing an offering is often confused with a number of other key concepts used in marketing when discussing how and why we set pricing levels, particularly cost and **value**.

Proposition Costs

To price an offering properly, we need some idea of what the offering costs us to make, produce, or buy. Cost represents the total money, time, and resources sacrificed to produce or acquire a good or service. For example, the costs incurred to produce the KFC meal will include the cost of heat and light in the restaurant, advertising and sales promotion costs, costs of rent or of the mortgage interest accrued from owning the restaurant, management and staffing costs, and the franchise fees paid to KFC's central headquarters to cover training, management,

Table 8.1	Examples of fixed and variable costs
Fixed costs	**Variable costs**
Manufacturing plant and equipment (in a business selling product)	Equipment servicing costs
Office buildings	Energy costs
Cars and other vehicles	Mileage allowances
Salaries	Overtime and bonus payments
Professional service fees (e.g. legal)	Professional services fees (e.g. legal) in a business with a strong regulatory regime (e.g. pharmaceuticals)

and marketing. Furthermore, there are costs associated with the distribution of the product components to and from farms and other catering suppliers to the restaurants. There are also the costs of computer systems and purchasing systems, and there are the costs of the packaging, bags, and any extras such as gifts and toys.

Typically, a firm will determine what its **fixed costs** are and what its **variable costs** are for each proposition. These items vary for individual industries, but Table 8.1 provides some indication of what these are in general. Fixed costs are costs that do not vary according to the number of units of goods made or services sold, so are independent of sales volume. In a KFC restaurant, this could include the cost of heating and lighting, rent, and staffing costs. In contrast, variable costs vary according to the number of units of goods made or services sold. For example, with the production of KFC meals, when sales and demand decrease, fewer raw goods such as chicken, product packaging, and novelty items such as toys are required, so less spending on raw materials occurs. However, when sales increase, more raw materials are used and spending rises.

Pricing and Costs

The relationship between price and costs is important, because costs should be less than the price assigned to a proposition, otherwise the firm will not sell sufficient units to obtain sufficient revenues to cover costs and make long-term profits. The price at which a proposition is set is strategically important, because increases in price have a disproportionately positive effect on profits and decreases in price have a disproportionately negative effect on profits. For example, in one study (Baker et al., 2010), it was identified that:

- a 1 per cent improvement in price brings an 8.7 per cent improvement in operating profit;
- a 1 per cent improvement in variable costs brings only a 5.9 per cent improvement in operating profit;

- a 1 per cent improvement in volume sales brings a 2.8 per cent improvement in operating profit; and
- a 1 per cent improvement in fixed costs brings only a 1.8 per cent improvement in operating profits.

Where we can, we should be looking to increase prices every time.

However, deciding how to price a proposition is not simple. Consider the example presented earlier for KFC. A firm like KFC might well have a hundred products on any one restaurant menu (including meals, individual burgers, ice creams, drinks, salads, etc.) in any one country. If we bear in mind that different countries have slightly different menus to incorporate food products for local tastes, then we can imagine that, worldwide, KFC must have an enormous menu of products. But how does it cost and price each individual product? The first step is to determine costs, but, in any one restaurant, how does it allocate fixed costs, such as heat and light, rent and tax, to each of the individual products sold? And once it has allocated the fixed costs, how does KFC determine the variable costs for each product? Once it has allocated fixed costs and determined the variable costs associated with a product, it sets the initial price of a product. But costs of components, such as heat and light, and other costs change constantly. How will KFC determine whether or not it needs to change its prices on any one item after it has set them because of the changes in component costs? After all, it can't keep changing prices every single time a component cost changes. So at what point does KFC decide to change a product price?

From this short example, we can see that determining a product's cost is a complex task. Because of the cost of information, to increase the accuracy of the cost data, we need to spend more time collecting and analysing the data. Determining costs is an exercise in which we trade off accuracy with the benefits and costs of data collection, storage, and processing (Babad and Balachandran, 1993). Determining costs and prices is made more difficult when organizations are divided into separate profit centres, selling on to other divisions within the same company—especially when these adopt inefficient transfer pricing mechanisms (Ward, 1993). For example, Airbus, the airline company owned by the European Aeronautic Defence and Space Company (EADS), assembles its planes using parts made in several European countries. When these parts are made by the respective divisions, they are sold on using a process known as **transfer pricing** to the main holding company, which assembles the plane from its component parts. But it's not only costs that matter; we might also observe changes in demand for our products, as customers' desires change. In setting pricing levels, we must also consider our customers' *perceptions* of prices.

Customer Perceptions of Price, Quality, and Value

Researchers are concerned with how individuals react to the way in which products are priced, questioning how consumers perceive prices and why they perceive them as they do. Here, we take into account individual perceptions of proposition quality and value, and their relationship to customer response to the pricing levels assigned to a product offering.

Proposition Quality
Quality is a very important concept when considering proposition pricing levels. 'Quality' is defined as 'the standard of something as measured against other things of a similar kind; the

degree of excellence of something; a distinctive attribute or characteristic possessed by some-one or something' (Anon., 2012). In this context, quality of offerings relates to standards to which that offering performs as a need-satisfier. For example, a very high-quality car will more than satisfy both our aesthetic needs for aerodynamic beauty and our ego and functional needs for high-performance road handling, speed, and power. But quality is not a single standard in a product or service; it encompasses many standards, since there are many levels at which our needs might or might not be satisfied.

Quality is multifaceted (that is, it comprises different functional and non-functional needs) and multi-layered (that is, it comprises differing levels or intensities of satisfaction). The American Society for Quality (ASQ) defines quality as a subjective term, suggesting that each person has his or her own definition of quality. So we prefer to talk of **perceived quality**. We find that consumers have differing views of the quality of the product offering that they have purchased: some might be very dissatisfied and some highly satisfied with exactly the same product offering.

The Relationship between Quality and Pricing Levels

The relationship between price and perceived quality is complex. There is an assumption that as price increases, so does quality, and that in general price reflects quality. But this is not always the case, even though 'snob' consumers in the fashion clothing and perfume sectors (see Amaldoss and Jain, 2005; Yeoman and McMahon-Beattie, 2006) assume that higher prices reflect higher-quality garments and fragrances. The general idea that price indicates quality (perceived quality) assumes that the prices are objectively determined by the inter-action of supply and demand in competitive markets (Sjolander, 1992). In truth, people within firms set prices, often dispassionately, so as to try to obtain the maximum profit possible. Various studies conducted to determine whether or not price bears a relation to quality have found that a general price–perceived quality relationship does not, in fact, exist (Zeithaml, 1988; Sjolander, 1992), except perhaps for wine and perfume (Zeithaml, 1988). However, a study specifically designed to understand the relationship between price and quality in a world in which price information is increasingly available online (Boyle and Lathrop, 2009) has found that US consumers believe that higher prices correspond with higher quality for **consumer durables** (such as cars and televisions), but are less likely to perceive this with **consumer non-durables** (such as foodstuffs).

The Relationship between Perceived Value, Product Quality, and Pricing Levels

'Value' is defined as 'the regard that something is held to deserve; the importance, worth or usefulness of something; principles or standards of behaviour; one's judgment of what is important in life' (Anon., 2012). In marketing terms, value refers to what we get for what we pay. It is often expressed as:

$$\textbf{Value} = \frac{quality}{price}$$

This approach to value indicates that, to increase a customer's perception of the value of a product offering, we must either lower the price or increase the quality. In some ways, this is a simplistic concept of value. There are other intervening effects on the value that we perceive a proposition to hold. Sometimes, our initial assessment is faulty, or needs to be reconsidered.

Sometimes, as customers, we are skilled to recognize or evaluate quality: for example, the average wine drinker would not regard himself or herself as knowledgeable about wine and so might find it hard to work out the product quality.

External Influences on Customer Price Perceptions

Reference Prices

Why do consumers see some prices as fairer than others and some products as of higher value than others? If we are to be able to price a good or service according to customer needs, we must have some idea of what customers think is a fair price to pay for that good or service, or what they expect to pay, or what they think others might pay.

Marketers call these prices **reference prices**. There is usually a price band against which customers judge the purchase price of goods and services in their own minds. Reference prices can be viewed as predictive price expectations in the consumers' own minds, brought about through prior experience with those products and services or through word-of-mouth discussions with others. They depend on brand choice, purchase quantity, purchase timing (for example, products bought at Christmas time in Western European markets tend to be more expensive than at other times), price history, promotion history, the shop visit history, whether or not the visit was planned, the store choice, whether or not the price was well advertised, whether or not the product is frequently purchased, whether there are different components of the product or service that make it easy to understand the pricing structure, and customer characteristics such as price sensitivity, brand loyalty, and so on. Reference prices do vary across consumers, and so there is a clear opportunity to segment and target consumers on the basis of reference price (Mazumdar et al., 2005).

But, in addition to deciding whether or not a price is fair (how products and services ought to be priced), or what they expect to pay ('expectation-based pricing'), or what significant others would pay (so-called 'aspirational pricing'), we also need to know whether or not customers are actually conscious of prices in a particular category or not. Most people do not have as good a knowledge of prices as they think. Think of your mum and dad, or a friend or a relative significantly older than you: do they know the ticket price for a gig? Do you know the price of a good-quality dining table? As an industrial buyer, how much should you pay for the installation and servicing of a new human resources (HR) computer system, say Peoplesoft, designed to keep records for about 5,000 staff? We use these examples to indicate that our experience of prices contributes to what we know about reference prices, but also to explain that our experience, by its very nature, is limited to what we have done in the past. In fact, there are certain groups of grocery items that supermarket shoppers are more likely to know, and it is these items that supermarkets frequently discount and advertise to attract shoppers, not the other lesser-known items, the prices of which may even be raised. Examples include everyday items such as bread, milk, and tins of baked beans. Shoppers assume that, because these items are discounted, all other items must be similarly discounted. So if people don't know the prices of goods and services, how can they possibly determine whether or not those prices are fair or reasonable?

To be fair to grocery shoppers, estimating reference prices is subject to seasonality for items such as flowers, fruit, and vegetables; quality and sizes of items are not universal across companies' offerings, product designs vary over time, and customers may not purchase some goods frequently (Anderson and Simester, 2003). Instead, when customers assess prices, they estimate value using **pricing cues**, because they do not always know the true cost and price of the item that they are purchasing. These pricing cues include sale signs, odd-number pricing, the purchase context, and price bundling and rebates.

Sale Signs

Sale signs act as cues by indicating to a potential customer that there is a bargain to be had. This entices the customer to purchase because it also suggests to the buyer that the item is desirable and so may be bought by another customer if he or she is not quick enough to buy it. The sale sign uses one of the most persuasive devices known in marketing: the notion of scarcity. The scarcer we perceive a product or service to be, the more we are likely to want it (Cialdini, 1993), often regardless of whether we even need it.

Odd-Number Pricing

Another pricing cue is the use of odd-number endings—that is, prices that end in '9'. Have you ever wondered why the Sony PlayStation that you bought was say US$199, or £149, or 749 (Polish) zloty? Why not simply round it up to US$200, £150, or 750 zloty? According to Anderson and Simester (2003), raising the price of a woman's dress in a national mail order catalogue from US$34 to US$39 increased demand by 33 per cent, but demand remained unchanged when the price was raised to US$44! The question is: why did the increase in demand take place when there was an increase in price? It is unlikely that there would have been such an increase if the item had been priced at US$38. The reason for this is that we perceive the first price as relative to a reference price of £30 (which is £33 rounded down to the nearest unit of ten) and more expensive, while the second price of US$39 we perceive as cheaper than a reference price of US$40 (which we rounded up to the nearest ten). (See Market Insight 8.1.)

Market Insight 8.1

Pricing Illusions

Consider the situation in which you are looking for a pair of sunglasses while shopping in the airport lounge. Let's say that you are flying to Thailand for your holidays and you're shopping at Frankfurt or Heathrow airport. You see two particular pairs of sunglasses at, say, Sunglass Hut that you consider buying: Pair A and B. Both are on sale, and both show the original and new discounted prices on their price tickets, as shown in Table 8.2. Which pair of sunglasses would you consider is the better bargain at the new discounted price: Pair A or Pair B? Don't think about it for too long; just decide which you think offers the best discounted price.

Table 8.2 Original and discounted prices

Sunglasses	Original price	Discounted price
Pair A	€79	€65
Pair B	€83	€69

The chances are that you picked Pair B. Not everyone does, but most of us do. But why is this? The difference in prices is actually the same (and some of us don't even bother to work this out—we still go for Pair B). We consider the left-hand digit before the right-hand digit in the

Specs appeal: how important is price when you buy a pair?

Source: © Tommazo Lizzul, Fotalia.com

prices. US$560 is read as five hundreds, six tens, and zero units, from left to right, rather than from right to left. So in this example we see a reduction in the price of Pair A from seven tens of euros to six tens of euros, whereas in the price of Pair B, we see a reduction from eight tens of euros to six tens of euros. For this reason, most of us regard Pair B as more of a bargain.

1 Next time you go to a shopping centre, have a look in the windows at how many products use a price ending in '9'.

2 When was the last time you bought a discounted product? What did you buy and why?

3 Try this example with your non-marketing friends or classmates and see which type, Pair A or Pair B, they prefer.

Purchase Context in Pricing

Another important element in pricing is the purchase context. In some cases, the purchase context can be used as a frame of reference by the customer in determining prices. Confused.com, an insurance comparison website, used this technique when advertising the message 'Save a pair of jeans on your car insurance', indicating that customers could get a cheaper deal by using its website and buy a pair of jeans with the difference saved. Our perception of risk is greater if we are continually reminded of it than if we consider it only at the point of purchase. For example, gyms use the technique of charging a monthly fee, even though they often demand a one-year membership agreement, for precisely this reason. In fact, a monthly price (instead of an annual, semi-annual, or quarterly charge) drives a higher level of gym attendance, because customers are more regularly reminded of their purchase. So the way in which you set your price does not only influence demand, but it also drives how buyers use your product and service (Gourville and Soman, 2002).

Research shows that if we are exposed to higher-priced items first, our reference prices are anchored at the higher level, whereas if we are exposed to lower prices first, they are anchored at the lower level (Smith and Nagle,

LA Fitness sells gym membership contracts from one month to two years in length

Source: LA Fitness

1995). Consequently, salespeople should show customers around product ranges by starting with products in *descending* price order rather than *ascending* price order. For example, in a car showroom, we should show the BMW 7 series first, then take the customer to the 3 series rather than vice versa. It makes sense also to redesign catalogues to include more expensive items in the earlier pages (Nunes and Boatwright, 2001) because of this effect.

Interestingly enough, location also has an impact on price perceptions. For example, we are prepared to pay more for a drink of, say, Absolut vodka from the hotel mini-bar than we are prepared to pay for it from the hotel bar or for an equivalent measure from a bottle from the supermarket. This indicates the context-specific nature of price perceptions.

Price Bundling and Rebates

Marketers highlight their prices to customers through bundling other products, services, and gains into an offering to make the price look more reasonable. For example, magazines frequently bundle CDs/DVDs and other gifts in with the magazine to make it appear more attractive, which is called **pure price bundling**. Sunday newspapers (in the UK, France, Thailand, and Sweden) often contain numerous supplements (on fashion, entertainment, property) to make the newspaper appear greater value for money. New cars are often sold with three years' warranty on parts to provide the customer with the peace of mind of knowing that he or she should not have to pay for any car parts to be repaired within the period of the warranty. Mobile phone manufacturers offer monthly price packages with international call packages and text message packages bundled in with different types of account, and these bundles are also available independently (so-called **mixed price bundling**).

But price bundles do not always mean the company giving the customer other products or services. We might simply be offered a rebate—that is, money back. Car manufacturers such as Ford have often used rebates to encourage customers to move from considering less-expensive base models to upgrade to higher-priced models. The lost revenues from purchases of the lower-priced models are often offset by the purchases of the higher-priced models even after the rebate (Cross and Dixit, 2005). Credit card companies often offer cashback schemes on money spent on their credit cards, as a proportion of the total amount spent.

Research Insight 8.1

To take your learning further, you might wish to read the following influential paper:

Smith, G. E. and Nagle, T. T. (1995) 'Frames of reference and buyers' perceptions of price and value', *California Management Review*, 38(1): 98–116.

This is a useful article summarizing in a practical way the psychological basis of how customers form frames of reference for prices, how they perceive risk, how current and past prices affect perceptions, the importance of context on price perception, and of odd price endings, and the implications that they have for marketing practice.

@ Visit the **Online Resource Centre** to read the abstract and to access the full paper.

Pricing Objectives

How a company prices its products depends on what its pricing objectives are. These can be financial, with offerings priced to maximize profit or sales, or to achieve a satisfactory level of profits or sales, or a particular return on investment. Companies may price by offering discounts for quick payment. A firm's pricing objectives could be marketing-based: for example, pricing to achieve a particular market share or to position the brand so that it is perceived to be of a certain quality. Sometimes, companies price their offerings simply to survive: for example, pricing to maintain sales volumes when competitors lower their prices. Alternatively, a company might price to avoid price wars, maintaining prices at levels similar to those of its competitors. Finally, a company may price to achieve certain social goals. There are many ways in which a company can price its offerings. Often, companies pursue more than one pricing objective simultaneously and some pricing objectives may be incompatible with each other. For example, pricing to increase cash flow by offering quick payment discounts is not compatible with maximizing profitability. It is, however, compatible with obtaining a satisfactory profitability, so long as the discounts offered are not greater than the cost of goods sold/services rendered.

Pricing Approaches

There are four types of pricing approach, as follows:

- the *cost-oriented approach*, in which prices are set based on costs;
- the *demand-oriented approach*, in which prices are set based on price sensitivity and levels of demand;
- the *competitor-oriented approach*, in which prices are set based on competitors' prices; and
- the *value-oriented approach*, in which prices set based on what customers believe to offer value.

The Cost-Oriented Approach

Considered to be the original theory of pricing, this approach advances the idea that the most important element of pricing is the cost of the component resources that make up the offering. So the marketer sells output at the highest price possible, regardless of the firm's own preference or costs. If that price is high enough compared with costs, the firm earns a profit and stays in business. If not, either the firm finds a way of increasing the price or lowering costs or both, or it goes out of business (Lockley, 1949). The cost-oriented approach considers the total costs of a proposition in the pricing equation, but does not take into account non-cost factors, such as brand image, degree of prestige in ownership, or effort expended.

One approach to determining price is using mark-up pricing, often used in the retail sector. This method operates on the base of a set percentage mark-up. When used, the cost-oriented method leads to the use of list prices, with single prices set for all customers. We simply add a mark-up to the cost of X per cent and this constitutes the price. In British supermarket retailing, the mark-up is around 6–8 per cent, but in American supermarket retailing, it is often even less: at around 4 per cent or less. Mark-ups on wine served in restaurants are typically between 200 per cent and 300 per cent. The cost-oriented approach requires us first to determine the price we set that just covers our costs. This is known as 'break-even pricing'. It represents the point at which our total costs and our total revenues are exactly equal.

To exemplify the concept of mark-up pricing further, we can use the example of a computer company selling high-quality laptop computers, at a cost of £1,000 per unit to make. Suppose that the computer company uses the mark-up pricing method and adds 40 per cent (or 0.4, when expressed as a decimal figure between 0 and 1). The final price set would be given by:

$$\textbf{Price} = \frac{\text{Unit item cost}}{(1 - \text{Mark-up})} = \frac{£1,000}{(1 - 0.4)} = \textbf{£1,667}$$

If we consider that, in a supply chain, there is typically more than one customer interaction, as we move along the supply chain, each partner takes their share, adding to the costs and the final selling price. So a toy, say a teddy bear, bought by a UK importer from a Chinese toy manufacturer based in Hong Kong, brought to Britain, warehoused, stored, financed, and eventually sold at £5.90 (in cases of twelve), may well have cost around £4.50 to that importer. The eventual retail price would probably be around the £10 retail price point—that is, £9.99. The mark-up here for the retailer is:

$$\frac{(£9.99 - £5.90)}{£5.90} = \textbf{69 per cent}$$

The mark-up for the importer is much lower at:

$$\frac{(£5.90 - £4.50)}{£4.50} = \textbf{31 per cent}$$

However, the importer may well buy a container of the teddy bears, comprising say 4,800 individual teddy bears (400 boxes, each containing twelve units), and sell these over three months between August until October for the Christmas retail season. The retailer, by contrast, may sell only six boxes of twelve during the period October–December, so the retailer has to make a higher profit on a smaller volume, with a wider range of items to give the customer some choice.

The cost-oriented approach does not always mean that we use a mark-up pricing approach. In some industries, prices are set based on fixed formulae, which are set with a supplier's costs in mind. For example, in the ethical prescription pharmaceutical industry in France, Italy, and Spain, government-fixed formulae dictate prices with limited scope for pharmaceutical manufacturers to negotiate, while in the UK and Germany, the tradition has been for the country's national health authorities not to fix individual product prices, but to set an overall level of profitability with which the pharmaceutical manufacturer must agree, based on a submission of its costs (Attridge, 2003).

The Demand-Oriented Approach

With the demand-oriented approach to pricing, the firm sets prices according to how much customers are prepared to pay. One of the best-known types of company to operate this approach to pricing is the airline industry, in which different groups of customer pay different amounts for airline seats with varying levels of service attached. Most airline companies operate three types of cabin service. Emirates, for example, offers first class, business class, and economy class, with fewer benefits as we move down the classes. By contrast, the low-cost carriers in Europe such as Ryanair and easyJet operate fairly sophisticated yield management systems, which set prices to ensure that planes operate at full capacity, but which usually price tickets at substantially less than the national airline carriers such as British Airways, Lufthansa, Air France, and so on, at least in the period during which tickets first become available. The result is a low-margin, yield-based pricing policy.

Companies operating a demand-oriented pricing policy should be wary of overcharging their customers, particularly when customers' requests are urgent. Examples include emergency purchases, such as funeral services, or prescription pharmaceutical products for life-threatening diseases. When companies do set charges that are perceived to be unfair, they are liable to claims of so-called **price gouging**. In the pharmaceutical industry, allegations of price gouging are frequent (Spinello, 1992; Hartley, 1993), because, unlike most industries, there are few or no alternative brands available. It is for this reason that governments regulate prices of pharmaceutical products, to ensure that those products reach all patients, not only those who can personally afford to pay for them privately.

The Competitor-Oriented Approach

With this approach, companies set prices based on competitors' prices—the so-called 'going rate'. The advantage of this approach is that when your prices are lower than your competitors, customers are more likely to purchase from you, provided that they know that your prices are lower (see Market Insight 8.2).

Market Insight 8.2

H & M: Pricing at the Margins

Hennes and Mauritz, better known as H & M, is a Swedish-based fashion retailer designing, manufacturing, and marketing clothing and sportswear for men and women, and cosmetics. It operates 2,472 stores in forty-three markets, and has online shopping operations in Norway, Sweden, Denmark, Finland, the Netherlands, Germany, Austria, and the UK. The mix of fashion, price, and quality is at the heart of H & M's offering.

Karl-Johan Persson, the company's chief executive has argued that the company's policy of offering quality clothes at prices lower than its competitors will strengthen H & M's long-term market position. The problem is that margins are also falling at the same time as cotton prices and its Asian production costs are rising. Accordingly, gross profit margin dropped in 2011 to 60.1 per cent from 62.9 per cent in 2010. Meanwhile, competitors are readily passing on their increased costs

in higher prices to their customers. Analysts are increasingly calling H & M's pricing strategy into question: the fear is that, by lowering its prices, it sends a signal to the marketplace that its clothes are lower quality and this could then allow the company to be undercut by even cheaper competitors. Of course, its customers might also perceive its clothes to be a bargain in times of austerity.

Sources: H & M (2012); Reuters (2012); Stothard (2012)

1 How do you think customers will perceive H & M's pricing strategy overall? What research would you undertake to determine their true perceptions?

2 To what extent are price and quality linked in fashion retailing? Does a high price always mean high quality?

3 Under what competitive conditions do you think it is possible to offer a high-quality product at a lower price?

John Lewis Partnership, a UK department store retailer, has for many years offered a price guarantee scheme, which it calls the 'Never knowingly undersold' commitment. The guarantee is that if a customer buys a product online and finds it cheaper with a high-street competitor (regardless of whether that is online or in-store), John Lewis will either match the price or refund the difference, as long as the competitor's service conditions are comparable.

John Lewis offers quality at value prices, a difficult combination to achieve
Source: © John Lewis 2012

Price guarantee schemes like this one are aimed at providing customers with the peace of mind of knowing that the company from which they are purchasing is competitive in price. In reality, such schemes are often expensive to operate, since they require continuous monitoring of competitors' prices and a strong focus on cost control to maintain those competitive prices in the first place. Adopting a competitor-oriented pricing strategy can, and often does, also lead to price wars.

Calculating and anticipating competitor response is important when price-setting. We should analyse consumer responses when a competitor starts to cut prices, but if purchase behaviour changes only modestly or temporarily, other marketing mix elements (for example, promotion, distribution or product differentiation) may be more likely to help us to win back customers (van Heerde et al., 2008). We do not always have to respond with a price cut either: instead, we might respond with improvements in the customer experience, or offer the customer greater value for money as a defensive strategy to offset the competitor's price reductions (Rust et al., 2000).

The Value-Oriented Approach

Even in the consumer durables category (for example, furniture, white goods), in which we might expect customers to be less price-sensitive, firms have long since practised pricing approaches with their customers' considerations in mind (Foxall, 1972). We term this the 'value-oriented approach' to pricing, because prices are based on buyers' perceptions of specific product/service attribute values rather than on costs or competitors' prices. It operates in direct contrast to the cost-oriented approach. The idea is that we no longer live in an era in which offerings are priced at what people can afford to pay, because resources used to make products and services are no longer scarce. Consumers are therefore more interested in obtaining more value from the offerings that they buy. With value-based pricing, the pricing process begins with the customer, determining what value he or she derives from the offering, then determining price, rather than the opposite approach used in cost-oriented pricing, in which costs are determined first, then price is set. (See Market Insight 8.3 for a discussion of this approach, among others.)

In value-based pricing, value determination is undertaken using customer research first. The result may be that the company does not necessarily offer a cheaper price. In fact, it could mean a higher-priced offering. If that offering is to represent true value to the customer, they must feel that it has more benefits than equivalent offerings. A good example of a brand using this approach is L'Oréal Paris, which has advertised its products using spokesmodels, such as Bollywood actress and former Miss World Aishwarya Rai, and British pop artist Cheryl Cole, on the basis that we should use their products 'Because [we're] worth it'. When a brand can generate revenues over and above those obtained by an own-label or generic version of the offering (so-called 'revenue premiums'), this acts as a useful measure for brand equity (Ailawadi et al., 2003). Brand equity is important, because it contributes to company valuations when they are sold, acquired, or merged. However, a price premium is no good if it's not considered fair.

Cheryl Cole, UK singer and songwriter, is the face of L'Oréal Paris

Source: Getty

Addleshaw Goddard's Billing Revolution

Since the economic downturn of 2008, it has been tough in the UK corporate legal services market. Law firms have come under considerable pressure to cut their prices. Supply has outstripped demand and clients have greater freedom than ever to shop around when looking for a law firm. Companies buying legal services (litigation, employment law advice, real estate, tax) are also increasingly becoming jaded with being offered only the conventional billable hour, not least because it's difficult to determine what the final price might be with this approach, and hourly billing has been said to lead to overstaffing, over-lawyering, and careless accounting. The problem therefore is: how can the industry develop new pricing approaches when lawyers work on legal problems based on the amount of hourly time that they have available at different levels of skill and expertise (for example, junior, associate, partner)? Clients seemingly want the certainty of knowing what the end cost will be and they want the service at a discount.

Addleshaw Goddard began its mission to reinvent pricing in the legal services market by establishing a dedicated pricing group, bringing together experts from finance, business development, and senior management to oversee pricing decisions over a certain financial threshold made for client bids and engagements. The group then tracks those decisions, obtaining feedback on bid wins and losses. However, simply advising on and monitoring pricing decisions wasn't enough; the firm also needed to understand how pricing mechanisms drawn from other industries might be applied to the corporate legal services sector. To do this, it worked with Cranfield School of Management to identify a menu of methods that its partners could then consider and offer to clients if they deemed these in the client's interests. Such pricing methods include fixed fees, capped fees, conditional fee agreements (for example, 'no win, no fee'), contingency fees (in which higher fees are charged based on a successful outcome), 'cap and collar' arrangements (in which minimum and maximum ceilings are set up-front for prices), price bundling arrangements (in which several services are undertaken with one or more charged at a lesser rate), risk-based pricing arrangements (for example, pricing the service based on the client's future share price), annual flat fees or monthly retainers, and a myriad of other possibilities. One firm, CMS Cameron McKenna, offers clients the opportunity to 'Pay what you think it's worth'—a brave move in tough economic times.

The question for Addleshaw's is: will its billing methods translate into higher profits? The firm believes that it will at least lead to higher client satisfaction and trust, and that, in the long term, this should lead to higher profits. Time will tell . . .

Sources: Leblebici (2007); Hollander (2010); Anon. (2011); Swift (2011); Addleshaw Goddard (2012)

1 **How do you think pricing practices affect the relationships that law firms have with their clients?**

2 **What are the marketing implications of moving from hourly billing to other approaches such as fixed fees?**

3 **What are the risks and rewards of allowing clients to pay what they think a legal service is worth?**

Pricing and Transactional Management

Over the past few decades, electronic technologies such as marketing information systems (MkIS), database technologies, and more recently Internet-enabled technologies, have been changing the rules of strategic pricing and pricing decisions. Pricing strategies such as 'real-time' or 'dynamic' pricing have increasingly developed in both consumer and B2B markets through online price comparison decision aids and online auctions. Electronic technologies influence how retailers manage stock pricing and how we actually buy or conduct a financial transaction—bringing into reality the idea of the cashless society.

go online

Visit the **Online Resource Centre** and follow the web link to Kelkoo to see an example of an online price comparison decision aid.

With the ease with which information can be exchanged, we are also seeing the proliferation of web-based information brokers with information offerings of product and price comparisons. In the Internet age, price comparison websites are an increasingly common feature of the electronic landscape. Examples in the UK include http://www.comparethemarket.com and http://www.gocompare.com. Like its counterparts in France (http://www.monsieurprix.com) and Sweden (http://www.pricerunner.se), these companies are rapidly developing large customer databases. Examples of compared services include complex services such as gas and electricity supply, insurance, mobile phone packages, and travel, as well as standard products such as cars and car breakdown cover. Therefore marketers now work in a much more price-transparent environment, in which both online and off-line customers want to know what the prices are, and want them presented as simply as possible. One company that does not allow its offerings to be compared on online websites is Direct Line, which even advertises on TV that customers can obtain a quote only directly with it (see Market Insight 8.4).

go online

Visit the **Online Resource Centre** and complete Internet Activity 8.2 to learn more about the role and importance of online auctions to price-setting and consumer decision-making.

Market Insight 8.4

To Compare or Not to Compare: Direct Line

For over five years, British insurer Direct Line has refused to appear on insurance price comparison websites such as gocompare.com, moneysupermarket.com, and comparethemarket.com. Its argument is that it deals with customers directly and price comparison websites are effectively digital middlemen, because they charge insurers (typically around £40) to be listed on their sites. In previous advertising, Direct Line, owned by Royal Bank of Scotland (RBS), warned consumers that price comparison websites are not accurate, independent, or comprehensive. In the motor insurance category, consumers are particularly price-sensitive because they leave the buying of their premiums until the last minute. Research also indicates that, by late 2009, over half of all motorists research insurers' prices via price comparison websites first before deciding from whom to buy. In many cases, consumers are already armed with at least one other quote when they contact an insurer directly for another.

For a couple of years between 2009 and 2011, Aviva also decided that it would not appear on price comparison websites, although has since changed its stance.

In response, price comparison websites have started to rank insurers not only on price, but on other non-price features (with motor insurance, this might be availability of courtesy cars in the event of an accident). In 2009, some companies such as Aviva moved to significantly increase their premiums, whilst in 2010 many insurers actually began to lower their premiums. With the motor insurance market forecast to increase by between 1–3 per cent between 2012 and 2015, but actually to decline in real terms once inflation is taken into account, by between 6 and 9 per cent, and with a likely shake-up after the UK government ordered RBS to divest its insurance businesses as part of its funding arrangement, the market is set to become even more competitive, and even more price-oriented.

The question is: will Direct Line continue to be able to resist the pressure to compete on price?

To view a copy of the Direct Line advert, visit http://www.youtube.com/watch?v=XnV5SDKPbQo

Moneysupermarket.com offers savings galore

Source: Courtesy of Moneysupermarket.com

Sources: Simon (2007); Steer (2009); Chynoweth (2011); Mintel (2011)

1 Why do you think price comparison websites have been so successful in capturing customers' attention?

2 What do you think are the key reasons why Direct Line and Aviva (for a time) refused to appear on price comparison websites?

3 What other offerings are typically compared on price comparison websites? Why do you think these offerings are selected?

Pricing Policies

When setting prices, the company has to trade off the factors associated with competition, such as how much competitors are charging, factors associated with cost, such as how much the individual components that make up the product/service cost, factors associated with demand, such as how much of this product or service will be sold at what price, and factors associated with value, such as what components of the product/service customers value and how much are they prepared to pay for them. Most pricing decisions are trade-offs between these and other factors. So while there are four main pricing approaches outlined in this chapter, there are in fact many different possible pricing policies that could be used, including the following.

- *List pricing*—This is an unsophisticated approach to pricing in which a single price is set for a product or service. Hotels frequently try to charge what they call 'rack rates' for hotel conferencing facilities, which combine residential accommodation for a set number of delegates with daytime accommodation for a seminar/workshop/conference, refreshments, and lunch.

- *Loss-leader pricing*—This occurs when the price is set at a level lower than the actual cost to produce it. This pricing tactic is often used in supermarkets on popular, price-sensitive items (such as baked beans and milk) to entice customers into the store. The loss incurred on these items is made up by increasing the prices of other less price-sensitive items, or absorbed as a short-term promotional cost on the basis that it brings in more customers.

- *Promotional pricing*—This occurs when companies temporarily reduce their prices below the standard price to raise awareness of the product or service, to encourage trial, and to raise brand awareness in the short term. Such pricing approaches incorporate the use of loss leaders, sales discounts, cash rebates, low-interest financing (some car manufacturers, such as Peugeot UK, have offered low or '0% finance' deals), and other price-based promotional incentives.

- *Segmentation pricing*—In this approach, varying prices are set for different groups of customers. For example, Unilever's ice cream is offered as various different ice cream products at differing levels of quality and price ranging from its superpremium (Ben & Jerry's ice cream, primarily available in video shops, cinemas, and elsewhere), to economy offerings (standard low-priced vanilla ice cream available in supermarkets). Economists refer to this approach as **price discrimination**.

- *Customer-centric pricing*—Cross and Dixit (2005) suggest that companies can take advantage of customer segments by measuring their value perceptions, measuring the value created, and designing a unique bundle of products and services to cater to the value requirements of each segment, and then continually assess the impact that this has on company profitability, taking advantage of up-selling (for example, offering a customer a more expensive product or service in the same category) and cross-selling (for example, selling other, different products and services to the same customer).

- *Pay-what-you-want pricing*—In retail situations, research has demonstrated that, under certain circumstances, customers are prepared to pay more if they are allowed to set their own prices than if prices are set for them (Kim et al., 2009). Radiohead, the band, released their album *In Rainbows* as a digital download direct from their own website and allowed their fans to pay whatever they wanted (Tyrangiel, 2007). Whilst the success of the experiment was kept secret by the band, the band's publisher indicated that sales of physical and digital albums numbered 3 million. So while many people will not have paid for *In Rainbows*, those same people were probably inspired to buy the album or merchandise, or to attend a gig (Geere, 2008).

Pricing for New Propositions

When launching new products and services, we adopt one of two particular pricing strategies. With the first approach, we charge a higher price initially and then reduce the price, recouping the cost of the research and development (R&D) investment over time from sales to the group of customers that is prepared to pay the higher price (hence it is known as 'skimming' the market). In the second approach, we charge a lower price in the hopes of generating a large volume of sales and recouping our R&D investment that way (hence it is known as 'market penetration').

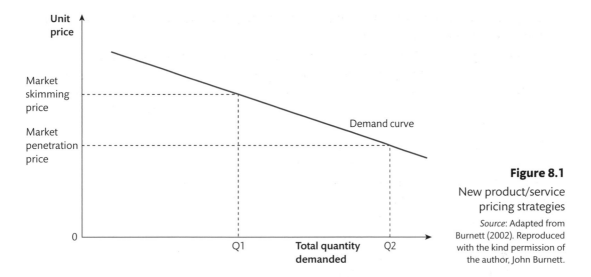

Figure 8.1

New product/service pricing strategies

Source: Adapted from Burnett (2002). Reproduced with the kind permission of the author, John Burnett.

Figure 8.1 shows both market penetration and market skimming price strategies, and their hypothetical impact on quantity demanded: Q1 and Q2, respectively. For any given demand curve, the market skimming price offers a higher unit price than the market penetration price. The actual amount sold at each of these unit prices depends on the price elasticity of demand: a more inelastic product demand curve would give greater revenue from a market skimming price than a market penetration price, since the quantity sold would not be so different between the two prices. On average, the market skimming price is likely to yield a lower quantity of goods/services sold than the market penetration price.

The market skimming approach is a fairly standard approach for high-technology goods and services or those products and services that require substantial R&D cost input initially, such as prescription pharmaceuticals. The skim pricing approach is particularly appropriate under certain conditions (Dean, 1950; Doyle, 2000), as shown in Table 8.3.

Table 8.3	Conditions for effective skim pricing
1	When companies need to recover their research and development investment quickly
2	When demand is likely to be price inelastic
3	Where there is an unknown elasticity of demand, since it is safer to offer a higher price and then lower it, than to offer a lower price and try to increase it
4	Where there are high barriers to entry within the market
5	Where there are few economies of scale or experience
6	Where product life cycles are expected to be short

Table 8.4 Conditions for effective market penetration pricing

1	Where there is a strong threat of competition
2	When the product/service is likely to exhibit a high price elasticity of demand in the short term
3	Where there are substantial savings to be made from volume production
4	Where there are low barriers to entry
5	Where product life cycles are expected to be long
6	Where there are economies of scale and experience of which to take advantage

The market penetration pricing approach is often used for fast-moving consumer good (FMCG) and consumer durable items, in which instances the new product introduced is not demonstrably different from existing formulations available. So if a car manufacturer were to introduce a new coupé that was relatively similar to its previous model and had no new features, and was not significantly better than competing models, it would probably be priced using the market penetration pricing approach. Similarly, items aimed at capturing price-sensitive customers might well adopt this approach. In a recessionary environment, customers are particularly sensitive to the value that they receive when purchasing consumer offerings or procuring business goods and services. The approach should be used under certain conditions when it is more likely to be most effective (Dean, 1950; Doyle, 2000), as outlined in Table 8.4.

Research Insight 8.2

To take your learning further, you might wish to read the following influential paper:

Dean, J. (1950) 'Pricing policies for new products', *Harvard Business Review*, Nov: 45–53; reprinted with retrospective commentary in (1976) *Harvard Business Review*, Nov–Dec: 0141–53.

This is a seminal paper introducing the reader to the concepts of price skimming and penetration pricing as pricing policies for pioneer product marketers. The author indicates that the new product should be priced through the customers' eyes, by consideration of the rate of return of a customer's investment. Reprinted twice since its original publication in *Harvard Business Review*, this article remains a classic, as true today as it was when it was first written.

@ Visit the **Online Resource Centre** to read the abstract and to access the full paper.

Pricing in the Business-to-Business Setting

Business-to-business markets exist on the basis that firms sell products and services to one another rather than to end users. The demand for their products and services comes from the demand for the finished goods and services required by the end user. Business markets are also different in the sense that buyers are usually professionally trained purchasing executives, who are often professionally accredited (for example, by the Chartered Institute of Purchasing and Supply, or CIPS, in the UK) and who have frequently attended training programmes to familiarize themselves with the offerings bought within their own organizations. Their function within the company as organizational buyers is a highly technical one, even for an apparently simple offering. The buyer–seller relationship is the fundamental component of the B2B marketing interaction. Pricing has an important function in this relationship. If a buyer thinks that he or she is being overcharged, he or she will quickly look elsewhere. Equally, if a seller is forced to make a sale too cheaply and is reprimanded for this by his or her superiors, he or she will not wish to sell at that lower price in future and the relationship may be equally damaged. Under such circumstances, the seller may then seek to sell elsewhere.

In the B2B context, the discussion of price takes place between the buyer and the seller in an atmosphere in which both are trying to make the best commercial decision for their organizations. The seller wants to sell at a high price to make the maximum profit, and the buyer wants to buy at a low price to lower his or her own costs and to maximize profits. Their task is to resolve their mutual needs in a win–win situation (for if one side is taken advantage of, the relationship is less likely to last in the longer term).

From the B2B seller's perspective, there are numerous approaches to pricing products and services, including the following.

- *Geographical pricing*—Prices are determined on the basis of customers' locations: for example, pharmaceutical companies often sell their prescription drugs at varying prices in different countries at levels set by the governments themselves rather than the pharmaceutical companies. This might include free on board (FOB) factory prices, in which case the price represents the cost of the goods and the buyer must pay for all transport costs incurred. Free on board (FOB) destination pricing occurs when the manufacturer agrees to cover the cost of shipping to the destination, but not that transport costs incurred on arrival at the port (air or sea).

- *Negotiated pricing*—Prices are set according to specific agreements between a company and its clients or customers (as in professional services, such as architectural or structural engineering practices, or IT installation and servicing). This approach typically occurs when a sale is complex and consultative, but sales and marketing representatives should beware of conceding on price too quickly before properly understanding a client's needs for the product or service (Rackham, 2001).

- *Discount pricing*—Companies reduce the price of a good or service on the basis that a customer is prepared to commit either to buying a large volume of that good or service now or in the future, or to paying for it within a specified time period. Large retailers work on the discount principle when buying goods for their stores. Their mighty procurement budgets and long experience ensure that they buy at cheaper prices from their manufacturer suppliers and so lower their costs. Consequently, they can set their own cheaper prices to their retail customers. Sometimes, discount pricing works on the basis of payment terms.

For example, in the British toy and gift market, in which retail buyers are used to buying their goods on credit, suppliers frequently offer their retail buyers discounts for quicker payment (for example, 5 per cent discount for payment within seven days, 2.5 per cent for fourteen days). However, each time a product or service price is reduced, we disproportionately reduce the operating profit (Baker et al., 2010).

- *Value-in-use pricing*—This approach focuses our attention upon customer perceptions of product attributes and away from cost-oriented approaches. It uses an approach that prices offerings according to what the customer is prepared to pay for different individual benefits received from that proposition (see Christopher, 1982, for a more detailed discussion). The approach is a particularly useful one for industrial products and services, although the actual process of price determination is complex.

- *Relationship pricing*—This approach to pricing is based on understanding a customer's needs and pricing the product or service according to these needs to generate a long-term relationship. This could mean offering good financial terms, perhaps credit or more lenient time periods for payment, or discounts based on future sales revenue. The difficulty with this approach is that it relies on a greater degree of trust and commitment between the two companies, particularly on the part of the seller in relation to the buyer. Where this trust is misplaced, the seller incurs an **opportunity cost**.

- *Transfer pricing*—This occurs in very large organizations in which there is considerable internal dealing between different divisions of the company and across national boundaries. Prices may be set at commercial rates, on the basis of negotiated prices between divisions, or using a cost-based approach. It entirely depends on whether each division is a cost or profit centre. The danger is that such internal dealings can sometimes mean that the final product or service is priced at too high a level for the customer. A good example of a company that adopts this approach is Airbus Industries, the European aircraft manufacturer, owned by the European Aeronautic Defence and Space Company (EADS), which constructs its planes built from components made in several different countries.

- *Economic value to the customer (EVC) pricing*—This approach works on the basis that a company prices an industrial good or service according to its value to the purchasing organization, typically through a comparison with a reference or market-leading product or service, taking into consideration not only the actual purchase price of the product or service, but also start-up and post-purchase costs, to give an overall indication of how much better the company's pricing structure is than that of a competitor.

Tendering and Bidding

In B2B markets, companies bid for the right to provide products and services for a fixed period of time through a competitive bidding process. In other words, a company sets up a form of competition (the 'tender process') in which it either asks a number of selected companies (its 'preferred suppliers') or sets an open competition in which it asks any number of companies to put together a proposal for a set of services or the supply of products and services (known as a 'bid'), which has to be submitted by a set deadline. When a company does not have a pool of preferred suppliers, or wants to widen its pool of potential suppliers, this phase is sometimes preceded by an initial phase during which the company invites 'expressions of interest' from interested potential suppliers. The submissions are then screened by the company, which removes those companies with which it does not want to deal, and the rest are advanced to the next phase of the competition. The company goes on to consider the individual full bids in some form of ranking process, often requiring the bid submitters to make a presentation and to discuss the detail of their bids individually. On the basis of those bids and the presentation, either the company will make a choice of who it wants to supply it, or it will take the process to a second or third round of bidding, and so on. Eventually, it will decide to which bidder it wants to award the temporary contract.

The tendering process is a set requirement for the provision of public services and goods in the European Union above certain financial values of contract, with strict rules on how the contracts must be promoted and awarded.

Private companies dealing with private companies tend to adopt the same forms of bidding and tendering, but without the same level of strict regulation. Generally, the formal tendering and bidding process takes a considerable period of time, effort, and expense. Bidding processes like that described are common in industrial markets and are used around the world as a means to introduce competition, particularly to the provision of public sector services, such as in telecommunications, public utilities (such as gas, electricity, and water), transport (train, underground, monorail, maglev), oil and gas exploration, defence contracting, and so on. The difficulty in designing, writing, and submitting a suitable contract is that the details of competitors' bids usually remain highly confidential. When trying to second-guess competitors' bid prices, it is important to use the sales force as a source of intelligence (since they often pick up information from talks with friendly companies that they supply and even colleagues in other companies at industry events). The manager should know his or her own profitability when determining the price, and aim to discover the winning bidder's name and price on lost jobs, although this is not always possible (Walker, 1967). Ross (1984) argues that it is often better not to ask 'What price will it take to win this order?', but follow up with 'Do we want this order, given the price that our competitors are likely to quote?' There is the notion of the 'winner's curse', which refers to the situation in which the winning bidder obtains an unprofitable contract that it is duty bound to deliver because the bid price was set so low so that it won the contract, but from which it makes only an insignificant (if any) profit.

Chapter Summary

To consolidate your learning, the key points from this chapter can be summarized as follows.

- **Explain the relationship between price, costs, quality, and value**

  Price, costs, quality, and value are all interrelated. Price is what a product or service is sold for and cost is what it is bought for. When value is added to a proposition, the price that can be obtained exceeds the cost. Price and cost are often confused, and assumed even by major international dictionaries to be the same thing; they are not. Quality is a measure of how well a product or service satisfies the need for which it is designed to cater. Value is a function of the quality of a good or service as a proportion of the price paid.

- **Describe how customers and consumers perceive price**

  Understanding how customers and consumers perceive pricing helps in setting prices. Customers have an idea of reference prices based on what they ought to pay for a good or service, what others would pay, or what they would like to pay. Their knowledge of actual prices is limited to well-known, and frequently bought and advertised, goods and services. Consequently, customers tend to rely on price cues such as odd-number pricing, sale signs, the purchase context, and price bundles when deciding whether or not value exists in a particular proposition.

■ **Explain cost-oriented, competitor-oriented, demand-oriented, and value-oriented approaches to pricing**

There are a variety of different pricing policies that can be used, dependent on whether you are pricing for a consumer or industrial proposition. They tend to be either cost-oriented (based on what you paid for it and what mark-up you intend to add), competitor-oriented (based on the so-called 'going rate' or on what price competitors sell a product or service at), demand-oriented (based on how much of a good or service can be sold at what price), or value-oriented (based on what attributes of the product or service are of benefit to your customer and what they will pay for them).

■ **Understand how to price new offerings**

The two dominant approaches to pricing new propositions are the market skimming pricing method and the market penetration pricing method. The former is favoured when a company needs to recover its research and development (R&D) investment quickly, when customers are price insensitive or of unknown price sensitivity, when product life cycles are short, and when barriers to entry to competitors are high. The latter is favoured when these conditions are absent.

■ **Explain how pricing operates in the business-to-business setting**

There are a variety of pricing approaches used in the B2B setting, including geographical, negotiated, discount, value-in-use, relationship, transfer, and economic value to the customer. Business-to-business pricing differs in the sense that buyers are frequently expert in purchasing goods and services for their organizations. They are likely to pay particular attention to the value that they derive from the offering. Companies and organizations, particularly government organizations, frequently purchase goods and services from suppliers through tenders inviting companies to submit bids, containing their proposals, terms and conditions, and prices.

❓ Review Questions

1 Define 'price', 'cost', 'quality', and 'value' in your own words.
2 Explain the concept of 'price elasticity of demand', giving examples of products that are price elastic and products that are price inelastic.
3 What pricing policies are most appropriate for which situations?
4 What are the main business-to-business pricing policies?
5 What are the main two approaches to pricing for new products and services?

@ Scan this image to go online and access the chapter's multiple-choice questions, web links, Internet activities, and more!

Worksheet Summary

Visit the **Online Resource Centre** and complete Worksheet 8.1. This worksheet looks at how external influences can affect our perceptions of the price for pizza and how we can use different approaches to set pizza pricing.

References

Addleshaw Goddard (2012) 'Alternative pricing', available online at http://www.addleshawgoddard.com/view.asp?content_id=5499&parent_id=5497 [accessed 16 September 2012].

Ailawadi, K., Lehmann, D. R., and Neslin, S. A. (2003) 'Revenue premium as an outcome measure of brand equity', *Journal of Marketing*, 67(Oct): 1–17.

Amaldoss, W. and Jain, S. (2005) 'Pricing of conspicuous goods: a competitive analysis of social effects', *Journal of Marketing Research*, 42(Feb): 30–42.

Anderson, E. and Simester, D. (2003) 'Mind your pricing cues', *Harvard Business Review*, Sept: 96–103.

Anon. (2011) 'The pricing revolution', *First Counsel Blog*, 5 July, available online at http://www.firstcounselblog.com/comment/2011/07/the-pricing-revolution.html [accessed 19 March 2012].

Anon. (2012) 'Price', 'Value', 'Quality', available online at http://oxforddictionaries.com/ [accessed 12 March 2012].

Attridge, J. (2003) 'A single European market for pharmaceuticals: could less regulation and more negotiation be the answer?', *European Business Journal*, 15(3): 122–43.

Babad, Y. M. and Balachandran, B. V. (1993) 'Cost driver optimisation in activity-based costing', *Accounting Review*, 68(3): 563–75.

Baker, W. L., Marn, M. V., and Zawada, C. C. (2010) *The Price Advantage*, 2nd edn, Hoboken, NJ: John Wiley and Sons.

Boyle, P. J. and Lathrop, E. S. (2009) 'Are consumers perceptions of price–quality relationships well calibrated?', *International Journal of Consumer Studies*, 33: 58–63.

Burnett, J. (2002) *Core Concepts in Marketing*, Chichester: John Wiley and Sons.

Christopher, M. (1982) 'Value-in-use pricing', *European Journal of Marketing*, 16(5): 35–46.

Chynoweth, C. (2011) 'There's no comparison with 30 years ago', *The Sunday Times*, 25 September, available online at http://www.thesundaytimes.co.uk/sto/public/roadtorecovery/article782735.ece [accessed 19 March 2012].

Cialdini, R. B. (1993) *Influence: The Psychology of Persuasion*, New York: Quill William Morrow.

Cross, R. G. and Dixit, A. (2005) 'Customer-centric pricing: the surprising secret for profitability', *Business Horizons*, 48: 483–91.

Dean, J. (1950) 'Pricing policies for new products', *Harvard Business Review*, Nov: 45–53.

Doyle, P. (2000) *Value-Based Marketing: Marketing Strategies for Corporate Growth and Shareholder Value*, Chichester: John Wiley and Sons.

Foxall, G. (1972) 'A descriptive theory of pricing for marketing', *European Journal of Marketing*, 6(3): 190–4.

Geere, D. (2008) 'Radiohead "pay what you want" numbers released', *TechDigest*, 16 October, available online at http://www.techdigest.tv/2008/10/radiohead_pay_w.html [accessed 29 April 2012].

Gourville, J. and Soman, D. (2002) 'Pricing and the psychology of consumption', *Harvard Business Review*, Sept: 90–6.

H & M (2012) *H & M Press Conference 26 January 2012: Full-Year Report*, available online at http://about.hm.com/content/dam/hm/about/documents/en/Presentations/Press%20conference%20presentation%202012-01-26_en.pdf [accessed 19 March 2012].

Hartley, R. F. (1993) *Business Ethics: Violations of the Public Trust*, New York: John Wiley and Sons.

Hollander, G. (2010) 'Camerons invites legal clients to pay what they want for legal work', *The Lawyer*, 5 August, available online at http://www.thelawyer.com/camerons-invites-clients-to-pay-what-they-want-for-legal-work/1005236.article [accessed 19 March 2012].

Kim, J.-Y., Natter, M., and Spann, M. (2009) 'Pay what you want: a new participatory pricing mechanism', *Journal of Marketing*, 73(1): 44–58.

Leblebici, H. (2007) 'Your income: determining the value of legal knowledge—billing and compensation practices in law firms', in L. Empson (ed.) *Managing the Modern Law Firm*, Oxford: Oxford University Press, pp. 117–40.

Lockley, L. C. (1949) 'Theories of pricing in marketing', *Journal of Marketing*, 13(3): 364–7.

Mazumdar, T., Raj, S. P., and Sinha, I. (2005) 'Reference price research: review and propositions', *Journal of Marketing*, 69(Oct): 84–102.

Mintel (2011) *Motor Insurance: UK—March 2011*, online at www.mintel.com [accessed 19 March 2012].

Nunes, J. C. and Boatwright, P. (2001) 'Pricey encounters', *Harvard Business Review*, July–Aug: 18–19.

Rackham, N. (2001) 'Winning the price war', *Sales and Marketing Management*, 253(11): 26.

Reuters (2012) 'H & M Hennes & Mauritz AB', available online at http://www.reuters.com/finance/stocks/companyProfile?symbol=HMb.ST [accessed 19 March 2012].

Ross, E. B. (1984) 'Making money with proactive pricing', *Harvard Business Review*, Nov–Dec: 145–55.

Rust, R. T., Danaher, P. J., and Varki, S. (2000) 'Using service quality data for competitive marketing decisions', *International Journal of Service Industry Management*, 11(5): 438–69.

Simon, E. (2007) 'Direct Line takes a swat at best buys', *The Telegraph*, 11 June, available online at http://www.telegraph.co.uk/finance/personalfinance/insurance/2810337/Direct-line-takes-a-swat-at-best-buys.html [accessed 19 March 2012].

Sjolander, R. (1992) 'Cross-cultural effects of price on perceived product quality', *European Journal of Marketing*, 26(7): 34–44.

Smith, G. E. and Nagle, T. T. (1995) 'Frames of reference and buyer's perceptions of value', *California Management Review*, 38(1): 98–116.

Spinello, R. A. (1992) 'Ethics, pricing and the pharmaceutical industry', *Journal of Business Ethics*, 11: 617–26.

Steer, B. (2009) 'Price comparison websites need to look beyond motor insurance', *On the Horizon: GfKNOP Newsletter*, September, available online at http://www.gfknop.com/imperia/md/content/gfk_nop/financial/onthehorrizon/othseptember09.pdf [accessed 19 March 2012].

Stothard, M. (2012) 'H & M defends pricing strategy as margins fall', *Financial Times*, 27 January, p. 23.

Swift, J. (2011) 'Addleshaws to spearhead client billing revolution', *The Lawyer*, 25(42): 1.

Tyrangiel, J. (2007) 'Radiohead says: pay what you want', *Time Entertainment*, 1 October, available online at http://www.time.com/time/arts/article/0,8599,1666973,00.html [accessed 29 April 2012].

van Heerde, H. J. Giisbrachts, E., and Pauwels, K. (2008) 'Winners and losers in a major price war', *Journal of Marketing Research*, 45(5): 499–518.

Walker, A. W. (1967) 'How to price industrial products', *Harvard Business Review*, Sept–Oct: 125–32.

Ward, K. (1993) 'Gaining a marketing advantage through the strategic use of transfer pricing', *Journal of Marketing Management*, 9: 245–53.

Yeoman, I. and McMahon-Beattie, U. (2006) 'Luxury markets and premium pricing', *Journal of Revenue and Pricing Management*, 4(4): 319–28.

Zeithaml, V. A. (1988) 'Consumer perceptions of price, quality and value: a means–end model and synthesis of evidence', *Journal of Marketing*, 52(July): 2–22.

An Overview of Marketing Communications

Learning outcomes

After reading this chapter, you will be able to:

- explain three models of communication and describe how personal influences can enhance the effectiveness of marketing communication activities;

- describe the nature and scope of marketing communications;

- understand the role and various tasks of marketing communications;

- consider issues associated with the nature and use of word-of-mouth communications; and

- understand the models used to explain how marketing communications is considered to work.

Helen Bull for the London Eye

The British Airways London Eye uses marketing communications in a number of interesting ways and has become the UK's most popular visitor attraction. We speak to Helen Bull to find out more.

The British Airways London Eye is the world's tallest observation wheel at 135 metres high, and, since opening at the turn of the century, has become an iconic landmark, with a status that can be compared with Tower Bridge, Big Ben, Eros, and the Tower of London. The London Eye has become the most popular paid-for UK visitor attraction, visited by over 3.5 million people a year—that is, an average of 10,000 a day.

At the London Eye, we use marketing communications in a number of interesting ways. During the construction phase, for example, we used public relations (PR) to build high pre-opening interest and awareness, and to challenge any negative perceptions associated with Ferris wheels or thrill rides. We gave the media access to key individuals and organizations throughout this period, in order to win public favour by involving them in the entire process and giving them ownership of what would become a global icon. For the same reason, the media was given access to the construction site at regular key stages of the build—the biggest day being the raising of the wheel from barges on the River Thames. The London Eye project was watched by millions of people on a daily basis, and we used regular, consistent media exposure to keep the public interested and to instill a sense of pride in Londoners. By the time the London Eye was scheduled to open, hundreds of thousands of people had already pre-booked their tickets.

Advertising is used as part of our marketing communications to drive both awareness and footfall. Building awareness with target audiences ensures that the London Eye, as a global icon, is at the forefront of everyone's mind. Through advertising, the London Eye targets audiences in London and the south-east, as well as visitors to London once they arrive in the capital.

Other marketing activity includes seasonal campaigns, sales promotions, and the tactical distribution of leaflets. Seasonal campaigns centre around key periods such as Easter, Christmas, and Halloween, when we target Londoners and the south-east market. This target makes it ideal to focus on local London media, such as the *Evening Standard*, all of the free London papers, and marketing emails.

Sales promotions are used to drive incremental off-peak revenue and visitors. These kinds of campaign are normally used tactically to encourage guests to trial additional products and also to extend brand communication. Leaflets are distributed via British Tourist Authority offices worldwide, trade clients, and tourist information centres throughout the UK. In addition, 'word-of-mouth' plays a key role to encourage visits to the London Eye. More than 30 per cent of London Eye guests visit as the result of a recommendation from family or friends. There is a definite consumer trend towards trusting word-of-mouth and personal recommendations above any form of advertising.

It is extremely important for us to build relationships with industry representative organizations, such as Visit London and Visit Britain, which actively go out to other territories around the world to promote London and Britain as a destination. Through working with these organizations, the London Eye is able to target audiences in desired countries and areas, as well as specific

The BA London Eye: the world's tallest observation wheel

demographics. At the London Eye, we also undertake a number of sales missions to different countries, where key salespeople will meet with travel agents and organizers in a small group or on an individual basis in order to communicate and educate buyers on the London Eye portfolio of products. In the world of

corporate events, as well as journalist familiarization trips, personal communications make a much bigger impact.

1 **We knew that our 25 millionth visitor would be arriving and two important questions emerged: how should we celebrate the occasion? And how should we use marketing communications to mark it?**

■ Introduction

Have you ever wondered how organizations manage to communicate with so many different people and organizations? Well, this is the first of two chapters that explain how this can be accomplished through the use of marketing communications. This chapter introduces and explains what marketing communications is; the following chapter considers each of the communication tools and media, and explains how marketing communications can be planned.

The overall purpose of this chapter is to introduce some of the fundamental ideas and concepts associated with marketing communications. In order to achieve this, the chapter commences with a consideration of communication theory. This is important because it provides a basis on which it is easier to appreciate the different ways in which marketing communications is used.

Following a definition, we explain the role and tasks of marketing communications. Again, this is important, because it specifies the scope of the subject and provides a framework within which to appreciate the various communication activities undertaken by organizations. The tools and media used by marketing communications are an important aspect of this topic. Although the next chapter is devoted to a fuller examination of each of them, a brief overview is presented here.

Marketing communications is about shared meaning and that means developing messages that can be understood and acted on by target audiences. We present some principles by which marketing messages are communicated and then consider how marketing communications might work.

■ Introducing Marketing Communications

Marketing communications, or **promotion** as it was originally called, is one element of the marketing mix. It is used to communicate elements of an organization's offering to a target audience. This offer might refer to an offering or the organization itself as it tries to build its reputation. However, this is a broad view of marketing communications, and we need to understand the various issues, dimensions, and elements that make up this important communication activity. For example, there are the communications experienced by audiences relating to both their use of products ('How good is this hairdryer?') and the consumption of associated services ('Just how good was the service when I was in IKEA?').

There are communications arising from unplanned or unintended experiences (empty stock shelves or accidents) and there are planned marketing communications (Duncan and Moriarty, 1997), which are the main focus of this and the following chapter. These are all represented in Figure 9.1 (Hughes and Fill, 2007), which is the point at which we start our exploration of marketing communications.

Figure 9.1 depicts the diversity and the complexity of managing marketing communications. However, this framework fails to provide any detailed understanding, particularly of the planned marketing communications element. This component is really important because it has the potential not only to present offerings in the best possible way, but also to influence people's expectations about both product and service experiences.

This chapter is intended to help you to understand some of the fundamental ideas associated with planned marketing communications. It sets out the broad scope of the subject and enables readers to appreciate the complexity and diversity of this fascinating subject. Visit the **Online Resource Centre** and follow the web link to the European Association of Communication Agencies (EACA) to find out more about marketing activities across Europe. You can also read Market Insight 9.1 for an example of marketing communications used to develop an entertainment brand.

go online

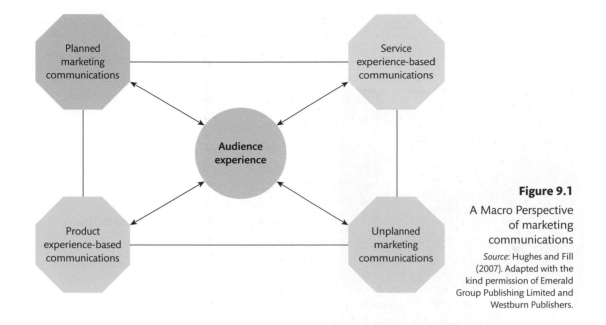

Figure 9.1

A Macro Perspective of marketing communications

Source: Hughes and Fill (2007). Adapted with the kind permission of Emerald Group Publishing Limited and Westburn Publishers.

Market Insight 9.1

Freefall Communication

Merlin Entertainments, which is second only to Disney in the visitor attractions sector, operates in thirteen countries across Europe, North America, and Asia. Alton Towers Resort in the UK is one of its major sites.

Among theme park customers, 23 per cent have previously visited a site, so the launch of new rides every few years encourages return visits. It is also a critical activity because new rides entice thrill seekers, drive interest and excitement for visitors, and enables conversations about Alton Towers.

In March 2010, the 'th13teen' ride was launched. This fulfilled new ride criteria at Alton Towers Resort—namely, that not only was it the world's first freefall drop rollercoaster, but it was also the first to use magnetic brakes. The planned communications to launch the ride started the previous year with public relations (PR) designed to build interest and mystery about what the ride was going to be. This meant keeping the freefall drop

element secret, and building anticipation and speculation. Press releases announced that Google Earth had been asked not to film over the site and *X-Factor* Simon Cowell's ex-bodyguard had been recruited for security reasons. Posters around the site referred to the new attraction with the strap lines 'Surrender' and 'Demon of the Dark Forest' to increase the interest. Activity in online forums increased, as users tried to fathom what the new ride was going to be.

The ride's name was announced at the beginning of the year, but even the name gave little away about the nature of the ride itself. In addition to print, a television ad was aired, and the website featured the new ride, but continued the anticipation and mystery by keeping the freefall drop element secret. Cage fighter Alex Reid, a recent winner of TV show *Celebrity Big Brother*, fronted a newspaper and online campaign to find the first members of the public to use the ride. A shortlist of thirty 'test riders' endured a pre-ride 'boot camp', consisting of endurance and psychometric tests, all of which was

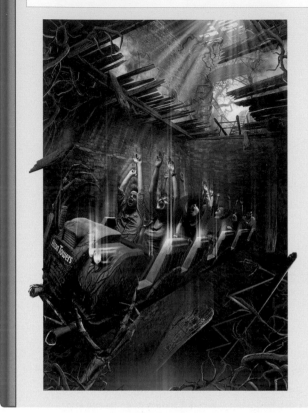

subject to great publicity. The winners experienced the inaugural ride, which was broadcast on television reaching an audience of several million and then posted on YouTube.

Sources: Based on Bainbridge (2010); Barda (2010); Campaignlive (2010)

1 **Identify the planned and unplanned communications used to launch the 'th13teen' ride.**

2 **How might a visitor's experience of the ride feed the communications activities?**

3 **Choose a theme park in your region or country, visit its website, and comment on its marketing communications.**

Marketing for the new ride TH13TEEN helped to create a sense of mystery, 'talkability' and tease before the grand reveal.

Source: TH13TEEN, at the Alton Towers Resort

■ Communication Theory

We start with a consideration of communication theory. This is important because it helps to explain how and why certain marketing communication activities take place. Communication is the process by which individuals share meaning. It is necessary, therefore, that participants in a communication event are able to interpret the meanings embedded in the messages that they receive and then, as far as the sender is concerned, are able to respond coherently. The act of responding is important because it completes an episode in the communication process. Communication that travels only from the sender to the **receiver** is essentially a one-way process and the full communication process remains incomplete. This form of communication is shown in Figure 9.2.

When Cadbury presents its Dairy Milk chocolate bar on a poster in the London Underground, the person standing on the platform can read it, understand it, and may even enjoy being entertained by it. He or she does not, however, have any immediate opportunity to respond to the ad in such a way that Cadbury can hear, understand, and act on the person's comments and feelings. When that same ad is presented on a website or a sales promotion representative

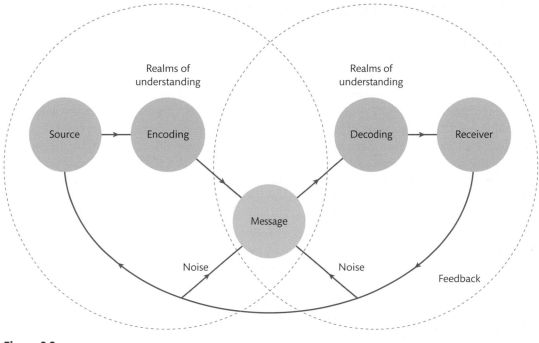

Figure 9.2

A linear model of communications

Source: Based on Schramm (1955), and Shannon and Weaver (1962)

offers that same person a chunk of Cadbury's Dairy Milk when he or she is shopping in a supermarket, there are opportunities to hear, record, and even respond to the comments that person makes. This form of communication travels from a sender (Cadbury) to a receiver (the person in the supermarket) and back again to Cadbury, and is referred to as a two-way communication and represents a complete communication episode. This type of communication is depicted in Figure 9.3.

These basic models form the basis of this introduction to communication theory. For those involved in managing and delivering marketing communications, it is important that these processes and associated complexities are understood. Through knowledge and understanding of the communications process, marketing managers are more likely to achieve their objective of sharing meaning with each member of their target audiences. This not only helps to create opportunities to interact with their audiences, but also encourages some people to develop a **dialogue**—the richest and most meaningful form of communication.

Understanding the way in which communication works therefore provides a foundation on which we can better understand the way in which marketing communications not only works, but also how it can be used effectively by organizations.

Visit the **Online Resource Centre** and follow the web link to the International Association of Business Communicators (IABC) to learn more about its work aimed at improving marketing communications effectiveness.

go online

Three main models or interpretations of how communication works are considered in this chapter: the linear model; the two-way model; and the interactive model of communication.

The Linear Model of Communication

The linear model of communication is regarded as the basic model of mass communications. First developed by Wilbur Schramm (1955), the key components of the linear model of communication are as set out in Figure 9.2.

The model can be broken down into a number of phases, each of which has distinct characteristics. The linear model emphasizes that each phase occurs in a particular sequence; hence it is a linear progression. The model and its components are straightforward, but it is the quality of the linkages between the various elements in the process that determines whether the communication will be successful.

The source is an individual or organization that identifies a problem requiring transmission of a message. The source of a message is an important factor in the communication process: first, the source must identify the right problem; second, a receiver who perceives a source to lack conviction, authority, trust, or expertise is not likely to believe the messages sent by that source.

Encoding is the process whereby the source selects a combination of appropriate words, pictures, symbols, and music to represent the message to be transmitted. The various bits are 'packed' in such a way that they can be unpacked and understood. The goal is to create a message that is capable of being comprehended easily by the receiver.

Once encoded, the message must be put into a form that is capable of transmission. It may be oral or written, verbal or non-verbal, in a symbolic form or in a sign. The channel is the means by which the message is transmitted from the source to the receiver. These channels may be personal or non-personal. The former involves face-to-face contact and word-of-mouth communications, which can be extremely influential. Non-personal channels are characterized by mass media advertising, which can reach large audiences. Whatever the format chosen, the source must be sure that what is being put into the message is what he or she wants to be **decoded** by the receiver.

Once the receivers, individuals or organizations, have seen, heard, smelt, or read the message, they decode it. In effect, they are 'unpacking' the various components of the message, starting to make sense of it and to give it meaning. The more clearly the message is encoded, the easier it is to 'unpack' and comprehend what the source intended to convey when it constructed the message. Decoding is therefore that part of the communication process during which receivers give meaning to a message.

Once understood, receivers provide a set of reactions referred to as a 'response'. These reactions may vary from an emotional response, based on a set of feelings and thoughts about the message, to a behavioural or action response.

Feedback is another part of the response process. It is important to know not only that the message has been received, but also that it has been correctly decoded and the right meaning attributed. However, although feedback is an essential aspect of a successful communication event, feedback through mass media channels is generally difficult to obtain, mainly because of the inherent time delay involved in the feedback process. Feedback through **personal selling**, however, can be instantaneous, through explicit means such as questioning, raising objections, or signing an order form. For the mass media advertiser, the process can be vague and prone to misinterpretation. If a suitable feedback system is not in place, then the source will be unaware that the communication has been unsuccessful and is liable to continue wasting resources. This represents inefficient and ineffective marketing communications.

Noise is concerned with influences that distort information and, which, in turn, make it difficult for the receiver to decode and interpret the message as intended by the source. So if a telephone rings or someone rustles sweet papers during a sensitive part of a film screened in a cinema, the receiver is distracted from the message.

The final component in the linear model concerns the 'realm of understanding'. This is an important element in the communication process, because it recognizes that successful communications are more likely to be achieved if the source and the receiver understand each other. This understanding concerns attitudes, perceptions, behaviour, and experience: the values of both parties to the communication process. Effective communication is more likely when there is some common ground—that is, the 'realm of understanding'—between the source and receiver.

One of the problems associated with the linear model of communication is that it ignores the impact that other people can have on the communication process. People are not passive; they actively use information, and the views and actions of other people can impact on the way in which information is sent, received, processed, and given meaning. One of the other difficulties with the linear model is that it is based on communication through mass media.

Developed at a time when first radio and then TV, with only a few channels, were the only media available, it can be seen why the model was developed. Today, there are hundreds of TV channels; audiences now use the Internet, mobile phones, and an increasing array of digital equipment to manage their work, leisure, and entertainment. Increasing numbers of people now engage with interactive communications, and in some circumstances organizations and individuals can be involved in real dialogue. For example, online games, such as World of Warcraft, had 10.2 million subscribers in February 2012, and Groupon, which offers vouchers for daily deals that can be used at local or national companies, was estimated to have some 150 million registered users in January 2012. Both of these examples can work only through interaction and dialogue. The linear model is therefore no longer entirely appropriate.

Groupon offers city deals, good offers, and getaways

Source: Courtesy of Groupon

The Two-Step Model of Communication

One interpretation of the linear model is that it is a one-step explanation: information is directed and shot at prospective audiences, rather like a bullet is propelled from a gun. However, we know that people can have a significant impact on the communication process and the **two-step model** goes some way towards reflecting their influence.

The two-step model compensates for the linear or one-step model because it recognizes the importance of personal influences when informing and persuading audiences to think or behave in particular ways. This model depicts information flowing via various media channels, to particular types of person to whom other members of the audience refer for information and guidance. There are two main types of influencer: the first is referred to as an **opinion leader**; the other is an **opinion former**. The first is simply an ordinary person who has a heightened interest in a particular topic; the second is involved professionally in the topic of interest. Both have enormous potential to influence audiences. This may be because messages from personal influencers provide reinforcement and message credibility, or it might be because this is the only way of reaching the end-user audience. (See 'Personal influencers' for more on these types of person.)

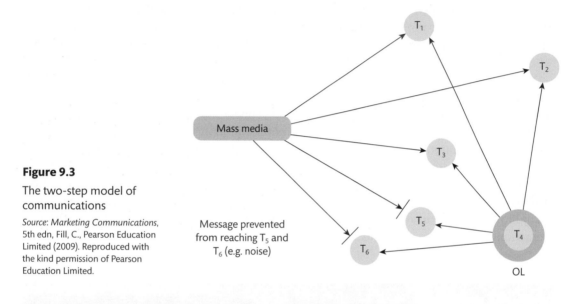

Figure 9.3

The two-step model of communications

Source: Marketing Communications, 5th edn, Fill, C., Pearson Education Limited (2009). Reproduced with the kind permission of Pearson Education Limited.

Message prevented from reaching T_5 and T_6 (e.g. noise)

The Interaction Model of Communications

The **interaction model** is similar to the two-step model, but it contains one important difference: in this interpretation, the parties are seen to interact among themselves and communication flows among all of the members in what is regarded as a communication network (see Figure 9.4). Mass media is not the only source of the communication.

Unlike the linear model, in which messages flow from the source to the receiver through a single channel, the interaction model recognizes that messages can flow through various channels and that people can influence the direction and impact of a message. It is not necessarily one-way, but interactive, communication that typifies much of contemporary communications.

Interaction is an integral part of the communication process. Think of a conversation with a friend: the face-to-face oral and visual communication enables both of you to consider what the other is saying, and to react in whatever way is appropriate. Mass communication does not facilitate this interactional element and so the linear model might therefore be regarded as an incomplete form of the pure communication process.

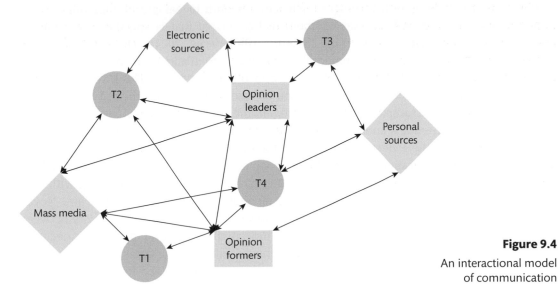

Figure 9.4

An interactional model of communication

Interaction is about actions that lead to a response and much attention is now given to the interaction that occurs between people. However, care needs to be taken because the content associated with an interactional event might be based on an argument, a statement of opinion, or a mere casual social encounter. What is important here is interaction that leads to mutual understanding. This type of interaction concerns 'relationship-specific knowledge' (Ballantyne, 2004)—that is, the interaction is about information that is relevant to both parties. Once this is established, increased levels of trust develop between the participants, so that eventually a dialogue emerges between communication partners. Interactivity therefore is a prelude to dialogue, the highest or purest form of communication.

Research Insight 9.1

To take your learning further, you might wish to read the following influential paper:

Ballantyne, D. (2004) 'Dialogue and its role in the development of relationship specific knowledge', *Journal of Business & Industrial Marketing*, 19(2): 114–23

This is an important academic paper in the field of marketing communications because it clarifies different forms of communication. Although set within a business-to-business (B2B) marketing context, the principles apply equally well within a consumer world. Ballantyne distinguishes between interaction and dialogue, and offers an understanding of how communication should be used within different relationships. He also avoids the tautology that is the awful phrase 'two-way dialogue'. Please avoid using this incorrect phrase yourself!

@ Visit the **Online Resource Centre** to read the abstract and to access the full paper.

Dialogue occurs through reasoning, which requires both listening and adaptation skills. Dialogue is concerned with the development of knowledge that is specific to the parties involved and is referred to as 'learning together' (Ballantyne, 2004). The development of digital technologies has been instrumental in enabling organizations to provide increased interaction opportunities with their customers and other audiences. Think of the number of times when watching Sky television that you are prompted to press the red button to get more information. For example, many news programmes now encourage viewers to tweet, to phone, or to send in emails and pictures about particular issues. This is an attempt to get audiences to express their views about a subject and, in doing so, to promote access to and interaction with the programme. Whereas interaction at one time really occurred only through personal selling, it is now possible to interact, and so build mutual understanding with consumers, through the Internet and other digital technologies. Indeed, Hoffman and Novak (1996) claim that interactivity between people is now supplemented by interactivity between machines. This means that the interaction, or indeed dialogue, that previously occurred through machines can now occur with the equipment facilitating the communication.

go online

Visit the **Online Resource Centre** and complete Internet Activity 9.3 to learn more about Internet advertising.

■ Personal Influencers

We have already mentioned the two main types of personal influencer that can be recognized: opinion leaders and opinion formers. These are now discussed in turn (see also Chapter 3).

Opinion Leaders

Studies by Katz and Lazarsfeld (1955) into American voting and purchase behaviour led them to conclude that some individuals were more predisposed to receiving information and then reprocessing it to influence others. They found that these individuals had the capacity to be more persuasive than information received directly from the mass media. They called these people 'opinion leaders' and one of their defining characteristics is that they belong to the same peer group as the people whom they influence; they are not distant or removed.

It has been reported in subsequent research that opinion leaders have a greater exposure to relevant media and, as a result, have more knowledge/familiarity and involvement with a product category than others. Non-leaders, or **opinion followers**, turn to opinion leaders for advice and information about offerings in which they are interested. Opinion leaders are also more gregarious and more self-confident than non-leaders, and are more confident of their role as an influencer (Chan and Misra, 1990). It is not surprising, therefore, that many marketing communication strategies are targeted at influencing opinion leaders, because they will, in turn, influence others.

This approach has been used to convey particular information and to help to educate large target audiences through TV and radio programmes. For example, television soap operas are popular not only in Western developed economies, but also in South America, Japan, India, Philippines, and South Korea. Apart from their entertainment value, shows such as *Coronation*

Street, *EastEnders*, and *Emmerdale*, and radio programmes such as *The Archers* in the UK, have been used as opinion leadership vehicles to bring to attention and open up debates about many controversial social issues, such as contraception, abortion, drug use and abuse, and serious illness and mental health concerns.

Opinion Formers

The other main form of independent personal influencer is the 'opinion former'. These people are not part of the same peer group as the people whom they influence. Their defining characteristic is that they exert personal influence because of their profession, authority, education, or status associated with the object of the communication process. They provide information and advice as part of the formal expertise that they are perceived to hold. For example, shop assistants in music equipment shops are often experienced musicians in their own right. Aspiring musicians seeking to buy their first proper guitar will often consult these perceived 'experts' about guitar brands, styles, models, and associated equipment such as amplifiers. In the same way, doctors carry such conviction that they can influence the rate at which medicines are consumed. Drug manufacturers such as GlaxoSmithKline and Pfizer often launch new drugs by enlisting the support of eminent professors, consultants, or doctors, who are recognized by others in the profession as experts. These opinion formers are invited to lead symposia and associated events, and in doing so to build credibility and activity around the new product.

Organizations target their marketing communications at opinion leaders and formers in order to penetrate the market more quickly than relying on communicating directly with the target audience. However, in addition to these forms of influence, reference needs to be made to spokespersons (see Market Insight 9.2). There are some potential problems of which advertisers need to be aware when considering the use of celebrities: first, does the celebrity fit the image of the brand and will the celebrity be an acceptable 'face' of the brand, to the target audience, now and in the long run? Interestingly, an NfpSynergy survey of more than 1,000 UK 11–25-year-olds named, as the top four celebrities most likely to influence them to support any charity that they endorsed, Cheryl Cole, David Beckham, Simon Cowell, and Stephen Fry (Cartmell, 2011).

The second problem concerns the impact that the celebrity makes relative to the brand. There is a danger that the receiver remembers the celebrity, but not the message or the brand. The celebrity becomes the hero, rather than the offering being advertised.

Market Insight 9.2

Celebrity 'Flowers' in Japan

The use of celebrity endorsers for personal care offerings is well established. Celebrity endorsers offer consumers trust, reassurance, and for some they act as a role model and provide guidance in terms of behaviour and aspirations. In many Western economies, this approach and use of the idealized appearance has been subject to much criticism and discussion. This is not the case in Japan and other parts of Asia.

The shampoo and conditioner market in Japan is relatively stable, with little significant change. Market share in 2008 was dominated by four major companies: Kao, Procter & Gamble, Unilever; and in fourth place Shiseido. Each has a similar portfolio of brands, but because the market is stable, rivalry is fierce and market entry a severe challenge. The most valued product features for Japanese consumers choosing haircare products are value for money, effectiveness, and sensory benefits. The influence of Western brands, values, and the desire for blonde hair had, until 2006, been very strong.

In order to establish a stronger market position, Shiseido launched Tsubaki, a luxury haircare series consisting of shampoo, conditioner, and an at-home hair treatment. *Tsubaki* is Japanese for the flower camellia. The brand rationale for Tsubaki was the anticipation that there was a fashion trend towards shiny black hair.

The key to the launch of Tsubaki was a heavyweight advertising campaign, costing ¥5 billion, the largest in the company's history. Rather than focus on the brand's attributes and its unique combination of oils and ingredients, an emotional positioning was adopted, one based on feelings of beauty. This was established through the use of six popular Japanese celebrities, women who symbolized Japanese beauty. Indeed the tagline, 'Japanese women are beautiful' has become synonymous with the brand. These and later campaigns included an Olympic figure skating gold medallist, a popular ex-news announcer, singers, and film actors. Many of the celebrities where shown wearing suits to foster an association with competence.

The brand was improved and refreshed in March 2009, and was again supported by a campaign, but this time it featured a new range of endorsers. This encouraged excitement and anticipation as consumers guessed who the new celebrities might be featured in the campaign. It also served to reinforce the brand's positioning and image of representing beautiful Japanese women. Even a film called *Flowers* featuring the six actors in the first ad has been made.

The Tsubaki brand has been extremely successful, its ads are well known throughout Japan, and they also win numerous awards.

Sources: AP (2007); Anon. (2010); Schilling (2010)

1 Why should the use of celebrity endorsers rather than ordinary people be a more effective form of brand communication?

2 If you were considering launching a brand into the personal care market and you did not have the resources necessary to support an advertising campaign, which marketing communications would you use?

3 Why do you think reassurance is necessary to help people to buy a personal care brand?

All of the models of communication discussed have a role to play in marketing communications. Mass media communication, in the form of broadcast TV and radio, is still used by organizations to reach large audiences. Two-way and interactional forms of communication are used to reach smaller, specific target audiences and to enable a range of people to contribute to the process. Interaction and dialogue are higher levels of communication, and are used increasingly to generate personal communication with individual customers. The skill for marketing practitioners is to know when to move from one-way, to two-way, to interactive, and then to dialogue-based marketing communications.

What is Marketing Communications?

Quite naturally, definitions of 'marketing communication' have evolved as the topic and our understanding has developed. Original views assumed that these types of communication were used to persuade people to buy offerings. The focus was on offerings, one-way communications, persuasion, and there was a short-term perspective. In short, an organization's offerings were *promoted* to audiences.

However, this perspective has given way to the term 'marketing communications'. This was partly a result of an increase in the tasks that the communications departments were expected to undertake, and a widening of the tools and media that could be used. At the same time, there has been a shift from mass to personal communications and a greater focus on integration activities. Fill (2011) offers a definition of marketing communications that reflects contemporary practice and focus: 'Marketing communications is an audience centred activity which aims to encourage engagement between participants and provoke conversations.' This definition has three main elements.

- The first concerns the *audiences* for marketing communications. Customers, both consumers and businesses, constitute the core audiences for most marketing communications activities. Within these groups and in addition to *current* customers, there are several other types of customer. *Lapsed* customers are those people who used to buy, but who have either defected to a competitor brand or have stopped buying as a result of changed circumstances. *Potential* customers are people who have never bought in the category; those who have only ever bought a competitor's brand are *rival* customers. Marketing communications should be varied in order to reach these different types of customer. This means that it is important that messages be based on a firm understanding of both the needs and environment of the audience. From this base, it is easier to present and position brands in order that they are perceived to be different and of value to the target audience.

- The second key word is *engage*. Good communication is characterized by participants sharing meaning. In order that this occurs, it is necessary that the communication stimulates engagement, a moment when a recipient actively considers a message and relates it to his or her circumstance. This might be reflected in getting his or her attention, provoking brand or message consideration, or even encouraging response, such as a request for more information, a click-through, or a text message.

  It is unrealistic to believe that all audiences always want a relationship with your organization/brand, and for some one-way communication is fine. However, messages should encourage individual members of target audiences to respond to the focus organization (or product/brand). This response can be immediate through, for example, purchase behaviour or use of customer care lines, or it can be deferred as information is assimilated and considered for future use. Even if the information is discarded at a later date, the communication will have attracted attention and consideration of the message. Engagement precedes response, yet response can be an integral part of engagement.

- The third element in the definition concerns *conversation*. The one-way mass communication model is no longer the dominant form of brand communication. Today, especially with the advent of social media and social networks, communication is largely two-way, with participation actively encouraged with a view to stimulating interactive communication and, in some cases, dialogue. This participation in the communication process is characterized by conversation, which occurs between people who have been sufficiently engaged and motivated to want to share ideas, thoughts, and feelings about a message with others. These conversations can be face-to-face, ear-to-ear, or electronic, but are rooted within word-of-mouth communication.

The response that a marketing communication event stimulates can be used as a measure of whether a communication event has been successful. There are essentially two key responses: cognitive and emotional. Cognitive responses assume an audience to be active problem-solvers and that they use marketing communications to help them in their lives, in purchasing offerings and in managing organization-related activities. For example, brands are developed partly to help consumers and partly to assist the marketing effort of the host organization. A brand can inform consumers quickly that, among other things, 'This brand means x quality', and through experience of similar brand purchases, consumers are assured that their risk is minimized. If the problem facing a consumer is 'which new soup to select for lunch', by choosing one from a familiar family brand, the consumer is able to solve it with minimal risk and great speed. Cognitive responses assume that audiences undertake rational information processing.

Emotional responses, on the other hand, assume that decision-making is not made through active thought processing but as a result of emotional reaction to a communication stimulus. 'Hedonic consumption' concerns the purchase and use of offerings to fulfil fantasies and to satisfy emotional needs. Satisfaction is based on the overall experience of consuming an offering. For example, sports cars and motorbikes are not always bought because of the functionality and performance of the vehicle, but because of the thrill of independence, power, and an adrenalin rush of freedom and excitement. Marketing communications in general—and content in particular—should be developed in anticipation of an audience's cognitive or emotional response.

Traditionally, marketing communications has been used to convey product-related information to customer audiences. Today, the use of **emotional appeals** has been shown to be more effective at engaging audiences (Binet and Field, 2007). In a customer-centric world, marketing communications should seek to provide value for the target audience, based on their needs and perception of the world. To be successful, marketing communications should therefore be grounded in the behaviour and relationship preferences and of the target audience. In many situations, the information-processing style of the audience can also be a significant factor. This is a reflection of their involvement with the product category and whether the brand that is subject to the communication event is of direct relevance to them at that particular point in time.

Although marketing communications is a complex activity and used by organizations with varying degrees of sophistication, it is undoubtedly concerned with engaging target audiences, and motivating them to respond and to develop conversations with other people.

■ The Role of Marketing Communications

Now that we have established ideas about how communication works and what marketing communications might be, it is time to examine the role of marketing communications and the tasks that it undertakes. Marketing communications is a relatively new term for what was previously referred to as promotion. As was discussed in Chapter 1, promotion is one of the 'P's of the marketing mix, and is responsible for the communication of the marketing offer to the target market. Although recognizing that there is implicit and important communication through the other elements of the marketing mix (for example, that a high price is symbolic of high quality), it is the task of a planned and integrated set of activities to communicate effectively with each of an organization's stakeholder groups.

Fundamentally, marketing communications comprises three elements: a set of tools, the media, and messages. The five common tools are advertising, sales promotion, personal selling, direct marketing, and public relations (PR). In addition, there are a range of media, such as TV, radio, press, and the Internet, which are used to convey messages to target audiences.

These various tools have been developed in response to changing market and environmental conditions. For example, PR is now seen by some to have both a product and a corporate dimension. Direct marketing is now recognized as an important way of developing closer relationships with buyers, both consumer and organizational, whereas new and innovative forms of communication through, for example, sponsorship, events, ambient media, video advertising, and gaming, plus the huge range of methods using social media, mean that effective communication requires the selection and integration of an increasing variety of communication tools and media. Communication is no longer restricted to promoting and persuading audiences; the tasks are now much broader and strategic.

Today, the term marketing communications is a more appropriate and established term than promotion with which to reflect an organization's communication activities.

Marketing communications are used to achieve one of two principal goals. The first concerns the development of brand values. Advertising, and to some extent PR, have for a long time concentrated on establishing a set of feelings, emotions, and beliefs about a brand or organization. Brand communication seeks to make us think positively about a brand, and helps us to remember and to develop positive brand attitudes, in the hope that, when we are ready to buy that type of offering again, we will buy brand X because we feel positively about it.

The alternative and more contemporary goal is to use communications to make us behave in particular ways. Rather than spend lots of money developing worthy and positive attitudes towards brands, the view of many today is that we should use this money to encourage people to behave in particular ways. This might be through buying the offering, or driving people to visit a website, to request a brochure, or to make a telephone call. This is called 'behaviour change' and is driven by using messages that provide audiences with a reason to act or what is referred to as a **call to action**.

So, on the one hand, communications can be used to develop brand feelings; on the other, they can be used to change or manage the behaviour of the target audience. These are not mutually exclusive: for example, many TV advertisements are referred to as **direct response advertising** because not only do they attempt to create brand values, but they also carry a website address, telephone number, or details of a special offer (sales promotion). In other words, the two goals are mixed into a hybrid approach.

The success of marketing communications depends on the extent to which messages engage their audiences. These audiences can be seen to fall into three main groups, as follows.

- *Customers*—These may be consumers or they may be end-user organizations.
- *Channel members*—Each organization is part of a network of other organizations, such as suppliers, retailers, wholesalers, value-added **resellers**, distributors, and other retailers, who join together, often freely, to make the offering available to end users.
- *General stakeholders*—These are organizations and people who either influence or are influenced by the organization, including shareholders, the financial community, trade unions, employees, local community, and others.

Marketing communications therefore involves not only customers, but also a range of other stakeholders.

The concept of 'exchange' is central to our understanding of marketing (see also Chapter 1). For an exchange to take place, there must be two or more parties, each of whom can offer something of value to the other and each of whom is prepared to enter freely into the exchange process—that is, a transaction. There are, of course, many types of exchange, but two are of particular importance: **transactional exchanges** and **collaborative exchanges**.

- *Transactional exchanges* (Bagozzi, 1978; Houston and Gassenheimer, 1987) are transactions that occur independently of any previous or subsequent exchanges. They have a short-term orientation and are primarily motivated by self-interest. So when a consumer buys an MP3 player, a brand that he or she has not bought before, then a transactional exchange can be identified.
- *Collaborative exchanges* (Dwyer et al., 1987) have a longer-term orientation and develop between parties who wish to build long-term supportive relationships. So when a consumer buys his or her third product from the same brand as the MP3 player, perhaps from the same dealer, collaborative exchanges are considered to be taking place.

These two types of exchange transaction represent the extremes of a spectrum. In mature industrial societies, transactional exchanges have tended to dominate commercial transactions, although recently there has been a substantial movement towards collaborative exchanges. Each organization has a mix of audiences, so it should not be surprising that they use a range of communication tools and media to suit different exchange preferences of customers, suppliers, and other stakeholder audiences.

The impact on marketing communications is essentially about the choice of tools, media, and messages. Audiences who prefer transactional exchanges might be better engaged with advertising and mass media-based communications, with messages that are impersonal and largely rational and product-focused. Audiences that prefer more collaborative exchanges should be engaged through personal, informal, and interactive communications, with messages that are generally emotional and relationship-oriented.

Shoes can be purchased from a range of different retail outlets and the store from which they are purchased is often insignificant, especially because price can be an important purchasing factor. The approach adopted by Clarks, the shoe company, recognizes the importance of building a long-term relationship with its customers. The 'First Shoes' campaign run by Clarks demonstrates good marketing communications, and is based on the significance of a child's first pair of shoes and what they can mean to the parents. These tiny shoes are often kept for years and years as a memento. Clarks now provide a souvenir of the occasion in the form of a free, framed Polaroid photograph of a child's very first shop visit and fitting. This is a simple campaign that engages audiences with an important event, but it also enables both the parents and Clarks to remember the event through the longer term. What might have been a transactional exchange is transformed into one that is more collaborative and relationship-oriented.

■ The Tasks of Marketing Communications

Promotion (essentially persuasion) alone is insufficient: marketing communications undertakes other tasks in the name of engaging audiences. So what is it that marketing communications does and why do organizations use it in varying ways? Fundamentally, marketing communications can be used to engage audiences by undertaking one of four main tasks, referred to by Fill (2002) as the **DRIP model** on the basis that communications can be used to *differentiate* brands and organizations, to *reinforce* brand memories and expectations, to *inform* (that is, to make aware and educate audiences), and finally to *persuade* them to do things or to behave in particular ways. Table 9.1 offers an explanation of each of these tasks.

These tasks are not mutually exclusive; indeed campaigns might be designed to target two or three of them (see Market Insight 9.3). For example, the launch of a new brand will require that audiences be informed, be made aware of its existence, and be enabled to understand

Table 9.1 The key DRIP tasks for marketing communications

Tasks	Explanation
To differentiate	In many markets, there is little to separate brands (e.g. mineral water, coffee, printers). In these cases, it is the images created by marketing communications that help to *differentiate* one brand from another and to position them, so that consumers develop positive attitudes and can make purchasing decisions.
To reinforce	Communications may be used to *remind* people of a need that they might have or of the benefits of past transactions, with a view to convincing them that they should enter into a similar exchange. In addition, it is possible to provide *reassurance* or comfort either immediately prior to an exchange or, more commonly, post-purchase. This is important because it helps to retain current customers and improve profitability. This approach to business is much more cost-effective than constantly striving to lure new customers.
To inform	One of the most common uses of marketing communications is to *inform* and make potential customers aware of the features and benefits of an organization's offering. In addition, marketing communications can be used to educate audiences, to show them how to use a product or what to do in particular situations.
To persuade	Communication may attempt to *persuade* current and potential customers of the desirability of entering into an exchange relationship.

how it is different from competitor brands. A brand that is well established might try to reach lapsed customers by reminding them of its key features and benefits, and offering them an incentive (persuasion) to buy again. For example, *Your M&S* is a bi-monthly magazine designed to showcase what is new in Marks and Spencer's stores, and to give fashion and style advice. However, it features only products available at M&S. The magazine is an integral part of the company's communication mix, and is used, among many things, to engage customers with the brand and drive readers into the store, or online, to shop. To that extent, an in-house survey found that 57 per cent of readers—that is, nearly 2.53 million people—visited an M&S store as a result of reading the magazine. It also found that 30 per cent of readers had bought a product featured in its magazine (Alarcon, 2008).

Market Insight 9.3

Phone-a-Stunt with T-Mobile

T-Mobile launched a campaign in 2009 that typifies the way in which marketing communications can now work. The campaign was audience-oriented, driven by digital media, yet incorporated traditional advertising through broadcast and outdoor media. The campaign also harnessed the power of PR.

The goal was to help people to see how they could create and share magical moments using T-Mobile.

This was achieved through two key events and YouTube, among other facilities. In January, a mass-choreographed dance (a 'flash mob'), involving unsuspecting commuters, was staged at Liverpool Street Station in London. A 2.5-minute advert, featuring footage from the dance, was delivered through broadcast media during Channel 4's *Big Brother*.

In April, another flash mob—this time, a mass singalong—was held in Trafalgar Square, with people invited to attend through Facebook, Twitter, and SMS. Over 13,000 people turned up for the event, which was filmed and again turned into an ad.

Videos from both events were hosted on T-Mobile's branded YouTube and received 23 million hits. The events were taken on a roadshow tour and one Facebook group re-enacted the dance with 2,000 people at Liverpool Street Station. As if that were not enough, outdoor advertising was used in the form of bus advertising and media

T-Mobile stages a mass choreographed dance with unsuspecting train commuters
Source: 2010 T-Mobile (UK) Ltd

relations, ensuring that the unusual events were mentioned in the news, entertainment, and business media.

The results? Handset sales rose by 22 per cent and T-Mobile stores experienced the highest ever recorded number of visitors.

Sources: Benady (2009); Byrne (2010)

1 What is the role of communications and which tasks do you think were being targeted in the T-Mobile campaign?

2 How does your mobile phone service provider use marketing communications?

3 Why was YouTube a central element in the campaign?

The Marketing Communications Mix

We learned earlier that marketing communications activities comprise three main elements: tools; media; and messages. These are considered here briefly, although a fuller exposition of the tools and media can be found in Chapter 10.

The traditional marketing communications mix consists of a set of five primary tools: advertising; sales promotion; direct marketing; PR; and personal selling. Additionally, these tools—and in particular advertising—use media in order to reach their audiences. Tools and media are not the same, because they have different characteristics and are used for different purposes.

The five primary tools of marketing communications are used in various combinations and with different degrees of intensity in order to achieve different communication goals with target audiences.

Media enable messages to be delivered to target audiences. Some media are owned directly by the organization advertising its services (a building or delivery van can constitute media), but in most cases media aiming to reach large audiences are owned by third-party organizations. As a result, clients have to pay media owners for the right to send their messages through their media vehicles.

For a long time, the range of available media was fairly limited, but since the early 1990s the array of media has been growing rapidly and changing the media landscape. Now, there is a huge choice of media, so that media selection has become crucial when trying to reach increasingly smaller audiences. The cost of some media can be immense, although in many cases fees are related to the number of people reached through a media vehicle. Space (or time) within traditional media is limited, and costs rise as demand for the limited space/time and audience size increases. As a generalization, space within digital media is unlimited and so contact costs fall as audience size increases.

Each of the tools, key media, and marketing communication messages is considered further in Chapter 10.

Word-of-Mouth

Planned marketing communications have traditionally used paid-for media to convey messages to target audiences. However, as mentioned previously in respect of opinion formers and leaders, some messages are best relayed through personal communications. This type of communication does not involve any payment for media, because communication is freely given through word-of-mouth conversation.

Word-of-mouth communication is 'interpersonal communication regarding products or services where the receiver regards the communicator as impartial' (Stokes and Lomax, 2002). Personal influence within the communication process is important. This is because customers perceive word-of-mouth recommendations to be objective and unbiased. In comparison to advertising messages, word-of-mouth communications are more robust (Berkman and Gilson, 1986). Word-of-mouth messages are used either as information inputs prior to purchase, or as a support and reinforcement of their own purchasing decisions. For example, websites such as TripAdvisor feature reviews and advice from those who have first-hand experience of hotels, resorts, flights, holiday rentals, and holidays.

People like to talk about their offering experiences. The main stimulus for behaviour is that the offering in question either gave them particular pleasure or displeasure. These motivations to discuss products, and their associative experiences vary between

Many travellers check TripAdvisor for reviews before booking a hotel or flight.
Source: TripAdvisor

individuals and with the intensity of the motivation at any one particular moment. One hotel gave away teddy bears to guests on the basis that the guests would be happy to talk about their stay at the hotel, with the teddy bear acting as a prompt to provoke or induce conversation.

Views about what gets talked about vary. One view holds that for every single positive comment, there are ten negative comments. A contrasting view holds that 85 per cent of **word of mouth** is positive about brand support. For this reason, word-of-mouth communication was once seen as negative, unplanned, and as having a corrosive effect on a brand's overall communications. Today, organizations actively manage word-of-mouth communications in order to generate positive comments and as a way of differentiating themselves in the market. 'Viral' marketing or 'word-of-mouse' communication is an electronic version of the spoken endorsement of an offering. Often using humorous messages, games, video clips, and screen savers, information can be targeted at key individuals, who then voluntarily pass the message to friends and colleagues, and in doing so bestow, endorse, and provide the message with much-valued credibility.

For organizations, it is important to target messages at those individuals who are predisposed to such discussion, because it is likely that they will propel word-of-mouth recommendations. The target is therefore not necessarily the target market, but opinion leaders within target markets, individuals who are most likely to volunteer their positive opinions about the offering, and who (potentially) have some influence over people in their peer group.

■ How Marketing Communications Might Work

Ideas about how advertising, and then promotion, works have been a constant source of investigation, endeavour, and conceptual speculation. To suggest that a firm conclusion has been reached would be misleading and untrue. However, particular ideas have stood out and have played a more influential role in shaping our ideas about this fascinating topic. Some of these are presented here.

The first important idea about how advertising works was based on how the personal selling process works. Developed by Strong (1925), the '**AIDA** model' has become extremely well known and used by many practitioners. AIDA refers to the need first to create *awareness*, second, to generate *interest*, and then to drive *desire*, from which *action* (a sale) emerges. As a broad interpretation of the sales process, this is generally correct, but it fails to provide insight into the depths of how advertising works.

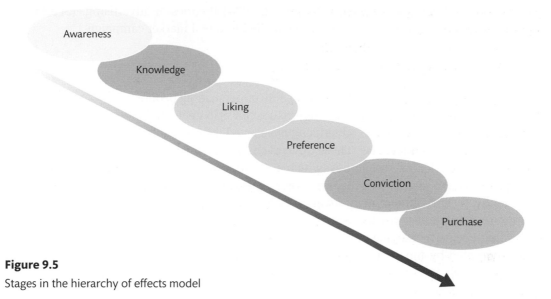

Figure 9.5
Stages in the hierarchy of effects model

Thirty-six years later, Lavidge and Steiner (1961) presented a model based on what is referred to as the **hierarchy of effects (HoE)** approach. Similar in nature to AIDA, it assumes that there are a series of steps through which a prospect must pass in order for a purchase to be made. It is assumed, correctly, that advertising cannot generate an immediate sale because there are a series of thought processes that need to be fulfilled prior to action. These steps are represented in Figure 9.5.

These models have become known as hierarchy of effects (HoE) models, simply because the effects (on audiences) are thought to occur in a top-down sequence. Some of the attractions of these HoE models and frameworks are that they are straightforward, simple, easy to understand, and, if creating advertising materials, provide a helpful broad template on which to develop and evaluate campaigns.

However, although attractive, this sequential approach has several drawbacks. People do not always process information, nor do they always purchase offerings, in a series of sequential steps. This logical progression is not reflected in reality when, for example, an impulse purchase is followed by an emotional feeling toward a brand. There are also questions about what actually constitutes adequate levels of awareness, comprehension, and conviction: how can it be known which stage the majority of the target audience has reached at any one point in time? And is this purchase sequence applicable to all consumers for all purchases?

■ The Strong and the Weak Theories of Advertising

So, if advertising cannot be assumed to work in just one particular way, what other explanations are there? Of the various models put forward, two in particular stand out—namely, the

Strong (Jones, 1991) and the Weak (Ehrenberg, 1974) theories of advertising. (See Market Insight 9.4 to see how these theories can be applied to a real market campaign.)

The Strong Theory of Advertising

According to Jones (1991), advertising is capable of persuading people to buy an offering that they have not previously purchased. Advertising can also generate long-run purchase behaviour. Under the **strong theory**, advertising is believed to be capable of increasing sales for a brand and for the **product class**. These upward shifts are achieved through the use of manipulative and psychological techniques, which are deployed against largely passive consumers, who, possibly as a result of apathy, are either generally incapable of processing information intelligently, or have little or no motivation to become involved.

This interpretation is a persuasion view and corresponds very well to the HoE models. Persuasion occurs by moving buyers towards a purchase by easing them through a series of steps, prompted by timely and suitable promotional messages. It seems that this approach correlates closely with new products for which new buying behaviours are required.

The Strong theory has close affiliation with an advertising style that is product-oriented, in which features and benefits are outlined clearly for audiences, and in which pack shots are considered important.

The Weak Theory of Advertising

Contrary to the strong perspective is the view that a consumer's brand choices are driven by purchasing habit rather than by exposure to advertising messages. One of the more prominent researchers in this area is Ehrenberg (1997), who believed that advertising represented a weak force and that consumers are active information processors.

Ehrenberg proposed that the 'awareness–trial–reinforcement' (**ATR**) framework is a more appropriate interpretation of how advertising works. Both Jones and Ehrenberg agree that awareness is required before any purchase can be made, although the elapsed time between awareness and action may be very short or very long. Out of the mass of people exposed to a message, a few will be sufficiently intrigued to want to try an offering (trial), the next phase. Reinforcement follows to maintain awareness and to provide reassurance to help customers to repeat the pattern of thinking and behaviour. Advertising's role is to breed brand familiarity and identification (Ehrenberg, 1997).

According to the **Weak theory**, advertising is employed as a defence, to retain customers, and to increase product or brand usage. Advertising is used to reinforce existing attitudes, not necessarily to change them drastically. This means that when people say that they 'are not influenced by advertising', they are, in the main, correct.

Both the Strong and the Weak theories of advertising are important, because they are equally right and they are equally wrong. The answer to the question 'How does advertising work?' lies somewhere between the two and is dependent on the context. For advertising to work, involvement is likely to be high, and so here the Strong theory is the most applicable. However, the vast majority of purchase decisions generate low involvement, and so decision-making is likely to be driven by habit. Here, advertising's role is to maintain a brand's awareness with the purchase cycle.

Market Insight 9.4

Dirt is Good . . . at least for Unilever

As companies introduce brands to different countries and regions, they often resort to an adaption strategy. This requires each brand to have an individual positioning, packaging, promise, and even name, to reflect local preferences. For Unilever, it had 'Ala' in Argentina, 'Surf' in India, 'Skip' in France, 'Breeze' in Thailand, 'Persil' in the UK, 'Rinso' in Indonesia, and 'Omo' in Africa, Brazil, China, the Middle East, and South America.

The idea that children should be able to play freely and that dirt was not bad, but indeed good, presented Unilever with the opportunity to standardize, and to create a global brand with one promise and one overall position.

Up until this point, advertising for detergent brands had been based on the premise that dirt is bad. Advertising used shots of stains being dissolved, clothing fibres being penetrated by the brand, and housewives relieved to have got their children's clothing clean and fresh. Informational claims that X brand 'comes to the rescue', 'washes whiter', and 'gets the best results ever' reinforced the heroic characteristics each brand portrayed.

Unilever's Omo brand in Brazil started to change this with the tagline 'There's no learning without stains'. This showed the brand as an integral part of a child's physical and mental growth, and that getting dirty by cooking, painting a picture, or having fun in the garden, water, or mud, is just a natural part of his or her development.

From here, a £54 million campaign was launched using different stories around the 'Dirt is good' proposition. For example, stories of strength and self-reliance have been used in economically challenged Turkey: in one ad, the closing moments of a football match show a man injured and replaced by his son. In wet, dark, and dank conditions, he fails to score, but he was brave enough to help.

In India, an ad showed a little boy getting dirty by 'punishing' a muddy puddle, after it had got his sister dirty. In parts of Latin America and Africa, an ad showed children getting their own ball and others, back from an eerie and derelict building. Although they had become stained and dirty in the process, they had overcome their anxiety about the building.

These and other campaigns enabled this group of brands to grow revenues from US$400 million to US$3 billion in ten years, in over sixty-four countries. This represents a substantial annual compound growth rate over the period.

Sources: Day (2005); Bidlake (2007); Gosling and Desai (2010); http://www.unilever.co.uk/

1 Is the Strong or the Weak theory of advertising most applicable to this campaign?

2 Choose a detergent brand and compare its advertising proposition with that of another.

3 Read the section on 'Attitudes' that concludes this chapter and then consider whether the 'Dirt is good' campaign works on a learn, feel, or do level.

■ A Composite Approach

Most of the frameworks presented so far have their roots in advertising. If we are to establish a model that explains how marketing communications works, a different perspective is required—one that draws on the key parts of all of the models. This is possible because the three key components of the attitude construct lie within these different models. Attitudes have been regarded as an important aspect of promotional activity and advertising is thought to be capable of influencing the development of positive attitudes towards brands (see also Chapter 3).

The three stages of attitude formation are that we learn something (a cognitive, or learning, component), we feel something (an affective, or emotional, component), and then we act on our attitudes (a behavioural. or the conative. component). So, in many situations. we learn something, feel something towards a brand, and then proceed to buy or not buy. These stages are set out in Figure 9.6.

The HoE models and the strong theory contain this sequential approach of learn—feel—do. However, we do not always pass through this particular sequence, and the Weak theory puts greater emphasis on familiarity and reminding (awareness) than the other components.

So, if we look at Figure 9.7, we can see that these components have been worked into a circular format. This means that, when using marketing communications, it is not necessary to follow each component in turn slavishly. The focus can be on what the audience requires, and this might be on the learning, feeling, or doing components, as determined by the audience. In other words, for marketing communications to be audience-centred, we should develop campaigns based on the overriding need of the audience at any one point in time, based on the need to learn, to feel, or to behave in particular ways.

Figure 9.6

Attitude construct: linear

Learn

Where learning is the priority, the overall goal should be to inform or to educate the target audience. If the offering is new, it will be important to make the target audience aware of the offering's existence, and to inform them of the brand's key attributes and benefits. This is a common use for advertising, because it has the capacity to reach both large and targeted audiences. Other than making them aware of the offering's existence, other tasks include showing the target audience how a brand is superior to competitive offerings, perhaps demonstrating how an offering works, and educating the audience about when and in what circumstances the brand should be used.

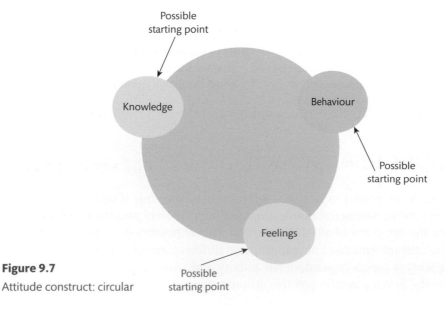

Figure 9.7

Attitude construct: circular

Feel

Once the audience is aware of a brand and knows something about how it might be useful to them, it is important that they develop a positive attitude towards the brand. This can be achieved by presenting the brand with a set of emotional values that it is thought will appeal to and be of interest to the audience. These values need to be repeated in subsequent communications in order to reinforce the brand attitudes.

Marketing communications should be used to involve and immerse people in a brand. So, for example, advertising or product placement within films and music videos will help to show how a brand fits in with a desirable set of values and lifestyles. Use of suitable music, characters that reflect the values of either the current target audience or an aspirational group, a tone of voice, colours, and images all help to create a particular emotional disposition and understanding about what the brand represents or stands for. For some people, advertising only works at an emotional level and the cognitive approach is irrelevant.

Do

Most organizations find that, to be successful, they need to use a much broader set of tools and that the goal is to change the behaviour of the target audience. This behavioural change may be about getting people to buy the brand, but it may often be about motivating them to visit a website, call for a brochure, fill in an application form, or simply visit a shop and sample the brand free of money and any other risk. This behavioural change is also referred to as a 'call to action'.

When the accent is on using marketing communications to drive behaviour and action, direct-response advertising can be effective, whether in print, on television, or online. It is commonly assumed that 40 per cent of TV ads have a telephone number or website address. However, sales promotion, direct marketing, and personal selling are particularly effective at influencing behaviour and calling the audience to act.

Research Insight 9.2

To take your learning further, you might wish to read the following influential paper:

Grönroos, C. (2004) 'The relationship marketing process: communication, interaction, dialogue, value', *Journal of Business and Industrial Marketing*, 19(2): 99–113.

Professor Grönroos is a leading researcher within the services marketing sector. In this paper, he suggests that if the interaction and marketing communications processes are geared towards customers' value processes, then a relationship dialogue may develop.

@ Visit the **Online Resource Centre** to read the abstract and to access the full paper.

Chapter Summary

To consolidate your learning, the key points from this chapter can be summarized as follows.

■ **Explain three models of communication and describe how personal influences can enhance the effectiveness of marketing communication activities**

The linear, or one-way, model of communication is the traditional mass media interpretation of how communication works. The two-way model incorporates the influence of other people in the communication process, whereas the interactional model explains how communication flows not only between sender and receiver, but also throughout a network of people. Interaction is about actions that lead to a response and, most importantly in an age of interactive communication, interactivity is a prelude to dialogue, the highest or purest form of communication.

■ **Describe the nature and scope of marketing communications**

Marketing communications, or promotion as it was originally called, is one of the 'Ps' of the marketing mix. It is used to communicate an organization's offer relating to an offering, or the overall organization. In broad terms, the management activity consists of several components. There are the communications experienced by audiences relating to both their use of products and the consumption of associated services. There are communications arising from unplanned or unintended experiences, and there are planned marketing communications.

■ **Understand the role and various tasks of marketing communications**

The role of marketing communications is to engage audiences and there are four main tasks that it can be used for. These tasks are summarized as the mnemonic 'DRIP'—that is, to differentiate, to reinforce, to inform, or to persuade audiences to behave in particular ways. Several of these tasks can be undertaken simultaneously within a campaign.

■ **Consider issues associated with the nature and use of word-of-mouth communications**

Word-of-mouth communication embraces interpersonal communication regarding offerings for which the receiver regards the communicator as impartial. Personal influence within the communication process is important, because customers perceive word-of-mouth recommendations as objective and unbiased. Word-of-mouth messages are used either as information inputs prior to purchase, or as a support and reinforcement of their own purchasing decisions.

■ **Understand the models used to explain how marketing communication is considered to work**

These models have evolved from sequential approaches, such as the awareness–interest–desire–action (AIDA) and the hierarchy of effects (HoE) models. The strong and the weak theories provide a vivid, yet polarized, contrast of different approaches. A circular model of the attitude construct helps us to understand the tasks of marketing communication—namely, to inform audiences, to create feelings and a value associated with offerings, and to drive behaviour.

Review Questions

1 Explain the key role of marketing communications and find examples to illustrate the meaning of each element in the DRIP framework.
2 Describe the main differences between opinion leaders and opinion formers.
3 What constitutes the marketing communications mix?
4 Using examples, discuss why word-of-mouth communication is important.
5 Why is the circular interpretation of the attitude construct better than the linear form?

Scan this image to go online and access the chapter's multiple-choice questions, web links, Internet activities, and more!

Worksheet Summary

Visit the **Online Resource Centre** and complete Worksheet 9.1. This will help you to learn about the role that marketing communications played in your decision as to which university to attend and who influenced your decision.

References

Alarcon, C. (2008) 'Customer titles extend reach', *Marketing Week*, 30 October, available online at http://www.marketingweek.co.uk/in-depth-analysis/customer-titles-extend-reach/2063120.article [accessed 12 September 2009].

Anon. (2010) 'Shiseido Tsubaki case study', *Datamonitor*, 5 February, available online at http://www.datamonitor.com/store/Product/shiseido_tsubaki_case_study_breaking_into_the_luxury_hair_care_market_with_an_effective_marketing_strategy?productid=CSCM0294 [accessed 9 October 2011].

AP (2007) 'Tsubaki shampoo's success reflects societal changes', *Taipei Times*, 29 August, available online at http://www.taipeitimes.com/News/worldbiz/archives/2007/08/29/2003376356 [accessed 9 October].

Bagozzi, R. (1978) 'Marketing as exchange: a theory of transactions in the market place', *American Behavioural Science*, 21(4): 257–61.

Bainbridge, J. (2010) 'Sector insight: UK theme parks', *Marketing Magazine*, 20 April, available online at http://www.campaignlive.co.uk/news/998079/Sector-insight-UK-theme-parks/?DCMP=ILC-SEARCH [accessed 8 October 2011].

Ballantyne, D. (2004) 'Dialogue and its role in the development of relationship specific knowledge', *Journal of Business & Industrial Marketing*, 19(2): 114–23.

Barda, T. (2010) 'Park life', *The Marketer*, July: 24–27.

Benady, D. (2009) 'Advertising to the YouTube generation', *Marketing*, 25 November, 34–5.

Berkman, H. and Gilson, C. (1986) *Consumer Behavior: Concepts and Strategies*, Boston, MA: Kent Publishing Co.

Bidlake, S. (2007) 'Sampling: Persil backs launch with sampling push', *Marketing*, 8 March, available online at http://www.marketingmagazine.co.uk/news/642734/Campaigns-Sampling---Persil-backs-launch-sampling-push/?DCMP=ILC-SEARCH [accessed 11 October 2011].

Binet, L. and Field, P. (2007) *Marketing in the Era of Accountability*, Henley-on-Thames: Institute of Practitioners in Advertising.

Byrne, C. (2010) 'Ad agency reputation survey reveals "disconnect" between advertisers and their clients', *The Guardian*, 22 March, available online at http://www.guardian.co.uk/media/2010/mar/22/advertising-reputation-survey [accessed 22 March 2010].

Campaignlive (2010) 'Alton Towers "th13teen" by DLKW', available online at http://www.campaignlive.co.uk/thework/992269/?DCMP=ILC-SEARCH [accessed 8 October 2011].

Cartmell, M. (2011) 'Celebrity endorsement of charity campaigns called into question', *PR Week*, 1 February, available online at http://www.prweek.com/news/1052346/ [accessed 13 November 2011].

Chan, K. K. and Misra, S. (1990) 'Characteristics of the opinion leader: a new dimension', *Journal of Advertising*, 19(3): 53–60.

Day, P. (2005) 'Dirt is good, despite the ads', *BBC News*, 21 July, available online at http://news.bbc.co.uk/1/hi/business/4702995.stm [accessed 10 October 2011].

Duncan, T. and Moriarty, S. (1997) 'A communication-based marketing model for managing relationships', *Journal of Marketing*, 62(Apr): 1–13.

Dwyer, R., Schurr, P., and Oh, S. (1987) 'Developing buyer–seller relationships', *Journal of Marketing*, 51(Apr): 11–27.

Ehrenberg, A. S. C. (1974) 'Repetitive advertising and the consumer', *Journal of Advertising Research*, 14(Apr): 25–34.

Ehrenberg, A. S. C. (1997) 'How do consumers come to buy a new brand?', *Admap*, Mar: 20–4.

Fill, C. (2002) *Marketing Communications: Contexts, Strategies and Applications*, 3rd edn, Harlow: FT/Prentice Hall.

Fill, C. (2009) *Marketing Communications: Interactivity, Communities and Content*, 5th edn, Harlow: FT/Prentice Hall.

Fill, C. (2011) *Essentials of Marketing Communications*, Harlow: FT/Prentice Hall.

Gosling, B. and Desai, R. (2010) 'Unilever: The alchemy of dirt', *Admap*, Nov: 10–13.

Grönroos, C. (2004) 'The relationship marketing process: communication, interaction, dialogue, value', *Journal of Business and Industrial Marketing*, 19(2): 99–113.

Hoffman, D. L. and Novak, P. T. (1996) 'Marketing in hyper computer-mediated environments: conceptual foundations', *Journal of Marketing*, 60(July): 50–68.

Houston, F. and Gassenheimer, J. (1987) 'Marketing and exchange', *Journal of Marketing*, 51(Oct): 3–18.

Hughes, G. and Fill, C. (2007) 'Redefining the nature and format of the marketing communications mix', *The Marketing Review*, 7(1): 45–57.

Jones, J. P. (1991) 'Over-promise and under-delivery', *Marketing and Research Today*, Nov: 195–203.

Katz, E. and Lazarsfeld, P. F. (1955) *Personal Influence: The Part Played by People in the Flow of Mass Communication*, Glencoe, IL: Free Press.

Lavidge, R. J. and Steiner, G. A. (1961) 'A model for predictive measurements of advertising effectiveness', *Journal of Marketing*, 25(6): 59–62.

Schilling, M. (2010) '"Flowers": you can't beat Japanese girls', *The Japan Times Online*, 25 June, available online at http://search.japantimes.co.jp/cgi-bin/ff20100625a3.html [accessed 9 October 2011].

Schramm, W. (1955) 'How communication works', in W. Schramm (ed.) *The Process and Effects of Mass Communications*, Urbana, IL: University of Illinois Press, pp. 3–26.

Shannon, C. and Weaver, W. (1962) *The Mathematical Theory of Communication*, Urbana, IL.: University of Illinois Press.

Stokes, D. and Lomax, W. (2002) 'Taking control of word of mouth marketing: the case of an entrepreneurial hotelier', *Journal of Small Business and Enterprise Development*, 9(4): 349–57.

Strong, E. K. (1925) *The Psychology of Selling*, New York: McGraw-Hill.

10

Managing Marketing Communications

Learning outcomes

After reading this chapter, you will be able to:

- describe the role and configuration of the marketing communications mix;

- explain the role and characteristics of each of the primary tools of the communication mix;

- outline the characteristics of the different media and explain how they can be categorized;

- consider the main issues associated with developing the right content for marketing communications;

- describe how digital marketing and media can enrich marketing communications; and

- explain how marketing communication activities are planned, implemented, and integrated.

James Bailey for ZSL London Zoo

London Zoo, located in Regent's Park in the centre of London, has changed its name to ZSL London Zoo. Why? We speak to James Bailey to find out more.

Following a segmentation exercise, it was revealed that 18 per cent of the UK population are what we call 'open conservationists'. These people would be more likely to visit zoos if they were aware of the conservation work that zoos do. This presented us with an opportunity: an opportunity to increase the potential audience within 90 minutes' drive time by 1.4 million people. We believe that if we could make London Zoo more synonymous with conservation, it would give these people permission to visit the Zoo.

So we changed the name to 'ZSL' to reflect the conservation work of the Zoological Society of London, a charity that operates London Zoo and the sister zoo, Whipsnade. ZSL carries out conservation work in thirty countries around the world, but there is very little awareness about ZSL. By using ZSL as a master brand, we hope to accelerate the awareness of ZSL and prompt people to ask the questions: what is ZSL and what does it do? Once people become more aware of ZSL and its work, they will associate the two zoos with conservation.

To attract visitors, ZSL uses a range of marketing communications tools and media. Public relations (PR) is very important, as it allows us to convey the wider message of ZSL's conservation work; personal selling has become more important recently as we strive to develop relationships with key customers in the travel trade industry, so that they sell more tickets to their own clients through various distribution outlets. Direct marketing is used to target specific consumer and trade groups, using a mixture of direct mail and email communications. Advertising is a key tool and is used to sell tickets. Sales promotion is not a key tool, as ZSL need to maintain high levels of per capita income, although we did discount heavily to get people back to the Zoo following the bombings in London in 2005.

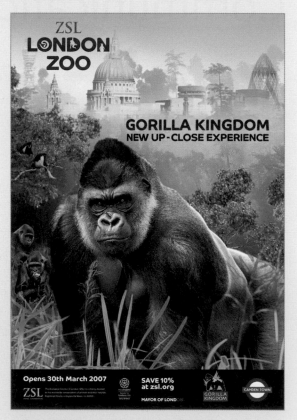

An advert for the rebranded ZSL London Zoo

Source: ZSL London Zoo

The main visitor season commences during spring each year and runs through to the end of September. In order to maximize the number of visitors in this period, the use of the various tools and media is very important. The objectives that we set ourselves also determine the mix. Budget constraints play a key part in determining the media used. We use a media agency to help and to advise on the mix, and to do this we provide the agency with information such as the demographics of the target market, which it then runs against TGI data. This analysis produces a whole range of different tactics that are appropriate for our target market. We then use our knowledge of the market to make the final decision.

When we launched 'Gorilla Kingdom', we needed to promote the exhibit as a key attraction. Once the product was named, the brand developed, and the creative direction established, the crucial question was: which tools and which media should we use?

1 Which tools and media would you use to attract visitors to see Gorilla Kingdom?

■ Introduction

What are the 'touchpoints' that you have with your mobile phone provider? Email, telephone, direct mail items, and snail mail for personal communications? What about TV ads, web pages, Facebook groups, articles and ads in magazines, posters, and perhaps news items that generate general brand awareness? In order that the right touchpoints are established, organizations need to research and plan their marketing communications activities. In this chapter, we consider two broad—yet interlinked—topics. The first are the elements that are used to configure the **marketing communications mix**. These elements consist of a variety of tools, media, and messages, including **digital media**. The role of the mix has changed from one based on persuading customers in the short term to buy offerings, to a longer-term perspective whereby the mix is intended to facilitate communication with a wide range of stakeholders and on a broader range of issues. New goals, such as developing understanding and preference, and reminding and reassuring customers, have now become accepted as important aspects of marketing communications. For example, an increasing number of organizations are reformulating the mixes used to support their brands in order to encourage customer retention, rather than acquisition.

The second topic concerns the development and implementation of the mix to optimize the use of resources, to ensure that audiences are engaged, and to accomplish goals. This requires the development of a marketing communications plan, so that the right blend of tools and media enable the delivery of the right messages in the right place, at the right time, for the right audience. To accomplish this, there are inevitably a series of issues that need to be addressed before decisions can be made. These 'issues' embrace a range of activities, such as developing strategy in the light of both audience and brand characteristics, agreeing communication objectives, and then formulating, implementing, and evaluating marketing communication strategies and plans, many of which need to be integrated—an important topic itself in contemporary marketing communications.

These two topics are now considered in turn.

■ The Right Mix of Tools

The five main tools of the marketing communication mix are **advertising**, **public relations (PR)**, **direct marketing**, **sales promotion**, and personal selling. Each has particular characteristics, as set out in Table 10.1, which means that they can play a particular role in a mix.

These primary tools subsume other tools, such as brand placement, **sponsorship**, and **exhibitions**. Although Table 10.1 suggests that the tools are independent entities, each with its own skills and attributes, a truly effective mix works when the tools are used to complement each other, the media, and the messages, and are designed to work as an interacting unit.

Table 10.1 The principal characteristics of the five main tools of the marketing communications mix

Marketing communication tools	Overview
Advertising	Advertising is a non-personal form of communication, in which a clearly identifiable sponsor normally pays for a message to be transmitted through media. One of the distinctive qualities that advertising brings to the mix is that it reaches large, often mass, audiences in an impersonal way.
Sales promotion	Sales and trade promotions offer a direct inducement or an incentive to encourage customers to buy an offering. These inducements can be targeted at consumers, distributors, agents, and members of the sales force. Sales promotions are concerned with offering customers additional value, in order to induce an immediate sale. The key forms of sales promotion are sampling, coupons, deals, premiums, contests and sweepstakes, and, in the trade, various forms of allowance.
Public relations (PR)	PR is used to influence the way in which an organization is perceived by various groups of stakeholders. One of the key characteristics that differentiate PR from the other tools is that it does not require the purchase of airtime or space in media vehicles, such as television magazines or online. This means that these types of message are low cost and are perceived to be extremely credible.
Direct marketing	The primary role of direct marketing is to drive a response and to shape the behaviour of the target audience with regard to a brand. This is achieved by sending personalized and customized messages, often requesting a 'call to action', designed to provoke a change in the audience's behaviour. In most cases, this is a media-based activity and offers great scope for the collection and utilization of pertinent and measurable data.
Personal selling	Personal selling involves interpersonal communication through which information is provided, positive feelings developed, and behaviour stimulated. It is a highly potent form of communication simply because messages can be adapted to meet the requirements of both parties. The role of personal selling is largely one of representation, but it is the most expensive tool in the mix and the reach of personal selling is the most limited.

One of the challenges facing marketing communication managers is to extract the full potential from the tools selected.

Although depicted individually, the elements of the mix should be regarded as a set of complementary instruments, each potentially stronger when it draws on the potential of the others. The tools are, to a limited extent, partially interchangeable and, in different circumstances, different tools should be used to meet different objectives. For example, in a business context, personal selling will be the predominant tool, whereas in a consumer market context, advertising has traditionally reigned supreme.

In addition to these five primary tools, there are numerous other tools, sometimes referred to as 'secondary', or 'support', tools. For example, sponsorship—normally associated with PR, but with strong associations with advertising—has become an important communication activity for many organizations. Sponsorship is a commercial activity, whereby one party permits another an opportunity to exploit an association with a target audience in return for funds, services, or resources (Fill, 2009). Organizations are using different forms of sponsorship activity to generate awareness, to form brand associations, and to cut through the clutter of commercial messages.

- Brand placement represents a relationship between film/TV producers and managers of brands. Through this arrangement, brand managers are able, for a fee, to present their brands 'naturally' within a film, television, book, or entertainment event. Such placement is designed to increase brand awareness, to develop positive brand attitudes, and possibly to lead to purchase activity.
- **Field marketing** provides support for the sales force and merchandising personnel. One of the tasks is concerned with getting free samples of a product into the hands of potential customers; another is to create an interaction between the brand and a new customer; another is to create a personal and memorable brand experience for potential customers.
- Exhibitions and trade shows enable organizations to meet their current and potential customers, to develop relationships, to demonstrate offerings, to build credibility, to place and take orders, to generate leads, and to gather market information. For customers, exhibitions enable them to meet new or potential suppliers, to find out about new offerings and leading-edge brands, and to get up to date with market developments.

■ The Right Mix of Media

Of the many available media, six main *classes* can be identified: broadcast; print; outdoor; digital; in-store; and 'other'. Within each of these classes, there are particular media *types*. For example, within the broadcast class, there are television and radio, and within the print class, there are newspapers and magazines. Within each type of medium, there are a huge number of different media *vehicles* that can be selected to carry an advertiser's message. For example, in print, there are business-oriented magazines such as *Business Today* in India and *Inc* in Sweden, and there are also an expanding number of specialist magazines such as the *Timber Trades Journal* and *ThirdSector*. Therefore there are three ways of categorizing the media: classes, types, and vehicles. Table 10.2 lists some examples of media for which advertisers have to buy time or space in order to place their ads, known as 'paid-for' media.

Table 10.3 provides an explanation of each of these different classes of 'paid-for' media.

Table 10.2 A summary of the main media classes, types, and vehicles in the UK

Class	Type	Vehicles
Broadcast	Television	*Coronation Street; The X Factor*
	Radio	Heart FM; Classic FM
Print	Newspapers	*Sunday Times; The Mirror; Daily Telegraph*
	Magazines: consumer	*Cosmopolitan; FHM; Woman*
	business	*The Grocer; Plumbing News*
Outdoor	Billboards	96- and 48-sheet
	Street furniture	Adshel
	Transit	London Underground; taxis; hot-air balloons
Digital media	Internet	Websites; email; intranet
	Digital television	Teletext; SkyText
	CD-ROM; DVD	Various: music; educational; entertainment
In-store	Point of purchase	Bins; signs; displays
	Packaging	The *Coca-Cola* contour bottle
Other	Cinema	*Pearl and Dean*
	Exhibitions	Ideal Home; The Motor Show
	Product placement	Films; TV; books
	Ambient	Litter bins; golf tees; petrol pumps
	Guerrilla	Flyposting

Source: Fill (2009). Used with permission.

Table 10.3 An overview of each class of media

Class	Overview
Print	Newspapers and magazines are the two main media in the **print media** class; others include custom magazines and directories. Print is very effective at delivering messages to target audiences, because it allows for explanation in a way that most other media cannot. This may be in the form of either a picture or a photograph demonstrating how a product should be used. Alternatively, the written word can be used to argue why a product should be chosen, and detail the advantages and benefits that consumption will provide for the user.
Broadcast	Advertisers use **broadcast media** (television and radio) because they can reach mass audiences with their messages at a relatively low cost per target reached. Broadcast media allow advertisers to add visual and/or sound dimensions to their messages. This helps them to demonstrate the benefits of using a particular offering, and can bring life and energy to an advertiser's message. Television uses sight, sound, and movement, whereas radio can use only its audio capacity to convey meaning. Both media have the potential to tell stories and to appeal to people's emotions when transmitting a message. These are dimensions that are hard to achieve effectively via the printed media within an advertiser's time and cost parameters.
Out-of-home	Out-of-home, or outdoor, media consist of three main formats: street furniture (such as bus shelters); billboards (which consist primarily of 96-, 48-, and 6-sheet poster sites); and transit (which includes buses, taxis, and the London Underground). The key characteristic associated with **outdoor media** is that they are observed by their target audiences at locations away from home and they are normally used to support messages that are transmitted through the primary media—namely, broadcast and print. Outdoor media can therefore be seen to be a secondary, but important, support media for a complementary and effective media mix.
In-store	There are two main forms of **in-store media**: point-of-purchase (POP) displays; and packaging. Retailers control the former; manufacturers, the latter. The primary objective of using in-store media is to get the attention of shoppers and to stimulate them to make purchases. There are a number of POP techniques, but the most used are window displays, floor and wall racks to display merchandise, and posters and information cards, plus counter and checkout displays. Packaging has to protect and preserve products, but it also has a significant communication role and is a means of influencing brand choice decisions.
Digital	Digital media enables two-way, interactive communication, with information flowing to and from the source and the receiver, as each participant adapts its message to meet the requirements of its audience. For example, banners and search can provoke a click, which can take the respondent to a new website where the source presents new information and the receiver makes choices, responds to questions (for example, registers at the site), and the source again provides fresh information. Indeed, the identity of the source and receiver in this type of communication becomes less clear. These interactions are conducted at high speed, low cost, and usually with great clarity. Space (or time) within traditional media is limited, so costs rise as demand for the limited space/time increases. To generalize, because space is unlimited on the Internet, so costs per contact fall as more visitors are received.

Class	Overview
	Table 10.3 (continued)
Other	Two main other media can be identified: cinema; and ambient.
	Cinema advertising has all the advantages of TV-based messages, such as the high-quality audio and visual dimensions, which combine to provide high impact. However, the vast majority of cinema visitors are people aged 18–35, so if an advertiser wishes to reach different age group segments, or perhaps a national audience, not only will cinema be inappropriate, but also its costs will be much higher than those for television.
	Ambient media are regarded as out-of-home media that fail to fit any of the established outdoor categories. Ambient media can be classified according to a variety of factors. These include posters (typically found in washrooms), distribution (e.g. ads on tickets and carrier bags), digital media (in the form of video and LCD screens), sponsorships (as in golf holes and petrol pump nozzles), and aerials (in the form of balloons, blimps, and towed banners).

Media can also be considered in terms of their purpose. For example, organizations use their assets, such as buildings, vehicles, work wear, and websites, to convey messages. These do not have to be rented and are referred to as **owned media**.

Some brand messages are shared by and among people through word of mouth and viral communications. This is known as 'earned' media.

This trio is referred to as **POEM** ('paid, owned, and earned media') and is useful because it encapsulates the contemporary use of media, beyond the paid-for-only approach. (See also Hughes and Fill, 2007, for a variation on this theme.)

Organizations use a variety of media in order to deliver their messages to a number of target audiences (see Market Insight 10.1). As a general rule, business marketers use print rather than broadcast media, simply because of the informational nature of the messages that they wish to convey and the (small) size and (large) geographic dispersion of their audiences. While choosing a single medium is reasonably straightforward, combining media and attempting to generate synergistic effects is far from easy.

One of the key tasks is to decide which combination of vehicles should be selected to carry the message to the target audience. First, it is necessary to consider the campaign goals and then use the main characteristics of each media type, in order that media planning decisions can be based on some logic and rationale. The fundamental characteristics concern the costs, delivery, and audience profile associated with a communication. Each media vehicle has a discrete set of characteristics that will also influence the way in which messages are transmitted and received, and meaning assigned.

Innocent: the honest and simple packaging pioneer

Source: Innocent

■ The Right Mix of Message(s)

The final element of the marketing communications mix is about the messages that are conveyed to, received from, and shared among audiences. Understanding what it is that needs to be said, and how to convey it with the right tone and with an insight into how audiences are expected to respond, is at the heart of marketing communications. However, this is not just about brand-sourced communications, because this is an age of interaction, in which individuals also create and share content with others.

Planned messages should reflect a balance between the need for pleasure or enjoyment and the need for information when consuming messages. At a broad level, messages can be considered to be product-oriented and rational- or customer-oriented, and based on feelings and emotions. All messages contain some information and some transformational (emotional) content. It is the balance between the two that needs to be managed, according to the task and context.

Messages in which there is high involvement require an emphasis on the information content—in particular, the key attributes and the associated benefits. This style is often factual and product-oriented. Where there is low involvement, the message should contain a high proportion of emotional content, and seek to develop brand values through imagery and associations. In business marketing, the factual and product-oriented approach can be observed more often.

Messages should be developed that enable recipients not only to respond to the source, but also to encourage them to talk to others through conversation, both offline or online, through forums, discussion boards, communities, and blogging. **Viral marketing**—that is, the passing on and sharing of content with others—has potential within business-to-business (B2B) marketing, although it is not as yet used as extensively as in consumer markets.

Digital media provides excellent opportunities to deliver rational, product-based information. On the other hand, conventional media are generally considered to be much better at developing brand values. The former have a dominant cognitive orientation; the latter, an emotional one. There are other differences, but the predominant message is that these types of medium are, to a large extent, complementary, suggesting that they should be used together, not independently of each other.

The credibility of the source of a message is considered important. High source credibility can occur when the source is perceived to be expert or knowledgeable, and whether they are objective and trustworthy. Branding can help to develop an organization's credibility, although perception of the individual people representing an organization is a critical factor. The use of spokespersons is common in consumer markets and four main ones can be identified: the expert; the celebrity; the chief executive officer (CEO); and the consumer.

Message Appeals

The main choice of presentation style therefore concerns the degree of factual information transmitted in a message (an information-based appeal) in comparison with the level of imagery thought necessary to make sufficient impact for the message to command attention and then be processed (an emotional, or transformational, appeal).

There are numerous presentational techniques associated with each of these two approaches, but the more commonly used appeals include:

- **informational appeals**, which include factual, demonstration, and comparative approaches; and

- **emotional appeals**, which include fear, guilt, humour, animation, sex, music, fantasy, and surrealism approaches.

The majority of consumer-oriented content is emotional, and uses humour, sex, music, and fear. Generally, B2B content is product-oriented, and uses factual and demonstration appeals. Traditionally, the focus is on the attributes of an offering, its characteristics and its performance qualities.

Market Insight 10.1

Eventful Marketing Communications

Events in the United Arab Emirates (UAE) are often targeted at a single section of a very diverse population. However, the area is extremely multicultural and the Abu Dhabi Authority for Culture and Heritage (ADACH) and the World of Music, Arts and Dance (WOMAD) agreed to stage the first WOMAD event in the Middle East, with the goal of bringing together a mix of UAE nationals, expatriate Arabs, expatriate Asians, and expatriate Westerners. The Media House (TMH) in Dubai was contracted to launch the three-day festival, during which twenty artists were to perform to a public audience that was to be admitted free of charge. TMH had just three months in which to attract 16,000 visitors to the April event.

The communications strategy was based on a three-level approach.

The base level consisted of a website in both Arabic and English, and online banners placed on websites visited by potential visitors, plus daily newspapers and periodicals. The website contained an email address and phone number, to enable contact and interaction with people seeking information about the festival. In addition to the print work, the awareness stage was supported through 60-second radio adverts, emails, and leafleting in Abu Dhabi and parts of Dubai. The interest stage was supported by 30-second, high-frequency radio ads, outdoor activity, and an SMS programme. The action stage was again supported by 60-second radio spots and more outdoor activity.

The second level was focused on differentiating the festival. This was approached by establishing marketing partnerships with Starbucks, Borders, and Virgin Megastores in Abu Dhabi and Dubai. For example, in-store screens at Virgin Megastores in all UAE outlets were used to play digital screen content on a loop during the week before the festival. Digital outdoor screens were also used to create a festival presence in stores and retail areas, and social media was used to induce conversations about the event. For example, images were uploaded to both Twitter and Facebook, prompting sharing, chat, and discussion.

The third level aimed to create standout reasons to attend the event. One thing that TMH did was to create a jukebox of the performing artists' songs by using the Blip FM functionality on Twitter. Followers were invited to upload their favourite music. Another was to mount a CD with the music of selected performing artists onto the cover of *TimeOut Abu Dhabi*. Public relations activity supported and built on these activities, and provided site maps, artist information, and interviews, plus, of course,

The WOMAD festival in UAW: promoted to a diverse section of the population
Source: TMH

the performance schedule. Television was used only in the final week, during which coverage was intense, culminating in a press conference the day before the festival itself.

Whilst the campaign achieved many different goals, the actual attendance was five times the target.

Source: Prakash and Sharma (2010)

1 Why was radio used throughout the campaign?

2 To what extent are the different levels in this campaign used to provide structure or to progress the communication goals?

3 Identify the elements of the marketing communications mix used in this campaign.

Digital Media and Marketing

Digital marketing encompasses a number of activities, which are depicted in Figure 10.1. These activities are changing as digital resources evolve in both functionality and marketing applications. Market and user adoption of digital resources, and their management cost, execution speed, and user experience, are driving the marketing profession's interest in these differing areas of digital marketing activities. Today, we see growth in search marketing, social web marketing, online **advergaming**, and both mobile and viral marketing, as market penetration and global reach of these digital resources grows. These are considered in turn.

Figure 10.1
Digital marketing activities

Internet Advertising

Internet advertising is a very important source of online consumer information, especially as the number of Internet users continues to increase. It is a form of marketing communications that uses Internet-based resources for the purpose of delivering messages to drive traffic to a website (measured by the **click-through rate**) and also to encourage trial, purchase, or repeat-purchase activity (measured by the **conversion rate**) (Cheng et al., 2009). Specific online advertising formats include display advertising (such as banner ads), rich media ads (for example, embedded multimedia ads, pop-up ads, and **interstitials**), online video-streamed ads, **search engine marketing (SEM)**, email advertising, and classified listings.

Used to achieve brand awareness and to encourage click-through to a target site, the major considerations for Internet advertising include the following.

- *Cost*—Internet adverts are relatively cheaper than those in other media.
- *Timeliness*—Internet adverts can be updated at any time, with minimal cost.
- *Format*—Internet adverts are richer and can effectively use the convergence of text, audio, graphics, and animation. In addition, games, entertainment, and promotions can be easily combined in online advertisements.
- *Personalization*—Internet adverts can be interactive and targeted to specific interest groups and/or individuals.
- *Location-based*—Using wireless technology and the global positioning system (GPS), Internet advertising can be location-based and targeted to consumers whenever they are at a specific time and location (for example, near a restaurant or a theatre).

- *Intrusive*—Some Internet advertising formats (such as pop-ups) are seen as intrusive and suffer more consumer complaints than other formats.

Visit the **Online Resource Centre** and follow the web links to the Interactive Advertising Bureau (IAB) to learn more about developments and standards for Internet advertising activities.

go online

Research Insight 10.1

To take your learning further, you might wish to read the following influential paper:

Winter, R. (2009) 'New communications approaches in marketing: issues and research directions', *Journal of Interactive Marketing*, 23(2): 108–17.

This article addresses the wider current context within which developing digital channels are influencing how organizations engage and participate in a dialogue with customers and their marketing activities. It reviews the challenges that these present from the perspective of the marketing manager.

@ Visit the **Online Resource Centre** to read the abstract and to access the full paper.

Search Marketing

The growth in digital content available through the Internet has given rise to search marketing, designed to help web users to locate data, information, and/or an organization's digital objects (pictures, videos). Search engine marketing (SEM) is one of the main forms of Internet advertising and aims to promote websites by increasing their visibility in search engine result pages (SERPs). SEM methods include **search engine optimization (SEO)**, **paid placement** (also known as 'pay per click', or PPC), **contextual advertising**, **digital asset optimization (DAO)**, sometimes also known as 'SEO 2.0', and **paid inclusion** (SEMPO, 2010), as outlined in Table 10.4.

All of these search marketing methods allow marketers to match specific users with specific content according to the users' interests. Search marketing is one of the most important and cost-effective methods of digital marketing, and is of increasing importance to digital marketers. This is not only because is it a highly effective way of matching content to user needs, or because the results are measurable, increasing its accountability, but also because search marketing methods (SEO, DAO, and PPC) are not perceived to be as invasive as other forms of online advertising, such as display and rich-media contextual advertising, such as pop-up ads, which are heavily disliked by consumers (Nail et al., 2005).

Table 10.4 Search engine marketing (SEM) methods

Method	Explanation
Search engine optimization (SEO)	A process used to structure a website, its contents, and links, so that search engines can match closely a searcher's key words/phrases with the content of registered web pages. The goal is to maximize the website's ranking within major search engines and directories.
Paid placement, or 'pay per click' (PPC)	Advertisers bid on keywords or phrases relevant to their target market, with sponsored/paid search engine listings to drive traffic to a website. Advertisers pay their host when their sponsored ad or link is clicked. The search engine ranks ads based on a competitive auction and other related criteria (e.g. popularity, quality).
Contextual advertising	An automated advertising system that scans a website for keywords and returns advertisements (e.g. banners, pop-ups) to the web page, based on the content being presented. Google AdSense was the first major contextual advertising programme.
Digital asset optimization (DAO), or SEO 2.0	The optimization of an organization's entire digital assets (e.g. Word files, pdfs, videos, **podcasts**, music files, images, and other digital media) for search, retrieval, and indexing.
Paid inclusion	Refers to the practice whereby search engine companies charge fees for the inclusion of websites in their search index. Some organizations mix paid inclusion with organic listings (e.g. Yahoo!); others do not allow for paid inclusion to be listed with organic lists (e.g. Google and Ask.com).

Email Marketing

Permission-based **email marketing** uses electronic mail to send messages to clearly defined groups and individuals who have consented to receive these communications. Email messages can be personalized and refined to meet the needs of individuals, and is regarded as a highly cost-effective form of digital marketing (Cheng et al., 2009).

Email can be used with varying levels of frequency and intensity, which is important when building awareness, reinforcing messages, or attempting to persuade someone into a trial or purchase. It is easy to use, costs little to produce or send, and has the potential to reach millions of willing prospects in a matter of minutes. It includes 'opt-in' and 'opt-out' mailing lists, email newsletters, and discussion list subscriptions, and, used effectively, email goes far beyond sending a sales message. This can help to build a brand's relationship with a consumer, to create a sense of trust, to retain loyal customers, and to generate revenue, as well as referrals.

A problem facing marketers is the sheer volume of emails and the information overload that it can cause. So, despite the enthusiasm of Cheng et al. (2009), Brennan (2010) notes that the reputation and use of email has fallen in recent years, based on usage and unsubscribe and opt-out rates. Rather than see social media as a threat, the integration of social media into email appears to be the way forward for many organizations (IAB, 2010).

Viral Marketing

Also referred to as 'electronic word-of-mouth' (eWOM), or 'word-of-mouse', the potency of viral marketing is based on the credibility and reach associated with word-of-mouth communications. Numerous definitions have been proposed, many of which can be found in Vilpponen et al. (2006). According to Simmons (2006: 1), the term 'viral marketing' refers to 'how the content—be it a joke, picture, game or video—gets around'. Developing this idea, Porter and Golan (2006: 33) refer to viral marketing in terms of how these materials are communicated and suggest that it commonly involves the 'unpaid peer-to-peer communication of provocative content originating from an identified sponsor using the internet to persuade or influence an audience to pass along the content to others'.

Market Insight 10.2 offers an excellent example of a viral advert in 2012.

Market Insight 10.2

Belgian Drama Goes Viral!

When TNT Benelux wanted to raise awareness of its new TV channel in Belgium, it decided on a unique approach: a viral publicity stunt, which it called 'A Dramatic Surprise'. Through agency Duval Guillaume Modern, TNT producers set up a scene in a small town in Belgium 'In a quiet square', where a large red button is placed with a sign 'Push to add drama'. When a passer-by finally musters the courage to press the button, a staged scene unfolds . . .

An ambulance drives into the town square and two paramedics emerge from a building, carrying a man on a stretcher—who tumbles as the trolley tips, to gasps from passers-by not yet sure what they're seeing. The paramedics pick the man up, wrangle him into the ambulance, and drive off—only for the trolley, and the poor patient, to fly out of the open back doors. The ambulance draws to a sudden stop, leading a passing cyclist to collide into its side—a cyclist who promptly picks himself up and hurls himself at the burly ambulance driver for a bout of fisticuffs. The surrealist spirit of the stunt escalates: a gorgeous girl barely dressed in red zooms past on a motorbike; police and gangsters screech up in cars, and start shooting at each other; bewilderingly, people are bundled into vehicles, leaving a bloodied gangster in their wake, who is hoisted aloft by a group of

American footballers and carried into the building—as the blonde biker bombs past once more . . . Finally, a banner unfurls: 'Your daily dose of drama from 10/4 on Telenet, TNT: We know drama.'

With content that was funny, shocking, and attention-grabbing, the YouTube clip (lasting for 1 minute and 46 seconds) was aimed at regular television viewers. The clip clocked up more than 30 million views on YouTube in its first two weeks, making it the second most shared advert ever at that time.

The problem with such an approach, of course, would be if the channel's TV programmes were to lack the thrill of the clip!

Sources: Anon. (2012); Chaffin (2012); http://www.youtube.com/watch?v=316AzLYfAzw

1 Visit the YouTube site for 'A dramatic surprise'. Why do you think the clip has clocked up so many views?

2 How else could TNT Benelux have raised awareness of the launch of the TNT channel in Belgium?

3 Search the web to find other highly viewed viral videos and make notes on their similarities and differences.

Social Web Marketing

The terms 'social media' and **social networks** refer to different activities and do not mean the same, yet are often used interchangeably. Kaplan and Haenlein (2009: 61) define 'social media' as 'a group of Internet based applications that build on the ideological and technological foundations of Web 2.0 and that allow the creation and exchange of user generated content'. In other words, the phrase refers to a broad range of web-based applications and social networking sites are but one of the many applications that are available. Others include **weblogs** ('blogs'), content communities (such as YouTube), collaborative projects (such as Wikipedia), podcasts, and virtual social worlds (such as Second Life).

There are a range of social media vehicles and some of the more prominent ones are explained in Table 10.5.

Table 10.5 Social media vehicles	
Form of social media	**Outline explanation**
Social networks	Social networks, e.g. Facebook and GooglePlus, and for professional and business use, LinkedIn, are about people using the Internet to share lifestyles and experiences. The participants in these networks not only share information and experiences, but they can also use the interactive capacity to build new relationships. The content is user-generated, which means users own, control, and develop content according to their needs, not those of a third party.
Weblogs	Blogs are professional or personal digital journals. A large proportion of blogs concern organizations and public issues, and they are virtually free. Blogging represents a simple, straightforward way of creating a web presence. Corporate blogs represent huge potential as a form of marketing communications for organizations. This is because blogs reflect the attitudes of the author and these attitudes can influence others. Organizations can set up *external* corporate blogs to communicate with customers, channel partners, and other stakeholders. *Internal* blogs focus on enabling employees to write about and discuss corporate policies, issues and developments.
Microblogging	Microblogging is a short format version of blogging. It's a form of eWoM and uses web social communication services (Jansen et al., 2009), of which Twitter is probably the best known. A microblog, or 'tweet', consists of a short comment, a post of 140 characters, which is shared with a network of followers. This makes production and consumption relatively easy in comparison to blogs. Microblogging offers huge potential to marketers and now ads are permitted on Twitter. These ads can become part of the conversations, and are referred to as 'promoted tweets'. These messages, limited to 140 characters, appear at the top of the page when a user has searched for that word and show up only in search results (Steele and Ahmed, 2010).

Table 10.5 (continued)

Form of social media	Outline explanation
Podcasting	Podcasting is a process whereby audio content is delivered over the Internet to iPods, MP3 players, and computers, on demand. A podcast is a collection of files located at a feed address, to which people can subscribe by submitting the address to an aggregator.
	Podcast material is pre-recorded and time-shifted, so that material can be listened to at a user's convenience, i.e. on demand. Listeners can take the material to which they have chosen to listen, and play it at times and locations that are convenient to them. They can listen to the content as many times as they wish simply because the audio files can be retained.
	Podcasting is relatively inexpensive and simple to execute. It opens up publishing to a host of new people, organizations as well as individuals, and it represents a new media channel for audio content. Users have control over what they listen to, when they listen to it, and how many times they listen to the content.
RSS	RSS stands for 'really simple syndication' and refers to the distribution of news content on the web. Rather than trawl all relevant web pages to find new content and updates, RSS allows for specific content to be brought together and made available to an individual without his or her always having to return to numerous sites. Just checking the RSS feed to see whether something new has been posted online can save huge amounts of time.
	From a marketing perspective, RSS feeds act as a media channel delivering a variety of information about news stories, events, headlines, project updates and even corporate information, often as press releases. This information is delivered quickly and efficiently to audiences who have signed up and effectively given express permission to be sent the information.

Social media enable users to generate, share, and comment on content (Van den Bulte and Wuyts, 2007).

- **User-generated content (UGC)** is content that is created by general users, not producers, although this raises questions about who is the producer. The contribution of user videos to YouTube is an example of UGC.

- In contrast, co-created content is more social. It is the act of interacting, creating content or applications, by at least two people (Trogemann and Pelt, 2006). Contributions to Wikipedia are a typical example of co-creation.

UGC and co-creation are important in that they provide evidence of consumer perceptions of the brand and brand attributes, are vivid examples of the most compelling marketing messages from the perspective of brand loyalists, and are only going to increase in frequency and prominence as social web channels and technologies develop (Muniz and Jensen Schau, 2007).

Social media also facilitate connectivity through online networks that arise from informal relations between people, enhancing a 'small world' phenomenon (Morlacchi et al., 2005). Social media enable individuals and organizations to connect to each other individually and

PR Grad Degree Online - Advance in Public Relations with a PR Focused Master's Degree Online.   From: Kent State University

People

« Go back to Home Page

Michel Eek (3rd) in ⚙
Passie voor Online & Social Media
Amsterdam Area, Netherlands | Online Media

Current	• **Sales Director Online Media** at **Semilo** ▢ • **Eigenaar** at **MF Produkties**
Past	• Sales Manager Online Advertising at Telegraaf Media Nederland • Sales Manager O.G. & Wonen at Telegraaf Classified Media • Sales Manager at Fortis ▢ <div align="right">see all…</div>
Education	• Christelijke Hogeschool Windesheim
Recommendations	**27 people have recommended Michel**
Connections	**500+ connections**
Websites	• Autoscout • Twitter
Twitter	michel_eek
Public Profile	http://nl.linkedin.com/in/micheleek

🔗 Share   📄 PDF   🖨 Print   ⚠ Flag

Add Michel to your network

Send InMail Free
Search for references
Save Michel's Profile   ⑦

Summary

Je hebt net Michel Eek gevonden op Linkedin. Sinds 9 jaar werk ik in de online media. Ik heb 6 jaar gewerkt voor Telegraaf Media Nederland. In die tijd heb ik een enorme passie voor, en expertise opgebouwd in internet en online media. Sinds april 2009 ben ik werkzaam voor Semilo, waar ik het voorrecht heb te mogen werken met top brands zoals Smulweb, Autoscout, buurtlink.nl, Expedia en gaspedaal.nl.

Binnen de online media ligt mijn expertise in online advertising, online publishing en social media. Ik heb een aantal succesvolle B2B communities ontwikkeld.

Ik heb mijn sporen ruimschoots verdiend binnen de disciplines sales, key account management, sales management, business development en publishing.

Ik beschik over een sterk netwerk binnen de online media, de bureauwereld in Nederland en diverse A-merken in FMCG en culinair.

Specialties

online marketing, online media, social media, B2B communities, online advertising, direct

How you're connected to Michel

You
↓
Ashley Pagán
Lindsay Olson
↓
Michel's connections
↓
(3rd) Michel Eek

Groups you share with Michel:

Linked in. Friends of LinkedIn

Viewers of this profile also viewed…

Andre Letsch
Manager met specialisatie inkoop in de…

LinkedIn: the social network valued at US$3 billion in 2011 now has over 100 million users

Source: LinkedIn Corporation © 2012

communally. For marketers, the challenge lies in deciding our level of engagement in online social forums, and how can we really participate in dialogue and add value. **Online communities** can develop around social media when groups of people come together freely to share a common interest. They interact, share information, develop knowledge and understanding, and build relationships. These communities can be set up, hosted, and run by an organization (a 'corporate community') or they can be driven by users, who meet independently of any corporate body. A good example of a brand community is Britain's Mumsnet, a website that offers parents peer-to-peer advice and support.

Online communities offer organizations opportunities to listen to and develop customer insight. Corporate-driven communities offer opportunities to test ideas and prototypes, and to explore ways in which a company's value proposition can be improved.

The development of social media has impacted not only on where we spend our marketing budget, but is also challenging the way in which we communicate, share information, interact, and create (or produce) an offering. When anybody who has access can create, comment on, or share information about what we do, what we represent, and how we do it, be it a person, organization, or brand, then we no longer have the power or **control** that we thought we had over the way in which we or our brand is perceived in the marketplace; instead, we tend to share control of our branding. 'Sharing control' refers to the ability of users in a computer-mediated environment, be they consumers, marketers, or competitors, to access content at will, to create and modify content to pertain to their needs, and to share this content with other consumers, companies, or third-parties. The brand manager who used to be the 'custodian' of the brand becomes a 'host', whose main role is not to control, but to facilitate sharing, participation, connectivity, and the co-creation of an offering, be it good or bad (Mitchell, 2001).

Online Advergaming

'Advergaming', or in-game advertising (IGA), is another form of digital marketing, often coupled with sales promotions that provide rewards in terms of incentives, fun, and entertainment. Advergaming is the use of computer and video games as a medium in which to deliver advertising. Advergames can consist of membership models of multiplayers (for example, *World of Warcraft*), applications downloaded to a mobile device or added to an online social network, or viral games in which the game is passed on from user to user on the web.

Most advergames require users to register, allowing for the collection of data for marketing research and other marketing initiatives, and mix interactivity, gaming, and advertising in a novel and innovative way. The huge increase in the number of gamers and research that shows the effectiveness of in-game advertising on brand recognition, recall, and revenue reflects the significance of this digital marketing activity.

Two rising digital gaming platforms are social networks and mobile phones. In May 2007, Facebook opened up its platform allowing outside web developers to create free software programs that members of the social networking site could use to entertain and inform each other. Gaming examples include applications such as *FarmVille* and *Bejeweled*, which induce users to play games with their friends. Facebook now has more than 7 million apps and websites integrated, allowing Facebook users to play games, share music recommendations, and send virtual hugs. Each day, an average of 20 million apps are installed on Facebook (Statisticsbrain, 2012).

Mobile Marketing

Increasingly, we are accessing digital technologies, sharing information, socializing online, and playing games away from the desktop computer. As the market for portable electronics grows (Anon., 2009b), new offerings emerge. For example, Netbooks (that is, notebooks), e-readers (for example, Kindle), smartphones (iPhone, Blackberry), media players (such as iTouch), gaming devices (for example, Wii), and tablet PCs (such as the iPad) have all helped to grow the number of mobile Internet users.

My Marriott Hotel: interactive gaming can also be used to recruit employees

Source: Marriott International Inc.

Mobile marketing is the set of practices that enables organizations to communicate and engage with their audience in an interactive and relevant manner through any mobile device or network (MMA, 2009). With the added benefits of store-and-send technology giving the option of message storage, mobile marketing is quick, inexpensive, and reaches markets wherever they are, despite limitations in message content. Whilst websites need to be tailored for mobile access, it is location-based services that add value. Through the use of apps, demonstrations, personalized information, and access to rich content and systems that enable them to do their work more effectively, mobile is perceived to be good for customer acquisition, as well as for developing relationships.

■ The Changing Role of the Media

For a long time, commercial media have been used to convey messages designed to develop consumers' attitudes and feelings towards brands. Today, many of the messages are designed to provoke audiences into responding, either physically, cognitively, or emotionally. The former is referred to as an 'attitudinal response'; the latter, an **emotional response**. It follows that attitude-oriented and emotion-oriented communications require different media.

Direct-response media are characterized by the provision of a telephone number, web, Twitter or email address, or a QR code. This is the mechanism through which receivers can respond to a message. Direct mail, telemarketing, and door-to-door activities are the main direct-response media, because they allow more personal, direct, and evaluative means of reaching precisely targeted customers. However, in reality, any type of media can be used, simply by including a telephone number, website or mailing address, or response card.

Direct-response media also allow clients the opportunity to measure the volume, frequency, and value of audience responses. This enables them to determine which direct-response media work best and so helps them become more efficient, as well as more effective. Estimates vary, but somewhere between 30 per cent and 40 per cent of all TV advertisements are now direct response. Direct-response TV (DRTV) is attractive to service providers, such as those in financial services (Aviva, National Accident Helpline, Injurylawyers4U) and entertainment (Jackpotjoy, National Lottery).

The complementary nature of TV and online media was revealed by a Deloitte/YouGov report published in 2009. This found that 44 per cent of consumers research a service online only after watching a TV ad. Over half of the respondents claimed to watch TV and use the Internet at the same time. The report revealed that TV was seen by consumers as the most impactful form of advertising (64 per cent), whereas search and online display were the least impactful (12 per cent and 8 per cent, respectively). What this reinforces is the notion that TV can drive people online because TV is good at display ads and brand building, whereas online advertising is best at search (Berne, 2009).

Visit the **Online Resource Centre** and follow the web link to the Radio Advertising Bureau (RAB) to learn more about the role of radio today.

go online

One aspect that is crucial to the success of a direct-response campaign is not the number of responses, but the conversion of leads into sales. This means that the infrastructure to support these activities must be well thought through and implemented; otherwise, the work and resources put into the visible level will be wasted if customers are unable to get the information that they require when they respond.

Another key area of change within the media concerns content. Traditionally, content is provided by a client organization, which uses the media to interrupt and transfer its message of persuasion to its target audience—usually, a mass audience. Digital media and changes in consumer behaviour now enable audiences not only to generate their own content, but also to discuss and consider the opinions and attitudes of others. This means that advertisers no longer have complete control over what is said about their brands, who says it, and when. The rise of online communities and social networking sites, blogging, wikis, and RSS feeds enable users to create content and to become more involved with a brand. Such brand participation presents clients such as Procter & Gamble with opportunities to enable and encourage their customers to become involved in a brand's development (see Silverman, 2006).

Research Insight 10.2

To take your learning further, you might wish to read the following influential paper:

Kent, M. L., Taylor, M., and White, W. J. (2003) 'The relationship between web site design and organisational responsiveness to stakeholders', *Public Relations Review*, 29(1): 63–77.

As the title indicates, this paper examines the relationship between website design and organizational responsiveness to stakeholder information needs. Written at a time when there was little or no empirical evidence about the extent to which new technologies can assist organizations to develop relationships, this paper provides an interesting and readable first insight.

Visit the **Online Resource Centre** to read the abstract and to access the full paper.

Marketing Communications Planning

Readers will appreciate the considerable number of changes occurring within the world of marketing communications. Planning in a context in which there is rapid change and dynamic advancements in media, consumer behaviour, and economic stability make the process of planning and managing marketing communications a significant challenge.

Planning is a systematic process involving a series of procedures and activities that lead to the setting of marketing **communications objectives** and the formulation of plans for achieving them. The aim of the planning process is to formulate and schedule the conveyance of messages utilizing the potential of the available resources to encourage target audiences to think, emote, behave, or respond in particular ways. It is the skill and responsibility of those in charge of marketing communications planning to ensure that there is the right blend of communication tools, that they create memorable messages, and that they convey them through a suitable media mix.

In order to better understand what a marketing communications plan should achieve, it is helpful to appreciate the principal tasks facing those who practise marketing communications —that is, answering the following questions.

- Who should receive the messages?
- What should the messages say?
- What image of the organization/brand are receivers expected to retain?
- How much is to be spent establishing this new image?
- How are the messages to be delivered?

- What actions should the receivers take?
- How do we control the whole process once implemented?
- What was achieved?

For many reasons, planning is an essential management activity, and if planned marketing communications are to be developed effectively, the use of a suitable framework is necessary. The framework for marketing communications plans presented in Figure 10.2 attempts to provide a structure within which rapid, dynamic changes can be accommodated, but not necessarily resolved.

The **marketing communications planning framework (MCPF)** provides a visual guide to what needs to be achieved and brings together the various elements into a logical sequence of activities. As with all hierarchical planning models, each level of decision-making is built on information generated at a previous level in the model. Another advantage of using the MCPF is that it provides a suitable checklist of activities that need to be considered. The MCPF represents a sequence of decisions that marketing managers make when preparing, implementing, and evaluating communication strategies and plans. This framework reflects a deliberate or planned approach to strategic marketing communications.

However, in practice, marketing communications planning is not always developed as a linear process, as depicted in this framework. Indeed, many marketing communications decisions are made outside any recognizable framework: some organizations approach the process as an integrative, and sometimes spontaneous, activity. The MCPF approach presented here does, however, highlight the tasks to be achieved, the way in which they relate to one another, and the order in which they should be accomplished.

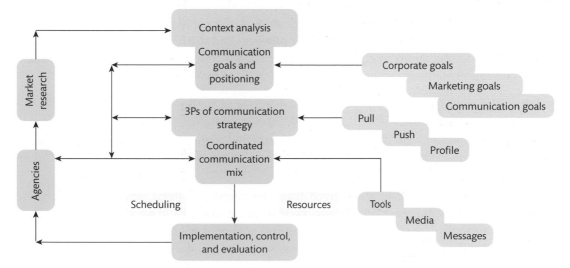

Figure 10.2

The marketing communications planning framework

Source: Marketing Communications, 5th edn, Fill, C., Pearson Education Limited (2009). Reproduced with the kind permission of Pearson Education Limited.

The Elements of the MCPF

A marketing communications plan should be developed for each level of communications activity, from strategy to individual tactical aspects of a campaign or ongoing activity. The difference between them is the level of detail that is included.

Context Analysis

The marketing plan is the bedrock of the **context analysis**. This will already have been prepared and contains important information about the target segment, the business and marketing goals, competitors, and the timescales in which the goals are to be achieved. The context analysis needs to elaborate and build on this information in order to provide the detail, so that the plan can be developed and justified.

The first and vital step in the planning process is to analyse the context in which marketing communications activities are to occur. Unlike a situation analysis used in general planning models, the context analysis should be communications-oriented and should use the marketing plan as a foundation. Care should be taken not to replicate the marketing plan. There are four main components to the communications context analysis: the customer, business, internal, and external environmental contexts.

The context analysis provides the rationale for the rest of the plan. It is from the context analysis that the **marketing objectives** (from the marketing plan) and the marketing communications objectives are derived. The type, form, and style of the message are rooted in the characteristics of the target audience, and the media selected to convey messages should be based on the nature of the tasks, the media preferences and habits of the audience, and the resources available.

Marketing Communications Objectives

Many organizations assume that their marketing communications goals are the same as their sales targets. This is incorrect, because there are so many elements that contribute to sales (such as competitor pricing, attributes of the offering, and distributor policies) that making marketing communications solely responsible for sales is naive and unrealistic. Ideally, marketing communications objectives should consist of three main elements, as follows.

- *Corporate objectives* are derived from the business or marketing plan. They refer to the mission and the business area in which the organization believes it should be.

- *Marketing objectives* are derived from the marketing plan and are sales-oriented. These might be market share, sales revenues, volumes, return on investment (ROI), and other profitability indicators.

- *Communications objectives* are derived from the context analysis, and refer to levels of awareness, perception, comprehension/knowledge, attitudes, and overall degree of preference for a brand. The choice of communications goal depends on the tasks that need to be accomplished.

These three elements constitute the overall set of marketing communications objectives. They should be set out in **SMART** terminology—that is, each should be specific, measurable, achievable, realistic, and timed. However, many brands need to refine the way in which they are perceived by customers, commonly referred to as a brand's 'position'. Positioning is not applicable to all communications plans: government-sponsored information campaigns, for example, do not have a positioning goal.

Market Insight 10.3 explores Renault's marketing communications objectives.

Marketing Communications Strategy

The marketing communications strategy is derived from the objectives and context analysis. There are a variety of influence strategies, but three generic strategies can be determined, based on the type of audience: end-user customers; trade and channel intermediaries; and all significant stakeholders. The DRIP roles of marketing communications (see Chapter 9) can be used to elaborate the relevant strategy to be pursued. For example, if a new brand is being launched, the first task will be to inform and differentiate the brand for members of the trade (known as a 'push' strategy), before informing and differentiating the brand for the target end-user customers (a 'pull' strategy).

Communications Methods

This part of the plan is relatively complex, because a number of activities need to be accomplished. For each specified target audience in the strategy, a creative or message needs to be developed. This should be based on the positioning requirements and will often be developed by an outside communications agency.

Simultaneously, it is necessary to formulate the right marketing communication mix. Here, integration is regarded as an important feature of the communication mix.

The Schedule

The next step is to schedule the way in which the campaign is to be delivered. Events and activities should be scheduled according to the audience's buying patterns, campaign goals, and the strategic thrust. So, if it is necessary to communicate with the trade prior to a public launch, those activities tied into the push strategy should be scheduled prior to those calculated to support the **pull strategy**.

Similarly, if awareness is a goal, then, funds permitting, it may be best first to use TV and poster ads offline, plus banners and search engine ads online, before using sales promotions (unless sampling is used), direct marketing, point of purchase, and personal selling.

Resources

The resources necessary to support the plan need to be determined. These refer not only to the financial issues, but also to the quality of available marketing expertise. This means that, internally, the right sort of marketing knowledge may not be present and may have to be recruited. For example, if launching a customer relationship management (CRM) system initiative, then it will be important to have people with knowledge and skills related to running CRM programmes. With regard to external skills, it is necessary that the current communications agencies are capable of delivering the creative and media plan.

Control and Evaluation

Campaigns, once launched, should be monitored. This is to ensure that, should there be any major deviance from the plan, opportunities exist to get back on track as soon as possible. In addition, all marketing communications plans should be evaluated. There are numerous methods to evaluate the individual performance of the tools and the media used, but perhaps the most important measures concern the achievement of the communication objectives.

Feedback

The marketing communications planning process is completed when feedback is provided. Information regarding not only the overall outcome of a campaign, but also the individual aspects of the activity, should be considered, For example, the performance of the individual tools used within the campaign, whether sufficient resources were invested, the appropriateness of the strategy in the first place, whether any problems were encountered during implementation, and the relative ease with which the objectives were accomplished are all aspects that need to be fed back to all internal and external parties associated with the planning process.

This feedback is vitally important, because it provides information for the context analysis that anchors the next campaign. Information fed back in a formal and systematic manner constitutes an opportunity for organizations to learn from their previous campaign activities—a point that is often overlooked and neglected.

Market Insight 10.3

Safety First: Attitude Change at Renault

When Renault decided that it needed to expand its German market share, several issues arose: one of these was the country of origin effect; another was consumer 'ethnocentrism'—that is, a tendency to evaluate domestic offerings as superior to all imported brands.

Planning the marketing communications activity was therefore crucial and started with a context analysis of the German car market. Primary and secondary research was undertaken, and the target market of 30–49-year-old males with a particular income was identified. It was also revealed that safety was the key criterion used by German consumers when planning to buy a new car. Unfortunately, Renault lagged behind both the leaders Mercedes and Volkswagen and others, including imports, in terms of perceptions of safety. Perceptions and reality are often far apart, and in this case eight of Renault's car models had won the European New Car Assessment Programme (NCAP) 'Crashtest' competition with five stars. Officially, therefore, Renault was the manufacturer

of the safest cars in Europe, yet the German market did not share this perception.

The objective of the new campaign was to increase market share. This was to be accomplished by first increasing awareness of Renault's unique safety features. The strategy was to position the brand as the safest car in the German market and, to do this, it was necessary to change German car buyers' attitudes towards Renault.

Renault appointed the well-established international advertising agency network Publicis, and Nordpol+ Hamburg, a young, small, yet highly regarded creative agency. The belief was that the experience of the former would complement the creative talent of the latter.

At this point in the process, the core message, 'The safest cars come from France', had to be configured for delivery through the marketing communications mix. Advertising was chosen as the lead discipline, using TV, cinema, and print as the main media. This was supported by a viral campaign and a new website.

It was decided to recreate the Euro NCAP Crashtest scenario for an ad called 'Crashtest'. The slight change was to film the crashes using stereotypical national food items, in slow motion, rather than dummies. The German cars were represented by a giant German sausage being driven into a barrier and exploding into thousands of pieces. Japanese sushi rolls and a Swedish crispbread suffered the same treatment. Only a soft French baguette survives the test, with a little crumpling to absorb the shock.

Media planning was undertaken and budgets revisited before the campaign was implemented. Controls ensured that the campaign performance was monitored during release and before evaluation was undertaken. Not only did Renault improve awareness, from 44 per cent to 52 per cent, but the campaign also achieved a 7 per cent increase in safety perceptions. So good were the outcomes that Renault's French headquarters planned to use the same approach in thirteen other territories.

Sources: Duncan (2006); Caemmerer (2009)

1 **To what extent should communications about safety issues rest solely with information, rather than an emotional approach?**

2 **Write notes identifying three conventional ways in which car manufacturers communicate car safety.**

3 **Think of two other countries and consider how their national foods might behave in the Crashtest.**

Evaluation and Measurement

Measurement and evaluation should be an ongoing activity, used throughout the development and implementation of a campaign (see also Chapter 5). The importance of measuring marketing communications activities should not be underestimated. The process can provide a potentially rich source of material for the next campaign and the ongoing communications that all organizations operate. Unfortunately, many organizations choose either to ignore, or not to devote too many resources or significance to, this aspect of their work. However, in an age of increasing accountability, measuring and determining just how well a campaign ran and what was accomplished is an essential part of marketing communications.

Table 10.6 sets out some of the commoner techniques used to measure marketing communications.

Integrated Marketing Communications

Having considered the different elements of the marketing communications mix, aspects of social media, and the planning process, it is clear that there are many strands and opportunities for inconsistency. So, for all of these elements to work most effectively and most efficiently, it makes sense to bring them together so that they work together as a unit. In doing so, they will have a greater overall impact and bring benefits to organizations, as well as audiences. This bringing together is referred to as **integrated marketing communications (IMC)**.

Integrated marketing communications has become a popular approach with both clients and communications agencies, although exactly what it is that is to be integrated is not

Table 10.6 Evaluation methods: marketing communications tools

Marketing communication tool	Method of testing
Advertising	Pretesting—*unfinished* ads—concept testing; focus groups; consumer juries
	Pretesting—*finished* ads—dummy vehicles; readability test; theatre tests
	Physiological—pupil dilation; eye tracking; galvanic skin response; tachistoscopes; electroencephalographs
	Post-testing—enquiry tests; recall tests; recognition tests; sales-tracking studies; financial analysis; likeability
Sales promotion	Trial; sales; stock turn; redemption levels
Public relations (PR)	Press cuttings; content analysis; media evaluation; tracking studies; recruitment levels
Direct marketing	Response rates; sales; opening/reading ratios; trial
Personal selling	Activities; costs; knowledge and skills; sales; performance ratios; territory analysis; team outputs; customer satisfaction

always as clear as it might be expected. One quite common use of an IMC approach can be seen in the use of the tools. For example, rather than use advertising, PR, sales promotions, personal selling, and direct marketing separately, it is better to use them in a coordinated manner. So organizations often use advertising or sales promotion to create awareness, involve PR to provoke media comment, and then reinforce these messages through direct marketing or personal selling. The Internet can also be incorporated to encourage comment, interest, and involvement in a brand, yet still convey the same message in a consistent way. Mobile communications are used to reach audiences to reinforce messages and to persuade audiences to behave in particular ways, wherever they are. However, the rise of digital media poses problems for IMC and for planning marketing communications activities. Some of these issues concern metrics and measurement, budgeting, brand control, and content development (Winter, 2009).

Another important aspect of integration concerns the question: 'What else should be integrated?' One element might be the planning and campaign development process. Using an integrated approach during the planning phase can serve to integrate clients, agencies, suppliers, and employees, as well as other resources.

Integrated marketing communications has emerged for many reasons, but two main ones concern customers and costs. First, organizations began to realize that their customers are more likely to understand a single message, delivered through various sources, rather than try to understand a series of different messages transmitted through different tools and a variety of media. Integrated marketing communications is therefore concerned with harmonizing the messages conveyed through each of the promotional tools, so that audiences perceive a consistent set of meanings within the messages that they receive. The second reason concerns costs: as organizations seek to lower their costs, it is becoming clear that it is far more cost-effective to send a single message, using a limited number of agencies and other resources, than it is to develop several messages through a number of agencies.

Market Insight 10.4 offers examples of integrated campaigns.

Market Insight 10.4

OK, Is This Integrated or What?

Many campaigns claim to be integrated, yet the only evidence appears to be that it is the tools and media that are combined so that the same message is conveyed through all media channels.

In July 2009, Samsung launched 'Jet', a super-fast smartphone, and used a £5 million integrated campaign, based on a marketing strategy designed to drive brand preference and loyalty. The campaign was called 'Impatience is a virtue' and illustrated different cases of people waiting, such as a person waiting to be served in a cafe and someone waiting for a bus. The voiceover informs us that we hate waiting, but that it can be a virtue, because it has driven civilization to build and to create things to rid us of waiting. Examples given included the jet plane, suggesting that the name of the new model further points to the function of the handset itself. The integrated campaign was based around TV as the lead medium, and included cinema, press, poster, digital, retail, PR, and below-the-line activity.

A quick scan of the marketing press shows that the word 'integrated' is used frequently to describe campaigns. For example, Nivea Sun ran a nationwide 'Sunwise' roadshow to promote sun safety and the brand's Children's Sun Spray range. The integrated programme was based on the Nivea Sun Bus, which

features areas for kids to explore. This was supported by TV and press activity.

Hotel company Ibis used an integrated campaign to drive leisure bookings, which included online promotions on several travel websites, as well as national press and outdoor ads.

And Volkswagen used an integrated campaign to illustrate how Volkswagen vans are a good investment in the recession. It used TV, radio, digital, experiential, retail, press, and PR elements.

Sources: Based on Alarcon (2009); Anon. (2009a); Charles-Kay (2009); Golding (2009); Wood (2009)

1 Just because a client wants an integrated programme does not mean that all agencies can deliver it. Go to the article in *Campaign* and see how one agency has approached the issue of integration: http://www.campaignlive.co.uk/news/941045/Close-up-Inside-MBA/?DCMP=ILC-SEARCH

2 Go to the article by Williams (2009b) in *Campaign* and write notes for and against the IMC concept: http://www.campaignlive.co.uk/news/912812/Close-Up-Does-UK-deliver-integration/?DCMP=ILC-SEARCH

3 How would you respond if you were asked to define an integrated campaign?

At first glance, IMC might appear to be a practical and logical development that should benefit all concerned with an organization's marketing communications. However, there are issues concerning the concept, including what should be integrated, over and above the tools, media, and messages. For example, what about the impact of employees on a brand, and the other elements of the marketing mix, as well as the structure, systems, processes, and procedures necessary to deliver IMC consistently through time? There is some debate about the nature and contribution that IMC can make to an organization, if only because there is no main theory to underpin the topic (Cornelissen, 2003).

Although IMC has yet to become an established marketing theory, the original ideas inherent in the overall approach are intuitively appealing and appear to be of value. However, what is integration to one person may be simply coordination and good practice to another, and until there is a theoretical base on which to build IMC, the phrase will continue to be misused, misunderstood, and used in a haphazard and inconsistent way.

Chapter Summary

To consolidate your learning, the key points from this chapter can be summarized as follows.

■ **Describe the role and configuration of the marketing communications mix**

The role of the marketing communication mix is to enable organizations to engage their various audiences. The mix consists of tools, media, and messages. Tools and media are not the same, because the former are methods or techniques, whereas the media are the means by which messages are conveyed to the target audience.

■ **Explain the role and characteristics of each of the primary tools of the communication mix**

Each of the tools communicates messages in different ways and achieves different outcomes. Advertising can differentiate, reinforce, and build awareness, but is not very good at getting responses or driving behaviour. Sales promotions are persuasive, and public relations can inform audiences and differentiate organizations and brands; direct marketing is strong at generating responses from target audiences—that is, persuading them to behave in particular ways. The final tool, personal selling, excels at persuading audiences.

■ **Outline the characteristics of the different media and explain how they can be categorized**

Each medium has a set of characteristics that enable it to convey messages in particular ways to a target audience. For example, TV uses sight and sound; radio, only sound; outdoor, usually only sight; and digital media can use sound, touch, and sight. Three media categories can be identified: classes, types, and vehicles. Media can also be categorized according whether it is paid, owned, or earned media (POEM).

■ **Consider the main issues associated with developing the right content for marketing communications**

Broadly, messages can be considered to be product-oriented and rational, or customer-oriented and based on feelings and emotions. All messages contain some information and some transformational (emotional) content. It is the balance between the two that needs to be managed, according to the task and context.

■ **Describe how digital marketing and media can enrich marketing communications**

Digital marketing encompasses a number of activities. These include Internet advertising, email marketing, search marketing, social media marketing, and advergaming, plus mobile and viral marketing. Market and user adoption of digital resources is encouraged by their lower costs, faster speeds of execution, and enhanced user experiences, all of which are driving the marketing profession's interest in these digital marketing activities.

■ **Explain how marketing communication activities are planned, implemented, and integrated**

Marketing communication planning is a systematic process that leads to the setting of marketing communication objectives and the formulation of plans for achieving them. The marketing communications planning framework (MCPF) provides a structure and checklist though which marketing managers can work when preparing, implementing, and evaluating communication strategies and plans. The framework reflects a deliberate or planned approach to strategic marketing communications, one that may not always occur in practice. Integrated marketing communications is concerned with the coordination of a campaign's tools, media, and messages in order to provide consistency each time a customer comes into contact with a brand. Various aspects of a campaign need to be integrated from both a strategic, as well as tactical, perspective.

Review Questions

1 Make brief notes about the nature and role of the marketing communications mix, and explain how the role has changed.

2 Write a definition for advertising, public relations, and one other tool from the mix. Identify the key differences.

3 Write a list that categorizes the media. Find a media vehicle to represent each type of media.

4 Draw the marketing communications planning framework. Refer to Figure 10.2 only if you get really stuck.

5 Explain the principles of integrated marketing communications.

Scan this image to go online and access the chapter's multiple-choice questions, web links, Internet activities, and more!

Worksheet Summary

Visit the **Online Resource Centre** and complete Worksheet 10.1. This will help you to learn about how we can use the different marketing communication tools and differing media channels to communicate information about a fast-moving consumer good (FMCG) to our target audiences.

References

Alarcon, C. (2009) 'Samsung launches Jet with integrated campaign', *Marketing Week,* 7 July, available online at http://www.marketingweek.co.uk/samsung-launches-jet-with-integrated-campaign/3002056.article [accessed 25 September 2009].

Anon. (2009a) 'Ibis in autumn break activity', *Marketing,* 2 September, available online at http://www.marketingmagazine.co.uk/news/931304/Ibis-autumn-break-activity [accessed 27 September 2009].

Anon. (2009b) 'Online advertising pushes through', available online at http://www.emarketer.com/Article.aspx?R=1007024&Ntt=online+ad&No=20&xsrc=article_head_sitesearchx&N=0&Ntk=basic [accessed 8 April 2009].

Anon. (2012) 'Brand barometer: TNT viral campaign reviewed', *Marketing,* 26 April, available online at http://www.marketingmagazine.co.uk/News/MostEmailed/1128485/Brand-barometer-TNT-viral-campaign-reviewed/ [accessed 29 April 2012].

Berne, S. (2009) 'Four in ten viewers driven online by TV ads', *New Media Age,* 19 August, available online at http://www.nma.co.uk/four-in-ten-viewers-driven-online-by-tv-ads/3003590.article [accessed 25 September 2009].

Brennan, J. (2010) 'Good email = Good customers', *B2B Marketing,* 7(10): 41.

Caemmerer, B. (2009) 'The planning and implementation of integrated marketing communications', *Marketing Intelligence and Planning,* 27(4): 524–38.

Chaffin, J. (2012) 'Ad deconstructed: TNT Benelux's viral publicity stunt', *Financial Times,* 17 April.

Charles-Kay, L. (2009) 'Volkswagen promotes commercial vehicles integrated campaign', *Marketing,* 1 July, available online at http://www.marketingmagazine.co.uk/news/917262/Volkswagen-promotes-commercial-vehicles-integrated-campaign [accessed 27 September 2009].

Cheng, J. M.-S., Blankson, C., Wang, E. S.-T., and Chen, L. S.-L. (2009) 'Consumer attitudes and interactive digital advertising', *International Journal of Advertising,* 28(3): 501–25.

Cornelissen, J. P. (2003) 'Change, continuity and progress: the concept of integrated marketing communications and marketing communications practice', *Journal of Strategic Marketing,* 11(Dec): 217–34.

Duncan (2006) 'Renault crash tests with sausage sushi and bread', *The Inspiration Room,* 14 July, available online at http://theinspirationroom.com/daily/2006/renault-crash-test/ [accessed 11 October 2011].

Fill, C. (2009) *Marketing Communications: Interactivity, Communities and Content,* 5th edn, Harlow: FT/Prentice Hall.

Golding, A. (2009) 'Nivea uses experiential events to promote children's sunscreen brand', *Marketing,* 7 May, available online at http://www.marketingmagazine.co.uk/news/904057/Nivea-uses-experiential-events-promote-childrens-sunscreen-brand [accessed 27 September 2009].

Hughes, G. and Fill, C. (2007) 'Redefining the nature and format of the marketing communications mix', *The Marketing Review,* 7(1): 45–57.

IAB (2010) 'Email marketing: IAB and ICD research', available online at http://www.iabuk.net/research/library/email-marketing-iab-and-icd-research [accessed 2 July 2012].

Jansen, B. J., Zhang, M., Sobel, K., and Chowdury, A. (2009) 'Twitter Power: tweets as electronic word of mouth', *Journal of the American Society for Information Science and Technology,* 60(11): 2169–88.

Kaplan, A. M. and Haelein, M. (2009) 'Users of the world unite! The challenges and opportunities of social media', *Business Horizons,* 53: 59–68.

Kent, M. L., Taylor, M., and White, W. J. (2003) 'The relationship between web site design and organisational responsiveness to stakeholders', *Public Relations Review,* 29(1): 63–77.

Mitchell, A. (2001) *Right Side Up: Building Brands in the Age of the Organised Consumer,* London: HarperCollins Business.

Mobile Marketing Association (MMA) (2009) 'Buy mobile research', available online at http://mmaglobal.com/about/content_category/research/10/341 [accessed 2 July 2012].

Morlacchi, P., Wilkinson, I. F., and Young, L. (2005) 'A network analysis of the evolution of personal research networks among IMP researchers', *Journal of Business to Business Marketing,* 12(1): 3–34.

Muniz, A. M. and Jensen Schau, H. (2007) 'Vigilante marketing and consumer-created communications', *Journal of Advertising,* 36(3): 35–50.

Nail, J., Charron, C., and Cohen, S. M. (2005) *The Consumer Advertising Backlash Worsens,* Forrester Research Report, available online at http://contentmarketingpedia.com/Marketing-Library/AdvertisingDoesn'tWork/AdvertisingBackLash_ForresterResearch_Jan2005.pdf [accessed 2 July 2012].

Porter, L. and Golan, G. J. (2006) 'From subservient chickens to brawny men: a comparison of viral advertising to TV advertising', *Journal of Interactive Advertising,* 6(2): 30–8.

Prakash, V. K. and Sharma, R. (2010) 'Megamarketing an event using integrated marketing communications: the success story of TMH', *Business Strategy Series,* 11(6): 371–82.

Search Engine Marketing Professional Organization (SEMPO) (2010) *The State of Search Engine Marketing Report*, 25 March, available online at http://www.sempo.org/news/03-25-10 [accessed 2 July 2012].

Silverman, G. (2006) 'How can I help you?', *FT Magazine*, 4–5 February, 16–21.

Simmons, D. (2006) 'Marketing's viral goldmine'. *BBC News*, available online at http://news.bbc.co.uk/1/hi/programmes/click_online/5179166.stm [accessed 2 July 2012].

Statisticsbrain (2012) 'Facebook statistics', available online at http://www.statisticbrain.com/facebook-statistics/ [accessed 2 July 2012].

Steele, F. and Ahmed, M. (2010) 'Twitter unveils advert tweets in bid for profits', *Times Online*, 13 April, available online at http://business.timesonline.co.uk/tol/business/industry_sectors/media/article7095914.ece [accessed 8 September 2011].

Trogemann, G. and Pelt, M. (2006) 'Citizen media: technological and social challenges of user-driven media', in *Proceedings of the Broadband Europe Conference*, 11–14 December, Geneva, Switzerland.

Van den Bulte, C. and Wuyts, S. (2007) *Social Networks and Marketing*, Relevant Knowledge Series, Boston, MA: Marketing Science Institute.

Vilpponen, A., Winter, S., and Sundqvist, S. (2006) 'Electronic word-of-mouth in online environments: exploring referral network structure and adoption behavior', *Journal of Interactive Advertising*, 6(2): 71–86.

Winter, R. S. (2009) 'New communications approaches in marketing: issues and research directions', *Journal of Interactive Marketing*, 23: 108–17.

Wood, R. (2009) 'Samsung rockets with new Jet', *Media Week*, 12 August, available online at http://www.mediaweek.co.uk/news/926809/Samsung-rockets-new-Jet/ [accessed 25 September 2009].

11

Retailing and Channel Management

After reading this chapter, you will be able to:

- define distribution channels and key considerations in managing a channel strategy;
- discuss the differing types of intermediary and their roles in the distribution channel;
- differentiate between different distribution channel structures and selection criteria;
- discuss the factors influencing channel design, structure, and strategy;
- discuss the role, function, and importance of retailers in the distribution channel; and
- compare and contrast the differing types of retailer.

Gennaro Castaldo for HMV

Founded in 1921, HMV opened its first store in Oxford Street, London. Long regarded as one of Europe's leading music retailers, today HMV is more a multiple entertainment hub than a pure music retailer. We speak to Gennaro Castaldo to find out how HMV is adapting to changing customer and market expectations.

With its origins in retailing, HMV has grown to comprise over 200 stores with sales of £1.1 billion in the UK and Ireland (HMV UK), with a further 130 stores throughout Canada, Hong Kong, and Singapore, with sales of £253.8 million (HMV International). However, HMV is far more than a music retailer. With rapid innovations in the development of technology coupled with changing customer preferences in entertainment consumption, HMV today is more a hub for entertainment. HMV's aim has always been to give customers access to the music and entertainment that they love, in the way that they want to enjoy it.

Over the last century, we have seen the way in which music and entertainment content is made available to customers continually change. However, today's digital technology has gone one step further and changed not only consumption patterns, but also the business model of music retailing forever. Digital technology has made downloads not only possible, but also a customer preference, with increased access via a variety of Internet-based PC and mobile platforms. CD albums still represent about 85 per cent of all legal sales in the UK, but there is a definite long-term downward trend to this market. In contrast, sales of singles have seen nine out of ten purchases made in digital form. Record labels and retailers alike are struggling to adapt their business models in light of this new digital landscape. Multi-category supermarket retailers also sell music and entertainment products, rendering increased competition across the sector. Questions continue to remain about

the long-term viability of selling recorded music and entertainment products.

To adapt, HMV is diversifying its product and channel offering, and further investing in adjacent businesses to provide a multi-channel entertainment experience for its customers. HMV's aim is to be seen *less* as a one-dimensional music retailer, and *more* as a multi-channel entertainment hub where consumers can 'get closer' to the music, film, and games that they love, however they wish to enjoy them.

With tens of millions of customers visiting our multiple channels and our HMV website generating over 55 million customer visits alone in 2009, we operate a multi-channel strategy. The HMV product portfolio includes not only music albums and singles, but also DVD and Blu-ray, games and technology, and related entertainment products such as licensed artist and film franchise merchandising. In the UK in 2009, 45 per cent of HMV sales came from visual (DVD and Blu-ray), 28 per cent from music, 24 per cent from games and technology, and 3 per cent from related entertainment products. Live in-store events include hundreds of artist personal appearances each year, ranging from album signings to live in-store performances. For online engagement, we use a website, email marketing, and social media strategy (Twitter, YouTube, Facebook), and a customer rewards programme across channels (pureHMV) to engage with customers' entertainment experiences. Critical to this is our employee strategy, spanning 6,500 employees in five countries, focused on providing specialist entertainment knowledge, with a staff ethos 'to be original, be fanatic and work hard together to get customers closer to the music, film, and games they love'.

HMV is also diversifying further the channels through which we offer our customers live entertainment

At HMV, retail is just one part of a multi-channel strategy

experiences. We continue to invest in entertainment venues, with eleven concert venues in total, co-owning (with MAMA Group) the legendary HMV Hammersmith Apollo and the HMV Forum (London), the HMV Picture House (Edinburgh), and investing in summer festivals such as Lovebox, Godskitchen, Global Gathering, and The Great Escape. We are also experimenting with cinema (in Wimbledon, south-west London) through a partnership with Curzon Artificial Eye, and rolling out an online gaming facility called Gamerbase across stores.

HMV is no longer a one-dimensional music retailer, but rather an entertainment hub using multiple channels to foster customer entertainment experiences—be it at home, in-store, online, or at live entertainment venues.

1 If you were to work for HMV, what would you do to manage its multi-channel entertainment hub to foster continued positive customer experiences?

■ Introduction

Where do you do your banking? How do you purchase tickets for a concert, a football match, or an airline flight? At what time of the day do you pay your electricity or phone bills? For many people, the time and place at which they deal with these things have changed. We can get cash 24 hours a day, 365 days per year, from automatic teller machines (ATMs). Bills can be paid and banking completed at any time, at home or at work, on the phone or through the Internet, and drink and snack dispensing machines appear on railway station platforms, airline terminals, in shopping malls, and hospital waiting rooms. These examples demonstrate that, in the last two decades, **place** (or distribution) has undergone substantial change.

Many organizations believe that they play a relatively small part in their marketing activities, seeing distribution as only the activities involved in transporting goods physically from where they are manufactured to the customer. However, as competition increases and margins are reduced, the focus on distribution efficiency and effectiveness continues to increase dramatically. If goods do not arrive in the proper place or in the proper condition, no sale can be made (Douglas et al., 1998).

This chapter demonstrates that distribution embraces a broader concept than only the delivery of goods; it includes understanding the strategic importance of **distribution channels**, of member roles in the channel, and of customer service. This chapter introduces you to the fundamental principle of 'place' in the marketing mix, and to management decisions concerning distribution channels, channel members, and **logistics management**. A detailed discussion of **retailing** is also provided.

■ Place

'Place', or distribution, concerns how to place the optimum amount of goods and/or services before the maximum number of a target market at the times and locations that they want them. The way in which distribution occurs can be physical, such as supplying a music CD or DVD through one of HMV's stores, or a service, such as training on how to use editing software to create your own music or video, or downloading the latest singles from iTunes. Irrespective of the mode used, distribution activities have a direct effect on other marketing elements. For example, Inditex, Europe's largest clothing maker and **retailer**, saw its clothing sales rise by over 11 per cent in the first quarter of 2011 as a result of its opening an additional 110 stores worldwide, a number of online launches, and because it updates stock in its Zara stores weekly with the latest fashion trends. It achieves this by manufacturing over 40 per cent of its stock in Spain or Portugal; although more costly in production, Inditex can get new trends into European and American stores twice as fast than if it has to wait for delivery for stock manufactured in Asia. This shows that distribution activities have a direct effect on Inditex and Zara's brand and retailing strategy.

Distribution activities are a vital element in creating customer value. A product will provide customer value and satisfaction only if it is available to the customer when and where it is needed, and in the appropriate quantity (Douglas et al., 1998). Sometimes, this requires organizations to think outside the box of traditional delivery channels. For example, in order to reach the 600,000 rural villages in India, Samsung partnered with the Indian Farmers Fertiliser Cooperative Ltd to sell its handsets. With this distribution channel, it can now reach over 90 per cent of the villages in India.

Factors that influence customer perceptions of distribution quality include:

- dependability (that is, consistency of service);
- time in transit;
- market **coverage**;
- the ability to provide door-to-door service;
- flexibility (handling and meeting the special needs of shippers);
- loss and damage performance; and
- the ability to provide more than a basic product delivery service.

Because product delivery has a direct effect on customer evaluations of service quality and satisfaction, we need to understand what it is customers want from our distribution activities. Do they want speedy delivery, a reliable supply of products, a good range of choice or product assortment, increased availability, convenience, service and support, a good price, or after-sales service? Insight to these questions helps to inform effective distribution and channel management strategies, but these too are dependent on the buyer type and type of product being delivered.

For more information on the role of distribution in the marketing of Chinese tea throughout Europe, see Market Insight 11.1.

Market Insight 11.1

For all the Tea in China

Every year, China exports about 20,000 tons of oolong tea to the world at a price of between US$2 and US$3 a kilogram. This value, however, is seen by many in China as not consistent with the true value of Chinese tea. Chinese tea is not simply a raw material for industrial processing; it is a symbol of the rise of China and, some 300 years ago, was a possession prized among the upper classes in Europe for its health benefits. The development of a new marketing centre for Chinese tea under the brand name 'Anxi Tieguanyin' in central Paris hopes to reposition how Europeans think about Chinese tea.

Eight Horses Tea Co., along with tea companies Empereur, Zhong Min Wei Shi, and Ping Shan from the Anxi county in Fujian province, have formed an agreement with European partner, Leblond Gregory, to operate the marketing centre jointly. The five companies have together committed to invest about 30 million yuan (US$4.76 million; €3.59 million) for the initial construction, management, and promotion of the centre. The centre's aim is to reposition Chinese tea so as to enter the high-end market in Europe, and to build up a

network of local and regional influence. The European market is a symbolic spot for Chinese tea companies to go global—especially Paris, which hosts many luxury brands. Tieguanyin (translated as 'Iron Goddess of Mercy') is a renowned variety of Chinese oolong tea; through this marketing centre, the company will fully promote Tieguanyin as a luxury good and look for a broader international market. The first container of Tieguanyin is to be priced at between €50 (US$64.60) and €500 per kilogram. The centre will be spread over 100 square metres and decorated with distinctive Chinese architecture, and divided into two areas: the sales zone and tasting zone. To promote Chinese tea culture, the centre will also hold various cultural activities, training courses, and tea-making performances, co-hosted with local Chinese communities.

The positioning of tea as a luxury product to be 'experienced' does, however, raise some doubts in that this trend of high-priced tea deviates from the nature of tea in Europe as an ordinary necessity of people's daily life. The main barriers for promotion of Tieguanyin in Europe include:

- introducing Chinese tea culture—previously, tea products have been mainly sold overseas in bulk, not as packaged tea, at a much higher price; and
- the tea-making process—Europeans are used to drinking the beverage with tea bags, with little understanding and education of Chinese tea culture.

Sources: Anon. (2011); Jing (2012)

1 **What were the reasons for the establishment of the marketing centre for Tieguanyin tea in Paris?**

2 **How does the approach of distributing Chinese tea through the marketing centre differ from how Chinese tea has been distributed in the past?**

3 **What effect do you think the establishment of this centre could have on the perceptions and purchase of Chinese tea in Europe?**

Tea at its finest
Source: © iStockphoto LP 2010

Distribution Channel Management

Distribution ranges from production and manufacturing to logistics, warehousing, and the final delivery of goods to the customer (Handfield and Nichols, 1999). Very few organizations are able to deliver products to all possible customers and thus they rely on other parties, such as distributors, for assistance. These organizations form what we call a 'distribution channel'—that is, an organized network of agencies and organizations that perform all of the activities required to link producers and manufacturers with purchasers and consumers (Bennet, 1988). The aim is the orderly flow of material, personnel, and information throughout the distribution channel to ensure product delivery (Russell, 2000). Distributors perform an important **intermediary** role in matching supply with demand through their interactions with suppliers, manufacturers, and end customers.

Management of distribution channels concerns two key elements: (1) managing the design of the channel and its activities; and (2) managing the relationship of members in the channel. First, we need to design an appropriate channel structure, including channel length, and select the members of the channel and their roles. This helps us to determine what is the most effective and efficient way in which to get the product to the customer. How can we reach the optimum number of customers? And what organizations do we need to help us to achieve this? Next, we turn our attention to managing the social, political, and economic relationships of channel members (Gandhi, 1979). A good understanding of the relationships in the channel will help us to improve the effectiveness and efficiency of product delivery.

Channel decisions are some of the most important decisions that a manager faces. An organization's pricing strategies will depend on whether the product is distributed through mass retailers or high-quality speciality stores. Likewise, sales force and advertising decisions will depend on how much persuasion, training, motivation, and support dealers in the channel need. If an organization does not pay sufficient attention to the distribution channel, it will be detrimental to its marketing efforts.

Key Considerations

When managing distribution channels, we need to consider balancing the three elements of economics, coverage, and control.

- *Economics* requires us to recognize where costs are being incurred and profits being made in a channel to maximize our return on investment.
- *Coverage* is about maximizing the product's availability in the market for the customer, satisfying the desire to have the product available to the largest number of customers, in as many locations as possible, at the widest range of times.
- *Control* refers to achieving the optimum distribution costs without losing decision-making authority over the product, how it is priced, how it is promoted, and how it is delivered in the distribution channel.

Sometimes, by covering a wide range of delivery times and locations through the use of intermediaries, the organization sacrifices some control in decision-making. Intermediaries start changing the price, image, display, and so on, as they seek to maximize sales of a whole range of products, including the products of competitors. Think about the positions of Nokia, Samsung, and Sony Ericsson. In order to get the maximum number of customers using their mobile phone handsets, they need to have the maximum number of retailers and mobile phone networks promoting and selling their phones. But the same networks and retailers also sell the handsets of their competitors. As the retailers and networks compete to sign up customers, they push for lower prices, or they demand advertising subsidies to help them to sell the phones. So Nokia, Samsung, and Sony Ericsson may discover that their phones are being sold at very low prices and that their brand image is being compromised by retailers and networks who are desperately seeking to maximize their own sales. What happens if Motorola reduces the number of retailers or networks with which it deals in order to increase control over its marketing mix? The danger, of course, is that its competitors will gain market share by continuing to deal with these retailers and networks.

go online

Visit the **Online Resource Centre** and follow the web link to the Institute of Supply Chain Management (ISM) to learn more about the profession and activities of managing the distribution and supply chain.

Intermediaries

Organizations often rely on intermediaries—independent organizations that provide a link between producers and end consumers, assisting the physical movement of the product and the transfer of legal title to the end consumer. They perform various functions, such as managing inventory, physical delivery, and financial services, enabling organizations to offer just about everything a buyer wants, including availability, speed of delivery, reliable supply, range of choice in product assortment, and so on. Figure 11.1 illustrates a number of the benefits offered by intermediaries.

The benefits of intermediaries include the following.

- *Improved efficiency*—Producers usually manufacture a small range of products in large quantities, whereas consumers consume a wide range of products in small quantities. An intermediary, such as a **wholesaler**, improves efficiency in the delivery channel by

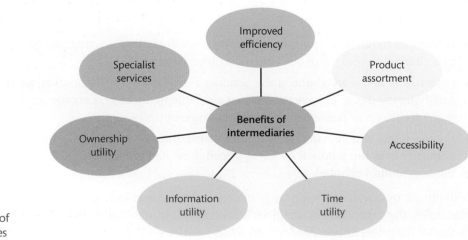

Figure 11.1

The benefits of intermediaries

breaking large deliveries from producers into single units and assorting them into a range of goods available for retailers, providing 'product assortment efficiency'.

- *Accessibility*—Usually, the location where production occurs is miles from the point of usage or consumption. Think about clothes purchased on the high street, which can be manufactured as far afield as China or India. Intermediaries assist by bringing the product to a more convenient location for purchase, providing 'place utility'.

- **Time utility**—Manufacturing, purchase, and consumption can also occur at differing points in time. The product might be manufactured during the day, but purchased and consumed at the weekend. Intermediaries, such as retailers, provide time utility.

- **Ownership utility**—Through intermediaries such as retailers, products are available immediately from the intermediaries' stocks, enabling ownership to pass to the consumer within a limited amount of time.

- *Specialist services*—Intermediaries might also provide specialist services such as after-sales, maintenance, installation, or training services to increase the effective use of the product. These services are best offered and performed by those closest to the purchaser or user of the product.

- **Information utility**—Sometimes, intermediaries also provide information about the product to aid sales and product usage. The Internet has further led to the development of a new type of intermediary, an information intermediary (for example, Expedia, Google, Tripadvisor), the key role of which is to manage information to improve the efficiency and effectiveness of the distribution channel.

These benefits are offset by certain disadvantages. With an increasing number of intermediaries and certain types of distribution channel, a lack of control over the product can result. Manufacturers are often at the mercy of intermediaries in terms of where their product is placed in-store and its final price. Furthermore, intermediaries might be susceptible to competitor inducement, such as trade promotions. For many manufacturers and producers, intermediaries often become a market in their own right, requiring considerable time, money, and personnel to support and develop a relationship with them. Sony provides a good example of the effect that a supplier's brand can have on the activities and behaviour of intermediaries, such as retailers in the electronics sector. Despite product similarity, Sony remains a premium electronics brand and any electrical retailer without the Sony brand in stock will suffer in terms of store traffic, because shoppers will expect to see it. Thus Sony has supplier power in this way, and can negotiate high margins and better shelf positioning for its products than its rivals (combining both pull and **push strategies**).

Visit the **Online Resource Centre** and complete Internet Activity 11.1 to learn more about the role of intermediaries in the supply chain within the film and TV industry.

go online

■ Member Channel Functions

Channel members perform a number of functions within the distribution channel. As shown in Figure 11.2, these functions have evolved since the 1980s from as few as five key functions

Figure 11.2

Evolution of the
channel member
functions

1980s	1990s	2000s
Sorting process	Distribution	Physical distribution
Mass distribution	Marketing research	Contact
Marketing research	Buying	Relationship management
Customer contact	Product services	Communications
Credit	Product promotion	Negotiation
	Pricing	Marketing research
	Product planning	Matching/customizing
		Risk taking
		Product assembly
		Financing
		Service

to as many as eleven (Michman, 1990). Managing the distribution functions involves managing the sourcing of organizational resources upstream from manufacturers, and suppliers and distributing resources downstream to customers. The aim is to provide a reliable and responsive service to meet customer orders with a guaranteed delivery date, of the right amount, with the expected level of quality. To achieve this, there is often a trade-off between the customer objectives of time, quality, and accessibility, and the cost to the supplier or distributor. The main strategy is to offer maximum flexibility in meeting customer requirements for a range of products, in any quantity, without incurring significant costs. Market Insight 11.2 offers an example of how channel members and technology help ASOS to meet customer needs throughout delivery.

Market Insight 11.2

ASOS on Foreign Soil

In 2011, UK-based fashion retailer ASOS.com began offering a combination of features designed to assure American consumers uncertain about buying from a foreign **merchant**. The company made free shipping and free returns standard on all orders, as well as keeping consumers informed of the status of their orders at every stage of the delivery process. Every US ASOS.com order ships from the e-retailer's **distribution centre** in the UK and is placed on a New York-bound flight from London. The order clears US customs electronically while in the air before being picked up by shipping carrier Newgistics Inc., which then delivers packages to the US postal service centre nearest to the consumer's delivery address. The postal service makes the home delivery.

At each stage, a consumer gets an email alerting him or her to the package's whereabouts, down to the flight number for the departure from London's Heathrow Airport. Newgistics Inc. sends the consumer an ASOS-branded email with domestic tracking information once the carrier receives the package in New York, which can then used by the consumer to track the package's progress through Newgistics' network. Newgistics sends another ASOS-branded alert when it delivers the package to the postal service; the message lets the consumer know that the package is in the area. ASOS.com receives the same tracking information.

Since ASOS began selling in the United States, US sales have grown 140 per cent over twelve months. Although it is difficult to assess whether this is only a result of shipping efficiencies, statistics do show that 'Where's my order?' enquiries from US consumers have dropped by more than 50 per cent since ASOS began sending the tracking alerts through Newgistics Inc.; the number of packages lost in transit has also dropped, while the number of repeat buyers has increased. The tracking service that ASOS provides has helped to build confidence with consumers.

Source: ASOS.com

1 Who are the channel members in ASOS's delivery strategy to the US?

2 What specific functions do these channel members serve for ASOS?

3 How did ASOS change its delivery strategy to better meet customer needs?

Distribution Channel Strategy

When devising a distribution channel strategy, several key decisions need to be made in order to serve customers and to establish and maintain buyer–seller relationships. These are summarized in Figure 11.3. The first decision is selecting how the channel will be structured. If the channel requires intermediaries, we need to consider the type of market coverage that we want, the number and type of intermediaries to use, and how we should manage the relationships between members in the channel. These choices are important, because they can affect the benefits provided to customers.

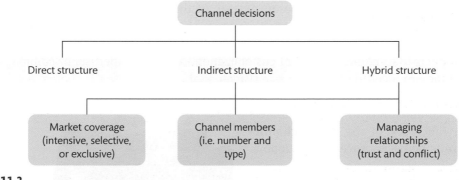

Figure 11.3
Distribution channel strategy decisions

Channel Structure

Distribution channels can be structured in a number of ways. Three examples of how relationships between producers, intermediaries, and customers can be structured include:

- a *direct* structure, which involves selling directly to customers, with minimal involvement from other organizations;

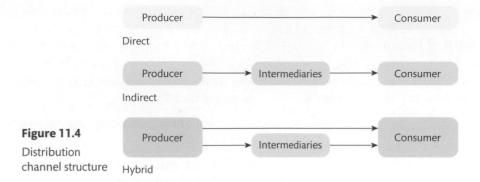

Figure 11.4
Distribution
channel structure

Direct: Producer → Consumer

Indirect: Producer → Intermediaries → Consumer

Hybrid: Producer → Consumer / Producer → Intermediaries → Consumer

- an *indirect* structure, which uses intermediaries; and
- a *hybrid* structure, which combines both.

These are displayed in Figure 11.4. The degree of efficiency that an intermediary can introduce to the performance of a distribution channel is what ultimately determines what form a channel structure will take.

We will now consider the advantages and disadvantages of each of type of channel structure.

Direct Distribution

In direct channels, the producer uses strategies to reach end customers directly rather than deals via an intermediary such as an **agent**, broker, retailer, or wholesaler (see Figure 11.4). Have you ever been to a farmers' market and purchased produce directly from a farmer, or listened to music from the Soundcloud profile or MySpace site of a local band? These are examples of direct distribution. The advantages of this structure include the producer or manufacturer maintaining control over their product and profitability, and building strong customer relationships. This structure is not suitable for all products; it is ideally suited to those products that require significant customization, technical expertise, or commitment on behalf of the producer to complete a sale (Parker et al., 2006).

Electronic technologies such as the Internet are, however, enabling more and differing product manufacturers to reach customers directly. Efficiency of the **direct channel structure** is being improved in the following ways.

- *Processing orders and distributing the product electronically directly to customers* —Adobe Reader is free universal software manufactured by Adobe Systems Inc. that enables users to read and share electronic documents. The organization employs a direct structure via the Internet, providing digital delivery, installation, and customer support.

Dell makes the switch
Source: Courtesy of Dell Inc

- *Supporting the physical distribution of the product offering directly to customers* —One of the most well-known examples of this is the Dell Computer Corp. system. Dell sells computer equipment through its website, using telesales for product ordering, database technology for order processing, tracking, and inventory management, and Twitter (@Dell) for customer service.

The disadvantages of a direct channel structure typically include the amount of capital and resources required to reach customers directly, resulting in the potential loss of economies of scale. Manufacturers might also suffer from offering a low variety of products, which are not consistent with the needs of the buyer. This is especially apparent in fast-moving consumer goods (FMCG) markets. Imagine having to shop for bread, milk, and a soft drink at three differing retail outlets owned by each product manufacturer. Few consumers today would purchase their products from individual manufacturers because of the inconvenience and time costs involved. Thus retailers fulfil the needs of end consumers for product variety.

Indirect Distribution

In an **indirect channel structure**, the producer concentrates on the skills and processes involved in producing the product, and will rely on one or more intermediaries for distribution. An example here is Procter & Gamble, which focuses its resources and expertise on developing new types of FMCG, and Sainsbury's, which alternatively focuses on making these new products available to end consumers. An intermediary must add some value that the producing organization cannot offer. Equally, the producing organization must add some value for the intermediary.

Using intermediaries often involves a trade-off between the benefits gained and the costs incurred, both financial and strategic. The benefits include reaching more of the target market by exploiting the networks and relationships of intermediaries. This further allows the producer to concentrate resources and skills on the areas in which it is most competent, and in which it can achieve maximum return. The main disadvantages can involve the sharing of profits, one of the major sources of **channel conflict**. Why should an intermediary spend further resources on managing the product in the way in which the producer would prefer if the return on investment (ROI) is not profitable?

Another source of channel conflict comes from the sharing of control between the producer and the intermediary. Sometimes, the producer has no direct relationship with the customer, and is therefore dependent on the intermediary for sales information and customer feedback. Electronic technologies such as scanning technologies, databases, and the development of radio frequency identification (RFID) have improved the efficiencies of data and information sharing throughout distribution channels. The Tesco Clubcard scheme is an excellent example in which producers such as Unilever and Procter & Gamble, as well as intermediaries such as transport carriers, receive a large stream of data and information about the sale and delivery of products.

Hybrid Distribution

An increasing number of organizations are adopting a multiple, or hybrid, channel structure to distribute goods and services (Park and Keh, 2003). Here, the producer controls some distribution channels and intermediaries control others. For example, many airlines sell their tickets directly to consumers through the Internet, but also rely on travel agents. Music labels can sell their music in album or single form directly using catalogues and their websites, or via music retailers such as HMV or iTunes, or can participate in music-sharing services such as Spotify.

Consider the options for the purchase of a mobile handset. This could occur directly from the Nokia website, from a service provider such as Orange, or perhaps while picking up some bread and milk at your local **supermarket** or **department store**. What we are seeing is growth in the use of hybrid channels in the mobile telecommunications industry. Samsung, Sony Ericsson, and Nokia are using service providers, electronic retailers, and wholesale discount clubs alongside their own direct Internet and telesales channels to market and deliver their mobile phone handsets.

The benefits of the **hybrid channel structure** include:

- increased reach to a target audience by exploiting existing direct networks, marketing efforts, and relationships of intermediaries;
- the producer has greater control over prices, communication, and promotion directly to customers;
- greater compliance from intermediaries, because the producer also acts like a competitor (although this could reduce the loyalty that the intermediary feels towards the producer);
- optimized margins to the producer (from the direct distribution channel) and increasing the bargaining power of the producer as dependence on the intermediary is reduced; and
- developing direct relationships with customers, a source of useful information.

The sharing of the profits among channel members can, however, create a source of distribution channel conflict, especially because intermediaries perceive the producer now as a competitor as well as a supplier. This structure may also confuse customers, who don't understand which distribution channel they should use.

▪ Members of Channel Intermediaries

Once we have decided to use a channel structure requiring intermediaries, we must then decide which type of intermediary to use. There are several different types of intermediary, including the following.

- *Agents, or brokers*—These act as a principal intermediary between the seller of a product and buyers, bringing them together without taking ownership of the product offering. These intermediaries have the legal authority to act on behalf of the manufacturer. For example, universities often use agents to recruit students in overseas markets (such as China, India).
- *Merchant*—A merchant performs in the same way as an agent, but takes ownership of the product.

- *Distributors, or dealers*—These distribute the product. They offer value through services associated with selling inventory, credit, and after-sales service. Often used in business-to-business (B2B) markets, they can also be found dealing directly with consumers, such as automobile distributors.

- *Franchise*—A franchisee holds a contract to supply and market a product to the requirements or blueprint of the franchisor, the owner of the original product. The contract might cover many aspects of the design of the product, such as marketing, product assortment, or service delivery. The uniformity of differing branches of McDonald's and KFC is an indication of franchisee contracts.

go online

Visit the **Online Resource Centre** and follow the web link to the European Franchise Association (EFA) to learn more about business franchise collaboration activities across Europe.

- *Wholesalers*—A wholesaler stocks goods before the next level of distribution, and takes both legal title and physical possession of the goods. In business-to-consumer (B2C) markets, wholesalers do not usually deal with the end consumer, but with other intermediaries (such as retailers). In B2B markets, sales are made direct to end customers. Examples include Costco Wholesalers in the US and Makro in Europe.

- *Retailers*—These intermediaries sell directly to end consumers and may purchase directly from manufacturers or deal with wholesalers. This is dependent on their purchasing power and the volume purchased. Leading retailers include Wal-Mart, Marks and Spencer, Carrefour, and electronics retailers such as Media-Saturn.

■ Intensity of Channel Coverage

With intermediaries, we further need to consider how many we may need to use. This is called the **intensity of channel coverage** and involves choosing between three basic types: intensive, exclusive, or selective distribution (see Figure 11.5).

- **Intensive distribution** is about placing a product in as many outlets or locations as possible, and is used most commonly for goods for which consumers are unlikely to search and which they purchase on the basis of convenience or impulse. Magazines and FMCGs such as soft drinks or confectionery are all examples. Retailers have increased control over the extent to which distribution is intensive. A manufacturer of a new brand of yoghurt, for

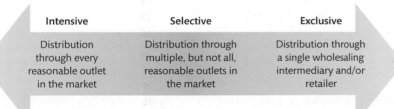

Figure 11.5

Intensity of the distribution continuum

example, might want its new brand put on the shelves of all supermarkets, but, owing to limited shelf space, the retailers might limit their assortment to the leading brands of yoghurt.

- **Selective distribution** involves some, but not all, available outlets being used. Typically, this is an attempt to balance a wider reach to the target audience at a lower cost than intensive distribution. Consumer shopping specialty goods and industrial equipment for which customers have a brand preference (for example, furniture or small appliance brands) are product categories that adopt this type of distribution. Sometimes, an organization might first use intensive distribution to increase awareness of its brand when entering a new market, but then move to a more selective strategy to improve control over product quality, and to manage costs and product price.

- **Exclusive distribution** occurs when intermediaries are given exclusive rights to market the product within a defined 'territory', using a very limited number of intermediaries. This is more useful for products for which significant support is required from the intermediary, and therefore the exclusivity is 'payback' for its investment and support. For example, high-prestige goods such as Ferrari sports cars and designer fashion apparel (Chanel, Gucci) adopt this type of distribution intensity.

The decision about the number of intermediaries is often driven by cost considerations. The costs of intensive distribution are higher because of the number of outlets that must be served. The implications of these three strategies for distribution are summarized in Table 11.1.

Table 11.1 Intensity of channel coverage

Characteristics	Exclusive	Selective	Intensive
Objectives	Strong image; channel control and loyalty; price stability	Moderate market coverage; solid image; some channel control and loyalty	Widespread market coverage; channel acceptance; volume sales
Channel members	Few in number; well-established, reputable stores	Moderate in number; well-established, better stores	Many in number; all types of outlet
Customers	Few in number; trend-setters; willing to travel to store; brand-loyal	Moderate in number; brand-conscious; somewhat willing to travel to store	Many in number; convenience-oriented
Marketing emphasis	Personal selling; pleasant shopping conditions; good service	Promotional mix; pleasant shopping conditions; good service	Mass advertising; nearby location; items in stock
Examples	Automobiles; designer clothes; caviar	Furniture; clothing; watches	Groceries; household products; magazines

Through the Internet, nearly all distribution is intensive because of the massive reach of the web. Even the smallest manufacturer can advertise and sell worldwide, using the same courier services to deliver its products as do major firms.

◼ Managing Relationships in the Channel

An important aspect in any channel strategy is managing relationships throughout the distribution channel. However, by their very nature, there is often a continuous struggle between channel members. Trust and channel conflict are the key issues here. Channel conflict arises when one channel member perceives another channel member to be acting in a way that prevents the first from achieving its distribution activities. Conflict in channels of distribution may involve intermediaries on the same level (tier), such as between retailers (**horizontal conflict**), or between members on different levels (tiers), thus between the producer, wholesaler, and the retailer (**vertical conflict**).

Member Incentives

Channel conflict can be reduced if manufacturers provide incentives to channel members, and if the risks, costs, and rewards of doing business are distributed fairly across the channel. Misaligned incentives are often the cause of channel conflict and also excess inventory, stockouts, incorrect forecasts, inadequate sales efforts, and even poor customer service (Narayanan and Raman, 2004). A historical example is Campbell's Soup. In the late 1980s, Campbell's Soup offered distributors discounts several times every year, hoping that the savings would be passed on to retailers. However, distributors bought more units than they sold to retailers, so Campbell's sales fluctuated wildly. The organization sold 40 per cent of its chicken noodle soup each year during the six-week promotional periods. This put a lot of pressure on the organization's distribution channel. Campbell invested in a system not only to track purchases of distributors, but also their sales, and with this system provided distributors with discounts on their sales as opposed to purchases. This helped to improve the performance of the distribution channel.

Grey Marketing

Another area of channel conflict is **grey marketing**—that is, the unauthorized sale of new, branded products diverted from authorized distribution channels or imported into a country for sale without the consent or knowledge of the manufacturer. What occurs is that the prices of authorized dealers in a market are undercut through unauthorized sales. This activity is not necessarily illegal, but could fall foul of licensing agreements or trade regulations (Myers and Griffith, 1999), as Tesco discovered when it attempted to stock and sell Levi's brand jeans, which it had purchased through an unauthorized supplier.

Market Insight 11.3

How Bazaar is Beauty!

Kazakhstan (population 15.4 million) is the wealthiest central Asian state and, in recent years, has been influenced by neighbouring Russia in terms of its growing spending pattern on personal care and cosmetic products. With total sales of US$660 million in 2008, the country's beauty market demonstrated healthy growth of 8.4 per cent in a five-year period to 2008. As a result, a legally structured retail industry and Western-style stores have been emerging, with Western-style retail spreading further into the regional centres such as Karaganda, Aktau, Atyrau, and other cities.

However, according to Kazakhstan's business portal (Kapital.kz), today 80–90 per cent of the country's population still prefers inexpensive cosmetics, with a significant number of customers switching to less expensive products or unofficial or unauthorized channels for the purchase of personal care products. A 'grey market' has emerged, seen in the unauthorized sale of branded cosmetics at open-air bazaars and markets selling both counterfeit alongside legitimate goods through local unauthorized distribution channels.

Source: Grishchenko (2011)

1 What is the grey market in the context of the Kazakhstan beauty market?

2 What are the benefits/disadvantages of a grey market for the sale of health and beauty products?

3 How could the presence of a grey market in Kazakhstan be the cause of channel conflict in the beauty industry?

Research Insight 11.1

To take your learning further, your might wish to read the following influential paper:

Webb, K. L. and Hogan, J. E. (2002) 'Hybrid channel conflict: causes and effects on channel performance', *Journal of Business and Industrial Marketing*, 17(5): 338–57.

This paper discusses the role of hybrid channel conflict not only in reducing channel performance, but also in serving as a mechanism for forcing internal channel coalitions to work harder and smarter to serve their market. The findings indicate that hybrid channel conflict is an important determinant of both channel performance and satisfaction.

@ Visit the **Online Resource Centre** to read the abstract and to access the full paper.

■ Logistics Management

Organizations must decide on the best way in which to store, handle, and move their product, so that it is available to customers in the right quantity, at the right time, and in the right place. Logistics includes the activities that relate to the flow of products from the manufacturer to the customer or end consumer. Although these are not traditionally marketing decisions or activities, they require marketing insight. The production schedule may mean that customers are asked to wait too long for products to arrive, which will affect product promotion. Inventory management may mean that there is not enough stock to meet urgent customer needs or unforeseen peaks in demand, which will affect customer satisfaction. So, although these areas are typically managed outside the marketing function, the need for everyone in the organization to share data and information about how a product is delivered is very important.

Importance of Logistics

Logistics management is the coordination of activities of the entire distribution channel. It addresses not only activities of moving products from the factory to customers (outbound distribution), but also moving products and materials from suppliers to the factory (inbound distribution). An example of an efficient inbound logistics system is provided by ASDA Wal-Mart, which uses computerized scanning to inform manufacturers very quickly of which products need delivery and in what quantities. More recent developments in electronic technologies, such as RFID tags, are further improving the efficiency and effectiveness with which the logistical activities are managed and implemented.

A core motivation for the growth in the management of logistics is an attempt to lower costs, given that about 15 per cent of an average product's price is accounted for in shipping and transport costs alone. IKEA can sell its furniture 20 per cent cheaper than competitors as it buys furniture ready for assembly, thereby saving on transport and inventory costs. The Benetton distribution centre in Italy is run largely by robots, delivering numerous goods to 110 countries within eleven days. Benetton also uses just-in-time (JIT) manufacturing, with some garments manufactured in neutral colours and then dyed to order, with very fast turnaround to suit customer requirements. However, beyond lowering costs, many organizations are increasing their focus on managing logistical activities as a result of demands for improved customer service, the explosion in product variety, and improvements in information and communication technologies.

Logistical Functions

Logistical activities or functions include order processing, inventory control, warehousing, and transportation (see Figure 11.6).

Order Processing
Accuracy and speed of billing and invoicing customers is vitally important, especially for customer relationships. Increasingly, we are seeing the use of information technology to help

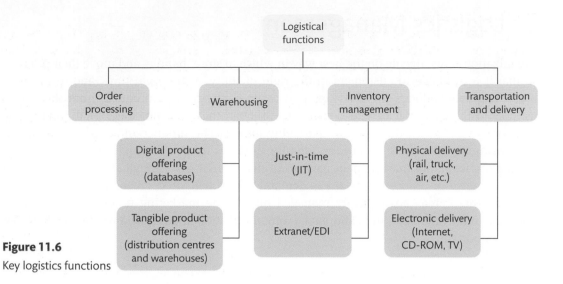

Figure 11.6
Key logistics functions

to manage order-processing activities. For example, automated emails are sent out to customers following online purchase of music from iTunes, a book from Amazon, or a train ticket from Eurorail.

In the retailing sector, order-processing technologies provide quick-response programmes to help to manage a retailer's inventory replenishment of products from suppliers. Kmart uses this kind of system, with electronic data interchange (EDI) systems/extranets to transmit daily records of product sales to suppliers, who analyse the information, create an order, and send it back to Kmart. Once in Kmart's system, the order is treated as though Kmart created it itself. Many technologies also speed up the billing cycle. For example, General Electric operates a computer-based system that, on receipt of a customer order, checks the customer's credit rating as well as whether and where the items are in stock. The computer then issues an order to ship, bills the customer, updates the inventory records, sends a production order for new stock, and sends a message back to the salesperson that the customer's order is on the way—all in less than 15 seconds. The hospitality industry also uses order-processing technology to improve service delivery efficiency. Fast food outlets such as McDonald's and KFC have for years recorded food orders through telecommunications systems, transmitting them to food preparation areas, with orders fulfilled within a matter of minutes, improving customer satisfaction in service delivery.

Warehousing and Materials Handling

Many organizations exchange tangible goods that require storage while they are waiting to be sold, largely resulting from the mismatch between when the product is produced and when it is sold and consumed. Books, dry goods such as sugar and canned goods, and even clothing, for example, require some degree of storage between the times when they leave the manufacturer and when they need delivery to customers. An organization must decide on how many and what types of warehouse it needs, and where they should be located. The type of warehouse is dependent on the type of product: tangible or digital; perishable or not.

Warehousing Tangible Goods

For the storage of tangible goods, such as FMCGs, an organization can use either **storage warehouses** or distribution centres. Storage warehouses store goods for moderate to long periods (for those that have a long shelf life), whereas distribution centres are designed to move goods, rather than only to store them. For products that are highly perishable with a short shelf life, such as fruit and vegetables, distribution centres are more appropriate. Grocery chains such as Woolworths in Australia and Tesco in the UK use large cold-store distribution centres to move perishable items such as fruit and vegetables to their various retail outlets. For products with a long shelf life or those that might require stockpiling to meet seasonal demands, storage centres are more appropriate.

Warehousing Digital 'Products'

Electronic warehousing systems, or database systems, are being used more and more for the storage of products (or product components) that can be digitized. These systems can be searched or browsed electronically, providing the user with immediate electronic delivery options. For example, emerald-library.com, ABI-Inform, or ScienceDirect are electronic databases accessible through the Internet that store a vast array of documents electronically in order to facilitate customers' search for information. In addition, many organizations use data warehousing facilities in which product information, or even actual products, are stored in digital form awaiting distribution. Apple iTunes is the largest entertainment retailer in the world, hosting over 225 million iTunes accounts worldwide in 2011. The online store has categorized over 15 million songs, sold over 15 billion songs, and serves over 425,000 apps, with 25 billion apps downloaded to March 2012. This does not include the thousands of games, videos, and podcasts electronically stored and shared. Customers can find, download, play, and sync in a fraction of the time it takes to drive to any store.

Inventory Management

Inventory management is an issue that arises from trying to balance responsiveness to customer needs with the resources required to store inventory. Zero-inventory, or JIT, production is ideal for many organizations, because this minimizes the use of resources that are often tied up in stock that doesn't sell. This must be balanced against the risk of not having the products available when customers want them.

Do we store the product so that it is available when customers need it, or do we produce the product when it is ordered or stock is low? A balance must be maintained between carrying too little inventory and carrying too much, as carrying larger-than-needed inventories can be expensive. Imagine the cost of storing all of the printed books that Amazon has listed for sale, or of storing fashion items in the spring ready for summer demand. With JIT systems, producers and retailers carry only small inventories of merchandise—often enough for only a few days' operations. New stock arrives exactly when it is needed, rather than being stored. ASDA Wal-Mart and even Burger King use these systems to track sales to service their outlets worldwide, automatically replenishing their ingredients according to product sales.

Transportation and Delivery

Transportation is considered to be the most important activity in logistics. Transportation is the physical movement of the product using truck, rail, air, pipeline, shipping, and so on.

Often, transportation is seen as concern only for supplying tangible goods, but it is just as relevant to many service organizations and delivery of electronic (or digital) products. Consultants, IT companies, and health organizations have to move staff around, incurring transport and accommodation costs. Transportation methods include physical transport modes (such as rail, truck, water, pipeline, and air) and electronic delivery modes (such as electronic vending machines, the telephone, the Internet, or EDI).

Physical Delivery

Information and communication technologies have improved physical product delivery. For example, where freight moves, the size of typical shipments and the time periods within which goods must be delivered has changed with significant economic benefits to all transportation activities. The top of the list of 'must have' systems for transportation are in-vehicle navigation and route guidance solutions to help to manage transport fleets, to track shipments, and to optimize transportation (Dreier, 2003). Amazon's tracking system assigns a tracking number and, using proprietary software, provides information to customers in real time about where the package or shipment is located, thereby managing customer satisfaction.

Electronic Delivery

As early as the introduction of the TV, radio, or even the telephone, electronic technologies have been used to deliver products electronically. Producers of music, games, video, or software are typically unconstrained by the needs of physical distribution as a result of product digitization; this has been increased with the development of the Internet. For example, Wall Street seemed at first to smirk at the E*Trade Group's invitation to investors to make their own trades on the Internet; then, the Charles Schwab Corporation jumped at the challenge and, by the late 1990s, other brokerages, such as Merrill Lynch and Bank of America Investment Services Inc., were scrambling to catch up. Organizations such as travel agents, banks, and insurance companies, which traditionally relied on customers coming to a branch or agency, have quickly moved to using telecommunications, ATMs, and the Internet to reach more customers. The Internet has clearly added to the capacity of these electronic distribution channels. In developed economies around the world, large numbers of customers now bank, trade stocks, and arrange insurance and travel through the Internet.

We will now look more closely at one type of intermediary used in B2C markets: the retailer and the activity of retailing.

■ Retailing

Retailing encompasses all of the activities directly related to the sale of products to the ultimate end consumer for personal and non-business use. These differ from wholesalers, which distribute the product to businesses, not to end consumers. For every successful large retailer, such as Carrefour or Tesco, there are thousands of small retailers, with all having two key features in common: they link producers and end consumers; and they perform an invaluable service for both.

Customer Value

In order to purchase a product, consumers must have access to it. The purpose of a retailer is to provide this access. As such, it is very important to find out what consumers actually want from a retailer in order to deliver value. Convenience is the primary concern for most consumers, with people increasingly being 'leisure time poor' and keen to trade off shopping time for leisure time (Seiders et al., 2000). Consequently, convenience has driven just about every innovation in retailing, such as supermarkets, department stores, shopping malls, the web, and self-scanning kiosks, in pursuit of providing customer convenience. As noted by Seiders et al. (2000), from a customer's perspective, convenience consists of the four key elements of access, search, possession, and transaction convenience (outlined in more detail in Table 11.2).

Retailer Types

There are numerous types of retailer. These can be classified according to the marketing strategy employed (that is, product, price, and service) and the store presence (that is, store or non-store retailing).

Table 11.2 Retailing convenience: a customer's perspective

Element	Description
Access convenience	• Accessibility factors include location, availability, hours of operation, parking, and proximity to other outlets, as well as telephone, mail, and Internet. • Convenience does not exist without access. • Increasingly, customers want access to products and services to be as fast and direct as possible, with very little hassle. • It is a global trend, e.g. the rise of **convenience stores** in Japan. • Direct shopping is driven by time and place utility.
Search convenience	• Identifying and selecting the products that you want is connected to product focus, intelligence outlet design and layout ('servicescape'), knowledgeable staff, interactive systems, product displays, package and signage, etc. • Solutions can be provided in the form of in-store kiosks, clearly posted prices, and mobile phones for sales staff linked to knowledge centres. • One example of good practice is German discount chain Adler Mode Market GmbH, which uses colour-coded tags to help customers to spot the sizes quickly.
Possession convenience	This is about having merchandise in stock and available on a timely basis, e.g. Nordstrom clothing store guarantees that advertised products will be in stock. However, possession convenience has its limitations for certain channels. The Internet scores highly for search convenience, yet is generally low in terms of possession convenience, unlike digital products.

Element	Description
Transaction convenience	• This relates to the speed and ease with which consumers can effect and amend transaction before and after the purchase. • A number of innovations in transactions and well-designed service systems—such as self-scanning in Carrefour, Tesco, and Metro—can mitigate the peaks and troughs in store traffic, as with the use of in-store traffic counters as in Sainsbury's to monitor store traffic. • Even queue design can contribute, e.g. single queues in post offices and banks differ from supermarkets as a result of space and servicescape design. • Transaction convenience is a significant issue on the Internet, with pure Internet retailers having problems with returns and customers not being prepared to pay for shipping and handling costs.

Marketing Strategy

Major types of retailer can be classified according to the marketing strategies employed, paying particular attention to three specific elements:

- product assortment;
- price level; and
- customer service.

Table 11.3, although not exhaustive, provides a useful summary of these elements across the differing types of retailing channel.

These retailing establishments can be further distinguished, as follows.

- *Department stores*—These are large-scale retailing institutions that offer a very broad and deep assortment of products (both hard and soft goods), and provide a wide array of customer service facilities for store customers. Debenhams has a wide array of products, including home furnishings, foods, cosmetics, clothing, books, and furniture, and further provides variety within each product category (brand, feature variety). Value-added services include wedding registries, clothing alterations, shoe repairs, lay-by facilities, home delivery, and installation.

- **Discount retailers**—This type of retailer is positioned based on low prices combined with the reduced costs of doing business. The key characteristics here involve a broad, but shallow, assortment of products, low prices, and very few customer services. Matalan in the UK, for example, Kmart in Australia, and Target in the US all carry a broad array of soft goods (for example, apparel), combined with hard goods such as appliances and home furnishings. To keep prices down, the retailers negotiate extensively with suppliers to ensure low merchandise costs.

Table 11.3 Marketing strategy and retail store classification

Retail store	Product assortment	Pricing	Customer service	Example
Department	Very broad, deep, with layout and presentation of products critical	Minimize price competition	Wide array and good quality	David Jones; Debenhams; Harrods
Discount	Broad and shallow	Low price positioning	Few customer service options	Pound Stretcher; Dollar Dazzlers
Convenience	Narrow and shallow	High prices	Avoids price competition	Co-op; 7-Eleven
Limited line	Narrow and deep	Traditional = avoids price competition; new kinds = low prices	Vary by type	Bicycle stores; sports stores; ladies fashion
Speciality	Very narrow and deep	Avoids price competition	Standard; extensive in some	Running shops; bridal boutiques
Category killer	Narrow, very deep	Low prices	Few to moderate	Staples and Office Works; IKEA
Supermarket	Broad and deep	Some = low price; others avoid price disadvantages	Few and self-service	Tesco plc (UK); Woolworths Ltd (Australia); Carrefour (Europe)
Superstores	Very broad and very deep	Low prices	Few and self-service	Tesco Extra; Asda Wal-Mart

- **Limited line retailers**—This type of retailer has a narrow, but deep, product assortment and customer services that vary from store to store. Clothing retailers, butchers, baked goods, and furniture stores that specialize in a small number of related product categories are all examples. The breadth of product variety differs across limited line stores and a store may choose to concentrate on: several related product lines (for example, shoes and clothing accessories), a single product line (shoes), or a specific part of one product line (sports shoes). Examples include bookstores, jewellers, athletic footwear stores, dress shops, newsagents, etc.

- *Category killer stores*—As the name suggests, these retailers are designed to kill off the competition and are characterized by a narrow, but very deep, assortment of products, low

Kmart in Australia is an example of a discount retailer

Source: Kmart

prices, and few-to-moderate customer services. Successful examples include IKEA in home furnishings, Staples in office supplies, and B&Q in hardware.

- *Supermarkets*—Founded in the 1930s, large self-service retailing environments offer a wide variety of differing merchandise to a large consumer base. Tesco Extra in the UK stocks products ranging from clothing, hardware, music, groceries, and dairy products, to soft furnishings. Operating largely on a self-service basis, with minimum customer service and centralized register and transactional terminals, supermarkets provide the benefits of a wide product assortment in a single location, offering convenience and variety. Today, supermarkets are the dominant institution for food retailing.

- *Convenience stores, or corner shops*—These offer a range of grocery and household items, and cater for convenience and the last-minute purchase needs of consumers. Key characteristics include long opening times (for example, '24/7'), being family-run, and belonging to a trading group such as 7-Eleven, Spar, or Co-op. Increasingly, we are seeing smaller local convenience stores threatened by large supermarket chains such as ASDA Wal-Mart and Tesco, especially as laws for longer open times for larger stores are being relaxed (including Sunday trading hours in the UK) and the main supermarket groups set up small, more convenient, 'express' store formats.

Store Presence

We can further categorize retailers according to their presence: 'store' or 'non-store' retailing. Most retailing occurs through fixed stores, with existing operators having 'sunk' investments in physical building. Several characteristics make store retailing unique from the customer viewpoint. The retail environment provides the sensation of touch, feel, and smell, which is very important for many product categories, such as clothing, books, or perfumes. Furthermore, the customer might interact with in-store staff, who provide purchase advice. Once the product is selected and the purchase decision made, the customer can walk out of the store with the merchandise in hand.

In contrast, retailing can also involve **non-store retailers**, retailing activities resulting in transactions that occur away from a fixed store location. Examples include automatic vending machines, **direct selling**, and Internet retailing (Bennet, 1988). Direct selling is one of the oldest forms of retailing methods, and is the personal contact between a salesperson and a consumer away from the retailing environment. Activities such as door-to-door canvassing and party plans (in which a sales presentation is made within the home to a party of guests) are examples. Examples include cosmetics companies, such as Avon, Nutri-Metics skincare, and Amway household products. **Telemarketing** or telesales is another form of non-store retailing in which purchase occurs over the telephone. During the 1990s, this form of non-store retailing grew extensively owing to rapid developments in computer-assisted and TV shopping networks.

A further development of non-store retailing is the **electronic kiosk**, which is being placed in shopping malls to assist the retailing experience. These computer-based retailing environments offer increased self-service opportunities, a wide array of products, and a large amount of data and information to help in decision-making. Somewhat different from the electronic kiosk is the automatic vending machine, providing product access 24 hours a day, seven days a week. From soft drinks and hot beverages, to newspapers and magazines, products distributed through vending machines are typical of low-priced products and convenience products. Perhaps an unusual example is the US Beverly Hills-based Sprinkles Cupcakes, which delivers cupcakes via the Cupcake ATM, the world's first cupcake vending machine (Stephens, 2012). However, we also see the wide adoption of automatic teller machines (ATMs) to facilitate the delivery of financial retailing services.

The Sprinkles ATM: now vending cupcakes
Source: Sprinkles Bakery

Another form of non-store retailing is Internet or online retailing, one of the fastest-growing markets in Europe. In 2011, online sales in the UK were £50.34 billion (€59.4 billion), or 12 per cent of UK retail trade. In 2008, online was equivalent to only 8.6 per cent of retail sales. For Europe (including UK), the total market was worth £169,880 million (€200.52 billion), up from £143,720 million (€169.63 billion) in 2010. Online retailers in only three countries, UK, Germany, and France, accounted for 71 per cent of European online sales (CRR, 2012).

go online

Visit the **Online Resource Centre** and complete Internet Activity 11.2 to learn more about the variety of Internet retailing sites and the importance of delivery information for this sector.

Market Insight 11.4 provides a specific snapshot of the impact that iTunes, the leading online music retailer, is having on the retail purchase of music.

Tuning into iTunes

Online shopping is set to account for nearly 40 per cent of all UK retail sales by 2020, with online sales reaching £50 billion in 2011 and set to quadruple to £162 billion by 2020. The most popular online purchases are holidays, films, and music.

One organization playing a key role in the facilitation of this growth of digital music sales is Apples iTunes Music Store (iTMS). The iTunes Store is an online business run by Apple Inc., which sells media files that are accessed through its iTunes application. Opened as the iTunes Music Store on 28 April 2003, it proved the viability of online music sales. The virtual record shop sells music videos, TV shows, movies, and video games in addition to music. iTunes now has several personalization options, one of which is 'Just for you'. Apple thoroughly dominates the market, controlling more than 70 per cent of the worldwide online digital music sales.

Apple's iTunes store allows the users to purchase songs and transfer them easily to the iPod through iTunes. The store began after Apple signed deals with the five major record labels at the time, EMI, Universal, Warner Bros, Sony Music Entertainment, and BMG (the latter two of which would later merge to form Sony BMG). Music by more than 600 independent label artists was added later, the first being Moby on 29 July 2003. The store now has more than 15 million songs, including exclusive tracks from numerous popular artists and, in early 2010, Apple celebrated the downloading of the 15 billionth song from Apple iTunes.

New songs are added daily to the iTunes catalogue and the iTunes Store is updated regularly. Apple also releases a 'Single of the Week' and usually a 'Discovery Download' on Tuesdays, which are available free for one week. Apple makes it possible for users to stream their digital music directly from the Internet (with iCloud). In the words of Steve Jobs:

> In 1984 we introduced the Macintosh. It didn't just change Apple, it changed the whole computer industry. In 2001, we introduced the first iPod and it didn't just change the way we all listen to music, it changed the entire music industry.

Sources: Allison and Palmer (2007); Apple (2007); Benson (2007); Wingfield and Smith (2007); Tabini (2010)

1 Why do you think offline retail selling of music is declining?

2 Why do you think iTunes has been such a success as an online music retailer?

3 Consider your own recent purchases of music. What retail channel did you use to purchase the music and why?

To take your learning further, you might wish to read the following influential paper:

O'Cass, A. and French, T. (2003) 'Web retailing adoption: exploring the nature of Internet users' web retailing behaviour', *Journal of Retailing and Consumer Services*, 10: 81–94.

In this paper, the authors provide a discussion of the nature of Internet retailing, its growth and importance. The authors further discuss the key elements that influence web retailing adoption and profile online users' web retailing behaviour.

Visit the **Online Resource Centre** to read the abstract and to access the full paper.

Chapter Summary

To consolidate your learning, the key points from this chapter can be summarized as follows.

■ **Define the distribution channels and key considerations in managing a channel strategy**

Distribution channels can be defined as an organized network of organizations, which, in combination, perform all of the activities required to link producers and manufacturers with consumers, purchasers, and users. Distribution channel decisions are about managing which channel best suits the organization's objectives. The key consideration that reveals itself here is the importance of optimizing the balance between the three elements of economics, coverage, and control.

■ **Define and discuss the differing types of intermediary and their roles in the distribution channel**

An intermediary is an independent business concern that operates as a link between producers and ultimate consumers or industrial end users. If using an indirect or hybrid channel structure, the next strategic decision is what type(s) of intermediary to use. The key difference between the various types is that not all intermediaries take legal title of the product offering or physical possession of it. There are several different types of intermediary, including agents, merchants, distributors, franchise, wholesalers, and retailers.

■ **Differentiate between differing distribution channel structures and selection criteria**

The relationship between producers, intermediaries, and customers will form a 'direct', 'indirect', or 'hybrid' channel structure. A direct structure involves selling directly to customers; an indirect structure involves using intermediaries; a hybrid structure will involve both. The degree of efficiency that an intermediary can introduce to the performance of distribution tasks determines what form a channel structure will take. At the simplest level, direct channels offer maximum control, but sometimes at the expense of reaching a target market. Indirect channels can maximize coverage, but often at the expense of control, as the intermediaries start 'playing' with the marketing mix strategies and demand a share of the profits in return for their involvement. Hybrid strategies often result in greater channel conflict because the intermediary feels that the organization that is supplying it is also competing with it.

■ **Discuss the factors influencing channel design, structure, and strategy**

In setting a distribution channel strategy, most organizations make key decisions in order to serve their customers and to establish and maintain buyer–seller relationships. The first decision is the selection of the structure of the channel. If it is decided that intermediaries will be required, management then needs to consider the type of market coverage that will be required, the number and type of intermediaries to use, and how to manage the relationships between channel members. These choices are important, because they can affect the value that is ultimately provided to customers.

■ **Discuss the role, function, and importance of retailers in the distribution channel**

Distributing consumer products begins with the producer and ends with the end consumer. However, between the two there is usually an intermediary called a retailer. 'Retailing' is all of the activities directly related to the sale of goods and services to the ultimate end consumer for personal and non-business use. This is also called the 'retail trade'. A retailer, or retail store, is a business enterprise the primary function of which is to sell to ultimate consumers for non-business use. However, they all have two key features in common: they link producers and end consumers; and they perform an invaluable service for both.

■ **Compare and contrast the differing types of retailer**

Types of retailing establishment can be classified as being differentiated by two key characteristics: the marketing strategy employed (that is, product, price, and service); and the store presence (that is, store or non-store retailing). Examples include department stores, discount stores, convenience stores, limited line retailers, specialty retailers, category killer stores, supermarkets, and superstores. In addition to the underlying marketing strategy, retailing establishments can be further characterized according to store or non-store presence.

Review Questions

1 Define what we mean by 'distribution channel management'.
2 What are the differing benefits of using intermediaries?
3 Why are economics, coverage, and control important when making distribution channel decisions?
4 What are the advantages and disadvantages of the three differing channel structures?
5 What are the differing types of retailer?

Scan this image to go online and access the chapter's multiple-choice questions, web links, Internet activities, and more!

Worksheet Summary

Visit the **Online Resource Centre** and complete Worksheet 11.1. This will explore the differing types of channel structure and different types of intermediary that could be used to distribute a technology product to a consumer market.

References

Allison, K. and Palmer, M. (2007) 'Into the pack: Apple takes risks in its bid to shake up the mobile market', *Financial Times*, 26 June, p. 11.

Anon. (2011) 'High-end Chinese tea makes new European inroads', *Jing Daily*, 26 April, available online at http://www.jingdaily.com/en/luxury/high-end-chinese-tea-makes-new-european-inroads/ [accessed 2 July 2012].

Apple (2007) 'iTunes store tops two billion songs', Apple Press Release, 9 January, available online at http://www.apple.com/pr/library/2007/01/09iTunes-Store-Tops-Two-Billion-Songs.html [accessed 11 January 2010].

Bennet, P. D. (1988) *Dictionary of Marketing Terms*, Chicago, IL: American Marketing Association.

Benson, C. (2007) 'Retail recovery', *Billboard*, 9 June, p. 119.

Centre for Retailing Research (CRR) (2012) 'Online retailing: Britain and Europe 2012', available online at http://www.retailresearch.org/onlineretailing.php [accessed 3 March 2012].

Douglas, M. L., James, R. S., and Ellram, L. M. (1998) *Fundamentals of Logistics Management*, New York: Irwin/McGraw-Hill.

Dreier, G. (2003) 'Technology that drives transportation', *Transport Technology Today*, July: 9.

Gandhi (1979) 'Marketing channels', *American Journal of Small Business*, 3(3): 50–3.

Grishchenko, G. (2011) 'Central Asia: cosmetics, culture and politics', *GCI Magazine*, 3 March, available online at http://www.gcimagazine.com/marketstrends/regions/easterneurope/117359933.html [accessed 12 January 2012].

Handfield, R. B. and Nichols, E. L. (1999) *Introduction to Supply Chain Management*, Upper Saddle River, NJ: Prentice-Hall.

Jing, L. (2012) 'Offering a blend of luxury and tea', *China Daily*, 6 January, available online at http://europe.chinadaily.com.cn/epaper/2012-01/06/content_14393397.htm [accessed 16 February 2012].

Michman, R. D. (1990) 'Managing structural changes in marketing channels', *Journal of Business and Industrial Marketing*, Summer/Fall: 5–14.

Myers, M. B. and Griffith, D. A. (1999) 'Strategies for combating grey market activity', *Business Horizons*, 42(6): 71–5.

Narayanan, V. G. and Raman, A. (2004) 'Aligning incentives in supply chains', *Harvard Business Review*, 82(11): 94–102.

O'Cass, A. and French, T. (2003) 'Web retailing adoption: exploring the nature of Internet users' web retailing behaviour', *Journal of Retailing and Consumer Services*, 10: 81–94.

Park, S. Y. and Keh, H. T. (2003) 'Modelling hybrid distribution channels: a game theory analysis', *Journal of Retailing and Consumer Services*, 10: 155–67.

Parker, M., Bridson, K., and Evans, J. (2006) 'Motivations for developing direct trade relationships', *International Journal of Retail and Distribution Management*, 34(2): 111–34.

Russell, S. W. (2000) *Marketing Management*, Englewood Cliffs, NJ: Prentice Hall.

Seiders, K., Berry, L. L., and Gresham, L. G. (2000) 'Attention retailers! How convenient is your convenience strategy?', *Sloan Management Review*, Spring: 79–89.

Stephens, L. (2012) 'It's pink: Sprinkles cupcakes gets vending debut', *Technorati*, 7 March, available online at http://technorati.com/business/article/its-pink-sprinkles-cupcakes-gets-vending/ [accessed 29 April 2012].

Tabini, M. (2010) 'iTunes store: more than 10 billion songs served', *Macworld*, 27(5): 63.

Webb, K. L. and Hogan, J. E. (2002) 'Hybrid channel conflict: causes and effects on channel performance', *Journal of Business and Industrial Marketing*, 17(5): 338–57.

Wingfield, N. and Smith, E. (2007) 'Jobs' new tune raises pressure on music firms: Apple chief now favors making downloads of songs freely tradable', *Wall Street Journal* (Eastern edn), p. A1.

Part 4

Principles of Relational Marketing

12

Services Marketing and CRM

Learning outcomes

After reading this chapter, you will be able to:

- explain what a service is, and describe the relationship between goods and services;

- explain the main characteristics of a service;

- understand the different service processes and outline each element of the services marketing mix;

- explain the term 'service encounters' and describe how to maintain service performance; and

- explain the ways in which organizations try to provide customer relationship management (CRM) and service support.

Banali Malhotra for RAKBANK

RAKBANK is the highly successful National Bank of Ras Al-Khaimah, in the United Arab Emirates. We speak to Banali Malhotra, Head of Marketing, to find out how they sought to improve relationships with their customers.

It is very difficult these days to get by without a credit card. Hotel bookings, car rentals, holidays, entertainment, and Internet purchases are nearly impossible to make without these pieces of plastic. At RAKBANK, our strategy involved entering the fiercely competitive credit card market. This market was dominated by our competitors' use of Gold and Platinum credit cards. These were positioned on a prestige platform, supported by a range of associated privileges, but they all required an annual fee and various extra charges.

The problem we faced was that customers resented paying these fees and were disenchanted with the financial services community. This dissatisfaction was rooted in the hidden charges and the service fees that were nearly always glossed over in the marketing communications used by our competitors. Their messages centred on financial freedom and desirable lifestyles, but there is no mention of their gratuitous annual fees, extortionate interest rates, complicated cancellation procedures and poor customer service.

RAKBANK was a late entrant into this overcrowded and disgruntled market and we needed to find a strong point of differentiation, something that would resonate with

our customers and encourage them to value and maintain their relationship with RAKBANK.

Our research indicated that there was a need for a premium product, one that offered the prestige perception and privileges, but at a cost advantage to customers. This suggested something between the Gold and Platinum cards that currently dominated the market might be successful. We also needed customers to evaluate the RAKBANK offering by comparing products on the basis of their features and benefits, and service, but not price.

RAKBANK identified four main segments. These are credit card customers, business entrepreneurs, high-net-worth individuals and local people who need personal loans. We developed our strategy on the well-established principle that the delivery of high product quality and above average service levels, leads to improved customer satisfaction levels. This, in turn, promotes higher levels of customer perceived value. We believed that once customers experienced our superior customer service, they would be more likely to take up other product offerings from RAKBANK. However, we needed to find a range of incentives to first attract and then retain customers, and so realize higher revenues from the life time value generated by these customers.

1 Suggest a name for a credit card that RAKBANK could use to enter the market. What might be the key product incentives necessary to attract and retain customers?

The RAKBANK logo

Introduction

Have you ever been frustrated trying to get through to **customer services** to sort out a mobile phone issue, or to the administrators at a university or college to get answers to important questions about your course or exam results? If you have, then you understand just how much better it would be if the provider were to deliver a better service. Services are important because they impact immediately on people and their perceptions of an organization. It is therefore important to understand how marketing activities can enhance the performance of service providers.

In this chapter, we consider the nature, characteristics, and issues associated with the marketing of services. Time is spent, first, considering the distinguishing characteristics, and then how the service marketing mix needs to reflect and deliver realistic marketing activities.

One of the critical aspects of services is the **service encounter**—that is, the point at which a service is provided and simultaneously consumed. Getting the service performance right each time the service is delivered—for example, each time you phone customer services at your mobile phone operator—is probably one of the most difficult aspects of service marketing management. Therefore consideration is given to branding, **internal marketing**, and the processes underlying customer relationship management (CRM), as key dimensions of services marketing.

What is a Service?

Services are different from goods (see also Chapters 1 and 7). One of the distinguishing dimensions of goods is that they have a physical presence; services do not have a physical presence and they cannot be touched. This is because their distinguishing characteristic is that they are an act or a performance (Berry, 1980). A service cannot be put in a bag, taken home, stored in a cupboard, and used at a later date. A service is consumed at the point at which it is produced. For example, watching a play at a theatre, learning maths at school, or taking a holiday all involve the simultaneous production and consumption of the play, new knowledge, and leisure and relaxation. (See Market Insight 12.1.)

Market Insight 12.1

Purity in Products and Services

Sweden's Tetra Pak revolutionized the food packaging industry, Finland's Huhtamäki Oyj is one of the world's leading manufacturers of paper cups and plates, Danish company Schur Technology is a leading North European total supplier of packaging solutions, and the Norwegian company Elopak is a leading global supplier of cartons for liquid food products. Rexam is one of the world's leading consumer packaging groups supporting the beverage, beauty, pharmaceuticals, and food markets.

What is common to all of these organizations? The answer: their skill and core competence in packaging. They make tangible goods to which, traditionally, there are few service additions.

Packaging firms like Tetra Pak manufacture a 'pure' product

Source: Courtesy of Tetra Pak packaging portfolio

Alternatively, Bain, McKinsey, Towers Perrin, and PricewaterhouseCoopers (PwC) are some of the leading management consulting organizations. Owned by IBM, PwC offers a huge range of services across many industries and sectors. Its approach to work is stated to be through 'connected thinking'. All of these organizations do not make or sell any products; they provide knowledge and skills—that is, pure services.

Sources: http://www.elopak.com/; http://www.huhtamaki.com/; http://www.pwc.com/; http://www.rexam.com/; http://www.schur.com/skabeloner/; http://www.tetrapak.com/

1 **Identify ways in which packaging might shape consumer experiences.**

2 **Think about the role of a marketing consultant and make a list of the different types of knowledge that might constitute 'connected thinking'.**

3 **Draw the product–service spectrum and place on it various product–service combinations.**

The service industry sector forms a substantial part of most developed economies. Not surprisingly, the range of services is enormous. and we consume services in nearly all areas of our work, business, home, and leisure activities. Table 12.1 indicates the variety of sectors and some of the areas in which we consume different types of service.

The sheer number of services that are available has grown, partly, because it is not always easy to differentiate products only on the basis of features, benefits, quality, or price. Competition can be very intense and most product innovations or developments are copied quickly. Services provide an opportunity to add value, yet not be copied, because each service is a unique experience.

Most products contain an element of service: there is a good–service combination designed to provide a means of adding value, differentiation, and earning a higher return. The extent to which a service envelops a tangible good varies according to a number of factors, including the level of tangibility associated with the type of product, the way in which the service is delivered, variations in supply and demand, the level of customization, the type of relationship between service provider and customer, and the degree of involvement that people experience in the service (Lovelock et al., 1999).

The good–service spectrum, explored at the beginning of Chapter 7, identifies that there are some goods that have very few services and some services that have little tangibility.

Table 12.1 Service sectors	
Sector	Examples
Business	Financial; airlines; hotels; solicitors and lawyers
Manufacturing	Finance and accountants; computer operators; administrators; trainers
Retail	Sales personnel; cashiers; customer support advisers
Institutions	Hospitals; education; museums; charities; churches
Government	Legal system; prisons; military; customs and excise; police

Many grocery products have few supporting services: only shelf-stocking and checkout operators. The purchase of new fitted bedroom furniture involves the cupboards, dressers, and wardrobes, plus the professional installation service necessary to make the furniture usable. At the other end of the spectrum, a visit to the dentist entails little physical product-based support, because the personal service is delivered by the service deliverer in the form of the dentist.

Visit the **Online Resource Centre** and complete Internet Activity 12.1 to learn more about the Professional Services Marketing Group (PSMG) and the marketing of professional services.

go online

■ The Nature of Services

In view of the foregoing comments about the range and variety of services, it is necessary to define what a 'service' is. As with any definition, there is no firm agreement, but, for our purposes, the following definition (derived from a number of authors) will be used: a service is any act or performance offered by one party to another that is essentially intangible. Consumption of the service does not result in any transfer of ownership, even though the service process may be attached to a physical product. Much of this definition is derived from the work of Grönroos (1990), who considered a range of definitions and interpretations. What this definition provides is an indication of the various characteristics and properties that set services apart from products.

The two sections that follow examine the key characteristics of services and the way in which the service mix, as opposed to the product mix, is configured.

Distinguishing Characteristics

Services are characterized by five distinct characteristics, as depicted in Figure 12.1: **intangibility**, **perishability**, **variability**, **inseparability**, and a lack of ownership. These are important aspects that shape the way in which marketers design, deliver, and evaluate the marketing of services.

Intangibility

The purchase of products involves the use of most of our senses. We can touch, see, smell, hear, or even taste products before we buy them, let alone use them. Think of a shopping trip

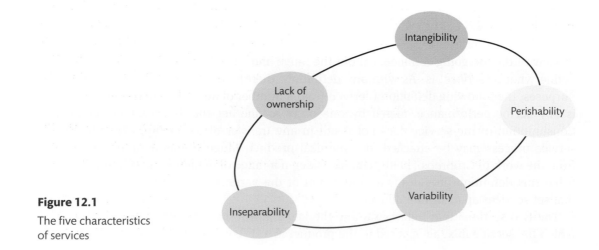

Figure 12.1

The five characteristics of services

to buy an MP3 player: it is possible to see the physical product and its various attributes, such as size and colour, to feel its weight, and to touch it. These are important purchasing decision cues and, even if the equipment fails to work properly, it is possible to take it back for a replacement. However, if a decision is made to buy additional insurance/support, this will be itemized on the receipt, but it is not possible to touch, taste, see, hear, or smell the insurance bought. Services are intangible and they are only delivered and experienced. Intangibility means that consumers use substitute cues to help them to make these purchasing decisions and to reduce the uncertainty because they cannot touch, see, smell, or hear the service. People make judgements based on a range of quality-related cues. These cues serve to make tangible the intangible service. Two types of cue can be identified: intrinsic and extrinsic cues (Olson and Jacoby, 1972). Intrinsic cues are drawn directly from the 'service product' itself and are regarded as difficult to change; extrinsic cues are said to surround the 'service product' and can be changed relatively easily. Brady et al. (2005) found that different types of service brand need different types of cue. Financial and investment-based brands prosper from the use of intrinsic cues, which stress objective information sources, such as a strong reputation, industry rankings, and favourable media reviews. The reverse is true for services that have a more tangible element, such as hotels and transport services. In these circumstances, more subjective communication, such as advertising and referrals through word-of-mouth, are more influential.

The use of cues is important because they often involve an assessment about the people delivering the service, the location, the equipment used, the messages and tone of the communications and associated branding devices, and, of course, price. Carbone and Haeckel (1994) refer to this process of 'tangibilizing the intangible' as 'customer service engineering'. This requires that the service organization first decides on what the customer experience should be like, by designing a service blueprint, and then designs a set of facilities and cues that lead customers to the required experience. Market Insight 12.2 offers an example of how an online service provider attempted to 'tangibilize' its service offering offline.

Service Blueprints
Service blueprints are used during the early stages of the design process, to help to specify the various components of a desired service. Developed by Shostack (1982; 1984; 1985), blueprints are used to identify sequentially and visually all of the activities necessary for designing and managing services effectively. Service blueprinting is a tool for depicting the service process, points of customer contact, and the evidence of the service as seen by a customer. This perspective reveals the overlapping layers that can be found in a service, ranging from the layer of physical evidence and customer interaction, to the layer of internal interaction within the service production process (Zeithaml et al., 2006).

According to Hara et al. (2009), service activities are arranged with respect to two lines: the first line of interaction concerns the point at which a customer and a service provider interact; the second is the line that separates the visible activities from the invisible activities performed by the provider.

Bitner et al. (2008) argue that there are five components that make up a typical service blueprint: customer actions; onstage/visible contact employee actions; backstage/invisible contact employee actions; support processes; and physical evidence. So, a five-star hotel will determine what constitutes a five-star hotel experience and then provide a series of context cues to be delivered by people ('humanics') and things ('mechanics'). These will include appropriate communication devices, such as brochures, and a website designed to position the hotel as a five-star brand and as a desirable place to stay. Staff will be trained and reservation systems installed such that the humanics and mechanics of customer handling are seamless and consistently high.

go online

Visit the **Online Resource Centre** and follow the web link to the Hotel Marketing Association (HMA) to learn more about marketing hotel services.

See Figure 12.2 for an example of a service blueprint for an overnight stay at a hotel.

Market Insight 12.2

eBay Inc. Pops up!

In December 2011, in a bid to tangibilize its service offering and to reach a wider consumer base, leading online auction service provider eBay Inc. experimented with bringing its pure online service offline. An eBay Inc. pop-up store was opened in London for the Christmas shopping period, enabling shoppers with mobile devices to browse and buy holiday gifts in a physical location. Branded the 'eBay Christmas Boutique', this was an attempt by the online marketplace to put its wares before consumers on the street, while also promoting its mobile commerce effort. The store represents the latest push by e-commerce operators to bring digital and bricks-and-mortar retailing services even closer. The shopping experience at the store relied on QR-Codes—that is, codes that consumers can scan using the appropriate app on their smartphones and then be automatically linked to the relevant mobile content. Shoppers could use the eBay app to capture codes from some 300 items on display in the store and then complete purchases on their mobile devices. If a customer had no smartphone, the store loaned handsets for shoppers to trial the service experience.

The pop-up store and the service experience received mixed reports, with many customers speaking of a string of faulty results, including many QR-Codes traversing to the website's home page or the wrong product. This was explained as a result of URLs on eBay being constantly updated owing to changing stock levels. One wonders why eBay used QR-Codes and not the more reliable product bar code scanners, which take you directly to the product itself.

The opening of the eBay Inc. pop-up store followed the opening of a similar storefront by eBay Inc. in New York City, the retail chain Wal-Mart Stores Inc. locating of e-commerce stores in two southern California malls, and Google Inc. launching a physical store in London where consumers can inspect and buy Chromebook computers featuring Google software.

Sources: Geere (2011); Rueter (2011); http://www.ebay.com

1 **List three main service differences between an online service experience and the offline experience described above.**

2 **Write notes explaining your interpretation of how eBay Inc. attempted to tangibilize the customer experience.**

3 **Prepare an outline blueprint for an online service that you experienced recently.**

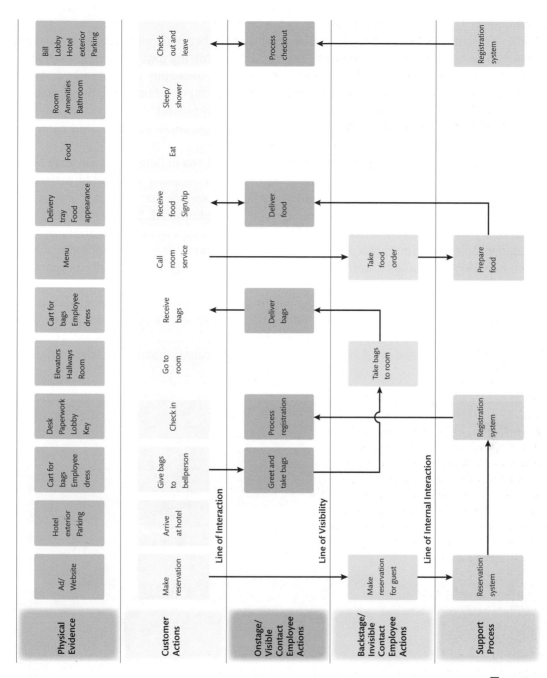

Figure 12.2

Blueprint for an overnight stay at a hotel

Source: From Bitner, Ostrom, and Morgan (2008). Used with permission.

Perishability

A bottle of shampoo on a supermarket shelf attracts a number of opportunities to be sold and consumed. When the store closes and opens again the following day, the bottle is still available to be sold and it remains available until purchased or the expiry date is reached. This is not the case with services. Once a train pulls out of a station, or a film starts, those seats are lost and can never be sold. This is referred to as 'perishability' and is an important aspect of services marketing. Services are manufactured and consumed simultaneously; they cannot be stored either prior to or after the service encounter.

The reason why these seats remain empty reflects variations in demand. These may be the result of changes in the wider environment and may follow easily predictable patterns of behaviour, as in family holiday travel. One of the tasks of service marketers is to ensure that the number of empty seats and lost-forever revenue is minimized. In cases of predictable demand, service managers can vary the level of service capacity: a longer train, or extra screenings of a film (multiplex facilities). However, demand may vary unpredictably, in which case service managers are challenged to provide varying levels of service capacity at short notice.

One of the main ways in which demand patterns can be influenced is through differential pricing. By lowering prices to attract custom during quieter times and raising prices when demand is at its highest, demand can be levelled and marginal revenues increased. Hotel and transport reservation systems have become very sophisticated, making it easier to manage

Wembley inspires huge football spectator audiences regardless of the ticket prices

Source: Wembley

demand, and to improve efficiency and, of course, customer service. Some football clubs categorize matches according to the prestige or ranking of the opposition and adjust prices in order to fill the stadium. In addition to differential pricing, extra services can be introduced to divert demand. Leisure parks offer family discounts and bundle free rides into prices to stimulate demand.

Variability

An important characteristic of services is that they are produced and consumed by people, simultaneously; one of the outcomes of this unique process is that it is exceedingly difficult to standardize the delivery of services. It is also difficult to deliver services so that they always meet the brand promise, especially because these promises often serve to frame customer service expectations. If demand increases unexpectedly and there is insufficient capacity to deal with the excess number of customers, service breakdown may occur: a flood of customers at a restaurant may extend the arrival of meals for customers who have ordered their meals; too many train passengers may mean that there are not enough seats. In both of these cases, it is not possible to provide a service level that can be consistently reproduced. A different way of looking at variability is to consider a live music performance: the singer, drummer, base guitarist, venue operator, and the audience all contribute to the quality of the performance experience, and each performance will be different. The variability of services does not mean that planning is a worthless activity. By anticipating situations in which service breakdown might occur, service managers can provide facilities. For example, entertainment can be provided for queues at cinemas or theme parks, in order to change the perception of the length of the time that it takes to experience the service (film or ride).

Inseparability

Tangible goods can be built, distributed, stored, and eventually consumed at a time specified by the ultimate end-user customer. Services, on the other hand, are consumed at the point at which they are produced. In other words, service delivery cannot be separated or split out of service provision or service consumption. This event in which delivery coincides with consumption means not only that customers come into contact with the service providers, but also that there must be interaction between the two parties. This interaction is of particular importance not only to the quality of service production, but also to the experience enjoyed by the customer.

Service delivery may be experienced as a mass service experience (the music experience) and as a solo experience (a visit to a doctor). The differences impact on the nature of the interaction process. In the mass service experience, the other members of the audience have the opportunity to influence the perceived quality of the experience. Audiences create atmosphere and this may be positively or negatively charged. A good performance can involve audiences in the music and keep them focused for the entire performance. However, a poor performance can frustrate audiences, leading to some members walking out, which influences the perception that others have of the performance and their experience of the musical artists.

Interaction within the solo experience (doctor–patient) allows for greater control by the service provider, if only because he or she can manage the immediate context within which the interaction occurs and not be unduly influenced by wider environmental issues.

Opportunities exist for flexibility and adaptation as the service delivery unfolds. For example, a check-in operator for an airline operates within a particular context, is not influenced by other major events during the interaction, and can adapt tone of voice and body language to meet the needs of particular travellers.

One final aspect of variability concerns the influence arising from the mixture of customers present during the service delivery. If there is a broad mix of customers, service delivery may be affected, because the needs of different groups have to be attended to by the service provider. Such a mixture may dilute the impact of the service actually delivered.

Lack of Ownership

The final characteristic associated with services marketing arises naturally from the other features. Services cannot be owned because nothing is transferred during the interaction or delivery experience. Although a legal transaction often occurs with a service, there is no physical transfer of ownership as there is when a tangible good is purchased. The seat in a theatre, train, plane, or ferry is rented on a temporary basis in exchange for a fee. The terms associated with the rental of the seat determine the time and use or experience to which the seat can be put. However, the seat remains the property of the theatre owner, rail operator, airline, and ferry company, respectively, because it needs to be available for renting to other people for further experiences.

■ The Service Mix

In the good–service spectrum, there are a range of services. These range from services attached directly to a tangible good to some that consist of a pure stand-alone service. It is therefore possible to identify a **services mix**. (Note that this is not the services marketing mix, which we consider later in this chapter and elsewhere in Chapter 1.)

- *Pure product*—In this, there are no services; the offering is purely a tangible good. Examples include salt, sugar, shampoo, and shower gel.
- *Product with some services*—This product is supported with a range of one or more services. The more technologically sophisticated the product, the more likely that it needs to be supported by services (Levitt, 1972). For example, cars require showrooms, delivery, warranties, and repair facilities, because without them 'sales will shrivel'.
- *Combination*—Here, products and services are used in equal proportion in order for customers' expectations to be met. So, in restaurants, service is expected as a complement to the food.
- *Service with some products*—The emphasis in this regard is on the service, but some products are a necessary part of the mix. For example, hotel guests rent a room, use leisure facilities, and seek relaxation, but in order for these to be experienced, some products, such as food and drink, Internet connections, and perhaps complementary stationery, are necessary to complete the experience.
- *Pure service*—Here, no products are involved in the service experience. Examples include dog walking, tax advice, and counselling.

Le Manoir aux Quat'Saisons, the two-Michelin-starred restaurant in Oxfordshire, UK, is as famed for its services as for its cuisine

Source: Copyright © Orient-Express Hotels Ltd

Services can also be understood in terms of other variables. One important variable concerns the significance and intensity of the equipment that is required to provide the service, as opposed to the intensity of people's contribution to the delivery of a service. So, at one extreme, a vending machine is an example of an equipment-intensive service and window cleaning an example of a person-intensive service. Other variables include the degree to which the customer needs to be present at the time that a service is delivered, for example a haircut in comparison with a car repair. Further, is the service directed at consumers (personal service) or at businesses (business services)?

Service Processes

Services are considered to be processes and a substantial part of the academic literature on services is based on a process perspective. A 'process' is a series of sequential actions that leads to predetermined outcomes. So a simple process might be the steps necessary to visit a dentist, whereas a complex process might be the actions necessary to manage passengers on a two-week luxury cruise.

If processes are an integral part of the operations performed by service organizations, in the general sense, what are they processing? Lovelock et al. (1999) argue that these processes are directly related to the equipment/people dimension referred to in 'The Service Mix'. On the one hand, a haircut is people-intensive, but the failure of a network server is intensely equipment-oriented. Lovelock et al. (1999) present a four-cell categorization of services based on tangible and intangible actions on people's bodies, minds, and physical assets. The categories involve four different processes: people processing; possession processing; mental stimulus processing; and information processing.

People Processing

In this type of processing, people have to present themselves physically, so that they become immersed within the service process. This involves their spending varying amounts of time actively cooperating with the service operation. So people taking a train physically have to go to the station, get on a train, and spend time getting to their destination. People undergoing dentistry work will have made an appointment prior to attending the dentist's surgery, will sit in the chair and open their mouths, and will cooperate with the dentist's various requests. They have physically become involved in the service process offered by their dentist.

From a marketing perspective, consideration of the process and the outcomes arising from participation in the service process can lead to ideas about what benefits are being created and what non-financial costs are incurred as a result of the service operation. For the dentistry example, a comfortable chair, background music, non-threatening or neutral to warm decor, and a pleasant manner can be of help.

Possession Processing

Just as people have to go to the service operation for people processing, so objects have to become involved in possession processing. Possessions such as kitchen gadgets, gardens, cars, and computers are liable to break down or to need maintenance. Cleaning, storing, and repairing, plus couriering, installation, and removal services, are typical possession-processing activities.

In these situations, people will either take an item to the service provider, or invite someone in to undertake the necessary work. In possession processing, the level of customer involvement is limited compared with that in people processing. In most cases, the sequence of activities is as follows.

1 In order for an object to be attended to, a telephone call is often required to fix an appointment.

2 The item then either needs to be taken to the service provider or the customer must wait for an attendant to visit.

3 A brief to explain the problem/task/solution is given to the service provider.

4 The customer then returns at an agreed time/location to pay and take away the renewed item.

This detachment from the service process enables people to focus on other tasks. The key difference here is that the quality of the service is not dependent on the owner or representative of the possession being present while the service operation takes place.

Mental Stimulus Processing

These types of service try to shape attitudes or behaviour. In order to achieve this, these services have to be oriented to people's minds; hence the expression 'mental stimulus' processing. So, examples of these types of service include education, entertainment, professional advice, and news. In all of these, people have to become involved mentally in the service interaction and give time in order to experience the benefits of this type of service.

Service delivery can be through one of two locations. First, services can be created in a location that is distant to the receiver. In this case, media channels are used to deliver the service. Alternatively, services can be delivered and consumed at the point at which they originate—that is, in a studio, theatre, or hall. One of the key differences here is the form and nature of the audience experience. The theatre experience is likely to be much richer than the distant format. Digital technology has enabled opportunities for increased amounts of interactive communication, even though the experience will be different from the original.

Information Processing

The final type of service concerns the huge arena of information processing, the most intangible of all of the services. Transformed by advances in technology in general, and computers in particular, information processing has become quicker, more accurate, and more frequent. The use of technology is important, but we should not exclude people, because individuals have a huge capacity to process information.

One key question that arises concerns the degree to which people should become involved in information processing. Some organizations deliberately route customers away from people processing and into information processing. EasyJet reduces costs by making it difficult for customers to telephone the company and seek advice from expensive staff. Their approach is to drive people to its website and to use the frequently asked questions (FAQs) to answer customer queries.

The Service Marketing Mix

The traditional '4P's marketing mix was developed at a time when product marketing was prevalent and the role of services was insignificant. As services marketing has become increasingly important, certain limitations regarding the utility of the '4P's approach have become apparent: the intangibility of services is normally ignored, for example, and promotion fails to accommodate the inseparability issue between the production and consumption of services.

As a result of these and other shortcomings, an extended marketing mix of '7P's has emerged. The three additional 'P's have been included in order to meet the express needs of the service context: people; physical evidence; and processes. The 7Ps mix can also be applied to business-to-business (B2B) and relationship marketing.

Product

Products are used to meet and satisfy customer needs, and today this can incorporate anything tangible or intangible. Services are now commonly referred to as 'products' in the widest sense. So holidays, insurance policies, and bank accounts are referred to as 'products', and they can all be categorized within a product mix.

Price

Because of the intangibility of services, price often becomes a means by which customers make a judgement about the quality of service. Because there is nothing to touch or feel, making considered opinions about the costs and benefits arising from a service interaction can be problematic.

Price can be an important instrument in managing demand. By varying price across different time periods, it is easier to spread demand and to ease pressure at the busiest of times. This also enables service providers to reach those customer segments who are willing and able to pay full price, and in doing so to deliver a service that meets the expectations of this type of customer.

Place

Place, in a traditional good-only context, refers to the way in which goods are distributed in order for customers to be able to access them at a time and place that is most convenient to them. In terms of services, place refers to two issues. The first concerns the reservation and information systems necessary to support the service proposition. Increasingly, this is undertaken remote from the service delivery point. The second refers to the simultaneous nature of the production/consumption interaction. Here, the service should be regarded as a function of direct supply, which suggests that place has little relevance in a service context. These interactions can occur at a customer's house or business location, or at the provider's location, such as a beautician's salon, an accountant's office, or a cinema.

Other interactions take place remotely over the Internet or telephone. One problem that arises for the provider is that this limits them in terms of their geographic coverage and the number of customers whom they can manage without suffering a decline in service performance.

Promotion

Promotion is concerned with the presentation of the marketing offer (goods and services) to target audiences. However, the promotion of services is essentially more challenging than that for goods, simply because of the intangibility issue. So promotion cannot convey size or volume, and images of the packaging or in-use pictures are also ruled out. In its favour, it is possible to depict or explain the benefits arising from the purchase of a service, and it is also possible to show physical evidence of people enjoying the service.

Perhaps the main goal of services-based promotional activity is to reduce the perceived uncertainty associated with the intangibility of a service. This can be achieved by providing tangible clues concerning the nature and quality of the service. First, make the service easy to recognize by providing a logo or brand identifier consistently in all communications. Examples include Google's multi-coloured, text-based image and, in the UK, the iconic red telephone and mouse used by Direct Line, the insurance company, in its television adverts. From this point, it should be possible to develop a reputation for trust, reliability, and quality that, hopefully, will spur positive word-of-mouth communication.

People

In the production of goods and manufactured items, the people element is removed from the customer at the point at which the product is purchased. It does not matter what the engineers look like, how they speak to one another in the factory, or how they dress. In service industries, this is an extremely important factor, because people representing the service provider have a direct impact on the perceived quality of the service itself.

Staff represent the service, and should deliver the service consistently to a level that matches the desired positioning and service blueprint. The recruitment, training, and rewarding of staff is an imperative if the required standards and expectations associated with customer interaction are to be achieved.

Physical Evidence

The intangibility of a service means that it is important to provide tangible cues for potential customers to deduce the product quality. One of the more common approaches is to use sales literature and brochures to give signs about the quality and positioning of the service. Staff deportment and dress also provide clues about a service provider's attitude and attention to tidiness, routines, safety, and customer orientation.

Shostack (1977) suggests that physical evidence can take one of two forms: essential evidence and peripheral evidence.

- *Essential evidence* refers to those few key elements that are important criteria when customers make purchasing decisions. For example, the quality of cars used by a car rental company or the location and architecture of cinemas provide essential information.
- *Peripheral evidence* is, by definition, less important to a customer's evaluation of the overall quality of the service provision. Very often these items, such as sales literature, can be taken away by the customer and used as a reminder of the service brand.

Processes

Understanding service-related processes is important, because customers are an integral part of service production. Processes include all of the tasks, schedules, activities, and routines that enable a service to be delivered to a customer. If the marketing of services is to be successful, then it is crucial that the processes customers use work effectively and appropriately.

The processes involved in getting a haircut involve making an appointment by phone, arriving at the salon, waiting for attention once booked in, being shampooed by the junior, discussing style and requirements, drinking tea or coffee, having the haircut, drying, paying and tipping, collecting belongings, and leaving. This is a relatively straightforward process; others can be more complex. Knowing these steps means that marketers can build benefits into key steps to avoid boredom or to enhance the experience. It is also an opportunity to provide differentiation and reposition service brands.

Service-dominant Logic

Some researchers believe that products alone are not capable of meeting all of a customer's needs (Grönroos, 2009), particularly in business markets. For customers to derive value from a product, they need to consume it, and that often requires a level of integration or coordination with a supplier's processes and systems. This, it is argued, resembles more of the characteristics of a service than a core product offering. Marketing should therefore be considered as a customer management process. This entails not only proposing how an offering might be of value to customers, but it also requires enabling and supporting them to create the value that they require through their use of the product.

This holistic idea of all offerings being inherently services (regardless of their physical or intangible nature) is referred to as the **service-dominant logic (SDL)** approach, and was first proposed by Vargo and Lusch (2004). The traditional marketing management approach can therefore be considered as product-dominant logic. (Those interested to know more about this approach should refer to Research Insight 12.2.)

Research Insight 12.2

To take your learning further, you might wish to read the following influential paper:

Vargo, S. L. and Lusch, R. F. (2004) 'Evolving to a new dominant logic for marketing', *Journal of Marketing*, **68(1): 1–17.**

This paper, one of the most highly cited in marketing journals, introduces the idea of service dominant logic (SDL) for marketing. It sets out the conceptual underpinning for the approach by tracking back and considering previous major marketing approaches. It explains that the new dominant logic for marketing should recognize that service provision, rather than goods, is fundamental to economic exchange, based on intangible resources, the co-creation of value, and relationships not tangible resources, embedded value, and transactions.

Visit the **Online Resource Centre** to read the abstract and to access the full paper.

Service Encounters

The development of service marketing strategies involves understanding the frequency and the ways in which customers contact service providers. Service marketing strategy should be based on insight into the ways in which customers interact or contact a service. The form and nature of the customer encounter is of fundamental importance.

Table 12.2 Levels of customer contact	
Contact level	**Explanation**
High-contact services	Customers visit the service facility so that they are personally involved throughout the service delivery process, e.g. retail branch banking and higher education.
Medium-contact services	Customers visit the service facility, but do not remain for the duration of the service delivery, e.g. consulting services, and delivering and collecting items to be repaired.
Low-contact services	Little or no personal contact between customer and service provider. Service is delivered from a remote location, often through electronic means, e.g. software repairs, and television and radio entertainment.

A service encounter is best understood as a period of time during which a customer interacts directly with a service (Shostack, 1985). These interactions may be short and encompass all of the actions necessary to complete the service experience. Alternatively, they may be protracted, involve several encounters, several representatives of the service provider, and indeed several locations, in order for the service experience to be completed. Whatever their length, the quality of a service encounter impacts on perceived service value, which, in turn, influences customer satisfaction (Gil et al., 2008).

Originally, the term 'encounter' was used to describe the personal interaction between a service provider and customers. A more contemporary interpretation needs to include all interactions that occur through people and their equipment and machines, with the people and equipment belonging to the service provider (Glyn and Lehtinen, 1995). As a result, three levels of customer contact can be observed: high-contact services; medium-contact services; and low-contact services (see Table 12.2).

One of the interesting developments in recent years is the decision by some organizations to move their customers from high-contact services to low-contact services. Clear examples of this are to be found in the banking sector, with first ATMs, then telephone, and now Internet banking, all of which either lower or remove personal contact with bank employees.

This demarcation of customer contact levels is necessary because it provides a sound base on which to develop services marketing. Market Insight 12.3 offers an example of how a business customer might encounter professional IT services.

The Softer Side of Opin Kerfi

Software can improve and protect a business, but it can't tell a customer the right strategy to succeed—or how to optimize its software for sustained return on investment. That's where professional IT service experts come in. Since 1985, Opin Kerfi has served as the IT partner for leading Icelandic companies, financial institutions, governmental agencies, and the healthcare and the educational industries. It is not only a computing business, but a professional services business, offering organizations both hardware and software advisory services to better meet their business needs. From articulated lorries to the Lagerinns chain of retail home furniture accessory stores in eight countries worldwide; to Reykjavik College, one of the oldest and most prestigious educational institutions in Iceland, Opin Kerfi provides a professional IT service. The company focuses on building and maintaining close relationship with its clients and affiliates, aiming to fulfil even the most demanding expectations with regards to specialist

OPIN KERFI

Opin Kerfi, the logo of the Icelandic IT services company

knowledge in the IT field. To maintain its diverse range of IT solutions, the Opin Kerfi team includes some of Iceland's leading IT experts and boasts affiliations to leading IT companies, including Cisco, Microsoft, and HP.

Source: http://dc.ok.is/

1 How would you classify the form of service encounter that customers would have with Opin Kerfi?

2 What level of customer contact do you think customers have with Opin Kerfi?

3 Visit the Opin Kerfi website. What characteristics in its marketing do you think help to position Opin Kerfi as a leading professional IT service provider?

▪ Key Dimensions of Services Marketing

Branding in a Services Context

The development of brand strategies for services is important simply because the intangibility of services requires that customers be helped to understand the value associated with the service offering (see also Chapter 7). Essentially, a brand provides a snapshot of the value and position offered by a service. Brands convey information about the standard of service and, in doing so, seek to achieve two main goals. First, brands can reduce the uncertainty associated with the purchase of services, especially when there are no tangible elements on which to base purchase decisions. Consider the complexity and risk associated with buying financial services, such as insurance, pensions, and savings products: developing strong brands enables these risks to be rolled up into a single identity—one that is familiar and trusted. Virgin is a relative newcomer to the financial service market, but today is already well established and still growing quickly.

The second goal is to reduce the amount of time that people spend searching for a particular service, especially when they are unfamiliar with a particular market or category. When travelling, many visitors to a city will stay at hotels such as Marriott, Motel One, Holiday Inn, Campanile, or Hilton because the brands say something about the standard of service that can be expected. Branding shapes customer expectations and can provide a quick answer to a purchase decision. Advertising can also be used to help to tangibilize the benefits of a service rather than the features, which can be limited or boring, or both.

Good branding involves the use of logos and symbols, plus straplines and slogans. These can also help to make the intangible more tangible by relating to some of the core benefits that a brand offers. However, care is required, because a strapline or term of identification might be perceived as generic to a category. For example, Sony lost a court case in Austria when the Supreme Court ruled that the word 'Walkman' had become a generic term and the common trade name for portable cassette players. The result of this was that Sony lost its right to use the name 'Walkman', which it had invented, invested in, and developed over many years (Meikle, 2002).

Motel One, the German hotel group offering high-quality rooms at low-budget prices
Source: Motel One

Many service providers use their physical facilities to shape the environment so that customers feel at ease and are attracted into the service process. Booms and Bitner (1981) term this the **servicescape**, and refer to the need to consider customer expectations and their emotional states. Branding the environment using signs, colours, clothing, and other physical items can provide recall of previous use of the service provider and also influence customer expectations. Consider the environment and overall design of fast food restaurants such as McDonald's and Burger King: these servicescapes are designed and replicated in high streets across the globe, are easily recognized, and convey immediately information about the type of food offered and the standard of service delivery.

Not all services are able to develop strong brands; they simply do not have the resources, or inclination. Communications should, however, still be an important part of their marketing. Those delivering services in which the credence properties are dominant and customers are unable to distinguish the quality of service can emphasize a service provider's professionalism. This can be achieved by displaying certificates, having a long list of professional qualifications on his or her business cards, and referring in sales literature and websites to the number and types of client with whom he or she has worked.

Internal Marketing

Branding is an important aspect in the marketing of services. Its overall role is to manage, by shaping and reinforcing customer expectations about the overall quality of the service itself, and to indicate what the service encounter will be like. It is important, however, that services are delivered by people who have been trained in delivering both brand values and the functional aspects of the service provision. The variability of service performance is a distinguishing characteristic and every effort needs to be made to ensure that each time the service is performed it is of a consistently high quality.

Some employees deliver the performance through interaction with customers. Other employees provide support facilities, or information to enable the service interaction. Therefore it makes sense to train, support, and motivate employees so that they deliver high-quality service performances each time they meet a customer.

Employees constitute an internal market in which paid labour is exchanged for designated outputs. For some, they are seen as a discrete group of customers with whom management, in order to develop and or maintain exchanges with external stakeholders, interacts (Piercy and Morgan, 1991). Although employees have the potential to add considerable value to manufactured goods, they are vitally important to the delivery of services. Indeed, the quality and perception of the way in which service-oriented employees interact with customers can be the crucial determinant concerning whether a customer will return at some point and whether he or she will speak positively about the service provider.

The role of the employee has changed. At one time, employees were regarded as only a part of an organization and were not required to have external orientation at all. Now, they are seen as brand ambassadors (Freeman and Liedtke, 1997; Hemsley, 1998). This is particularly important in service environments, in which employees represent the interface between an organization's internal and external environments, and in which their actions can have a powerful effect in creating images among customers (Schneider and Bowen, 1985; Balmer and Wilkinson, 1991). Employees are important to external stakeholders not only because of the tangible aspects of service and production that they provide, but also because of the intangible aspects, such as attitude and the way in which service is provided: 'How much do they really care?' Images are often based more on the intangible than the tangible aspects of employee communications.

The values transmitted to customers, suppliers, and distributors through external marketing communications need to be reinforced through the values expressed by employees, especially those who interact with these external groups. Internal marketing is necessary in order to motivate and involve employees with the brand, such that they are able to present a consistent and uniform message to stakeholders. This process whereby employees are encouraged to communicate with stakeholders in order for an organization to ensure that what is promised is realized by customers is referred to as 'living the brand'. Employees are required to deliver both the functional aspects of an organization's offering and the emotional dimensions, particularly in service environments. In order to engage customers in this way, attention needs to be given to the intellectual and emotional elements in internal communications.

The level of interaction into which customers are prepared to enter can hamper the degree to which employees can deliver the service promise. For example, a customer who doesn't tell the dentist where the pain is restricts the quality of performance that the dentist is likely to give. Therefore employees need to be trained to communicate with customers in such a way that they provide sufficient information to avoid **service failure**.

Service Failure and Recovery

Measuring the quality of a service encounter has become a major factor in the management of service-based organizations. **Service quality** is based on the idea that customer expectations of the service that they will receive shape their perception of the actual service encounter. In essence, therefore, customers compare perceived service with expected service. So if the perceived service meets, or even exceeds, expectations, then customers are deemed to be satisfied and are much more likely to return at some point in the future. However, if the perceived service falls below what was expected, then customers are more likely to feel disappointed and be less likely to return.

All organizations have times when things go wrong. Where a customer's expectations are not met, then the result is 'service failure' (Bell and Zemke, 1987). Service failures, according to Bitner et al. (1990), arise from one of three main areas: failure in the delivery system; failure in response to customer requests; and failure through employee actions. Table 12.3 provides a brief explanation of these three types of service failure.

The problem with service failure is not the failure itself, but how managers and customers react. Whereas some customers will tell a few people about exceptionally good service performance, service failure can result in a disproportionate number of people hearing about the lost bag, the slow service, or the cold food. Negative word-of-mouth increases the more dissatisfied customers become (Rananweera and Prabhu, 2003). Dissatisfied customers are unlikely to come back, so it is really important to ensure that service performance is correct in the first place. Should a failure occur, steps have to be taken immediately to correct the situation and to turn a potentially negative situation into one that leads to positive outcomes for all involved—known as **service recovery**.

Table 12.3 Sources of service failure

Type of service failure	Explanation
Failures in the delivery system	Links between service personnel and service process break down because of service unavailability (e.g. swimming pool closed), slow service (e.g. airport queues and delays), and core service failure (e.g. undercooked food).
Failure in response to customer requests	Explicit customer requests (e.g. a room with a sea view) or implicit customer requests (e.g. that children be excluded from quiet areas) are ignored or overlooked. Alternatively, customers make errors (e.g. a forgotten PIN number).
Failure through employee actions	Unexpected, non-standard employee actions may occur in which delivery of the service is perceived to be rude, dismissive, or unfair.

Source: Adapted from Bitner et al. (1990)

Service recovery is concerned with an organization's systematic attempt to correct a problem following service failure (Grönroos, 1988) and to retain a customer's goodwill (Lovelock, 2001). By acting quickly, demonstrating empathy with the customer's perception of the failure, and enabling employees to instigate corrective actions and to award appropriate compensation, well-managed organizations are able to overcome service failure and to develop positive reputations. Indeed, it has been found that successful service recovery, in which customer satisfaction was maximized and negative word of mouth minimized, only occurred when the service recovery process was handled by employees who reacted quickly, courteously, and in a caring way (Hocutt et al., 2006). A survey of 540 travellers found that the most successful recovery strategies involved senior personnel. A fast response by a senior manager, a fast response with a full refund plus some compensation, and a large amount of compensation delivered by a high-ranking manager were considered the best forms of recovery. What was not acceptable was an apology, unless accompanied by some form of tangible compensation (Boshoff, 1997). See Market Insight 12.4 for an example of the negative impact of service recovery when managers did not take responsibility in a serious case of service failure.

Market Insight 12.4

Costa Concordia: Making it Right!

What happens when a service encounter results in service failure that is near-fatal or when the customer has been wronged? When something fails during service delivery as a result of the actions of the employees affecting not one customer, but a multitude of customers, what is the right response? On Friday 13 January 2012, *Costa Concordia*, a luxury Italian cruise ship full of pleasure-seeking tourists, struck a reef, gouging a huge gash in her side and causing her to capsize just off the Tuscan island of Isola del Giglio. Apparently, the ship's captain had allegedly ignored computer equipment in a bid to take the ship closer to the shoreline than authorized in order to give the residents of local islands a 'show they'd never forget'. The cruise ship was carrying more than 3,200 people when it ran aground off Italy. Reports confirm that at least seventeen people died in the incident, including fifteen passengers and two crewmen; sixty-four others were injured (three seriously), sixteen are missing, and thousands lost personal possessions and were traumatized by the event.

The *Costa Concordia* entered service for Costa Cruises, a subsidiary of the Carnival Corporation, in July 2006 as the largest ship built in Italy at the time, measuring 114,137 gross tonnage, 290.2 metres (952 feet) long, and costing €450 million. By tonnage, it is the largest passenger ship ever to sink. Passengers claimed that crew had failed to give instructions on how to evacuate the ship and that, during the evacuation, the ship's captain and second commander left the ship, leaving passengers and crew members to organize their own evacuations. Local service recovery teams aided in the effort and citizens of the island of Isola del Giglio opened their homes, schools, and church to help the survivors. The incident has resulted in criminal charges being brought against the ship's captain and his second in command for abandoning the ship, and a class action lawsuit by the passengers against Costa Cruises for negligence.

When service failure results in harm to others, the service provider has a choice between 'making it right' or pursuing the least costly alternative with which it thinks it can get away. It is the former resolution that will lead to the most desirable result. Following the incident, it was reported that Costa Cruises had offered passengers a 30 per cent discount on future cruises—an offer that was met with disdain not only by passengers, but also by the general public.

Source: BBC News (2012)

1 How would you classify the type of service failure experienced by the passengers of *Costa Concordia*?

2 What role did the captain and his second in command play during the service recovery process?

3 What course of action should Costa Cruises take to ensure that it *makes it right* to the passengers and their families?

Customer Service and Relationship Management

The idea that providing a superior customer service might help in the (repeat) purchase decision process is something important to service organizations. For a long time, it was assumed that product quality and pricing were sufficient differentiators. However, product quality is no longer a viable means of establishing competitive advantage, simply because of shortening life cycles and improved technologies. In contrast, customer service is very difficult to replicate and is becoming an important aspect of customer management.

The management of relationships has long been regarded as the responsibility of the sales force. However, this perspective has also changed and it is now expected that a range of employees have a responsibility for satisfying customer needs. Managing trust and reputation, reducing risk, and providing high levels of customer satisfaction are now regarded as an expectation that all suppliers need to meet.

Two elements of customer management are considered here: first, customer contact centres; and second, **customer relationship management (CRM) systems**.

Customer Contact Centres

Many organizations try to help their customers to contact them. This can be achieved via a call centre, or 'customer contact centre', as they are now known. Instead of customers contacting a variety of people in different offices and perhaps receiving assorted messages, all of which require training and support, it makes sense to have a single point of contact. Very often, this task is outsourced to a specialist company, which is trained in product support and company policy. Specialist organizations can reduce costs, improve efficiency, and enhance a client's reputation through the quality of interaction with customers. Using digital technology to manage voice, web, interactive TV, email, mobile, and fax-originated messages, contact centres enable customers to complain about a product performance and related experience, to seek product-related advice, to make suggestions regarding product or packaging development, and to comment about an action or development concerning the brand as a whole. Very often, this access is referred to as a 'careline'—a dedicated telephone and email connection.

In addition, organizations can use contact centres to provide outbound calls, often to generate sales leads or to provide market information.

Carelines and contact centres have enormous potential to support brands. The majority of calls to carelines are not about complaints, but are from people seeking advice or help about products. Food manufacturers provide cooking and recipe advice; cosmetic and toiletries companies provide healthcare advice and application guidelines; white goods and service-based organizations can provide technical and operational support. By dealing with complaints in a prompt, courteous, and efficient manner, people are more likely to repurchase a brand than if the service was not available. Carelines are essentially a post-purchase support mechanism, which facilitates feedback and intelligence gathering. They can warn of imminent problems (product defects), provide ideas for new products or variants, and, of course, provide a valuable method to reassure customers and improve customer retention levels.

Customer Relationship Management Systems

The development of CRM systems has been a significant development in the way in which organizations have attempted to manage their customer interactions. CRM applications were originally developed as sales force support systems (mainly, sales force automation), and later applications were designed for supplier organizations to enable them to manage their end-user customers. They have subsequently evolved as a more sophisticated means of managing direct customers and are an integral part of customer contact centres.

The principal aim of CRM systems is to provide superior value by enabling suppliers' access to real-time customer information. This helps suppliers to anticipate and satisfy customers' needs effectively, efficiently, and in a timely manner. To make this happen, a complete history of each customer needs to be available to all staff who interact with customers. This is necessary in order to answer two types of question: questions prompted by customers about orders, quotations, or products; and questions prompted by internal managers concerning, for example, strategy, segmentation, relationship potential, sales forecasts, and sales force management.

The customer value concept provides the grounding for CRM (Flint et al., 2002). Acceptance of the notion that different customers represent differing levels of importance to a firm suggests that different customer segments represent different profit potential and hence different value. So if different groups of customers represent different levels of profit potential, it is important to manage this variability in order to maximize the use of a firm's resources.

CRM applications typically consist of call management, lead management, customer record, and sales support and payment systems. Ideally, they should be incorporated as part of an overall strategic approach (Wightman, 2000). However, such systems are invariably treated as add-on applications that are expected to resolve customer interface difficulties. Unsurprisingly, many clients have voiced their dissatisfaction with CRM, because many of the promises and expectations have not been fulfilled.

Problems have arisen with CRM implementation because technology vendors have not properly understood the need to manage all relationships with all major stakeholders (O'Malley and Mitussi, 2002). Disappointment with CRM systems can also be regarded as a failure to understand the central tenets of a customer-focused philosophy and the need to adopt a strategic business approach to managing customer relationships. If the centrality of concepts such as trust and commitment are not understood, nor a willingness displayed to share information and to achieve a balanced relationship, the installation of databases and data warehouses will not change—and to date has not changed—the quality of an organization's relationships with its customers. O'Malley and Mitussi (2002) also refer to the failure of CRM systems in terms of internal political power struggles, and associated issues about who owns particular systems and data. Where an organization has neither established a customer-oriented culture nor begun to implement enterprise-wide systems and procedures, it is probable that access to certain data might be impeded, or at least made problematic.

Good customer management requires attention to an organization's culture, training, strategy, and propositions and processes. Regretfully, too many organizations focus on the interface or fail to understand the broader picture. It is important to understand that even the most sophisticated CRM systems are based on data about an organization's contacts and interactions with them. Although these can be processed to supply one-touch, real-time multidimensional views of any relationship, they do not manage it. That, as ever, is the challenge for the people involved.

Visit the **Online Resource Centre** and follow the web link to CRM Today to learn more about CRM systems, applications, news, and research.

go online

Chapter Summary

To consolidate your learning, the key points from this chapter can be summarized as follows.

■ **Explain what a service is, and describe the relationship between products and services**

A service is any act or performance offered by one party to another that is essentially intangible. Consumption of the service does not result in any transfer of ownership, even though the service process may be attached to a physical product. There is a spectrum of product–service combinations. At one extreme, there are pure goods with no services, such as grocery products. At the other end of the spectrum are pure services, in which there is no tangible product support, such as education and dentistry. In between, there is a mixture of product–service arrangements.

■ **Explain the main characteristics of a service**

Unlike goods, services are considered to be processes, and products and services have different distinguishing characteristics. These are based around their intangibility (you can touch a product, but not a service), perishability (products can be stored, but you cannot store a service), variability (each time a service is delivered, it is different, but products can be identical), inseparability (services are produced and consumed simultaneously), and a lack of ownership (you cannot take legal possession of a service).

■ **Understand the different service processes and outline each element of the services marketing mix**

A process is a series of sequential actions that leads to predetermined outcomes. Four main service process categories can be identified: people processing; possession processing; mental stimulus processing; and information processing. As a result of various shortcomings of the traditional marketing mix, an extended version has been developed in order to account for the particular characteristics associated with services. The three additional 'P's are people, physical evidence, and processes.

- **Explain the term 'service encounter' and describe how management should seek to maintain service performance**

  A service encounter is best understood as a period of time during which a customer interacts directly with a service (Shostack, 1985). There are three levels of customer contact: high-contact services; medium-contact services; and low-contact services. As more services are introduced, so opportunities for service variability and service failure also develop. Responses for maintaining service performance include branding, the way in which a service is identified and understood, and internal marketing, the processes and communications used to develop employees as part of the brand.

- **Explain the ways in which organizations try to provide customer relationship management (CRM) and service support**

  The principal aim of customer contact centres and CRM systems is to provide both buyers and sellers with superior value by enabling suppliers to gain access to real-time customer information, in order to satisfy their customers' needs appropriately.

❓ Review Questions

1 Using the product–service spectrum, explain how a service is different from a product.

2 Set out in your own words the essential characteristics of services and find examples of each.

3 Explain the term 'service encounter'.

4 Explain the ways in which service managers could seek to maintain service performance.

5 Discuss the two main approaches used for customer relationship management (CRM).

@ Scan this image to go online and access the chapter's multiple-choice questions, web links, Internet activities, and more!

📋 Worksheet Summary

Visit the **Online Resource Centre** and complete Worksheet 12.1. This will help you to learn about the five gaps between actual and expected service quality: reliability; responsiveness; assurance; empathy; and tangibles.

References

Balmer, J. M. T. and Wilkinson, A. (1991) 'Building societies: change, strategy and corporate identity', *Journal of General Management*, 17(2): 20–33.

BBC News (2012) 'Italy cruise ship *Costa Concordia* aground near Giglio', 14 January, available online at http://www.bbc.co.uk/news/world-europe-16558910 [accessed 3 February 2012].

Bell, C. R. and Zemke, E. (1987) 'Service breakdown: the road to recovery', *Management Review*, Oct: 32–5.

Berry, L. L. (1980) 'Services marketing is different', *Business*, May–June: 24–30.

Bitner, M. J., Booms, B. H., and Tetreault, M. S. (1990) 'The service encounter: diagnosing favorable and unfavorable incidents', *Journal of Marketing*, 54(Jan): 71–84.

Bitner, M. L., Ostrom, A. L., and Morgan, F. N. (2008) 'Service blueprinting: a practical technique for service innovation', *California Management Review*, 50(3): 66–94.

Booms, B. H. and Bitner, M. J. (1981) 'Marketing strategies and organization structure for service firms', in J. H. Donnelly and W. R. George (eds) *The Marketing of Services*, Chicago, IL: American Marketing Association, pp. 47–51.

Boshoff, C. (1997) 'An experimental study of service recovery options', *International Journal of Service Industry Management*, 8(3): 110–30.

Brady, M. K., Bourdeau, B. L., and Heskel, J. (2005) 'The importance of brand cues in intangible service industries: an application to investment services', *Journal of Services Marketing*, 19(6): 401–10.

Carbone, L. P. and Haeckel, S. H. (1994) 'Engineering customer experiences', *Marketing Management*, 3(3): 8–19.

Flint, D. J., Woodruff, R. B., and Gardial, S. F. (2002) 'Exploring the phenomenon of customers' desired value change in a business-to-business context', *Journal of Marketing*, 66(4): 102–17.

Freeman, R. E. and Liedtke, J. (1997) 'Stakeholder capitalism and the value chain', *European Management Journal*, 15(3): 286–96.

Geere, D. (2011) 'eBay to open pop-up shop in London', *Wired UK*, 18 November, available online at http://www.wired.co.uk/news/archive/2011-11/18/ebay-high-street [accessed 13 January 2012].

Gil, I., Berenguer, G., and Cervera, A. (2008) 'The roles of service encounters, service value, and job satisfaction in business relationships', *Industrial Marketing Management*, 37(8): 921–39.

Glyn, W. J. and Lehtinen, U. (1995) 'The concept of exchange: interactive approaches in services marketing',

in W. J. Glyn and J. G. Barnes (eds) *Understanding Services Management*, Chichester: John Wiley and Sons, pp. 89–118.

Grönroos, C. (1988) 'Service quality: the six criteria of good perceived service quality', *Review of Business*, 9(Winter): 10–13.

Grönroos, C. (1990) *Service Management and Marketing: Managing the Moment of Truth in Service Competition*, Lexington, MA: Lexington Books.

Grönroos, C. (2009) 'Marketing as promise management: regaining customer management for marketing', *Journal of Business and Industrial Marketing*, 24(5/6): 351–59.

Gummesson, E. (1991) 'Marketing-orientation revisited: the crucial role of the part-time marketer', *European Journal of Marketing*, 25(2): 60–75.

Hara, T., Arai, T., and Shimomura, Y. (2009) 'A CAD system for service innovation: integrated representation of function, service activity, and product behaviour', *Journal of Engineering Design*, 20(4): 367–88.

Hemsley, S. (1998) 'Internal affairs', *Marketing Week*, 2 April, pp. 49–50.

Hocutt, M. A., Bowers, M. R., and Donavan, D. T. (2006) 'The art of service recovery: fact or fiction?', *Journal of Services Marketing*, 20(3): 199–207.

Levitt, T. (1972) 'Production-line approach to service', *Harvard Business Review*, 50(5): 20–31.

Lovelock, C. (2001) *Services Marketing: People, Technology, Strategy*, 4th edn, Upper Saddle River, NJ: Prentice Hall.

Lovelock, C., Vandermerwe, S., and Lewis, B. (1999) *Services Marketing: A European Perspective*, Harlow: FT/Prentice Hall.

Meikle, E. (2002) 'Lawless branding: recent developments in trademark law', available online at http://www.brandchannel.com/features_effect.asp?pf_id=103#more [accessed 25 March 2007].

Olson, J. C. and Jacoby, J. (1972) 'Cue utilization in the quality perception process', in M. Venkatesan (ed.) *Proceedings of the Third Annual Conference of the Association for Consumer Research*, Iowa City, IA: Association for Consumer Research, pp. 167–79.

O'Malley, L. and Mitussi, D. (2002) 'Relationships and technology: strategic implications', *Journal of Strategic Marketing*, 10: 225–38.

Parasuraman, A., Zeithaml, V., and Berry, L. L. (1988) 'SERVQUAL: a multiple-item scale for measuring consumer perceptions of service quality', *Journal of Retailing*, 64(1): 5–37.

Piercy, N. F. and Morgan, N. A. (1991) 'Internal marketing: the missing half of the marketing programme', *Long Range Planning*, 24(2): 82–93.

Rananweera, C. and Prabhu, J. (2003) 'On the relative importance of customer satisfaction and trust as determinants of customer retention and positive word of mouth', *Journal of Targeting, Measurement and Analysis for Marketing*, 12 September, pp. 82–91.

Rueter, T. (2011) 'eBay brings its online marketplace to a London storefront', *Internet Retailer*, 17 November, available online at http://www.internetretailer.com/2011/11/17/ebay-brings-its-online-marketplace-london-storefront [accessed 12 January 2012].

Schneider, B. and Bowen, D. E. (1985) 'Employee and customer perceptions of service in banks: perception and extension', *Journal of Applied Psychology*, 70: 423–33.

Shostack, G. L. (1977) 'Breaking free from product marketing', *Journal of Marketing*, 41(Apr): 73–80.

Shostack, G. L. (1982) 'How to design a service'. *European Journal of Marketing*, 16(1): 49–63.

Shostack, G. L. (1984) 'Design services that deliver', *Harvard Business Review*, 62(Jan–Feb): 133–9.

Shostack, G. L. (1985) 'Planning the service encounter', in J. A. Czepiel, M. R. Solomon, and C. F. Suprenant (eds) *The Service Encounter*, Lexington, MA: Lexington Books, pp. 243–63.

Vargo, S. L. and Lusch, R. F. (2004) 'Evolving to a new dominant logic for marketing', *Journal of Marketing*, 68(1): 1–17.

Wightman, T. (2000) 'e-CRM: the critical dot.com discipline', *Admap*, April: 46–8.

Zeithaml, V. A., Bitner, M. J., and Gremler, D. D. (2006) *Services Marketing: Integrating Customer Focus across the Firm*. Boston, MA: McGraw-Hill/Irwin.

Glossary

a priori segmentation Market segmentation that is not empirically based; involves segmenting markets on the basis of assumptions, custom, or hunches.

access panel A panel used in online survey research to provide samples for survey-style information; made up of targets who have been invited by email to take part, with a link to the online survey.

adoption process The process through which individuals try to use new products; the different stages in the adoption process are sequential and each is characterized by different factors.

advergaming The use of video and online games to advertise a product, organization, or an idea; encourages repeat website traffic and reinforces brand loyalty.

advertising A form of non-personal communication, by an identified sponsor, which is transmitted through the use of paid-for media.

affective A psychological term meaning our emotional state of mind; values are affective because they are linked to our feelings about things.

agent A person or organization that acts as principal intermediary between the seller of a product and buyers, bringing them together without taking ownership of the product offering. Cf **merchant**

aggregated demand Demand calculated at the population level rather than at the individual level.

AIDA Standing for 'awareness, interest, desire, and action'; a hierarchy of effects, or a sequential model, used to explain how advertising works.

ATR Standing for 'awareness–trial–reinforcement'; a framework developed by Ehrenberg to explain how advertising works.

attitude The mental state of an individual that underlies his or her perceptions and guides his or her behavioural response.

backward integration The situation in which a company takes over one or more of its suppliers. Cf **forward integration**

behavioural economics An approach to economics that incorporates psychology—particularly consumers' fear of loss or failure—in order to understand consumer decision-making.

benefits sought A behavioural segmentation criterion that focuses on the motivations that customers have for making purchases, which offers insight into the benefits that they seek from product use.

blog See **weblog**

Boston box A popular portfolio matrix based on two key variables—market growth and relative market share—developed by the Boston Consulting Group and hence also known as the 'BCG matrix'.

brand association A device, such as a name, packaging, price, marketing communications, and other mechanism, which enables an individual to make mental linkages to give meaning to a brand.

brand extension The process by which a successful brand is used to launch a new product into a new market.

brand personality The set of human characteristics that some individuals associate with a brand.

breakdown method An approach to market segmentation based on an assumption that the market consists of customers who are essentially the same; thus the task is to identify groups that share particular differences. Cf **build-up method**

broadcast media Those audio-visual means by which audio and video content distribution can be distributed to a dispersed audience; usually used to refer to television and radio.

build-up method An approach to market segmentation based on an assumption that a market consists of customers who are all different; thus the task is to find similarities among them. Cf **breakdown method**

business market A market characterized by organizations that consume products and services for use within the manufacture or production of other products, or for use in their daily operations.

business-to-business (B2B) market segmentation Market segmentation based on identifying a group of present or potential customers with some common characteristic.

buyclass A type of buying situation faced by the decision-making unit within an organization.

buyer A role that involves selecting suppliers and managing the buying process through which the required products and services are purchased once a decision has been made to procure them.

buying centre See **decision-making unit (DMU)**

buyphase One of a series of sequential activities or stages through which organizations proceed when making purchasing decisions.

call to action The part of a marketing communication message that explicitly requests that the receiver act in a particular way.

capitalism The political system in which private (as opposed to governmental) capital and wealth is the predominant means of producing and distributing goods.

category killer A large retail outlet, typically positioned in an out-of-town location, specializing in selling one type of product with the aim of killing off the competition, such as DIY stores such as Homebase in the UK; characterized by a narrow, but very deep, product assortment, low prices, and few-to-moderate customer services.

causal research A technique used to investigate the relational link between two or more variables by manipulating the independent variable(s) to see the effect on the dependent variable(s) and comparing effects with a control group in which no such manipulation takes place.

celebrity endorsement Endorsement by a famous or respected individual who is perceived to be expert or knowledgeable in his or her field, or who displays particular attractive qualities; used to market specific goods and services.

channel conflict Arises when one member of a distribution channel perceives another channel member to be acting in a way that prevents the first member from achieving its distribution activities.

choice criterion One of the principal dimensions on which we select a particular product or service; when choosing a hairdresser, for example, this might be price, location, range of services, level of expertise, friendliness, and so on.

classical conditioning A theory of learning propounded by Russian physiologist Ivan Pavlov, who carried out a series of experiments with dogs, which learned to associate the sound of a bell (the conditioned stimulus) with the presentation of food (the unconditioned stimulus) and so would begin to salivate on hearing a bell ring—that is, the natural response to the unconditioned stimulus was triggered by the conditioned stimulus.

click-through rate A measure of the amount of traffic on a website.

co-branding A process by which two established brands work together, on one product or service, the principle being that the combined power of the two brands generates increased consumer appeal and attraction.

co-creation The process by which organizations work with customers to generate new forms of customer value.

cognition Knowledge or perception of something, typically as a result of rational thought.

cognitive dissonance A psychological theory proposed by Leon Festinger in 1957, which suggests that we are motivated to re-evaluate our beliefs, attitudes, opinions, or values if an event, circumstance, or action intervenes to alter the position that we previously held.

collaborative exchange One of a series of economic transactions between parties who have a long-term orientation towards, and are primarily motivated by, concern for each other.

communication The sharing of meaning created through the transmission of information.

communications objective One of a set of communication effects at which a marketing communications campaign may aim; normally a change in levels of awareness, perception, comprehension/knowledge, attitudes, and overall degree of preference for a brand.

competitive advantage Advantage achieved in the marketplace when an organization achieves a sustainable edge over its competitors on factors that are important to customers.

computer-assisted personal interviewing (CAPI) An approach to interviewing that is administered by means of a computer-based survey; CAPI software can streamline the interview process.

computer-assisted telephone interviewing (CATI) An approach to interviewing that is conducted over the telephone between a consumer and a computer; CATI software will increase call centre productivity.

computer-assisted web interviewing (CAWI) An approach to interviewing in which the respondent accesses questions online in a set location; questions are set automatically based on the respondent's answers.

conative A psychological term meaning related to our motivations; attitudes are conative because they are linked to our motivations.

concentrated marketing strategy Also known as a niche marketing strategy, an approach to marketing that recognizes that there are segments in the market and which focuses on only one or no more than a few of those segments.

conceptual equivalence The degree to which interpretation of behaviour, or objects, is similar across countries.

consumer The user of a product, service, or other form of offering.

consumer durable A manufactured consumer product that is relatively long-lasting, such as a car or a computer. Cf **consumer non-durable**

consumer jury A qualitative approach to market research in which a collection of target consumers are asked to rank ideas or concepts and to explain their choices.

consumer non-durable A consumer product that has only a short shelf life, such as foodstuffs. Cf **consumer durable**

context analysis The first stage of the marketing communications planning process; involves analysing four main contexts (or situations)—the customer, business, internal, and external environmental contexts—in order to shape the detail of the plan.

contextual advertising A form of online targeted advertising in which advertisements are selected and served by automated systems based on the content displayed to the user.

control *(Of digital media)* The ability of users in a computer-mediated environment to access content at will, and to create, modify, and share the content; *(Of distribution)* the achieving of optimum distribution costs without losing decision-making authority over the product offering and the way in which it is marketed and supported—that is, maximizing capacity to manage all marketing mix decisions.

control group A sample group used in causal research that is not subjected to manipulation of some sort.

convenience sampling A method of selecting respondents for market research that is based only on the judgement of the researcher; the likelihood of selection is thus is unknown beforehand.

convenience store Also known as a 'corner shop', a business that offers a range of grocery and household items, catering for convenience and the last-minute purchase needs of consumers; key characteristics include long opening times ('24/7'), that it is usually family-run, and that it often belongs to a trading group.

conversion rate A measure of the prospects or visitors to a website who become active customers.

corporate objective One of a set of overall business goals towards which an organization has agreed to aim.

corporate strategy The means by which an organization attempts to match its current or future resources with the needs of the environment in which it operates.

cost leadership A corporate strategy involving the production of goods and services for a broad market segment, at a cost lower than that of all other competitors.

counter-implementation The behaviour that employees exhibit when they resist tasks associated with the implementation of strategic programmes, whether intentionally or unintentionally; often motivated by anxiety.

coverage A measure of the amount of contact and value (or benefits) for the customer (in terms of product offering availability); the marketer desires the product to be available to the maximum number of customers, in the maximum number of locations, across the widest range of times.

credit crunch A period of economic turbulence during which economies around the world entered recession; caused by lax regulation in banking markets and the improper securitization of sub-prime mortgage debt, which led to very low rates of inter-bank lending and difficulties in obtaining consumer and wholesale credit (hence its name).

crowdsourcing A method of outsourcing a function originally undertaken by employees to a group ('crowd') of external contributors either as an open call or in a more restricted way.

customer A person who purchases and pays for (or initially requests and specifies, in the case of a non-financial transaction) a product, service, or other form of offering from a company or organization.

customer relationship management (CRM) system A software system that provides all staff with a complete view of the history and status of each customer.

customer relationship marketing Marketing activities and strategies that are used to retain customers, usually by providing customers with relationship-enhancing products and/or services that are perceived to be of value and superior to those offered by a competitor.

customer services The services provided to customers before, during, and after a purchase.

customized targeting strategy A marketing strategy that is developed to target each customer, rather than each market segment.

cut The cartoon format in which an advert is initially produced, complete with dialogue, before it is produced, filmed, and edited.

decider A person who makes organizational purchasing decisions; often very difficult to identify.

decision-making unit (DMU) structure A means of segmentation in which the attitudes, policies, and purchasing strategies used by organizations are used as the basis on which organizations can be clustered.

decision-making unit (DMU) Also known as a 'buying centre', a group of people, or sometimes a single person, who make purchasing decisions on behalf of an organization.

decoding The part of the communication process in which receivers unpack and begin to make sense of the various components of the message, and give the message meaning.

demographics Key variables concerning age, sex, occupation, level of education, religion, and social class, many of which determine a potential buyer's ability to purchase a product or service.

department store A large-scale retailing institution that has a very broad and deep product assortment (of both hard and soft goods), and which provides a wide array of customer service facilities for customers.

descriptive research A research technique used to test, and confirm, hypotheses developed from a management problem.

desk research See secondary research

dialogue An interaction between the parties to a communication event involving listening, adapting, and reasoning with one another about a specific topic, during which knowledge develops as a result.

differentiated targeting strategy An approach to targeting in which a different marketing strategy is developed for each of several market segments that are attractive to the marketing organization.

differentiation A corporate strategy involving offering products and services to broad particular customer groups, who perceive the offering to be significantly different from, and superior to, those of the organization's competitors.

diffusion (In marketing) The way in which an offering is slowly accepted or not by customers over time as they become socialised in relation to its purchase and/or use.

digital asset optimization (DAO) Sometimes known as 'SEO 2.0', a method of search engine marketing in which all of an organization's digital assets are optimized for search, retrieval, and indexing.

digital media The various means by which data can be stored and transmitted electronically as either information or 'products'.

digital value The enhanced product and service value that can be offered to customers as a result of digital processes and systems.

direct channel structure A distribution channel structure in which the product is sold directly by the producer to the final customer.

direct marketing A marketing communications tool that uses non-personal media to create and sustain a personal and intermediary-free communication with customers, potential customers, and other significant stakeholders; usually a media-based activity.

direct selling Also known as 'in-home personal selling', one of the oldest forms of retailing, which involves personal contact between a salesperson and a consumer away from the retailing environment.

direct-response advertising A form of advertising that contains mechanisms such as a telephone number, a website address, and email and postal addresses; designed to encourage viewers to respond immediately to the advert; most commonly seen in the form of direct-response television (DRTV).

direct-response media Marketing communications media characterized by the inclusion of a response mechanism (such as a telephone number, website, email, or postal address, or a response card).

discount retailer A type of retailer that combines a comparatively low price as a major selling point with reduced costs of doing business.

distribution centre A facility that is designed to move goods, rather than only to store them.

distribution channel An organized network of agencies and organizations that, in combination, perform all of the activities required to link producers and manufacturers with consumers, purchasers, and users, to accomplish the marketing task of product distribution.

distributor brand Also known as an 'own-label brand', a brand developed by one of the wholesalers, distributors, dealers, and retailers that make up the distribution channel.

distributor An organization that buys goods and services, often from a limited range of manufacturers, and sells them on to retailers or resellers.

diversification A corporate strategy that requires an organization to grow outside its current range of activities, which growth brings new value chain activities because the firm is operating with new products and in new markets.

divest A strategic objective that involves selling or killing off a product when it continues to incur losses and to generate negative cash flows.

DRIP model Standing for 'differentiate, reinforce, inform, and persuade', a model of the four primary tasks that marketing communications can be expected to accomplish.

dyadic Meaning two-way; a dyadic commercial relationship is an exchange between two people—typically, a buyer and a seller.

early adopter As part of the process of diffusion, a person who enjoys being at the leading edge of innovation and who buys into new products at an early stage.

early majority As part of the process of diffusion, a group of people who need to be reassured that a product works and has been proven in the market before they are prepared to buy it.

electronic kiosk A computer-based retailing environment, often found in a shopping mall, that offers consumers increased self-service opportunity, wide product assortments, and large amounts of data and information to help in their decision-making; mediated by hypermedia web-based interfaces.

email marketing A form of direct marketing using email as a means of communicating messages directly, increasing loyalty, and building relationships with an audience, each member of which has given his or her permission to be contacted in this way.

emotional appeal The lure of a marketing communication message that is designed to provoke sensations, feelings, and sentiments.

emotional response The set of feelings and thoughts that an individual experiences when exposed to an emotional appeal.

encoding The part of the communication process in which the sender selects a combination of appropriate words, pictures, symbols, and music to represent a message to be transmitted.

environmental scanning The management process undertaken within an organization to identify external issues, situations, and threats that may impinge on its future and its strategic decision-making.

ethnographic study An approach to market research that involves the collection of data through observation of members of a specific sub-cultural grouping.

evoked set of products The group of goods, brands, or services of which someone thinks when he or she contemplates a particular purchasing situation and from which he or she chooses which product, brand, or service to buy.

exclusive distribution A form of distribution in which intermediaries are given exclusive rights to market the good or service within a defined 'territory'; thus a limited number of intermediaries are used.

exhibition An event at which groups of sellers meet collectively, with the key purpose of attracting buyers.

exploratory research An approach to research that aims to generate ideas and to develop hypotheses based around a management problem.

face validity A measure of the successful implementation of a research instrument based only on the researcher's or expert's subjective judgement.

feedback A part of the communication process in which receivers offer their opinions and experiences.

field marketing A marketing communications activity that aims to provide support for the sales force and merchandising personnel.

firmographics An approach to the segmentation of business-to-business markets using criteria such as company size, geography, standard industrial classification (SIC) codes, and other company-oriented classification data.

fixed costs The costs that do not vary according to the number of units of product made or service sold; in the pharmaceutical market, for example, these would include manufacturing plant costs; in a service business such as the airline industry, fixed costs include the cost of purchasing the plane.

focus group See group discussion

focus strategy A corporate strategy based on finding gaps in broad market segments or in competitors' product ranges.

forward integration The situation in which a company takes over one or more of its buyers. Cf backward integration

franchise A branch within a business model in which a company offers a complete brand concept, supplies, and logistics to a franchisees, who invest an initial lump sum and thereafter pay regular fees to continue the relationship.

full-service agency An advertising agency that provides its clients with a full range of services, including strategy and planning, designing the advertisements, and buying the media.

functional equivalence A measure of whether or not a concept has the same function in different countries.

gatekeeper A person who controls the type and flow of information into an organization, and in particular to members of the decision-making unit.

generic brand A brand sold without any promotional material or any means of identifying the originating company.

geodemographic segmentation An approach to segmentation based on the assumption that there is a relationship between the type of housing and location in which people live and their purchasing behaviours.

geographic segmentation An approach to segmentation based on the assumption that, in many situations, the needs of potential customers in one geographic area are different from those in another area, perhaps as a result of climate, custom, or tradition.

grey marketing The unauthorized sale of new, branded products diverted from authorized distribution channels or imported into a country for sale without the consent or knowledge of the manufacturer.

gross domestic product (GDP) A measure of the output of a nation and the size of its economy;

calculated as the market value of all finished goods and services produced in a country during a specified period, typically annually or quarterly.

group discussion A method of market research in which a group of between eight and twelve people are encouraged to express their own views on a pre-selected series of topics introduced by a moderator.

habit A repetitive behaviour, often performed without conscious rational thought in a routine way as a result of routinization that voluntary (controllable) rather than reflexive (uncontrollable).

harvest A strategic objective based on maximizing short-term profits and stimulating positive cash flow; often used in mature markets as firms or products enter a decline phase.

hierarchy of effects (HoE) A general sequential model, popular in the 1960s–1980s, used to explain how advertising works; provides a template that encourages the development and use of communication objectives.

hold A strategic objective based on defending an organization or product against attacks from aggressive competitors.

horizontal conflict Arises between members of a channel on the same level of distribution.

hybrid channel structure A distribution channel structure in which some products are sold directly from producer to customers and others are sold through intermediaries.

in-depth interview A qualitative research method used to identify respondents' hidden feelings, memories, attitudes, and motivations by means of a face-to-face interview.

indirect channel structure A distribution channel structure in which the product is sold from the producer to the customer via an intermediary, or series of intermediaries, such as a wholesaler, retailer, franchisee, agent, or broker.

influencer A person who helps to set the technical specifications for a proposed purchase and helps to evaluate alternative offerings by potential suppliers.

information utility The extent to which information about the product offering is provided before and after sales; it can further provide information about those purchasing it.

informational appeal The lure of a marketing communication message that is designed to provide factual information.

initiator A person who starts the organizational buying decision process.

innovator As part of the process of diffusion, a person who likes new ideas and who is most likely to take risks associated with new products.

inseparability A service characteristic that refers to the instantaneous and inextricable nature of its production and consumption.

in-store media Devices used in retail establishments that are designed to convey messages to shoppers; the two main forms are point-of-purchase displays and packaging.

intangibility A service characteristic that refers to the absence physical attributes, meaning that the service cannot be perceived by the senses— that is, it cannot be tasted, seen, touched, smelt, or possessed.

integrated marketing communications (IMC) Marketing communications that are characterized by the coordinated development and delivery of consistent marketing communication message(s).

intensity of channel coverage A measure of the number of intermediaries within a distribution channel.

intensive distribution A method of distribution that focuses on placing the product or service in as many outlets or locations as possible, to maximize the opportunities for customers to find it.

interaction model A model of the flow of communication messages that leads to mutual understanding about a specific topic.

intermediary An independent business concern that operates as a link between producers and ultimate consumers or industrial end users; it renders services in connection with the purchase and/or sale of the product offering moving from producers to consumers.

internal marketing The application of marketing concepts and principles within an organization; normally targeted at employees with a view to encouraging them to support and endorse the organization's strategy, goals, and brands.

interstitial A webpage that is displayed before an expected content page, often used to display advertisements.

involvement A measure of the personal importance that a person attaches to a given communication message.

laggard As part of the process of diffusion, a person who is suspicious of all new ideas and whose opinions are very hard to change.

late majority As part of the process of diffusion, a group of people who are sceptical of new ideas and who adopt new products only because of social or economic factors.

licensing A commercial process whereby the trademark of an established brand is used by another organization over a defined period of time, in a defined area, in return for a fee, to develop another brand.

lifestage analysis Analysis that is based on the principle that people need different products and services at different stages in their lives (for example, childhood, adulthood, young couples, retired, etc.).

limited line retailer A type of retailer with a narrow, but deep, product assortment and customer services that varies from store to store.

logistics The process of transporting the initial components of goods, services, and other forms of offering, and their finished products, from the producer to the intermediary or customer and the end consumer.

logistics management The coordination of activities of the entire distribution channel to deliver maximum value through the suppliers of raw materials to the manufacturer of the product, to the wholesalers who deliver the product, to the final customers who purchase it.

management problem A statement that outlines a situation faced by an organization that requires further investigation and subsequent organizational action.

manufacturer brand A brand created and sustained by a producer that seeks widespread awareness and distribution as a result of high demand.

market development A corporate strategy that involves increasing sales by selling existing or 'old' products in new markets, either by targeting new audiences domestically or by entering new markets internationally.

market orientation A principle relating to the development of a whole-organization approach to the generation, collection, and dissemination of market intelligence across different departments and the organization's responsiveness to that intelligence.

market segmentation The division of customer markets into groups of customers with distinctly similar needs.

market sensing An organization's ability to gather, interpret, and act on strategic information from customers and competitors.

marketing communications mix The specific combination of particular tools, media, and messages designed to achieve a set of marketing communications objectives and so to fulfil a communication strategy.

marketing communications planning framework (MCPF) A model of the various decisions and actions that are undertaken when preparing, implementing, and evaluating communication strategies and plans; reflects a deliberate or planned approach to strategic marketing communications.

marketing information system A system incorporating ad hoc and continuous market and marketing research surveys, together with secondary data and internal data sources, to aid marketers in decision-making.

marketing mix The list of factors that a marketing manager should consider when devising plans for marketing products, including product decisions, place (distribution) decisions, pricing decisions, and promotion decisions (the '4Ps'); later extended to include physical evidence, process, and people decisions to account for the lack of physical nature in service products (the '7Ps').

marketing objective A marketing aim to be accomplished within a particular period of time; usually specified in terms of market share, sales revenues, volumes, return on investment (ROI), and other profitability indicators.

measurement equivalence A measure of the extent to which the methods by which the researcher collects and categorizes essential data and information from two or more different sources are comparable.

media usage An indicator of what media channels are used, by whom, when, where, and for how long, which provides useful insight into the reach potential for certain market segments through differing media channels, and also insight into the segments' media lifestyles.

media vehicle An individual medium used to carry advertising messages.

merchant A person or organization that acts as principal intermediary between the seller of a product and buyers, bringing them together and taking ownership of the product offering. Cf **agent**

microblog Also known as a nanoblog or a tweet (when posted via Twitter), a short-format version of the weblog comprising only 140 characters that is shared with a network of followers.

mixed price bundling The offering of a product or service together with another, typically complementary product or service, which is also available separately, to make the first product or service seem more attractive, such as a mobile phone package that includes text messages and international call packages in its price.

mobile marketing The set of practices that enable organizations to communicate and engage with their audience in an interactive and relevant manner through any mobile device or network.

modified rebuy The organizational processes associated with the infrequent purchase of products and services.

mystery shopping A form of research designed to evaluate standards of customer service performance received by customers either within one's own organization or within a competitor's organization.

near-field communications A form of short-range wireless communication technology that allows data transfer between two enabled communication devices when they are brought into close contact with each other.

new task The organizational processes associated with buying a product or service for the first time.

niche (In marketing) A small segment or specialist target market.

niche market A small part of a market segment that has specific and specialized characteristics that make it uneconomic for the leading competitors to enter.

niche marketing strategy See concentrated marketing strategy

noise The influences that distort information in the communication process and which, in turn, make it difficult for the receiver to decode and interpret a message correctly.

non-probability sampling An approach to sampling in which the probability of selection of the sample elements from the population is unknown, such as quota, snowball, and convenience sampling.

non-store retailer A retailer that engages in activities resulting in transactions that occur away from a retail store.

observational study A market research study in which behaviours of interest are recorded, such as mystery shopping or a mass transit study.

online community A group of people who come together freely to share a common interest via the Internet, which involves interacting, sharing information, developing knowledge and understanding, and building relationships.

operant conditioning A learning theory developed by B. F. Skinner that suggests that when a subject acts on a stimulus from the environment (the antecedents), this is more likely to result in a particular behaviour (the behaviour) if that behaviour is reinforced through reward or punishment (the consequence).

opinion follower A person to whom opinion leaders and formers turn for advice and information about products and services that they are interested in purchasing or using.

opinion former A person who exerts personal influence because of his or her profession, authority, education, or status associated with the object of the communication process; not part of the same peer group as the people whom he or she influences.

opinion leader A person who is predisposed to receiving information and then reprocessing it in order to influence others; belongs to the same peer group as the people whom he or she influences—that is, is not distant or removed.

opportunity cost The difference between the revenues or benefits generated from undertaking one particular activity and the possible revenues or benefits of another feasible revenue-generating activity that is discarded.

organizational goal One of a set of outcomes at which the organization's various activities are aimed, often expressed in terms of market share, share value, return on investment (ROI), or numbers of customers served.

organizational size segmentation A method of grouping organizations by their relative size—such as multinational corporations (MNCs), international, large, or small and medium-sized enterprises (SMEs)—which enables the identification of design, delivery, usage rates, or order size and other purchasing characteristics.

organizational values The standards of behaviour expected of an organization's employees.

outdoor media Sometimes referred to as 'out-of-home media', media that enable advertising messages to reach consumers in public places, in transit and waiting areas, and in specific commercial locations; the three primary formats are billboards, street furniture, and transit.

overt search The point in the buying process at which a consumer seeks further information in relation to a product or buying situation, according to the Howard–Sheth model of buyer behaviour.

owned media Organizational assets such as buildings, vehicles, work wear, and websites used to convey messages without payment of a fee.

ownership utility The extent to which goods are available immediately from the intermediaries' stocks, meaning that ownership passes to the purchaser.

packaging The enclosing, protecting, and communication of products for distribution, storage, sale, and use; the materials within which products are enclosed.

paid inclusion A method of ensuring that a website is included in a search engine's natural listings, by means of a fee.

paid placement Also known as 'pay per click' (PPC), advertising that uses sponsored search engine listings to drive traffic to a website; the advertiser bids for search terms and the search engine ranks ads based on a competitive auction, as well as other factors.

panel study A market research study that uses information collected from a fixed group of respondents over a defined period of time.

perception A mental picture that is based on existing attitudes, beliefs, needs, stimulus factors, and factors specific to a situation, which governs a person's attitude and behaviour towards an object, an event, or a person.

perceptual mapping The illustration of the differences in perceptions that customers, consumers, or the general public have of different products, services, or brands in general by means of a (typically two-dimensional) diagram depicting the 'image-space' derived from attitudinal market research data.

perceived quality A relative subjective measure of product or service quality, for which there is no truly objective absolute measure.

perishability A service characteristic that recognizes that spare or unused capacity cannot be stored for use at some point in the future.

personal selling The use of interpersonal communications to encourage people to purchase particular products and services, for personal gain and reward.

PESTLE Standing for 'political, economic, socio-cultural, technological, legal, and ecological', a framework that allows an organization to examine the factors comprising its external environment.

picking In the context of consumer behaviour, the process of deliberative selection of a product or service from among a repertoire of acceptable alternatives, even though the consumer believes the alternatives to be essentially identical in their ability to satisfy his or her need.

place Now more commonly referred to as 'distribution', the element of the marketing mix that focuses on getting the optimum amount of goods and/or services before the maximum number of members of the target market, at times and locations that optimize the marketing outcome—that is, sales.

podcast An audio or video file that can be downloaded over the Internet on demand.

POEM Standing for 'paid, owned and earned media', a way of categorizing the different types of medium that can be used to convey marketing messages.

political environment That part of the macro environment concerned with government policies, and impending and potential legislation, and how they may affect a particular firm.

positioning The way in which an audience of consumers or buyers perceives a product or service, particularly as a result of the marketing communications process aimed at a target audience.

post hoc segmentation Market segmentation in which the segments are deduced from research.

price The amount of money that the customer has to pay to receive a good or service.

price discrimination Discrimination that arises when the price of a good or service is set differently for certain groups of people.

price elasticity A measure of the extent to which a change in price will change the volume of a product or service demanded, usually expressed as a negative number; a score close to 0 indicates that a product or service price change has little impact on quantity demanded; a score of −1 indicates that a product or service price change effects an equal percentage quantity change; a value above −1 indicates a disproportionately high change in quantity demanded as a result of a percentage price change.

price gouging A practice whereby a seller sets the price of a good or service at a level far higher than is considered reasonable.

price sensitivity A measure of the extent to which a company (or consumer) increases or lowers its purchase volumes in relation to changes in price; a customer is price insensitive when the drop in unit volumes is proportionately lower than the increases in prices.

pricing cue A proxy measure used by customers to estimate a product or service's reference price, such as quality, styling, packaging, sale signs, and odd-number endings.

primary research A technique used to collect for the first time data that has been specifically collected and assembled for the current research problem.

print media Those text- and image-based means of conveying meaning in marketing communications, primarily comprising newspapers, magazines, custom magazines, and directories.

probability sampling A sampling method in which the probability of selection of the sample elements from the population is known, such as simple random, stratified random, and cluster sampling.

procurement The process of purchasing (buying) in a firm or organization.

product class A broad category referring to various types of related product, such as, 'cat food', 'shampoo', or 'cars'.

product differentiation A corporate strategy in which a company produces offerings that are different from those of competing firms.

product life cycle (PLC) The pathway through which a product passes during its lifetime, comprising five main stages: development; introduction; growth; maturity; and decline.

product placement The planned and deliberate appearance3 of brands within films, TV, and other entertainment vehicles with a view to developing awareness and brand values.

product usage segmentation A form of segmentation based on analysing a markets' usage of the product offering, brand, or product category, in the form of usage frequency, time of usage, and usage situations.

product Any good that is capable of satisfying customer needs.

projective technique An indirect approach to questioning that encourages the subject to reveal his or her hidden feelings and values, by means of word association, role playing, pictorial construction, and completion tests, for example.

promotion The use of communications to persuade individuals, groups, or organizations to purchase products and services.

proprietary panel A method of market research set up of commissioned by a client firm in which the panel comprises only the company's customers.

psychographics A term used in market segmentation to describe market segments on the basis of their mental (that is, psychological) characteristics.

psychological reactance The extent to which, when a consumer perceives his or her freedom to pursue a particular decision alternative to be blocked, wholly or partially, he or she will become more motivated to pursue that decision alternative.

public relations (PR) A non-personal form of communication used by companies to build trust, goodwill, interest, and ultimately relationships with a range of stakeholders.

pull strategy A marketing communications strategy used to communicate directly with end-user customers, whether consumers or other organizations within a business-to-business context.

purchase situation segmentations An approach to segmenting organizational buyers that focuses on the way in which a buying company structures its purchasing procedures, the type of buying situation, and whether buyers are in an early or late stage in the purchase decision process.

purchasing power parity (PPP) A measure of the relative wealth of the population based on the cost of an identified basket of goods, which can be used to compare the wealth of one population with that of another.

pure price bundling The offering of a product or service together with another, typically complementary product or service, which is not available separately, to make the original product or service seem more attractive (such as a CD with a music magazine).

push strategy A marketing communications strategy used to communicate with channel intermediaries, such as dealers, wholesalers, distributors, and retailers, otherwise referred to as the 'trade', or 'channel buyers'.

qualitative research A type of exploratory research using small samples and unstructured data collection procedures, designed to identify hypotheses, possibly for later testing in quantitative research; the most popular examples include in-depth interviews, focus groups, and projective techniques.

quantitative research A type of research that is designed to provide responses to predetermined, standardized questions from a large number of respondents and which involves the statistical analysis of the responses.

quota sampling A sampling method used to select respondents in which the criteria for selection are restricted, but the final selection of the respondents is left to the judgement of the researcher and the chance of selection beforehand is unknown.

random digit dialling A computer-based form of telephone sampling that pulls telephone numbers at random, whether listed or not, to provide a representative survey sample.

receiver An individual or organization that has seen, heard, smelled, or read a message.

recognition The process whereby new images and words presented are compared with existing images and words in memory, and a match is found.

reference group A group that an individual uses to form his or her own beliefs and attitudes; can be positive, if the individual aligns his or her opinions, attitudes, values, or behaviour with those of the group, or negative, if he or she is repelled by the group's behaviour and seeks to dissociate his or her opinions, attitudes, values, and behaviour from those of the group.

reference price A price band that a customer has in mind for a particular product or service and against which he or she judges the actual purchase price.

relationship marketing The development and management of long-term relationships with customers, influencers, referrers, suppliers, recruiters, and employees.

reliability The degree to which the data elicited in a study is replicated in a repeat study.

research and development (R&D) The process of using basic and applied science to develop new technologies, in turn used to develop new product, process, and service specifications, which can be leveraged into the development of new or reformulated customer propositions; the department within the organization responsible for the process.

research brief A formal document prepared by the client organization and submitted to either an external market research provider (a market research agency or consultant) or an internal research provider (an in-house research department) outlining a statement of the management problem and the perceived research needs of the organization.

research proposal A formal document prepared by an agency, consultant, or in-house research manager and submitted to the client to outline what procedures will be used to collect the necessary information, including timescales and costs.

reseller An organization that purchases goods and services from wholesalers, distributors, or even directly from producers and manufacturers, and makes these available to organizations for consumption.

retailer An organization that purchases goods and services from wholesalers, distributors, or even directly from producers and manufacturers, and makes these available to consumers.

retailing Also known as the 'retail trade', all of the activities directly related to the sale of goods and services to the ultimate end consumer for personal and non-business use.

reverse engineering The process of developing a product from the finished version (for example, from a competitor's prototype), working backwards to its constituent parts rather than from component parts to a finished product, as is more usual.

RSS Standing for 'really simple syndication', the distribution of specific news content on the Internet.

sales promotion A communication tool that adds value to a product or service with the intention of encouraging people to buy now rather than at some point in the future.

sample A group that is selected as a representative of the true population for a given research experiment.

sampling equivalence The extent to which samples representative of their populations are comparable across countries.

sampling frame A list of population members from which a sample is generated, such as a telephone directory or membership list.

search engine marketing (SEM) A set of marketing methods aiming to increase the visibility of a website in search engine results pages (SERPs).

search engine optimization (SEO) A technique that attempts to improve rankings for relevant keywords in search results by improving a website's structure and content.

secondary research Also known as 'desk research', a technique used to collect data that has been previously collected for a purpose other than the current research situation.

segmentation base The key customer, product or situation-related criterion (or criteria) used to determine the markets from which information will be collected.

selective distribution A method of distribution in which some, but not all, available outlets for the good or service are used.

selective exposure The process during which consumers screen out that information which they do not consider meaningful or interesting.

semiotics (In marketing) this is a specialist sub-discipline of marketing research that seeks to analyse signs in marketing communications and consumer culture in order to deconstruct promotional propositions, and thereby to identify new communication approaches, messages and styles.

service encounter An event that occurs when a customer interacts directly with a service.

service failure An event that occurs when a customer's expectations of a service encounter are not met.

service quality A measure of the extent to which a service experience exceeds customers' expectations.

service recovery An organization's systematic attempt to correct a service failure and to retain a customer's goodwill.

service-dominant logic (SDL) A core orientation that considers marketing to be a customer logic management process, in which services (not products) are the principal consideration for value creation.

services mix A combination of different service elements, including products.

servicescape The set of stimuli impacting on the customer in the service environment; a similar concept to the atmospherics present in a retail environment.

simple random sampling A sampling method used to select respondents from a known population frame using randomly generated numbers assigned to population elements.

SMART Standing for 'specific, measurable, achievable, realistic, and timed', an approach used to write effective objectives.

snowball sampling A sampling method used to select respondents from rare populations in which the criteria for selection are based on referral from an initial set of respondents typically generated through newspaper advertisements or some other method, in response to which one set of respondents refers another set—and the process repeats.

social entrepreneur A leader of an organization who seeks not only to earn a profit, but also to make a social change in the world.

social learning theory Advocated by Albert Bandura, this suggests that we can learn from observing the experiences of others and that, in contrast with operant conditioning, we can delay gratification and even administer our own rewards or punishment.

social network A social structure comprising interconnected individuals and organizations that choose to share lifestyles and experiences, and to build relationships, often through the Internet.

sponsorship A marketing communications activity in which one party permits another an opportunity to exploit an association with a target audience in return for funds, services, or resources.

Statistical Package for the Social Sciences (SPSS) A software package used for statistical analysis marketed by SPSS, a company owned by IBM.

stakeholder A person or organization with an interest—that is, a 'stake'—in the levels of profit that an organization achieves, its environmental impact, and its ethical conduct in society.

standard industrial classification (SIC code) One of a set of codes that are used to identify and categorize all types of industry and business.

storage warehouse A facility used to store goods for moderate to long periods.

storyboard An image-based outline, prepared before advertisements are made, depicting the advertisement's key themes, characters and story (if any), and messages.

STP process Standing for 'segmentation, targeting, and positioning', the method by which whole markets are subdivided and tackled.

straight rebuy The organizational processes associated with the routine reordering of good and services, often undertaken from an approved list of suppliers.

strategic business unit (SBU) An organizational unit that, for planning purposes, is sufficiently large to exercise control over the principal strategic factors affecting its performance; might incorporate an entire brand and/or its sub-components, or a country region, or some other discrete unit of an organization.

strategic market analysis The starting point of the marketing strategy process, involving analysis of three main types of environment: the external environment; the performance environment; and the internal environment.

strategic procurement The long-term agreement with a single supplier, or a few suppliers, to develop mutually beneficial purchasing relationships.

stratified random sampling A sampling method used to select respondents from known homogeneous sub-groups of the population determined on the basis of specific criteria.

Strong theory A persuasion-based theory aiming to explain how advertising works.

supermarket A large self-service retailing organization that offers a wide variety of differing merchandise to a large consumer base.

sustainable competitive advantage Advantage achieved in the marketplace when an organization is able to offer a superior product to those of competitors, which is not easily imitated, and enjoys significant market share as a result.

switching costs The psychological, economic, time, and effort-related costs associated with substituting one product or service for another, or changing a supplier from one to another.

SWOT analysis Standing for 'strengths, weaknesses, opportunities, and threats', a framework used by an organization to determine the key issues arising from, and the fit between, its internal capability (strengths and weaknesses) and the external situation (opportunities and threats).

systematic random sampling A sampling method used to select respondents from a known population using an initial random number generated to determine the first sample respondent, but in which each subsequent sample respondent is selected on the basis of the nth respondent proceeding, where n is determined by dividing the population size by the sample size and rounding up.

tangibility A characteristic relating to the extent to which something is physical—that is, can be touched, has form, and has physical presence.

telemarketing Also known as 'telesales', a form of non-store retailing in which purchase occurs over the telephone.

test marketing A stage in the new product development process undertaken when a new product is tested with a sample of customers, or is launched in a specified geographical area, to judge customers' reactions prior to a national launch.

test market A region within a country used to test the effects of the launch of a new product or service, typically using regional advertising to promote the service and pre- and post-advertising market research to measure promotional effectiveness.

time utility The extent of the gap between manufacture, purchase, and consumption, which occur at differing points in time.

transactional exchange A short-term economic transaction between parties who are primarily interested in products and prices, and who are primarily motivated by self-interest.

transfer pricing The pricing approach that typically occurs in large organizations when one unit of a company sells to another unit within the same company.

translation equivalence The degree to which the meaning of one language is represented in another after translation.

transvections A term proposed by Alderson and Miles to denote the relationships (transactions) that occur in the development of a product or service that cross between company (that is, product/service) ownership boundaries to produce a finished product or service; now more likely to be considered, in manufacturing from the perspective of supply chain management, to be vertical integration or cooperation.

t-test A statistical test of difference used for small randomly selected samples with a size of less than thirty.

two-step model A communication model that reflects a receiver's response to a message.

undifferentiated approach An approach to marketing that does not distinguish between market segments, but instead views the market as one mass market and subjects it to a single marketing strategy.

user-generated content (UGC) Content made publicly available over the Internet that reflects a certain amount of creative effort and is created by users rather than professionals.

user A person, or group of people, who uses business products and services once they have been acquired, and who then evaluates their performance.

validity The extent to which an instrument measures exactly the construct that it is attempting to measure.

value The amount that something is held to be worth, often expressed in financial terms.

values The beliefs of a social group or an individual, held with some conviction, often learned from parents and formed early in life, and tending to change less and less with age, which define how we ought to behave.

variability A service characteristic that refers to the amount of diversity allowed in each step of service provision.

variable costs Costs that vary according to the number of units of product made or service sold; variable costs in the pharmaceutical market would include plastic bottles in which to place the pills; in a service business such as the airline industry, variable costs would include airline meals.

vertical conflict Arises between sequential members in a distribution network, such as producers, distributor, and retailers, over matters such as carrying a particular range or price increases.

viral marketing The unpaid, peer-to-peer communication, often of provocative content, which originates from an identified sponsor and uses the Internet to persuade or influence an audience to pass along the content to others.

Weak theory A view of advertising that suggests that it is a weak force and works only by reminding people of preferred brands.

weblog More commonly known as a 'blog', a personal online diary that provides web visibility for an individual or organization; open to the public, who are free to respond as appropriate.

wholesaler An organization that stocks products, not services, before the next level of distribution.

word of mouth A form of communication founded on interpersonal messages regarding products or services sought or consumed; the receiver regards the communicator as impartial and credible, because he or she is not attempting to sell the products or services.

z-test A statistical test of difference used for large, randomly selected samples with a size of thirty or more.

Index

Twitter 116, 117–18, 306
two-step model of communication
    267, 268, 269–70, 401

U

understanding 269
undifferentiated targeting
    strategy 188, 401
Unilever 44, 228, 229, 285, 335
updator purchasing strategy 89
usage segmentation 179–80, 397
user 84, 401
user-generated content (UGC) 307,
    311, 401

V

validity 113, 114, 401
    face validity test 114, 392
value 239, 401
    digital 206, 391
    perceived 239–40
    pricing relationship 239–40
    see also values
value creation 83
value-based pricing approach 248
value-in-use pricing 256
values 78, 131–2, 396, 401
    brand values 230
    see also value
Vargo, S. L. 19, 374

variability of services 367, 402
variable costs 237, 402
vending machines 349
vertical conflict 339, 402
ViiV Healthcare 54
viral marketing 282, 299, 305, 402
Virgin 227, 229, 376
vision 129–30
Visual Attention Service (VAS)
    202–3
Vodafone 18, 194
VOIP (voice over Internet
    protocol) 54
Volkswagen 179, 319
Volvo 53, 70, 71, 143

W

wage inflation 40
Waitrose 147
Wal-Mart 21, 175, 228, 337
Walkers Crisps 223
Walls 136
warehousing 342–3
    digital products 343
    tangible goods 343
weak theory of advertising 284,
    286, 402
weaknesses 139–40, 141
    competitors 136–8
Webb, K. L. 340
Weber Shandwick 39

weblogs 306, 402
White, W. J. 312
wholesalers 330–1, 337, 402
WikiLeaks 38
Wikipedia 306
Wilkie, W. L. 26
winner's curse 22, 257
Winter, R. 303
Woolworths 343
word-of-mouse communication 282,
    305
word-of-mouth messages 79, 281–2,
    402
    electronic (viral marketing) 305
World of Music, Arts and Dance
    (WOMAD) 300–1
World of Warcraft 269, 309

Y

Yoplait Dairy Crest (YDC) 174
YouTube 307

Z

z-tests 113, 402
Zara 49, 147, 174, 327
zero-inventory 343
Zhejiang Geely Holding Group 143
ZSL London Zoo 292–3